国际贸易专业应用型本科精选系列教材

省级精品课程教材

国际贸易理论与实务

双语教程（第三版）

Theory and Practice of International Trade

A Bilingual Course

傅龙海　郑佰青　陈剑霞　主　　编

傅安妮　周宝玉　执行主编

对外经济贸易大学出版社

中国·北京

图书在版编目（CIP）数据

国际贸易理论与实务双语教程：汉英对照 / 傅龙海，郑佰青，陈剑霞主编. —3 版. —北京：对外经济贸易大学出版社，2022.8　（2024.8 重印）
国际贸易专业应用型本科精选系列教材
ISBN 978-7-5663-2411-5

Ⅰ. ①国… Ⅱ. ①傅…②郑…③陈… Ⅲ. ①国际贸易理论–双语教学–高等学校–教材②国际贸易–贸易实务–双语教学–高等学校–教材 Ⅳ. ①F740

中国版本图书馆 CIP 数据核字（2022）第 112032 号

国际贸易理论与实务双语教程（第三版）
Theory and Practice of International Trade：A Bilingual Course

傅龙海　郑佰青　陈剑霞　**主编**
责任编辑：张俊娟

出版发行：对外经济贸易大学出版社　　邮政编码：100029
社　　址：北京市朝阳区惠新东街 10 号　　邮购电话：010 – 64492338
网　　址：www.uibep.com　　发行部电话：010 – 64492342
资源网址：www.uibepresources.com　　E-mail：uibep@126.com

成品尺寸：185mm×260mm　　印　　刷：北京市泰锐印刷有限责任公司
印　　张：20　　版　　次：2022 年 8 月北京第 3 版
字　　数：462 千字　　印　　次：2024 年 8 月第 2 次印刷
ISBN 978-7-5663-2411-5　　定　　价：45.00 元

前　言

由傅龙海老师主编的《国际贸易理论与实务》一书在出版后短短不到三年的时间里，又出了第五版，可想而知这本书受欢迎的程度。根据教育部的要求，高校需要有一定比例的双语教学。现在很多高校已经在国际贸易实务或是国际贸易理论课程教学中采用双语授课形式，但是目前国际贸易理论与实务双语教材还是比较缺乏。为了满足广大高校师生的热切愿望，编者在原中文书稿的基础上推出该书的双语教程。

《国际贸易理论与实务双语教程》在编写过程中始终坚持“人才是第一资源”“为党育人、为国育才”的指导，将其有机融入国际贸易理论与实务双语教学的学科知识体系中。党的二十大报告指出：“教育、科技、人才是全面建设社会主义现代化国家的基础性、战略性支撑。必须坚持科技是第一生产力、人才是第一资源、创新是第一动力，深入实施科教兴国战略、人才强国战略、创新驱动发展战略，开辟发展新领域新赛道，不断塑造发展新动能新优势。要坚持教育优先发展、科技自立自强、人才引领驱动，加快建设教育强国、科技强国、人才强国，坚持为党育人、为国育才，全面提高人才自主培养质量，着力造就拔尖创新人才，聚天下英才而用之。”

《国际贸易理论与实务双语教程》既介绍了国际贸易的理论知识，又介绍了国际贸易的实务知识。本书结合当代国际贸易的一些新情况和新问题，将理论性与实际操作性相结合，突出实务操作，力求达到内容新颖、重点突出、概念准确、简明扼要，以便更好地适合教师课堂教学和学生学习的需要。需要指出的是，本书采用中英文一一对应的呈现形式，极个别中英文没有完全对应是基于表述更容易让学生理解，更符合国际贸易惯例。

《国际贸易理论与实务双语教程》主要作为经济类和非外贸类专业学生学习经贸基础知识之用，如营销、会计、经济管理、物流和电子商务等专业均可以把本课程当作公共课程来学习，也可以作为相关专业的社会培训用书。本书共16章，分为两个部分。第一部分1—6章为国际贸易的理论部分，第二部分7—16章为国际贸易的实务部分。教师在使用时，可根据需要或分别使用，或综合使用。

本书的作者既有长期从事外贸一线工作的经历，又有从事教学工作的经验，在写作本书时，本着通俗易懂又不乏深度的原则，结合了目前最新的法律法规、惯例以及国际贸易的新形势、新特点来论述。本书不论是理论部分还是实务部分，都结合了目前最新的理论动向和大量的实际案例，使得纯理论的内容变得生动、活泼、通俗易懂。实务部分，萃选精华，深入浅出，使学生更容易掌握国际贸易的最新知识。

本书具体编写人员及分工如下：傅龙海，第1章；陈剑霞，第2章；傅安妮，第3章；倪昌源、倪玮佳，第4章；周宝玉，第5章；刘宝华，第6章；郑佰青，第7章；傅安妮，第8章；张壁芬、陈剑霞，第9章；刘建华，第10章；陈剑霞，第11章；詹小琦，第12章；刘小华，第13章；傅安妮，第14章；周金铁，第15章；傅丹妮、郑佰青，第16章。全书由傅龙海统稿。

本书的出版得到了对外经济贸易大学出版社刘传志副总编和郭华良主任的大力支持和帮助。特别要感谢对外经济贸易大学原副校长、博士生导师贾怀勤教授。同时，还要感谢福建阳光集团傅瑞翔先生和王琳女士以及福建省旅游贸易公司进出口部许鲁江经理的大力支持，为我们提供了丰富的案例和单据资料。在本书编写过程中，对外经济贸易大学英语学院的郑佰青老师对本书英文部分的编写及审校做了大量工作。

本书在编写过程中，作者见识难免有限，加之时间仓促，不足之处敬请同行和广大读者不吝赐教。

2024 年 7 月

目　录

Part One

Part Two

Part One

Chapter 1

International Trade Theories and Policies 国际贸易理论及政策

Lesson 1 Basic Concepts of International Trade 国际贸易的基本概念

1. International Trade, Foreign Trade and Overseas Trade 国际贸易、对外贸易和海外贸易

1.1 International Trade 国际贸易

International trade (also named world trade), is the exchange of goods and services happening between the countries or regions across world, including visible products (substantial products) and invisible products (such as labor, technology, consultation etc.). For the traditional international trade, it only refers to the exchange of the goods in variety between countries and regions, not including services; in a modern international trade, the exchange covers the goods as well as services of different countries and regions over the world.

国际贸易又称世界贸易，是指世界各国（或地区）之间货物和服务的交换活动。它既包含有形产品（实物产品）交换，也包含无形产品（劳务、技术、咨询等）的交换。传统的国际贸易，仅指国家间各类货物的交换，不包括服务；现代的国际贸易是指世界各国（或地区）之间货物和服务的交换。

1.2 Foreign Trade 对外贸易

Foreign trade (also named import and export business), refers to the exchange activity about the goods and services operated by one country or region with other countries or regions.

Foreign trade means the business activity regarded on the side of one country. For example, the trade between China and other countries, is usually called Chinese Foreign Trade. International trade is the business activity regarding all over the world.

对外贸易，又称进出口贸易，是指国际贸易活动中的一国（或地区）同其他国家（或地区）所进行的货物和服务的交换活动。

对外贸易是从一个国家的角度去看待它与其他国家或地区的产品与劳务的贸易活动。如中国与别国的贸易，则称为中国对外贸易。国际贸易是站在世界的角度，从整个国际范围来看这种商品和服务的交换活动。

1.3 Overseas Trade 海外贸易

The foreign trade developed by the insular countries such as Japan, UK is named as overseas trade.

某些海岛国家，如日本、英国等国的对外贸易则称为海外贸易。

2. Export Trade, Import Trade, Transit Trade 出口贸易、进口贸易、过境贸易

According to the different movement directions of the goods, international trade is classified into export trade, import trade, and transit trade.

依据货物的移动方向不同来划分，国际贸易可分为出口贸易、进口贸易和过境贸易。出口贸易与进口贸易是每一笔贸易的两个方面，对卖方是出口贸易，对买方则是进口贸易。

2.1 Export Trade 出口贸易

The business of selling the merchandise including services produced or proceeded in domestic market to abroad market is called export trade or output trade.

出口贸易是将本国所生产或加工的商品（包括劳务）输往国外市场进行销售的商品交换活动，称为出口贸易或输出贸易。

2.2 Import Trade 进口贸易

The business of buying the merchandise (including services) from overseas market, and inputing them to domestic market is called import trade or input trade.

进口贸易是将外国的商品（包括劳务）购买后，输入本国市场进行销售的贸易活动，称为进口贸易或输入贸易。

2.3 Transit Trade 过境贸易

During the business between the country of production and the country of consumption, the transportation will be carried out usually through a third country while the third country charges for the transportation. Then the business is regarded as the transit trade by the third country. For instance, the business trade between the inland country and the non-neighboring countries has to be completed through the third country's frontier, and consequently the kind of business will be classified as the transit trade by the customs of the third country.

商品生产国与商品消费国之间进行的商品买卖活动，其货物运输过程必须要通过第三国的国境。第三国则对此批货物收取一定的费用，这对第三国来说就构成了该国的过境贸易。比如，内陆国与不相邻的国家之间的商品交易，就必须通过第三国国境，对第三国海关来说，则会把这类贸易归入过境贸易。

3. Direct Trade, Indirect Trade, Entrepot Trade 直接贸易、间接贸易、转口贸易

Depending on whether the third party gets involved in the trade, international trade is classified into direct trade, indirect trade and entrepot trade.

依据是否有第三者参与来划分，国际贸易可分为直接贸易、间接贸易和转口贸易。

3.1 Direct Trade 直接贸易

The direct trade is the business trade happening between the country of production and the country of consumption without the involvement of a third country. Both parties of a direct trade make negotiation, conclude a deal and make settlement directly. When the merchandise is exported directly to the country of consumption from the country of production, it is direct export for the producing country and direct import for the consuming country.

直接贸易是指商品生产国与商品消费国不通过第三国而直接买卖商品的贸易活动。直接贸易的双方直接谈判、直接签约、直接结算、货物直接运输。生产国商品出口到消费国，从生产国来说，是直接出口；从消费国来说，是直接进口。

3.2 Indirect Trade 间接贸易

The indirect trade is the business trade made by the producing country and the consuming country through a third country. For some reasons such as political reasons and the inconvenience of communication between the two countries, when the negotiation, contract conclusion and settlement in the business cannot be carried out directly between the export country and the import country without the involvement of the third country, the indirect trade is necessary.

间接贸易是指商品生产国与商品消费国通过第三国所进行的商品买卖行为。此类贸易

因为各种原因，出口国与进口国之间不能直接进行洽谈、签约和结算，而必须借助于第三国。间接贸易有些是出于政治方面的原因，有些是由于交易双方的信息不通畅造成的。

3.3 Entrepot Trade 转口贸易

The Entrepot Trade is the business involving three parties which are the country of production, the country of consumption and the country of making entrepot trade. Sometimes, the merchandise is transported to the country of consumption from the country of the production, though the two countries are not in direct business relationship, as a third country has business relationship with the two countries respectively.

The countries or regions engaged in entrepot trade usually boast the advantages of superior geographic location, well-developed traffic, convenient settlement instruments and free trade policies, which are suited to being distribution centers such as Hong Kong of China, Rotterdam of Holland and the like.

The difference between entrepot trade and indirect trade originates from the different points of view: so far as the country of production or the country of consumption is concerned, the trade made through a third country is indirect trade, and for the third country it is entrepot trade.

The difference between entrepot trade and transit trade is as follows: for entrepot trade, the ownership of the merchandise is firstly moved to the party of a third country or region from the country of the production, then to the party of the country of consumption; for transit trade, the ownership of the merchandise is not moved to the party of a third country. Entrepot trade takes making profits as its main purpose and usually has an addition to the price while transit trade usually takes a bit of extra charges.

转口贸易是指商品生产国与商品消费国通过第三国进行商品买卖，对第三国来说是转口贸易。转口贸易亦包括下述情况，即商品直接从生产国运往消费国，但两国并没有发生直接贸易关系，而是由第三国分别与两国发生贸易关系。

从事转口贸易的大多是地理位置优越、交通便利、结算方便、贸易限制较少的国家或地区，适合于作为商品的集散、销售中心，例如中国香港、荷兰鹿特丹等。

转口贸易与间接贸易的区别在于看问题的角度不同：商品生产国与消费国通过第三国进行的贸易对生产国和消费国而言是间接贸易；对第三国（地区）而言，则是转口贸易。

转口贸易与过境贸易的区别如下：在转口贸易中，商品的所有权先从生产国出口者转到第三国（或地区）商人手中，再转到最终消费该商品的进口国商人手中。而在过境贸易中，商品所有权无须向第三国商人转移。转口贸易以营利为目的，通常有一个正常的商业加价，而过境贸易只收取少量的手续费。

4. General Trade and Special Trade 总贸易和专门贸易

According to the different standards of import and export, international trade may be divided into general trade and special trade. Both are statistical systems.

依据进出口标准的不同，国际贸易可分为总贸易和专门贸易。总贸易与专门贸易是国际货物贸易的统计方法。

4.1 General Trade 总贸易

It is a statistical method to classify import and export by country's border. General trade is divided into general import and general export. All the merchandise moving into the border of a country counts toward the general import including what are consumed in domestic and what are transited or passed through the territory of the country; all the merchandise moved out of the border of a country counts toward general export including the export of the home-made products, the re-export of foreign merchandise and transited goods or the goods passing through the border. The total sum of general import and general export is general trade. Currently, there are more than 90 nations and regions adopting general trade as the statistical method, covering the United States, UK, Japan, Canada, Australia etc. China also adopts general trade system as the statistical method.

总贸易是指以国境为标准划分进口与出口的一种统计方法。总贸易可分为总进口和总出口。凡是进入一国国境的商品一律列入总进口，包括进口后供国内消费的部分和进口后成为转口或过境的部分；凡是离开一国国境的商品一律列入总出口，包括本国产品的出口、外国商品复出口及转口或过境的部分。总进口额与总出口额之和即为总贸易额。目前，采用总贸易统计方法的有美国、英国、日本、加拿大、澳大利亚等 90 多个国家和地区。我国采用的是总贸易体系。

4.2 Special Trade 专门贸易

It is a statistical method to classify import and export by a country's customs frontier. Special trade is divided into special import and special export. Special import is the goods moving into the customs frontier after paying tariff and making customs clearance; according to the standard, the goods which are moved into the border of a country but kept in the bonded warehouse, or in the duty-free export processing zone are not taken as the import. Special export is the home-made goods moved out of the customs area and the re-exported goods which are moved out of the customs area after being imported and processed. Therefore, the exported goods within the border but out of the customs area are not taken as the export of the country. Special trade of a country consists of special import and special export. For the time being, there are more than 80 nations and regions adopting special trade system, including Germany, Italy, Switzerland, France and so on.

The customs area and country's area are usually consistent entirely. However, occasionally there are inconsistency, such as the countries with special economic zone in which the customs area is smaller than the country's area because the special economic zone is out of the customs area but within the country's border. In case that several countries are allied into a customs union, the territories of the countries are united into one unified customs frontier. In this case, the customs area is bigger than any country's area.

专门贸易是指以关境作为划分进口和出口标准的统计方法。专门贸易又可分为专门进口和专门出口。专门进口是指进入关境并向海关缴纳关税由海关放行的外国商品；根据这个标准，虽然进入了国境，但如果只是放在海关的保税仓库之内，或者只是进入到免税的出口加工区进行加工，则不被统计为进口。专门出口是指从国内运出关境的本国产品及进口后经加工又运出关境的复出口商品。可见，从关境外国境内出口到其他国家的商品，则不被统计为出口。专门进口额加专门出口额构成一国的专门贸易总额。目前，采用专门贸易统计方法的国家有德国、意大利、瑞士、法国等 80 多个国家和地区。

一般情况下，一国关境与国境完全重合，但也有不一致的情况，如设经济特区的国家，关境的范围要小于国境，因为，经济特区虽然在国境内，但却在关境之外。当几个国家结成关税同盟，参加关税同盟的国家的领土合并成为一个统一的关境，这时，关境范围要大于其中某一国的国境。

5. Visible Trade and Invisible Trade 有形贸易和无形贸易

According to the forms and contents of merchandise, international trade may be classified into visible trade and invisible trade.

依据商品的形式与内容的不同来划分，国际贸易可分为有形贸易和无形贸易。

5.1 Visible Trade 有形贸易

It is also named as cargo trade, referring to the trade of substantial merchandise in import and export, in which the goods are visible and touchable. The import and export of visible merchandise have to go through customs, and to be indicated in the statistical data of import and export, constituting the total amount of the foreign trade of a country for a period of time. At the same time, for convenience of statistics, UN makes a classification of visible merchandise, which can be categorized into 10 sorts. The No.0–No.4 are named as primary products, and No.5–No.8 are named as manufactured products. No.9 is named as other articles unclassified.

有形贸易也称货物贸易，是指在进出口贸易中进行的实物商品交易，因为这些实物商品看得见、摸得着，故称为有形贸易。有形商品的进口和出口都要办理海关手续，并在海关的进出口统计中反映出来，从而构成一个国家一定时期的对外贸易总额。同时，联合国为便于统计，把有形商品分为 10 类。0—4 类商品称为初级产品，5—8 类商品称为制成品。9 类为没有分类的其他商品。

5.2 Invisible Trade 无形贸易

It refers to all the trades of non-material merchandise in international business, including trade of service and trade of technology. Usually, the invisible trade is not indicated in the statistics of customs as it needn't go through customs, but instead shown on the international balance sheet as an important part of it.

The main differences between visible trade and invisible trade are as follows: (1) the visible merchandise can be stored while the invisible merchandise cannot; (2) the visible trade is the main part in the international balance sheet which can be indicated in customs statistics. As to the invisible trade, it is only indicated on the international balance sheet without indication in the customs statistical data.

无形贸易是指在国际贸易活动中所进行的所有非物质形态的商品贸易，无形贸易包括服务贸易和技术贸易。通常不办理海关手续，在海关的进出口统计中不反映，而在国际收支中反映出来，是国际收支的重要组成部分。

有形贸易与无形贸易的区别主要有：有形商品是可以储存的，而无形商品是无形的、不可储存的；有形贸易额也就是货物贸易额是各国国际收支的主要组成部分，并在各国海关统计中能查到，而无形贸易额在各国国际收支表中只得到部分反映，在海关统计中查不到。

6. Free-liquidation Trade and Barter Trade 自由结汇贸易和易货贸易

In accordance with payment ways, international trade may be divided into free-liquidation trade and barter trade. 依据清偿方式的不同来划分，国际贸易可分为自由结汇贸易和易货贸易。

6.1 Free-liquidation Trade 自由结汇贸易

It is also named as cash-liquidation trade, referring to the trade on the payment by currency, on the condition that the payment currency must be convertible in international financial market. The characteristic of it is to make settlement in trade through bank as scheduled. For the time being, in international trade, the payment currencies are mainly Dollar, Euro, Pound, Yen, and Swiss Franc etc.

自由结汇贸易又称为现汇贸易，是指以货币作为清偿工具所进行的贸易，其前提条件是作为支付的货币必须能够在国际金融市场自由兑换。其特色是银行逐步支付货物款项，以结清债权、债务。在当今国际贸易中，能作为国际支付工具的货币主要有美元、欧元、英镑、日元、瑞士法郎等。

6.2 Barter Trade 易货贸易

It refers to the trade based on the barter trade agreement or barter contract concluded by both parties, on the payment with the valuated goods.

Free-liquidation trade is the most common one in the current international trade. Barter trade is more suitable for the countries which cannot carry out free-liquidation trade because of scarcity of foreign exchange or for other reasons.

易货贸易是指商品交易的双方依据相互间签订的易贸协定或易货合同，以经过计价的货物作为清偿工具所进行的贸易。

自由结汇贸易是目前国际贸易活动中最普通的一种。易货贸易比较适用于那些外汇不足或因其他各种原因无法以自由的结汇方式进行相互交易的国家。

7. Foreign Trade Volume, International Trade Volume, Quantum of Foreign Trade 对外贸易额（值）、国际贸易额（值）、对外贸易量

7.1 Foreign Trade Volume 对外贸易额（值）

Foreign Trade Volume consists of the total import volume and the total export volume of a country for a period of time. It is an important indicator to reflect the foreign trade situation of a country, measuring the scale of the import and export volume in form of currency amount. In calculation, the export volume is calculated in terms of FOB price, and import volume is calculated in terms of CIF price. For a period of time, the difference between the total export volume and the total import volume is called the balance of foreign trade. In case that the total export volume is larger than the total import volume, the balance is called trade surplus or favorable trade balance; on the contrary, in case that the total import volume is larger than the total export volume, the balance is called trade deficit or adverse trade balance; when the total volumes of import and export are the same, it is called trade balance.

对外贸易额（值）是由一国一定时期内从国外进口的商品总额加上该国同一时期内向国外出口的商品总额构成。这是用货币金额表示的一国一定时期内的进出口的规模，是衡量一国对外贸易状况的重要指标。在计算时，出口额要以 FOB 价格计算，进口额则以 CIF 价格计算。一定时期内一国出口总额与进口总额之间的差额，则称为对外贸易差额。当出口商品总额超过进口商品总额时，差额部分称为“贸易顺差”，也可称为“贸易出超”；反之，当进口商品总额超过出口商品总额时，差额部分称为“贸易逆差”，也可称为“贸易入超”，或称贸易赤字；如进出口商品总额相等，则称为“贸易平衡”。

7.2 International Trade Volume 国际贸易额（值）

It is the total trade volume of countries all over the world indicated in form of currency, the total sum of the export volumes of all countries and regions. In order to avoid repeat calculation, international trade volume cannot be calculated by simply gathering the total sum of import volumes and export volumes of all countries because the export of one country (or region) is also the equivalent import of the other country (or region).

In UN statistics, the total export volume of all countries is taken as International Trade Volume. For most countries, the import volume is calculated at CIF price, that is to say, cost plus freight and insurance. Obviously, it is not exact enough to take the total import volume as international trade volume. On the other hand, the export volume is calculated at FOB price, namely free on board, comparatively more exact than at CIF price. CIF price is higher than FOB price by the freight and insurance, and consequently the total import volume of the world is bigger than the export volume.

国际贸易额（值）是指以货币表示的世界各国的对外贸易总额。这是计算和统计世界各国对外贸易总额的指标，是把世界上所有国家和地区的出口额相加得出的数额。但是，在计算国际贸易额时，不是简单地把世界各国的出口额与进口额加在一起。因为一国（或地区）的出口，就是另一国（或地区）的进口，若两者相加等于重复计算。

在联合国统计中，通常采用各国出口额相加作为国际贸易额。因为世界上绝大多数国家（或地区）都是用 CIF 价格计算进口额的，即成本加运费、保险费。显而易见，把进口值加起来作为国际贸易额是不准确的。而出口额一般采用 FOB 价格，即装运港船上交货，相对于 CIF 而言，是比较准确的。CIF 价格比 FOB 价格多了运费和保险费，所以，世界进口额会大于世界出口额。

7.3 Quantum of Foreign Trade 对外贸易量

The foreign trade volume indicated in currency cannot exactly reflect the actual scale of a country's foreign trade as it is often influenced by the fluctuation of price. As a result, the volumes of foreign trade for different periods cannot be compared directly. In actual practice, in order to eliminate the influence of price's fluctuation, and reflect more exactly the actual variation of a country's foreign trade, the quantum of foreign trade is adopted to indicate the actual scale of foreign trade of a country.

The specific calculation is as follows:

Quantum of Foreign Trade = foreign trade/price index of Im./Ex. goods

Price Index = price of current period/price of base period ×100%

Example:

1) Export Volume, generally on the basis of FOB price, the export volume of China in 2020 is 17.93 trillion dollars.

2) Import Volume, generally on the basis of CIF price, the import volume of China in 2020 is 14.23 trillion dollars.

3) Foreign Trade Volume: Import Volume + Export Volume. The total foreign trade volume of China in 2020 is 32.16 trillion dollars.

4) Trade Balance: Export Volume – Import Volume.

- Trade Surplus: Export Volume > Import Volume. Trade surplus of China is 3.7 trillion dollars.
- Trade Deficit: Export Volume < Import Volume.
- Trade Balance: Export Volume = Import Volume.

对外贸易量以货币表示的对外贸易额经常受到价格变动的影响，因而不能确切地反映一国对外贸易的实际规模，不同时期的对外贸易额是不能直接比较的。所以，在实际工作中，为剔除价格变动的影响，并能准确反映一国对外贸易的实际数量变化，制定了对外贸易量这一指标，它能确切地反映一国对外贸易的实际规模。

具体计算方法是：以固定年份为基期计算的进口或出口价格指数去除报告期的进口或出口总额，得到的是相当于按不变价格计算的进口额或出口额。

对外贸易量=对外贸易额/进出口价格指数

价格指数=报告期价格/基期价格×100%

例如：

1）出口额，一般以 FOB 统计，2020 年中国出口额为 17.93 万亿美元。

2）进口额，一般以 CIF 统计，2020 年中国进口额为 14.23 万亿美元。

3）对外贸易额：出口额+进口额。2020 年中国对外贸易额为 32.16 万亿美元。

4）贸易差额：出口额　进口额。

- 贸易顺差：出口额＞进口额。2020 年中国贸易顺差为 3.7 万亿美元。
- 贸易逆差：出口额＜进口额。
- 贸易平衡：出口额=进口额。

8. Terms of Trade 贸易条件

It refers to the proportion of the quantity of the imported merchandise exchanged per unit of exported merchandise.

The trade condition index for the current year = Price Index of Export/Price Index of Import ×100%.

The rise of the trade condition index (>100), indicating the export price is rising compared with the import price, means the increase of the quantity of the imported exchanged for one unit of the exported, that is to say, the trade condition is improved. The decline of the trade condition index (<100), indicating the drop of the export price compared with the import price, means the decrease of the quantity of the imported exchanged for one unit of the exported. That is to say, the trade condition is becoming worse.

贸易条件是指一定时期内一国出口一单位商品可以交换多少单位外国进口商品的比例。

当年贸易条件系数=出口价格指数/进口价格指数×100

贸易条件指数的上升（大于 100），表明出口价格较进口价格相对上涨，意味着每出口一单位商品能换回的进口商品数量比原来增加，即贸易条件改善；贸易条件指数下降（小于 100），则表明出口价格比进口价格相对下跌，意味着每出口一单位商品能换回的进口商品数量比原来减少，即贸易条件恶化了。

9. Foreign Trade Dependence 对外贸易依存度

Foreign Trade Dependence, namely foreign trade index, a proportion of the import and export volumes of one country for a period of time to the general domestic product, is an indicator measuring the dependence degree of a country's economy on foreign trade. Due to the different development levels, different open-up degrees, different domestic market scales of countries, there is a great discrepancy.

Example:

1) Export dependence: export volume/GDP =32.16/101.59×100%=31.67%

2) Import dependence: import volume/GDP = 17.93/101.59×100%=17.65%

3) Foreign trade dependence: foreign trade volume/GDP= 14.23/101.59×100%=14%

对外贸易依存度又称对外贸易系数，是指一个国家在一定时期内进出口贸易值同该国同期国内生产总值的对比关系，是衡量一国国民经济对进出口贸易的依赖程度的一个指标。由于各国经济的发展水平不同，对外开放的程度不同，国内市场的大小不同，导致各国的对外贸易依存度有较大的差异。

例如：2020 年我国外贸依存度如下：

1）出口依存度：出口额/GDP×100%=32.16/101.59×100%=31.67%

2）进口依存度：进口额/GDP×100%=17.93/101.59×100%=17.65%

3）外贸依存度：对外贸易额/GDP×100%=14.23/101.59×100%=14%

10. Foreign Trade Structure and International Trade Structure 对外贸易商品结构和国际贸易商品结构

10.1 Foreign Trade Structure 对外贸易商品结构

It refers to the shares of the variety of merchandise in the total import and export volume. The foreign trade structure of a country results from the economic development situation, trade policy, industrial structure, natural resource. The foreign trade structure of developed countries is presented as dominantly the export of industrial finished products and import of primary products; the foreign trade structure of developing countries is characterized mainly as the export of primary products and import of finished products. According to Standard International Trade Classification (SITC), the commodities are classified into 10 categories as follows: food and edible living animals (0); beverages and tobacco (1); non-edible raw materials expected for fuels (2); mineral fuels, lubricant oil and products (3); animal or vegetable fats and waxes (4); chemicals and chemical products (5); finished products categorized by raw materials (6); mechanical appliances and transport equipment (7); manufactured articles (8); other articles unclassified (9). In international trade statistics, generally the commodities from (0)–(4) are called primary products and the commodities from (5)–(8) are named as finished products.

Example: data of China in 2011

For example, in accordance with SITC, the export of the primary products of China is 100.5 billion dollars in 2011, occupying 5% of the total export volume with the increase of 23%, and the export of manufactured products is 1,798.05 billion dollars occupying 95% of the total export volume with the increase of 20.2%. In the export of primary products, food and living animals, beverages and tobacco, non-edible materials, mineral fuels, lubricating oil and the materials, animal and vegetable fats and oils and wax have respectively increased for 22.7%, 19.4%, 29.1%, 21% and 47.9%. In the manufactured products, chemical products and the allied products, the manufactured products based on various materials, mechanical and transportation equipment, and other miscellaneous manufactured articles (including prefabricated houses, furniture, travel articles, costumes and shoes etc.) have respectively increased for 31.1%, 28.3%, 15.6% and 21.6%.

对外贸易商品结构是指一个国家一定时期内各类商品占整个进出口贸易额的份额。一个国家的对外贸易货物结构，主要是由该国的经济发展水平、贸易政策、产业结构状况、自然资源状况决定的。发达国家对外贸易货物结构是以出口工业制成品和进口初级产品为主；发展中国家的对外贸易货物结构的特征则是以出口初级产品和进口工业制成品为主。联合国国际贸易标准分类法将商品分为 10 类：食品及主要供食用的活动物（0）；饮料及烟类（1）；燃料以外的非食用原料（2）；矿物燃料、润滑油及有关原料（3）；动植物油脂及蜡（4）；化学品及有关产品（5）；主要按原料分类的制成品（6）；机械及运输设备（7）；各项制品（8）；没有分类的其他产品（9）。在国际贸易统计中，一般把（0）—（4）类商品称为初级产品，把（5）—（8）类商品称为制成品。

10.2 International Trade Structure 国际贸易商品结构

It refers to the shares of a variety of commodities in the general international trade volume, generally indicated with the proportion in the total export volume or import volume of world. The study of international trade structure mainly focuses on the proportion of primary products and industrial finished products in the world trade volume. The international trade structure is a reflection of worldwide economic development, industrial structure and service development.

国际贸易商品结构是指各类商品在整个国际贸易额中所占的比重，通常以它们在世界出口总额或进口总额中的比重来表示。研究国际贸易商品结构，通常是看初级产品和工业制成品两大类别占世界贸易额的比重。国际贸易商品结构可以反映出整个世界的经济发展水平、产业结构状况和服务发展水平。

Lesson 2 General Introduction to International Trade Policies
国际贸易政策概述

For a period of time, a nation will implement a variety of basic policies on import and export to develop foreign economic relationship, which is called as foreign trade policy. It serves the economy basis and foreign policies of all countries.

对外贸易政策是各国在一定时期内对进口贸易和出口贸易所实行的政策，是各国发展对外经济关系的基本政策，是为各国经济基础和对外政策服务的。

1. Goals of Foreign Trade Policies 对外贸易政策的目的

The goals of foreign trade policies are as follows:

1) To protect the domestic market. In order to avoid the competition against the foreign merchandise, a nation may adopt tariff measures and non-tariff barriers to restrict the import of foreign commodities and services.

2) To enlarge the export market. A variety of foreign policies and measures are adopted to encourage exporters to increase export volume, further to enlarge the export scale of the whole country.

3) To drive the improvement and upgrade of industrial structure.

4) To accumulate capital and fund. With the implementation of tariffs and domestic taxation, a nation's revenue increases.

5) To maintain a good foreign economic and political relationship. It will help exporters to enjoy a good foreign trade environment.

各国制定对外贸易政策的目的如下。

（1）保护本国的市场。通过关税和各种非关税壁垒措施限制外国商品和服务的进口，使本国商品和服务免受外国竞争。

（2）扩大本国产品的出口市场。通过各种鼓励出口的措施来促进本国出口商增加出口，使本国的出口市场不断扩大。

（3）促进本国产业结构的改善和升级。

（4）积累资本或资金。通过关税、国内税等，使国家财政收入增加。

（5）维护本国对外的经济、政治关系。促使出口商获得良好的外贸环境。

2. Types of Foreign Trade Policies 对外贸易政策的类型

2.1 Free Trade Policy 自由贸易政策

When free trade policy is implemented, the goods and services are input and output freely with the cancel of the restrictions and barriers on export and import trade, and the elimination of various privileges and special treatments on the import and export of domestic commodities and services, to carry out free competition and cooperation in world market.

自由贸易政策是指国家取消对进出口贸易的限制和障碍，取消对本国进出口商品和服务贸易等的各种特权和优待，使商品和服务自由地输出和输入，在世界市场上实行自由竞争与合作。

2.2 Protective Trade Policy 保护贸易政策

When protective trade policy is carried out, the nation adopts a variety of policies and measures to intervene the foreign trade and protect the domestic market from the competition of the goods and services from other countries, restricting the import of the goods and services abroad, and granting privilege and allowances to the exported goods and services of homeland.

保护贸易政策是指国家采取措施干预对外贸易，限制外国商品和服务的进口，保护本国市场免受国外商品和服务等的竞争，并对本国出口商品和服务贸易给予优待和补贴。

2.3 Managed Trade Policy 管理贸易政策

Managed trade is the type of trade between free trade and protective trade, focusing on coordination, dominated by government intervention, with negotiation as the measure. The managed trade policy is carried out by the government with measures of intervention, in coordination and management.

管理贸易介于自由贸易和保护贸易之间，以协调为中心，以政府干预为主导，以磋商为手段，管理贸易政策就是政府对外贸进行干预、协调和管理的措施。

3. Establishment of Foreign Trade Policy 对外贸易政策的制定

During the establishment of foreign trade policy, governments have to take the following points into consideration.

各国在制定贸易政策的过程中，要考虑到以下因素。

3.1 Economic Power 经济力量的强弱

Generally, developed and competitive economies are more likely to take free trade policies, standing for free competition and cooperation. Contrarily, the developing and weak economies intend to take protective policies to make more restrictions on foreign trade.

一般来说，经济发达、国际竞争力强的经济体，总体上倾向于自由贸易政策，主张在世界范围内进行自由竞争与合作。反之，发展中的、竞争力较弱的经济体则倾向于保护贸易政策，对对外贸易加以诸多限制。

3.2 Economic Development Strategy 经济发展战略

The nations which adopt the extroversive-oriented strategy will make more open and free policy. The more important the foreign trade is for a nation, the more likely the nation is to support worldwide competition and cooperation.

采取外向型经济发展战略的国家会制定比较开放和自由的外贸政策。对外贸易对一个国家的经济发展越是重要，就越会主张在世界范围内进行竞争和合作。

3.3 International Political Environment and Diplomatic Policy 国际政治环境和一国的外交政策

For a nation, the foreign trade policy and the diplomatic policy are in a close relationship, mutually serving and driving each other. Occasionally foreign trade has to comply with the diplomatic need, whereas more often diplomatic policy is made to develop and protect foreign trade.

外贸政策和外交政策关系密切，两者之间存在着相互服务、相互促进的关系。在某些场合，对外贸易要服从外交的需要。在更多的场合下，外交政策为外贸打通道路、提供保护。

3.4 Influence of Foreign Trade Policy on Interest Groups 外贸政策对利益集团的影响

Foreign policy is the result of the contradictions and conflicts of different interest groups. In case that an interest group is on predominant position politically and economically, the need of the group will be taken into consideration sufficiently by the foreign policy maker, to boost or discourage the import and export of some commodities seeking for the biggest interest of it.

外贸政策是不同利益集团之间矛盾和斗争的产物。当某一集团在政治和经济方面占上风时，制定外贸政策的过程中就会充分考虑该集团的需要，以促进或阻碍某些特定商品的进出口，从而谋求最大的利益。

Lesson 3 Evolution of Free Trade Theories and Policies 自由贸易理论和政策的演变

1. Classic Theories of Free Trade 古典自由贸易的理论学说

1.1 Absolute Advantage Law of Adam Smith 亚当·斯密的绝对优势理论

Adam Smith (1723–1790): A well-known economist of UK, one of the main founders of capitalist classic economics school, and the father of the theory of international specialization and international trade.

One of the masterpieces of Adam Smith is *The Wealth of Nations*, the initial publishment of which symbolized the birth of the economics as an independent knowledge playing an important role in the development of capitalist society.

In the middle of the eighteenth century, with the coming of industrial revolution and the handicraft industry in workshop as the leading production form as well as the invention of primary machines, the boosting market demand from the internal and external required the rapid growth of capitalism. The emerging industrial capitalists required the further expansion of international trade, the extension of overseas markets with more raw material sources, settling substantial foundation for the government to adopt free trade policies. Since the theories and policies of Mercantilism had been the obstacles for emerging capitalism to gain, Adam Smith's theory, standing on the side of capitalism, brought the law of absolute advantage in his book, giving an expatiation on how to go on with trade to increase wealth and develop economy more efficiently, explaining the strengths of free trade, and advancing the theory of absolute advantage.

亚当·斯密（1723—1790）：英国著名经济学家，资本主义古典经济学派的主要奠基人之一，国际分工及国际贸易理论的创始者。

亚当·斯密的代表作之一《国民财富的性质和原因的研究》（简称《国富论》）的首次出版，标志着经济学作为一门独立学科的诞生，对资本主义社会的发展起到了重大的促进作用。

18世纪中期，英国的产业革命逐渐展开，工场手工业已成为工业生产的主要形式，且有一些早期的机器发明，国内外迅速膨胀起来的市场需求要求资本主义迅速发展，新兴的工业资产阶级迫切要求扩大对外贸易，扩大海外市场和原料来源，也为政府采取自由贸易政策奠定了物质基础。重商主义的贸易理论和政策限制了新兴资产阶级的利益，亚当·斯密站在产业资产阶级的立场上，从理论上阐述如何进行贸易才能有效地积累财富和发展经济，说明自由贸易对经济发展的好处，提出了绝对优势的理论。

1.1.1 Major Points of Absolute Advantage Law 绝对优势论的主要论点

In the "Absolute Advantage Law" of Adam Smith, it is stated as follows: with different natural conditions owned by every country and consequently different production conditions of every country, based on its most favorable condition, it is beneficial to every country if every country makes exchange of the commodities produced in the absolutely low production cost with other countries. The theory is also called "Law of Absolute Cost" as he stressed but the commodities in absolutely low cost can be exchanged internationally.

The theory, calling for every country to take the free trade policy, thinks that every country could enjoy the benefit from the absolute cost difference resulting from the natural specialization.

亚当·斯密提出了他的"绝对优势理论"——每一个国家先天所拥有的自然条件是不同的，后天所获得的生产条件也很不一样，如果各个国家都根据自己的有利条件，用生产成本比别的国家绝对低的商品进行国际交换，这对各个国家是有利的，由于他强调生产劳动成本绝对低的商品才能进行国际交换，所以这一理论又被称为"绝对成本论"。

这一理论思想要求一国实行自由贸易政策，认为只有这样各国才能充分享受自然分工导致的绝对成本差异所带来的利益。

1) Specialization Leading to the Enhancement of Productivity 分工导致劳动生产率提高

Adam Smith's argument about free trade was based on his theory of international specialization. The reasons for the enhancement of productivity, Adam Smith thought, are as follows.

First, specialization has made workers more skillful on their jobs. Second, specialization has avoided the time loss caused by labour transition. Third, specialization has resulted into the invention of machines which made work easier and shortened working time, further advancing the improvement of working tools, and making one person able to finish the work of several persons, consequently to enhance the productivity. Smith took the factory of handmade pins as example. Every worker made 20 pins at the most in case that there's no specialization under the working condition of that time, while in case of specialization, every worker made 4,800 pins per capita everyday, which means the productivity of every worker had been raised for hundreds of times. Therefore, he argued that productivity could be promoted through specialization when the production factors were kept invariable.

亚当·斯密主张自由贸易的思想是建立在他的国际分工学说基础上的。分工之所以能够提高劳动效率，亚当·斯密认为存在以下几个原因：

其一，分工可以提高劳动者的熟练程度；其二，分工避免了不同劳动转移而造成的时间损失；其三，分工导致了许多简化劳动和缩减劳动投入的机械的出现，有利于发明创造和改进工具，使一个人能够完成多个人完成的任务，因此能够提高劳动生产力。斯密以手工制扣针的工厂为例，认为根据当时的情况，在没有分工的情况下，一个工人每天最多制作 20 根针。而在分工的情况下，平均每人每天可制针 4 800 根，每个人的工作效率提高了几百倍。因此，他认为在生产要素不变的条件下，依靠分工，劳动生产率可以得到提高。

2) The Absolute Advantage of Cost Is the Principle of Specialization 分工的原则是成本的绝对优势

In case that one nation may produce a kind of product at absolutely lower cost than the other nations, the nation has the absolute advantage on the product.

Since division of labour can spur the productivity greatly, Adam Smith thought, every person should get engaged into the production in which he specialized, and then made exchange of the products with other persons, which is beneficial to everyone at the most. It's written in his book: "It is the maxim of every prudent master of a family, never to attempt to make at home what it will cost him more to make than to buy. The tailor does not attempt to make his own shoes, but buys them from the shoemaker. The shoemaker does not attempt to make his own clothes, but employs a tailor." "What is prudence in the conduct of every private family, can scarcely be a folly in that of a kingdom. If a foreign country can supply us with a commodity cheaper than we ourselves can make it, better buy it of them with some part of the produce of our own industry, employed in a way in which we have some advantages." He extended the idea of individual specialization to social specialization further to international specialization.

绝对优势是指如果一国生产某种商品的成本绝对低于另一国，则该国在这一产品上有绝对优势。

由于分工可以极大地提高生产率，所以亚当·斯密认为，每个人都应该在自己最具优势的领域从事产品生产，然后再用这种产品和他人交换物品，这样对每个人都最有利。

他写道：“每一个精明的家长都会遵循以下准则：从不在家里生产那些比购买的还贵的产品。裁缝不会试图自己做鞋，而是从鞋匠那里买鞋……”“在每一个私人家庭中堪称精明的事情，在一个大国的行为中不大会是荒唐的。如果外国能以比我们自己制造还便宜的商品供应我们，那么，我们最好就用我们具有某些优势的行业中生产出来的部分产品来向他们购买。”他由个人分工推及社会分工进而到国际分工。

3) International Specialization Is Based on Natural Advantage or Acquired Advantage Owned by a Nation 国际分工是建立在一个国家所拥有的自然优势或获得性优势的基础之上

The advantage is determined after comparing the production costs of nations, which is resulted from rich natural resources (such as geographic, environmental, soil, climate, mineral conditions etc.) and the acquired advantages (such as highly skilled craft owned by local people).

Depending on the above stated, Adam Smith brought the "Law of Absolute Advantage"—every country owns some absolute advantageous production conditions for some particular products, and the production cost of these products consequently is lower absolutely than other countries, so it is absolutely beneficial for the country in the production and trade of the products. Every country shall make international specialization according to the absolute difference of production cost and trade, which will make full use of the resources, labor, and capital of every country most efficiently, and then enhance the productivity and increase wealth greatly. In accordance with the theory, every country is required to carry out free trade policy so as to enjoy the benefits brought from the absolute cost difference due to the natural specialization.

优势是通过比较生产成本确定的，优势的来源是自然禀赋（如地理、环境、土壤、气候、矿产等自然条件）和后天获得的某些有利条件（如民众特殊的技巧和生产工艺）。

据此亚当·斯密提出了他的“绝对优势理论”——每一个国家都有其适宜生产某些特定产品的绝对有利的生产条件，因而生产这些产品的成本会绝对低于别国，因而在该产品的生产和交换上处于绝对有利地位。各国应按照绝对成本差异进行国际分工，然后进行贸易，这将会使各国的资源、劳动力和资本得到最有效的利用，从而大大地提高劳动生产率和增加物质财富。这一理论思想要求每一个国家实行自由贸易政策，这样各国才能充分享受自然分工导致的绝对成本差异所带来的利益。

1.1.2 Argument of the Law of Absolute Advantage 绝对优势论的论证

Productivity is promoted with specialization resulting from division of labor for trade. Every country shall produce the products which are at the lowest cost, and gain more through free trade. To illuminate the theory, Smith took two examples as follows:

It's presumed that Britain and Portugal both go into production of wine and wool, which is as follows.

Before specialization, the labor needed for every unit of product (Table 1-1).

交换形成分工，分工能导致专业化，提高劳动生产率。各国应生产成本绝对低的产品，通过自由贸易，取得更大的收益。为了说明这一理论，斯密举出下面的例子。

假定英国和葡萄牙两国都生产葡萄酒和羊毛，生产情况如下所示。

分工前，生产一单位产品所需的劳动量见表 1-1。

表 1-1

Country 国家	Wool 羊毛		Wine 酒	
	Labor (P/Y) 劳动量（人/年）	Output (unit) 产量（单位）	Labor (P/Y) 劳动量（人/年）	Output (Unit) 产量（单位）
Britain 英国	80	1	120	1
Portugal 葡萄牙	120	1	60	1

According to the above data, Britain has absolute advantage on the production of wool while Portugal has absolute advantage on the production of wine, so the two countries may get into specialization.

After specialization, the production of both countries (Table 1-2).

根据以上数据，英国在生产羊毛上有绝对优势，而葡萄牙在生产酒上具有绝对优势，所以两国可进行分工。

分工后，两国的生产情况见表 1-2。

表 1-2

Product 产品 / Country 国家	Wool 羊毛	Wine 酒
Britain 英国	（80+120）÷80＝2.5	
Portugal 葡萄牙		（60+120）÷60＝3

The two countries go into trade at 1:1, and Britain gets one unit of wine in return with one unit of wool.

After trade, the products owned by the two countries are as follows (Table 1-3).

两国按 1:1 进行交换，英国用 1 单位的羊毛换取葡萄牙 1 单位的酒。

贸易后，两国拥有的产品情况见表 1-3。

表 1-3

Product 产品 / Country 国家	Wool 羊毛	Wine 酒
Britain 英国	1.5 (0.5 unit more than before specialization) 1.5（比分工前多 0.5 单位）	1 (Imported) 1（进口）
Portugal 葡萄牙	1 (Imported) 1（进口）	2 (1 unit more than before specialization) 2（比分工前多 1 单位）

1.2 The Law of Comparative Advantage of David Ricardo 大卫·李嘉图的比较优势论

David Ricardo (1772–1823): a great British classic political economist, born in a rich capitalist Jewish family in Britain. At his time, it happened that industrial revolution was growing rapidly in Britain with emerging capitalists. When the major contradiction in British society was between industrial capitalists and landlords in that time, David Ricardo advocated free trade in opposition to Corn Laws and argued to amend election laws.

大卫·李嘉图（1772—1823）：英国资产阶级古典政治经济学的杰出代表和完成者，生于英国犹太族大资产阶级家庭。李嘉图所处的时代正是英国工业革命及新兴资本家迅速发展的时代。当时英国社会的主要矛盾是工业资产阶级同地主贵族阶级的矛盾，李嘉图代表新兴产业资产阶级的利益和要求，提倡自由贸易，反对谷物法，主张修改选举法。

1.2.1 The Historical Background for the Theory Forming 该理论产生的历史背景

In 1815, the Britain parliament passed the amended Corn Laws which was a protectionist trade policy to restrict the import of foreign grain, leading to other countries to obstruct the export from Britain through imposing high tariff on the British industrial products, hence cutting down the competition of industrial products. In order to protect the benefits of British capitalists, it was urgent and necessary to give argument for the advantage of free trade for corn.

David Ricardo, as a British capitalist classical political economist, standing on the side of industrial capitalist, argued that Britain shall import corn from abroad in large quantity because Britain's production advantage on textile is bigger than on corn. Therefore, Britain shall get engaged in the production of textile specially and export them to trade for corn, to get comparative benefit to enhance the production of commodity.

As a successor of Adam Smith's absolute cost theory, in his masterpiece named *Principles of Political Economy and Taxation*, he developed the law of absolute cost. Making use of analysis model of two countries (Britain and Portugal) and two products (wool and wine), he gave the argument that it was comparative advantage that formed the basis for trade instead of absolute advantage, established relative cost theory based on free trade and formulated all countries in different development stages may gain from international trade.

英国议会于 1815 年通过了修订的限制外国粮食进口的保护贸易政策——谷物法，招致外国以高关税阻止英国向他们出口工业品，削弱了工业品的竞争能力。为了维护英国工业资产阶级的利益，迫切需要从理论上论证谷物自由贸易的好处。

英国资产阶级古典政治经济学者大卫·李嘉图站在工业资产阶级一边。他主张，英国不仅要从外国进口玉米，而且要大量进口，因为英国在纺织品上所占的优势比在玉米生产上所占的优势还大。故英国应该专门进行纺织品生产，以其出口换取玉米，取得比较利益，提高商品生产数量。

李嘉图在《政治经济学及赋税原理》一书中，继承和发展了亚当·斯密的绝对成本论，运用两个国家（英国和葡萄牙）、两种产品（羊毛和葡萄酒）这种分析模型，提出决定国际贸易的基础是比较而不是绝对优势这一命题，建立了以自由贸易为前提的比较成本理论，解释了发展程度不同的国家，都能通过参与国际贸易获得利益。

1.2.2 Major Arguments of the Law of Comparative Advantage 比较优势理论的主要论点

In the law of comparative advantage, it takes the opinion that the gaps of productivity between two countries are not the same in all products. For the country which is more efficient in the production of all products, it shall concentrate on the production of the products with bigger efficiency while the country with absolute disadvantage shall focus on the production of the products with smaller disadvantage, then both countries could save labor and gain in international trade.

比较优势理论认为，在两国间，劳动生产率的差距并非在任何商品上都是相等的。对处于绝对优势的国家，应集中力量生产优势较大的商品；处于绝对劣势的国家，应集中力量生产劣势较小的商品。然后，通过国际贸易，互相交换，彼此都节省了劳动，都得到了益处。

1) The Principle of Specialization Is Comparative Advantage 分工的原则是比较优势

The definition of comparative advantage: in case that the opportunity cost (measured with other products) to produce a kind of product in one country is lower than the opportunity cost occurred in other countries, the country owns the comparative advantage on the products.

比较优势的定义：如果一个国家在本国生产一种产品的机会成本（用其他产品来衡量）低于在其他国家生产该产品的机会成本的话，则这个国家在生产该种产品上就拥有比较优势。

2) The Core of Comparative Advantage Theory Is to Engage in the Production for Which One's Advantage over Others Is the Largest or His Disadvantage Is the Smallest 比较优势的核心内容是“两优取其重，两劣取其轻”

David Ricardo gave the example: if both persons could manufacture shoes and hats, one person is 1/3 more capable of making shoes than the other person, and 1/5 more capable of making hats, then the former would specialize in shoes, and the latter makes hats only, so they exchange, which is beneficial to each one.

He demonstrated the theory by extending the economic relationship between individuals to that of two countries. Even if one country's efficiency of production on every product is under the other country, namely on absolute disadvantage, as long as both countries concentrate on the production of the products with the largest advantage to engage in international trade, the two countries still can gain and save labors as well as increase social wealth.

It is determined for the two countries to gain by the structure chain as follows: comparative low cost→comparative advantage→comparative benefit. Comparative benefit is the basis of international specialization and international trade, which is due to the difference of productivity and production costs between the countries.

李嘉图举例说：如果两个人都能制造鞋和帽，其中一个人在制鞋时强 1/3，在制帽时强 1/5，那么这个较强的人专门制鞋，而那个较差的人专门制帽，然后进行交换，这样对双方都有利。

他采用了由个人之间的经济关系推及国家之间的经济联系这种实证的方法。一国与另一国相比，其劳动生产率在任何商品的生产中均低于另一国，处于绝对劣势。但只要本国集中生产那些绝对优势最大的产品，即按照“两优取其重，两劣取其轻”的原则，进行国际分工与国际贸易，在同样交易中双方不仅都可从中获益和实现社会劳动的节约，而且会增加社会财富。

这样，两国进行贸易从而获得利益是由比较成本低→比较优势→比较利益这一结构链决定的。比较利益是发生国际分工和国际贸易的基础，而产生比较利益的原因则是各国间劳动生产率的差异及由此产生的劳动成本的差别。

1.2.3 Argumentation for the Law of Comparative Advantage 比较优势理论的论证

Before specialization, the labor to produce one unit of product (Table 1-4).

分工前，生产 1 单位产品所需的劳动量见表 1-4。

表 1-4

Product 产品 / Country 国家	Wool 羊毛		Wine 酒	
	Labor (P/Y) 劳动量（人/年）	Output (unit) 产量（单位）	Labor (P/Y) 劳动量（人/年）	Output (unit) 产量（单位）
Britain 英国	100	1	120	1
Portugal 葡萄牙	90	1	80	1

On the side of Britain, the efficiencies of the two products are both lower than Portugal. The cost of wool is 1.1 times of Portugal while the cost of wine is 1.5 times of Portugal. It's obvious that the production efficiency of wool is comparatively higher, therefore Britain shall specialize in the production of wool.

On the side of Portugal, the country produce both products more efficiently over Britain. The cost of wool is 90% of Britain while the cost of wine is 67% of Britain. So, Portugal shall specialize in the production of wine as the efficiency of the production of wine is higher compared with the production of wool.

After specialization, the production of the two countries is shown in the following table (Table 1-5).

从英国方面看，两种产品的生产都比葡萄牙效率低、成本高，但是高的程度不同。羊毛的成本是葡萄牙的 1.1 倍，而酒的成本是葡萄牙的 1.5 倍。可见，英国生产羊毛的效率相对高一些。所以，英国把全部劳动力都用于生产羊毛。

从葡萄牙方面看，两种商品的生产都比英国效率高。羊毛的成本相当于英国的 0.9，而酒的成本相当于英国的 0.67。可见，葡萄牙生产酒的效率相对生产羊毛更高些。所以，葡萄牙把全部劳动力都用于生产酒。

国际分工后，两国的生产情况见表 1-5。

表 1-5

Product 产品 / Country 国家	Wool 羊毛	Wine 酒
Britain 英国	（100+120）÷100＝2.2	
Portugal 葡萄牙		（90+80）÷80＝2.125

To trade the goods at 1:1, Britain exchanges one unit of wool for one unit of wine with Portugal.

两国按 1:1 进行交换，英国用 1 单位的羊毛换取葡萄牙 1 单位的酒。

After the trade, the goods owned by the two countries are as follows (Table 1-6).

贸易后，两国拥有产品的情况见表 1-6。

表 1-6

Product 产品 / Country 国家	Wool 羊毛	Wine 酒
Britain 英国	1.2 unit (0.2 unit more than before specialization) 1.2 单位（比分工前多 0.2 单位）	1 unit (imported) 1 单位（进口）
Portugal 葡萄牙	1 unit (imported) 1 单位（进口）	1.125 units (0.125 unit more than before specialization) 1.125 单位（比分工前多 0.125 单位）

Depending on the above table, it is obvious that the total output of the two countries increases though labor input by both countries does not change. The two countries gain the comparative benefits after trade.

从表中可看出，分工后，两国的劳动投入并没有增加，但是两种产品的总量却增加了，其中羊毛增加了 0.2 个单位，葡萄酒增加了 0.125 个单位。两国进行交换，双方都得到了比较利益。

2. The Evolution of Free Trade Policies 自由贸易政策的演变

There are two phases in history in which free trade policies were prevailing: the first phase is the time of laissez faire capitalism with Britain as the leading country to carry out free trade policy from the middle of the 19th century to World War I; the second phase is from 1950s to the beginning of 1970s with the spread of global trade freedom.

自由贸易政策盛行的时期主要有两个阶段：第一个阶段是 19 世纪中叶至第一次世界大战前的资本主义自由竞争时期，英国带头实行自由贸易政策；第二个阶段是 20 世纪 50 年代到 70 年代初期，出现了全球范围的贸易自由化。

2.1 Free Trade Policy in the Period of Laissez Faire Capitalism 资本主义自由竞争时期的自由贸易政策

Britain which is the earliest country finishing industrial revolution, and Netherlands which is advanced in marine industry, are countries carrying out free trade policies entirely.

Since the middle of the 18th century, Britain has gone through industrial revolution. Up to the beginning of the 19th century, Britain has won and reinforced its position as "world factory" with its cheap and quality goods which were strongly competitive in international market. Moreover, British industry desired to export to overseas market and import cheap raw materials and grain in large quantity from abroad (the cheap grain is the basis of low wage).

Upon the situation, the mercantilist trade protectionist policy has become a big obstacle to the development of British economy and expansion of British industrial capitalists. Consequently, British capitalists appealed for laissez faire policy and free market policy worldwide and required other countries to supply grain, raw materials and market with Britain offering industrial products as a return.

In 1920s, based on London and Manchester, a free trade campaign sponsored by British industrial capitalists spread in large scale advocating for the repeal of Corn Laws. And after struggling for nearly 30 years, industrial capitalists finally won over landlords and nobilities to carry out free trade policy gradually.

最早完成工业革命的英国和航海业发达的荷兰是全面实行自由贸易政策的国家。

英国自 18 世纪中叶开始进入产业革命。到 19 世纪初，“世界工厂”地位已经确立并得以巩固，其产品物美价廉，具有强大的国际竞争能力。而且，英国的工业迫切需要国外市场，需要从国外进口大量廉价的原料和粮食（廉价粮食是低工资的前提条件）。

在这种状况下，重商主义的贸易保护政策便成为英国经济发展和阻碍英国工业资产阶级对外扩张的一大障碍。这时，英国工业资产阶级便要求在世界市场上实行无限制的自由竞争和自由贸易政策。他们要求其他国家供给英国粮食、原料和市场，而由英国向它们提供工业制造品。

在 19 世纪 20 年代，以伦敦和曼彻斯特为基地的英国工业资产阶级开展了一场大规模的自由贸易运动。运动的中心内容是废除谷物法。工业资产阶级经过近 30 年的斗争，最终战胜了地主、贵族阶级，使自由贸易政策逐步取得胜利。

2.2 Trade Liberalization from 1950s to the Beginning of 1970s 20 世纪 50 年代至 70 年代初期的贸易自由化

After World War II, a new era of free trade was started, symbolized by Bretton Woods Conference which was held in New Hampshire, United States. The planners at Bretton Woods established the International Monetary Fund (IMF) and the International Bank for Reconstruction and Development (IBRD), which today are parts of the World Bank Group. In 1947, with the General Agreement on Tariffs and Trade (GATT) being signed, free trade was boosted again worldwide. The purpose of GATT was the "substantial reduction of tariffs and other trade barriers and the elimination of preferences, on a reciprocal and mutually advantageous basis" and pushed for free trade. GATT had been replaced by WTO (World Trade Organization) since Jan.1, 1995.

In this period, there were two sides indicating the trade liberalization:

1) Substantial reduction of tariff. Inside the parties signing GATT, the tariff was cut down greatly for each other; EU eliminated tariffs for EU members and reached tariff cut agreements with other countries through negotiation; since the beginning of 1971, more than 20 developed countries have granted General System of Preference treatment to over 170 developing countries on manufactured and semi-manufactured products.

2) Gradual reduction of non-tariff restrictions. With the resumption and growth of Japan and Western European countries, the import restrictions on these countries was decreased. Until the beginning of 1960s, the rate of import liberalization between western major economies reached over 90%.

第二次世界大战结束后，以布雷顿森林会议为标志，又一次自由贸易的新时代开启，以美国为首的20多个国家在美国新罕布什尔州召开了著名的布雷顿森林会议，成立了三个国际组织：国际货币基金组织（IMF）、国际复兴开发银行（IBRD）和关税及贸易总协定（简称关贸总协定、GATT），从而拉开了自由贸易的大旗。关贸总协定的宗旨就是大幅度降低关税，提倡自由贸易。关贸总协定已于1995年1月1日被世界贸易组织（WTO）替代。

这段时期贸易自由化的表现主要有两个方面。

（1）关税大幅度降低。关贸总协定缔约方内部关税大幅度降低；欧共体对内取消关税，对外通过谈判达成关税减让协议，使关税大幅度降低；从1971年开始，20多个发达国家对170多个发展中国家实施制成品和半制成品的普惠制待遇。

（2）非关税壁垒逐渐减少。随着日本和西欧经济的恢复和发展，它们在不同程度上放宽了进口数量限制。到20世纪60年代初，西方主要国家间进口自由化率已达到90%以上。

Lesson 4 Development of Theories and Policies of Protectionism
贸易保护理论和政策的演变

1. Classical Protectionism 古典贸易保护理论

1.1 Theories of Mercantilism 重商主义对外贸易学说

Besides exploiting domestic farmers, Western European countries also accumulated their original capital by international trade and overseas plunder. The wealth was mainly captured in the form of gold. Those countries had so limited gold mining and reserves at that time that they were desperate to fulfill their “gold need” by trading and plundering gold abroad. Engels mentioned this in *The Disintegration of the Feudal System and the Rise of the Bourgeoisie* that “the Portuguese traced gold in coast of Africa, India and the Far East; gold has become the wizard that drove Spaniards to sail far across Atlantic; gold was also the first important thing that Caucasians pursued when they just set their foot on the coast of the newly discovered continent.” This change of social economy will definitely aroused echoes in the superstructure. In terms of economic thought and policy, the echo was the rise of the mercantilism.

西欧国家资本原始积累的手段除了在国内剥削农民之外，还有就是进行国际贸易和海外掠夺，当时积累财富的主要手段是获取黄金，而当时西欧本身黄金的开采和储备已很有限，迫切需要通过国际贸易和对外掠夺来满足当时在西欧国家中出现的“黄金渴望”。恩格斯在《论封建制度的解体及资产阶级的兴起》中提到：“葡萄牙人在非洲海岸、印度及整个远东地区搜寻着黄金；黄金这两个字变成了驱使西班牙人远渡大西洋的符咒；黄金也是白种人刚踏上新发现的海岸时所追求的最重要的东西。”社会经济的这种变化，必然要反映到上层建筑中来，在经济思想和政策方面，就表现为重商主义的兴起。

Mercantilism Views on Trade 重商主义的贸易观点

The mercantilism, emerging in the time of primitive accumulation of capital in Europe in 15–17 century, is the system of economic thought and policy on behalf of the interests of the commercial capital. It reveals the need for trade protection, and it’s the first theory of trade protection. The mercantilism considered money as the only form of wealth, and it can be divided into two phases.

The early mercantilism was popular from the 15th century to mid-16th century; it was also called the balance of bargains. In this period, the mercantilism believed that noble medal was the only form of wealth, and people could gain it by buying cheap and selling dear in commodity exchange. Commodity exchange in domestic marketplace was realized by a group of people paying money to another group, which could cause no increase of the total wealth of the community as a whole but only the reallocation of wealth among domestic groups. Therefore, in order to obtain noble medal from commerce, a country had to embark on foreign trade. Exportation could bring gold and silver currency from abroad which would enrich the country, while importation would cause the monetary output and loss of national wealth as a result. The early mercantilists advocated high tariffs to block importation.

The later mercantilism was popular from the mid-16th to mid-17th century; it was also known as the theory of the balance of trade. The mercantilism in this period advocated abolishing the ban on monetary output which would cause other countries to take equipotent measures of retaliation that may lead to the reduction or even elimination of the home country’s trade. It was argued that as long as a country was able to maintain a trade surplus, its monetary wealth would be increased.

Historically, protectionism was prevalent mainly in four periods: mercantilism in

16th–18th century, protective policy in the 1870s to World War I, ultra protective policy between the two world wars and the new protectionism emerged after the mid-1970s.

重商主义是15—17世纪欧洲资本原始积累时期，代表商业资本利益的经济思想和政策体系，该思想揭示了贸易保护的必要性，是最早的贸易保护理论。重商主义认为货币是财富的唯一形态，可分为早期和晚期。

早期的重商主义流行于15世纪至16世纪中期，又称为货币差额论。这一时期的重商主义认为，财富的唯一表现形式是贵金属，人们在商品的交易中可以通过贱买贵卖来获得贵金属财富。国内市场上的贸易是由一部分人支付货币给另一部分人，其结果只是社会财富在国内不同集团之间的再分配，整个社会财富的总量并没有增加。因此，一国要想从商业中获得贵金属财富，则必须开展对外贸易。出口贸易可以使一国从国外获得金银货币从而使国家致富，而进口外国产品则会造成货币输出从而使国家丧失财富。早期的重商主义者主张实行高关税以阻止进口。

晚期的重商主义流行于16世纪中期至17世纪中期，又称为贸易差额论。这一时期的重商主义主张取消禁止货币输出的禁令，因为对方国家会采取对等措施进行报复，使本国贸易减少甚至消失，认为只要该国能够保持贸易收支的顺差，一国的货币财富就会增加。

从历史上看，保护贸易政策盛行的时期主要有以下四个阶段，即16—18世纪的重商主义的保护贸易政策，19世纪70年代至第一次世界大战前的保护贸易政策，两次世界大战之间的超保护贸易政策，20世纪70年代中期以后出现的新贸易保护主义。

1.2 List Trade Protectionism 李斯特贸易保护主义

After the 1970s, the United States and several Western European countries had been shifting from free trade to protective trade, gradually implementing a series of protective measures to restrict imports and to encourage exports. The main driver behind it was the big gap of the levels of industrial development between those countries and the United Kingdom. With little economic strength and goods advantage to compete with the United Kingdom, those countries had to protect their own emerging industries as infants from the competition of British goods.

List is the active advocator of infant industry protection policy, who is a German politician, theorist and economist. In the book *The National System of Political Economy* he published in 1841, he systematically propounded a theory of infant industry protection for less economically developed countries, based on the productivity theory with the stages of economic development as index and protective tariff at the core.

19世纪70年代以后，美国和西欧的一些国家纷纷从自由贸易转向保护贸易，逐步实施了一系列限制进口和鼓励出口的保护性措施，其主要原因是这些国家的工业发展水平与英国相比还存在很大差距，经济实力和商品竞争力都难以与英国抗衡，需要采取强有力的贸易保护政策来保护本国的新兴工业即幼稚产业，使之免受英国商品的竞争。

保护幼稚工业政策的积极倡导者是德国政治家、理论家、经济学家李斯特，他是保护贸易的积极倡导者。他在1841年出版的《政治经济学的国民体系》一书中，系统地提出了以生产力理论为基础、以经济发展阶段为依据、以保护关税制度为核心、为经济落后国家服务的保护幼稚工业的学说。

1.2.1 Key Points of List Trade Protectionism 李斯特贸易保护主义的主要内容

1) Advocating the Protection of Infant Industries 主张保护幼稚工业

List founded his infant industries protection theory on his understanding of the relationship between productivity and wealth. "Productivity of wealth than the wealth itself, I do not know how many times more important it is", wealth is inherent in the development of productivity.

Exchanging for cheap foreign goods may bring gains in the short term, but more losses in the long run in industry in Germany because it will make Germany backward and subordinate to foreign nations. If Germany imposes protective tariffs, the prices of industrial products will rise in the beginning, but after a period of time, the industry will be fully developed, the production will be empowered, the cost will be cut and the commodity prices will be eventually lower than those of the imported.

李斯特关于生产力与财富关系的认识是保护幼稚工业论的理论基础。"财富的生产力比之财富本身，不知要重要多少倍"，因为有了生产力的发展，就有了财富本身。

购买国外的廉价商品，从眼前利益看，可能会得到一些实惠，但是从长远利益看，则会影响德国工业的发展。因为这样做会使德国长期处于落后和从属于外国的地位。如果德国采取保护关税政策，一开始会使工业品的价格提高，但经过一段时期，德国工业将得到充分发展，生产力将会提高，商品生产费用将会下跌，商品价格甚至会低于从外国进口的商品的价格。

2) Stages of Economic Development 经济发展阶段论

List theorized that nations pass through five stages of economic development according to their economy accomplishments. These are: uncivilized stage, pastoral stage, and stages of agriculture and agriculture united with manufactures, and when agriculture, manufactures and commerce are combined. Nations should use corresponding trade policies in the progress through these stages. Nations in agriculture stages should stimulate its agriculture by using free trade policies to encourage export of agriculture products and import of foreign industrial products, and should nurture its basis of industrialization.

For the nations in the stage of agriculture combined with manufactures, whose home industries already have basic development but are not enough to compete with foreign industries, protection should be used to save them from being overpowered by the competition. When a nation have grown into a stage that agriculture, manufactures and commerce are combined, this competition is not a threat as the home industries are equipped with competitive strength; free trade should again become the rule to enjoy the best interests and stimulate the further development of the domestic industries.

李斯特根据国民经济完成程度，把国民经济的发展分为五个阶段，即"原始未开化时期、畜牧时期、农业时期、农工业时期、农工商业时期”。各国经济发展阶段不同，应采取的贸易政策也应不同。处于农业阶段的国家应实行自由贸易政策，以利于农产品的自由输出，并自由输入外国的工业产品，以促进本国农业的发展，并培育工业化的基础。

处于农工业阶段的国家，由于本国已有工业发展的基础，但并未发展到能与外国产品相竞争的地步，故必须实施保护关税制度，使它不受外国产品的打击。而处于农工商业阶段的国家，由于国内工业产品已具备国际竞争能力，国外产品的竞争威胁已不存在，故应实行自由贸易政策，以享受自由贸易的最大利益，刺激国内产业进一步发展。

1.2.2 Aim and Object of Trade Protection Policy 贸易保护政策的目的与对象

List’s trade protection policy aims to promote the growth of productive power. After some relative comparison, List argued that the industry manufacturing with power and machines in large scale was far more productive than agriculture. He argued that a nation focusing on agriculture tended to have listless people with conservative habits and manners, lack of cultural well-being and freedom; while a nation depending on developed manufacturing and commerce had its people inspired and talented. He claimed the justification for protection object includes that:

① Its agriculture doesn’t need protection. Only those nations that have entered the agriculture life but far away from industrial maturity are suitable for protection.

② If there is no compelling competitor, even a nation’s industry is infantile, it doesn’t need protection.

③ Only those infant industries at the beginning of development and facing fierce competition from foreign competitors are justified for protection. List defined a 30-year maximum for the period of protection.

李斯特保护贸易政策的目的是促进生产力的发展。经过比较，李斯特认为使用动力与大规模机器的制造工业的生产力远远大于农业。他认为着重农业的国家，人民精神萎靡，一切习惯与方法偏于守旧，缺乏文化福利与自由；而着重工商业的国家则不然，其人民充满增进身心与才能的精神。他提出保护对象的条件是：

① 农业不需保护。只有那些刚从农业阶段跃进的国家，距离工业成熟时尚远，才适宜于保护。

② 一国工业虽然幼稚，但在没有强有力的竞争者时，也不需要保护。

③ 只有刚刚开始发展且有强有力的外国竞争者的幼稚工业才需要保护。 李斯特提出的保护时间以 30 年为最高限期。

1.2.3 Major Methods of Protection 保护政策的主要手段

To protect infant industries by prohibition of importation and high tariffs, to encourage importation of complex machines by exemption or minor import duties. To protect infant industries, List proposed that “importation of certain industrial products can be prohibited or imposed tariffs”. Meanwhile, he pointed out that “countries that haven’t possessed specialties and advancement in machine manufacturing should exempt or only impose minor duty on import of all complex machines”.

通过禁止输入与征收高关税的办法来保护幼稚工业，以免税或征收轻微进口税方式鼓励复杂机器进口。为保护幼稚工业，李斯特提出“对某些工业品可以实行禁止输入，或规定的税率事实上等于全部、或至少部分地禁止输入”。同时，对“凡是在专门技术与机器制造方面还没有获得高度发展的国家，对于一切复杂机器的输入应当允许免税，或只征收轻微的进口税”。

1.2.4 Evaluation of List Protectionism 对李斯特保护主义理论的评价

1) Positive Effect 积极作用

His advocacy of protective tariffs is for the purpose of squeezing out manual labor by machine, replacing patriarchal production with modern production. It restricts the protection to the promising infant industries, and recognizes the benefits of international division of labor and free trade. It stimulates the development of capitalism in Germany, and is conducive to the struggle of the bourgeoisie against the feudal forces.

In other words, he claimed that protective trade is a transition while free trade is the ultimate aim. The protection should be limited. List's theory is of significant reference value to the less developed economies.

它主张保护关税，是为了用机器挤掉手工劳动，用现代的生产代替宗法式的生产。其保护的对象以将来有前途的幼稚工业为限，对国际分工和自由贸易的利益也予以承认。它促进了德国资本主义的发展，有利于资产阶级反对封建主义势力的斗争。

换言之，他主张以保护贸易为过渡时期，而以自由贸易为最后目的。其保护也是有限度的，不是无限度的。李斯特的理论对经济欠发达国家是有重大参考价值的。

2) The Limitations 局限性

Theory of protecting infant industries has received little practical effectiveness. Although developing countries attached great importance to the protection of infant industries, most of them didn't bring about the desired result but paid painful prices. China used to protect a number of industries, such as automobile, which resulted in the domestic companies lying back and growing slowly.

保护幼稚工业的理论在实践中成效不大。虽然发展中国家都很注重对幼稚产业的保护，但多数未达到预期效果，反而付出惨痛代价。而我国曾经保护了多个像汽车这样的产业，结果却使得国内企业安于现状，发展不快。

2. Keynesianism Protectionist Trade Policy 凯恩斯的超保护贸易主义

After the Great Depression of 1929, due to the unprecedented severe economic crisis sharpening market problems, many countries raised tariffs in large scale, adopted the restriction measures widely on foreign exchange and import quantity to prevent the import from abroad. On the other hand, the economies such as Britain and Germany had implemented the relevant policies to encourage export. In this fierce war of market competition, all nations had been engaging in it and took every conceivable means to protect home trade including the adoption of forbidding tariff and foreign exchange war etc. In the year of 1930, United States raised its tariff as much as 52.2% on average for the imported commodities, hence leading to a tariff war among big economies worldwide.

The theory of Keynesianism had a great influence on the implementation of the trade policies of capitalism countries. Being the founder of the school of thoughts of Keynesianism, John Maynard Keynes was a well known British economist with magnum opus *The General Theory of Employment, Interest and Money*. Before the falling of the Great Depression, Keynes was a supporter of laissez faire, and then turned to supporting mercantilism after economic crisis, arguing that mercantilist protectionist trade policy can ensure economic prosperity and boosting employment, further coming up with his own Keynesianism protectionist trade theory.

1929 年的大萧条开始之后，空前严重的经济危机使市场问题进一步尖锐。一方面，许多国家大幅提高关税，广泛采用外汇管制、数量限制等手段，阻止外国商品的输入。另一方面，英国和德国等都加强了奖励出口的政策。在激烈的商品战中，各国政府在对外贸易方面无所不用，采用禁止性关税、外汇战争等。1930 年，美国把关税税率首先提升到极高的水平，进口商品的平均税率达 52.2%，由此引发了世界主要国家之间的一场关税战。

凯恩斯的超保护贸易学说对资本主义各国执行超保护贸易政策影响很大。凯恩斯是英国资产阶级经济学家，凯恩斯主义经济学的创始人，其代表作是《就业、利息和货币通论》。经济危机前凯恩斯是一个自由贸易论者，经济危机后他转而推崇重商主义保护贸易政策。他认为，重商主义保护贸易政策确实能保证经济繁荣和促进就业，形成颇具影响的超保护贸易政策理论。

2.1 Key Points of Keynesianism Protectionist Trade Policy 凯恩斯超保护贸易主义的主要内容

1) Criticism on Classical Free Trade Theory 对古典自由贸易理论的批评

The full employment at home is the base for classical free trade theories, while mass unemployment is not in accordance with the classical free trade theories.

国内充分就业是古典自由贸易理论建立的基础，而现在发生的大量失业现象明显不合乎古典自由贸易理论。

2) Enlarging the Effective Demand to Relieve Crisis and Unemployment 扩大有效需求的目的在于救治危机和失业

The employment level of one nation is decided by the effective demand. The government of a nation shall intervene in the economy through setting a variety of policies to stimulate the effective demand, aiming to reach trade surplus which can enhance the effective demand in domestic market and relieve crisis and unemployment.

一国的就业水平由有效需求决定，国家应干预经济生活，制定一系列的政策来刺激有效需求，而贸易顺差可以提高国内的有效需求，缓和危机，增加就业。

3) Investment Multiplier Theory 投资乘数理论

In order to prove the benefit of increased investment to employment and national income, Keynes put forward the investment multiplier theory indicating the dependent relationship between the increase of investment and the increase of general national income.

According to the theory of investment multiplier, the increased investment will bring the increase of demand for production goods, then leading to income increase of the people (entrepreneurs and workers) who get engaged in the production of production goods, and thereafter the increase of their income will increase their demand for consumable products, further leading to the increase of the income of the people who produce consumable products. The result of this deduction is that the increase in general national income will be equal to several times of the original increase in investment.

Multiplier is dependent on the proportion of consumption in the increased income. Investment multiplier formula is as follows:

multiplier K=1/(1-marginal propensity of consumption)

marginal propensity of consumption = 0–all increased income to be saved to bank, then the general national income remain invariable

marginal propensity of consumption = 0–all increased income to be consumed, then the general national income is infinite

the increased amount of national income (ΔY) = multiplier (K) × the increased investment (ΔI)

为了证明增加新投资对就业和国民收入的好处，凯恩斯提出了投资乘数理论。投资乘数理论反映了投资增长和国民收入总量增加之间的依存关系。

投资乘数理论是指新增加的投资引起对生产资料需求的增加，从而引起从事生产资料生产的人们（企业主和工人）的收入增加，收入的增加又使他们对消费品的需求增加，进而引起从事消费品生产的人们的收入增加；如此推演下去，结果由此增加的国民收入总量会等于原增加投资量的若干倍。

乘数（即倍数）的大小取决于人们增加的收入中有多大比例用于消费、有多大比例用于储蓄。投资乘数理论的计算公式是：

乘数 K=1/(1–边际消费倾向)

边际消费倾向=0–增加的收入全部储蓄，则国民收入不变

边际消费倾向=1–增加的收入全部消费，则国民收入无限大

国民收入的增加额(ΔY)=乘数(K)×投资的增加量(ΔI)

4) Theory of Foreign Trade Multiplier 对外贸易乘数理论

The followers of Keynes, F. Machlup and Harrod established the theory of foreign trade multiplier. The meaning of theory of foreign trade multiplier is as follows: the export as well as the domestic investment of one country can increase the national income; the import and domestic savings can decrease national income. The foreign trade of one country can promote the employment and enhance national income so long as the trade or international balance is surplus. In this case, the increased national income is times of trade surplus.

For instance, export of goods and services→increase of export industry income→increase of consumption→promotion of the production of other products→further promotion of employment→increase of income... the increase of national income will be times of trade surplus.

Therefore, in order to protect domestic employment and obtain trade surplus, the government of a country shall intervene in foreign trade through fiscal policies, increasing the public investment and government expense, and then further protect trade surplus to promote employment and enhance production.

凯恩斯的支持者马克卢普和哈罗德等人建立了对外贸易乘数理论。对外贸易乘数理论的含义为：一国的出口和国内投资一样，有增加国民收入的作用；进口则和国内储蓄一样，有减少国民收入的作用。只有当贸易为顺差或国际收支为顺差时，对外贸易才能增加一国就业，提高国民的收入。此时，国民收入的增加量将为贸易顺差的若干倍。

例如：商品和劳务出口→相应出口产业的收入增加→消费增加→引起其他产业生产增加→就业进一步扩大→收入增加……国民收入的增加量将为贸易顺差的若干倍。

因此，为保护国内就业，实现贸易顺差的目标，国家应对外贸进行干预，采用财政政策，增加公共投资和政府开支，保护贸易顺差，以促进就业和产出的增加。

2.2 Characteristics of Keynesianism Trade Policy 凯恩斯超保护贸易政策的特点

In comparison with the protectionism before World War I, it has the following characteristics:

- The range of protection is enlarged, not only of infant industries but also of highly developed industries as well as declining monopoly industries.
- The goal of protection has changed, from developing competitive ability to strengthening monopoly power.
- The protection strategy has changed from the restriction of import to expansion of home market and overseas market.
- The protection measures have been diversified, with the adoption of tariff as well as various measures to encourage export and restrict import.

The protection policy of this time has become the major means to occupy global market, which has become the weapon taken to defeat the rival countries instead of defending.

与第一次世界大战前贸易保护主义相比，超保护贸易主义有以下特点。

- 保护的对象扩大了。不仅保护幼稚工业，而且保护高度发达的工业和出现衰落的垄断工业。

- 保护的目的变了。从培养自由竞争的能力到着重于加强垄断能力。
- 保护的战略方式改变。从防御性地限制进口到进攻性扩张国内外市场。
- 保护的措施多样化。保护措施不仅采用关税，还有各种各样的奖出限入措施。

这个阶段的保护政策成为争夺世界市场的手段，成为攻击而不是防卫的武器。因此，这种保护政策被称为超保护贸易政策。

2.3 Comments on Keynesianism Protectionist Trade Policy 对凯恩斯超保护贸易主义的评价

The theory of foreign trade multiplier under Keynesianism has indicated the inner law between foreign trade and national economy, which is scientific in some senses. However, Keynesianism stressed too much on the role of foreign trade surplus on the increase of national income. If every country diminishes import from other countries, no country can increase its export. As a result, due to the prevailing trade protection measures and tariff to stimulate export and restrict import, international trade will be damaged.

凯恩斯主义的对外贸易乘数理论在一定程度上揭示了对外贸易与国民经济之间的内在规律性，且具有一定的科学性。但凯恩斯主义过于强调对外贸易顺差对增加国民收入的作用。如果各国都减少进口，那么一国出口量的增加就无法实现，可能导致国际上各国过度地强调出口而限制进口，导致关税和其他贸易保护手段盛行，最终则不利于国际贸易的健康发展。

3. New Trade Protectionism 新贸易保护主义

New trade protectionism, coming up in the middle and late 1970s, being relative to the trade protectionism in laissez-faire era, is the basis of the coordinated managing trade, namely the “organized free trade”. It is a new international trade system, centering around coordination, government intervention oriented, in form of negotiation and consultation, to intervene, in coordinate and manage internation trade and relationship.

20 世纪 70 年代中期以后出现的新贸易保护主义是相对于自由竞争时期的贸易保护主义而言的，在此新贸易保护主义的基础上，形成了协调管理贸易，即“有组织的自由贸易”。它是以协调为中心，以政府干预为主导，以磋商谈判为轴心，对本国进出口贸易和全球贸易关系进行干预、协调和管理的一种国际贸易体制。

3.1 Characteristics of New Trade Protectionism 新贸易保护主义的主要特点

3.1.1 The Range of Protected Merchandise Is Enlarged 被保护的商品范围不断扩大

The protected merchandise has been enlarged from traditional products (such as steel, textile products etc.), agricultural products to advanced industrial products (such as cars, airplanes, digital machines, semi-conductors, computers etc.), service trade (such as visa application, investment rules, restrictions on income remittance) and intellectual property as well. The protected objects are developed from goods to investment, technology and environmental protection.

被保护的商品从传统产品（如钢铁、纺织品等）、农产品转向高级工业品（如汽车、飞机、数控机床、半导体、计算机等）、服务贸易（如签证申请、投资条例、限制收入汇回）和知识产权。保护对象从商品发展到投资、技术知识和环境保护。

3.1.2 Trade Protection Measures Are Diversified 贸易保护措施多样化

In accordance with the effective tariff ratio, many countries have set step tariff and strengthened the levy of anti-subsidy and anti-dumping. From 1980 to 1985, there were as many as 283 cases about anti-dumping involving 44 countries. Meanwhile, the non-tariff barriers have increased from over 800 sorts of non-tariff barriers in 1970s to more than 1,000 sorts at the beginning of 1980s.

按照有效保护税率，许多国家设置了阶梯关税，加强了征收“反补贴税”和“反倾销税”。从 1980 年到 1985 年，“反倾销”案多达 283 起，涉及 44 个国家。非关税壁垒不断增高，已从 20 世纪 70 年代末的 800 多种增加到 80 年代初的 1 000 多种。

3.1.3 Trade Protection System Has Been More Complete and Perfect 贸易保护制度转向更全面、更完美

The laws on foreign trade in developed countries have integrated the single law of foreign trade with other domestic laws and legalized the foreign trade policies to support export and protect foreign trade in legislation.With the continuous enrichment and adjustment to foreign trade management, the trade protection measures have been an important integral part of the foreign trade system of a country.

发达国家管理外贸的法律已将单一的外贸法律与其他方面的国内法整合，把外贸政策法律化，再通过立法为出口提供支持，以保护对外贸易。随着对外贸管理的不断加强和调整，贸易保护措施已成为一个国家对外贸易体制中的重要组成部分。

3.1.4 The Emphasis of Foreign Trade Protection Has Been Turned to the Stimulation on Export from the Restriction on Import 外贸保护措施的重点从限制进口转向促进出口

Many countries have strengthened the fiscal and legal measures to boost export and import, in an economic way, implementing the policies of export subsidy, export loan and establishing export processing zone; forcing other countries to open market in a legal way. For instance, in 1989, the United States adopted “super 301 rules” to require Japan to open markets for computers, secondary planets, and agricultural products to the United States within one year.

各国加强了财政和法律措施以促进进出口。在经济方面，实行出口补贴、出口信贷、建立出口加工区等措施；在法律方面，强迫外国开放市场。例如，1989 年美国对日本动用“超级 301 条款”，要求日本在一年内向美国开放计算机、卫星、农产品等市场。

3.1.5 Trade Protection Has Turned into Regional Trade Barrier from National Trade Barrier 贸易保护从国家贸易壁垒转变为区域贸易壁垒

With the development of regional economy, trade protectionism has evolved into regional protection from single country's protection. Free trade policy is carried out between the counties within one region and common tariff barrier is implemented towards the countries out of the region.

随着区域经济集团化的发展，贸易保护主义也由一国的贸易保护演变为区域贸易保护。在区域范围内的国家之间实行自由贸易，而对区域范围外的国家则实行共同的关税壁垒。

3.2 The Reasons for the Reinforcement of New Trade Protectionism 新贸易保护主义加强的原因

There are profound economic and political background for the appearance and reinforcement of new trade protectionism. The reasons are as follows:

新贸易保护主义的出现与加强有着深厚的经济和政治根源，新贸易保护主义不断加强的原因主要有以下几个方面。

3.2.1 The Rapid Rising of the Trade Deficit of U.S. Makes U.S. an Important Origin of New Trade Protectionism 贸易逆差急剧上升使美国成为新贸易保护主义的重要发源地

Since the middle of the 1970s, the foreign trade in major industrially developed countries has been not in balance so much, and the U.S. trade deficit has faced strong competition from Japan and western European countries as well as newly emerging industrial countries. In order to reduce the trade deficit, the United States forced the countries like Japan which enjoyed great trade surplus to open market and strengthen the import restriction as well.

20 世纪 70 年代中期以后，主要工业发达国家的对外贸易发展并不平衡，美国对外贸易逆差不断扩大。在世界制成品市场和国内市场上不但面临日本、西欧国家的激烈竞争，还面临新兴工业化国家的竞争。为了减少贸易逆差，美国一方面迫使对它有巨额贸易顺差的日本等国开放市场，另一方面加强限制和报复的进口措施。

3.2.2 The Declining Economic Growth Ratio of Major Industrial Countries and Rising Unemployment Rate 主要工业国家经济增长率下降，失业率上升

Since the 1980s, the average annual growth ratio of GNP of industrially developed countries has been in a low level except for a few years, lower than 3.5% in 1968–1977. But the unemployment rate is higher than 3.7% of 1968–1977 while inflation and unemployment rate rised. The stagflation forced many counties to give up the free trade and turn to trade protection.

20 世纪 80 年代以来，工业发达国家国民生产总值的年平均增长率除个别年份外一直低速增长，低于 1968—1977 年的 3.5%；而失业率却大大高于 1968—1977 年的 3.7%。通

货膨胀率和失业率上升。滞涨迫使这些国家放弃自由贸易而转向保护贸易。

3.2.3 The Disorder of International Monetary System 国际货币体制的失调

The long term disorder of foreign exchange has influenced the healthy development of international trade, leading to the boost of trade protection. Floating exchange ratio pressed traders to purchase futures and hedges to avoid the exchange risk, which brought more dealing costs and the change of prices, investment benefits and competition situations. In addition, the great fluctuation of exchange rates has made many countries implement trade protection in order to defend the impact of exchange rate fluctuation on the domestic economies.

汇率长期失调影响了国际贸易的正常发展，导致了贸易保护主义的盛行。浮动汇率迫使贸易商购买期货和进行套期保值来规避汇率风险，增加了交易成本，又引起价格、投资效益和竞争情况的变化。此外，汇率的大幅波动使许多国家为减少汇率波动对国内经济的影响而实行贸易保护。

3.2.4 Political Requirements 政治上的需要

High unemployment rate, stronger power of labour union and government image's maintenance have intensified the pressure of trade protection. For instance, from the late of the 1980s to the end of the 20th century, the United States had been taking excuse of human right to bring troubles to China on Most Favored Nation clause.

高失业率、工会力量的壮大以及对政府形象的维护，大大加剧了贸易保护主义的实施。如 20 世纪 80 年代末至 20 世纪末，美国以“人权”问题为借口，在给予中国最惠国待遇的问题上大做文章。

Lesson 5 Cross-border Electronic Commerce 跨境电子商务

On May 22, 2020, when Premier Li Keqiang delivered the government work report at the National People's Congress, he proposed to "accelerate the development of cross-border e-commerce and other new formats, and enhance the international freight transport capacity". He emphasized in particular we should speed up the development of cross-border e-commerce, a new form of foreign trade, and accelerate the development of China's foreign trade.

2020 年 5 月 22 日，李克强总理在全国人民代表大会上做《政府工作报告》时，提出“加快跨境电商等新业态发展，提升国际货运能力”，特别强调要加快发展跨境电子商务这一外贸新业态，加速我国外贸事业的发展。

1. Definition and Significance of Cross Border E-commerce 跨境电子商务的定义和意义

Cross-border Electronic Commerce（Cross-border e-commerce）as a new type of trade, refers to the transaction subjects belonging to different national boundaries or regions, through the Internet, intelligent mobile and other related information platforms, with two main modes of B2B and B2C to achieve transactions between enterprises and enterprises or end consumers, complete payment and settlement, and deliver goods through cross-border logistic mode of trade.

This new mode of trade makes foreign trades become more and more "order fragmentation", products and market closely combined, marketable. In the face of fierce international market competition and disappearing export cost advantage, some foreign trade enterprises timely obtain new development space from the new global supply chain with the help of cross-border e-commerce. Compared with the traditional trade model, cross-border e-commerce can effectively bypass the restrictions of trade barriers and directly face foreign consumers with fewer intermediate links, low channel cost, virtual transaction and all-weather marketing, which helps manufacturers and end consumers to reach a win-win situation. According to data released by the National Bureau of Statistics on January 17, 2020, China's online retail sales in 2019 totaled 1.06 billion yuan, up 16.5 percent over the previous year. In 2019, cross-border e-commerce transactions accounted for 33.29 percent of China's total import and export value of 31.54 trillion yuan. The penetration rate has steadily increased compared with last year, and the role of cross-border e-commerce in boosting the development of traditional foreign trade has become increasingly prominent.

Cross border e-commerce (export) is a comprehensive innovation of the traditional trade mode. It bypasses the traditional trade middlemen and directly sells products to end customers in the way of independent brand, which changes the value distribution of the global trade chain and is an effective way to achieve high-quality development of foreign trade.

跨境电子商务（简称跨境电商）作为一种新型贸易方式，是指分属不同国界或地区的交易主体，通过互联网、智能移动及其他相关信息平台，以 B2B 和 B2C 两种主要模式实现企业与企业或终端消费者之间达成交易、完成支付结算，并通过跨境物流送达商品的一种新型贸易方式。

这种新型贸易方式，使得外贸交易越来越趋向于“订单碎片化”，产品与市场紧密结合，适销对路。面对激烈的国际市场竞争和逐渐消失的出口成本优势，一些外贸企业适时借助跨境电商从新型全球供应链中获得新的发展空间。跨境电商与传统贸易模式相比，可以有效地绕过贸易壁垒的限制，直接面对国外消费者，中间环节少，渠道成本低，交易虚拟化，营销全天候，这有助于制造商和终端消费者达成双赢局面。国家统计局 2020 年 1 月 17 日发布的数据显示，2019 年全年全国网上零售额达 10.6 亿元，比上年增长 16.5%。2019 年跨境电商交易规模占中国进出口总值 31.54 万亿元的 33.29%。渗透率相比去年稳步提升，跨境电商在助推传统外贸发展上起到的作用愈加凸显。

跨境电商（出口）是对传统贸易方式的全面革新，它绕过传统贸易中间商以自主品牌的方式直接将产品销售给终端客户，改变了全球贸易链条的价值分配，是实现外贸高质量发展的有效途径。

The first is "face-to-face terminal". It has changed the traditional OEM processing mode and directly sells to end customers, making it possible for Chinese manufacturing brands to be internationalized.

The second is to "control the channel". Have your own sales channels to control the pricing power of the product.

The third is direct dialogue. Foreign users' evaluation of products can be directly fed back to domestic manufacturers, so as to actively optimize products at the first time, so as to enhance market competitiveness.

These are the bottlenecks that traditional foreign trade has been unable to break through. In other words, cross-border e-commerce is a kind of trade mode innovation and process reengineering, rather than simply facilitating the trade process, which can play a more important role in the high-quality development of China's foreign trade.

一是“直面终端”。改变了传统贴牌加工模式，直接面向终端客户进行销售让中国制造品牌国际化成为可能。

二是“掌控渠道”。拥有自己的销售渠道从而能掌控产品的定价权。

三是“直接对话”。国外用户对产品的评价可以直接反馈到国内厂家，以便第一时间对产品主动进行优化从而提升市场竞争力。

这些都是传统外贸一直无法突破的瓶颈。也就是说，跨境电商是一种贸易方式的创新和流程再造，而不是简单的贸易过程便利化，从而对我国外贸高质量发展更能发挥重要作用。

2. Classification of Cross Border E-commerce 跨境电商的分类

According to the direction of import and export, it can be divided into export cross-border e-commerce and import cross-border e-commerce. In terms of import and export structure, in 2019, China's cross-border e-commerce's import and export structure, export accounted for 76.5%, and import accounted for 23.5%; but the import proportion is expanding.

According to the transaction mode, it can be divided into B2B cross-border e-commerce and B2C cross-border e-commerce. Under the B2B mode, enterprises mainly use e-commerce to publish advertisements and information, and the transaction and customs clearance processes are basically completed offline. In essence, it is still a traditional trade and has been included in the general trade statistics of customs. Under the B2C mode, Chinese enterprises directly face foreign consumers and mainly sell personal consumer goods. In terms of logistics, they mainly use air parcels, mail, express delivery and other means. The main body of customs declaration is postal or express delivery company. At present, most of them are not included in the customs registration. Cross border e-commerce began to develop towards refinement, branding, localization and diversification. In 2019, China's cross-border e-commerce transaction mode, cross-border e-commerce B2B transaction accounted for

80.5%, and cross-border e-commerce B2C transaction accounted for 19.5%.

依据进出口方向分为出口跨境电子商务和进口跨境电子商务。在进出口结构上，2019年中国跨境电商的进出口结构上出口占比达到 76.5%，进口比例 23.5%；但进口比例正不断扩大。

依据交易模式分为 B2B 跨境电子商务和 B2C 跨境电子商务。B2B 模式下，企业运用电子商务以广告和信息发布为主，成交和通关流程基本在线下完成，本质上仍属传统贸易，且已纳入海关一般贸易统计。B2C 模式下，我国企业直接面对国外消费者，以销售个人消费品为主，物流方面主要采用航空小包、邮寄、快递等方式，其报关主体是邮政或快递公司，目前大多未纳入海关登记。跨境电商开始向精细化、品牌化、本土化以及多元化发展。2019 年中国跨境电商的交易模式跨境电商 B2B 交易占比达 80.5%，跨境电商 B2C 交易占比 19.5%。

3. Differences between Cross Border E-commerce and Traditional Trade 跨境电商与传统贸易的区别

3.1 Different Ways of Negotiation 交易磋商方式的不同

In the traditional international trade, our buyers and sellers contact each other by means of telephone, email and other instant communication tools and software. They usually go through the process of preparation (Market Research), inquiry, quotation, counter-offer, acceptance, contract signing, goods preparation, chartering and space booking, insurance purchase, customs declaration and inspection, transportation of goods, buyer's receipt and payment, etc. Compared with the traditional international trade model, cross-border e-commerce has the characteristics of mobility, multilateral, small order, high frequency and low cost. And can do: (1) Delivery before trading, trading mode from offline to online, greatly reducing the transaction time and cost, improve the efficiency of the transaction. (2) It omits many links of middlemen, which can make manufacturers and consumers directly linked, and has the characteristics of less links, low cost, high efficiency, high profit and high frequency. (3) The whole process of cross-border e-commerce can be operated on the cross-border e-commerce platform from the initial transaction negotiation to the transaction. For example, bank transfer, freight forwarding, commodity inspection, customs declaration and other businesses all adopt online application and offline processing, which greatly saves time, speeds up the processing time, simplifies the negotiation process and improves efficiency.

在传统国际贸易中，我们的买卖双方都是通过电话、邮件等即时通信工具及软件等方式来联系，一般会经历交易前的准备（市场调研）、询价、报价、还盘、接受、签订合同、备货、租船订舱、购买保险、报关报检、运输货物、买方收货付款等过程。而跨境电商相比传统的国际贸易模式，具有可移动、多边化、订单小、频率高、低成本等特点。并且能够做到：（1）先交货后交易，交易模式从线下转到线上，大大缩减了交易时间及成本，提高了交易效率。（2）省略了很多中间商的环节，可以让生产商与消费者直接挂钩，具备环节少、低成本、高效率、利润高、频率高等特点。（3）跨境电商从最开始的交易磋商到成交整个过程都可以在跨境电商平台上进行操作，比如银行转账、货代、商检、报关等业务都采用线上申请、线下办理的方式，极大地节省了时间，加快了办理时间，简化了协商程序，提高了效率。

3.2 Different modes of transportation 运输方式的不同

The traditional modes of international trade transportation mainly include ocean transportation, air transportation, railway transportation, container transportation and so on. Among them, the container ocean transportation mode accounts for nearly 80%. Among the cross-border e-commerce, the most common mode of transportation is international express in postal transportation. According to the data of the national e-commerce Research Center, the number of cross-border e-commerce is increasing 70% of the export business is international express.

传统的国际贸易运输方式主要包括海洋运输、航空运输、铁路运输、集装箱运输等运输方式，其中集装箱海洋运输模式就占了将近 80%的比例，而跨境电商中，最惯常的运输方式是邮政运输中的国际快递，国家电子商务研究中心的数据显示，跨境电商 70%的出口业务走的都是国际快递。

3.3 Different Types of Transportation Insurance 运输保险险别的不同

In the traditional trade, the insurance clauses for marine transportation are ICC formulated by London Insurance Association and CIC clauses issued by China. These clauses include W.P.A., F.P.A., all risks and war risks. In cross-border e-commerce, the main mode of transportation is postal transportation. Obviously, the contents of these terms are no longer applicable. For postal transportation, express insurance is used more often.

在传统的贸易中，针对海洋运输所设置的保险条款分别是英国伦敦保险业协会所制订的 ICC 和我国颁布的海洋运输保险条款 CIC 条款，这些条款包括水渍险、平安险、一切险以及战争险等，而在跨境电商中，由于运输方式主要是邮政运输，这些条款的内容显然就不再适用，对于邮政运输更多采用的是一些快递类的保险。

3.4 Different Payment Methods 支付方式的不同

In traditional trade, after delivery, the buyer and the seller will directly accept payment by letter of credit, remittance and collection. There are many intermediate links, complicated procedures and complicated bills involved. In cross-border e-commerce platform transactions, most of them are online or electronic payment methods, such as credit cards, online banking, electronic transfer, mobile phone payment, third party payment PayPal and China Alipay. The new payment method is not only low cost, but also fast. It also greatly improves the efficiency of the transaction, enhances the trust of both sides, and helps the seller to facilitate the completion of the transaction.

在传统贸易中买卖双方在完成交货之后，会直接采用信用证、汇款和托收等支付方式收受货款，中间环节较多，并且办理手续麻烦，涉及的票据较繁杂。在跨境电商平台交易，大多数采用的是线上或电子支付方式，比如信用卡、网上银行、电子转账、手机支付、第三方支付方式 PayPal 和中国支付宝等，新型的支付方式不仅成本低、速度快，而且还大大提高了交易效率，增强双方的信任，有助于卖方促成交易的完成。

3.5 Different Order Completion Efficiency 订单完成效率的不同

In traditional international trade, exporters usually spend a lot of money to participate in exhibitions around the world, search for information about relevant companies on the international official website or get yellow pages from commercial counselors, and then make business contact with each other, which is inefficient. In the cross-border e-commerce mode, the buyer and the seller do not need to negotiate for a long time. As long as the online communication is conducted, and the online buyers basically have demand, the transaction time is short, the cost is very low and the efficiency is greatly improved

在传统国际贸易中，出口商一般需花费巨额的成本去参加全球各地的展销会，或者在国际官网上搜索相关公司的信息或从商务参赞处获得国外公司的黄页，再进行业务联系，效率较低。而在跨境电商模式下，买卖双方不需长时间交涉，只要在线上交流，而且线上的买方基本上都有需求的，所以交易时间很短，成本很低，也大大提高了效率。

Questions 思考题

1. What is international trade? And what is its studying object and contents?
什么是国际贸易？它的研究对象及内容是什么？

2. What are the differences between direct trade and indirect trade, and between entrepot trade and transit trade?
直接贸易和间接贸易、转口贸易和过境贸易的区别是什么？

3. What is the difference between general trade system and special trade system?
总贸易体系与专门贸易体系有何区别？

4. How to calculate Foreign Trade Volume and Quantum of Foreign Trade?
对外贸易值和对外贸易量如何计算？

5. How to calculate Trade Condition Index?
贸易条件指数如何计算？

6. What is the difference in the calculation of foreign trade volume and international trade volume?
对外贸易额与国际贸易额的计算有什么不同？

7. What is Quantum of Foreign Trade?
什么是对外贸易量？

8. What is the goal of making foreign trade policies?

各国制定对外贸易政策的目的是什么？

9. What are the types of foreign trade policies?

各国对外贸易政策有哪些？

10. What are the differences between new trade protectionism and classical trade protectionism?

试比较新贸易保护主义与古典贸易保护主义的不同。

11. What are the characteristics of List's theory of trade protection?

李斯特的保护贸易学说有什么特点？

12. What is the theory of foreign trade multiplier? Where did it evolve from?

什么是对外贸易乘数理论？从何演变而来？

Chapter 2

Instruments of International Trade Policy

国际贸易措施

Lesson 1 Tariffs 关税措施

1. General Introduction to Tariff 关税概述

Tariff is a tax or customs duty levied on a commodity by the customs of a country when it is imported or exported. As one kind of revenue, on the one hand, tariff is compulsory, un-reimbursing and fixed etc as same as other kinds of taxes; on the other hand, tariff has its own characteristics as follows.

关税是进出口商品经过一国关境时，由该国海关向本国进出口商人所征收的一种税。关税作为国家税收的一种，一方面具有和其他税赋相同的特点，即强制性、无偿性和预定性等；另一方面，关税又有其自身的特点。

1.1 Tariff Is a Sort of Indirect Tax 关税是一种间接税

The tariff is taken as part of the commodity cost and added to the price finally by the importer or exporter although the payer of tariff is importer or exporter. The bearer of tariff is the buyer or consumer at the end.

关税是作为商品成本的一部分，最终由进出口商打入货价。虽然关税由进出口商支付，但是关税负担最后还是转嫁给买方或消费者承担。

1.2 Subject of Tariff and Object of Tariff 关税的税收主体和税收客体

Subject of taxation: the taxpayer of tariff, the importer or exporter of the commodity
Object of taxation: the imported or exported commodity
税收主体——本国进出口商品（即关税的纳税人）

税收客体——进出口商品

1.3 The Levy Scope of Tariff Is Bounded by Custom Border and the Levier Is Customs 关税的征收范围是以关境为界，关税的征收机构是海关

Customs is a national administrative organization set on the customs boundaries, with the function of supervision and management of merchandise conveyance and personal items, levy of tariff, banning of smuggling, temporary storage of goods as well as working out import and export statistics etc. The place where customs executes its function is called customs area.

The customs area is usually as same as the country's area with some exceptions, such as the countries with the free trade zone, export processing zone or bonded warehouse which are out of customs boundaries, in which case, the customs area is smaller than the country's territory; or several countries are united to form an economic integration like tariff union, common market etc., which have a uniformed customs area, so the customs area of the country members is bigger than any one country's territory.

海关是设立在关境上的国家行政管理机关，对进出口商品、运输工具和个人物品等进行监督管理、征收关税、查禁走私、临时保管通关货物和编制进出口统计等。海关执行其职能的领域叫关境。

一般情况下，关境和国境是一致的，但也有不一致的情况，如有些国家在国境内设有自由贸易区、出口加工区或保税仓库，此时，关境小于国境。另一种情况是几个国家结成关税同盟、共同市场等区域经济一体化组织，参加这些组织的国家即成为统一的关境，这时关境就大于国境。

2. Functions of Tariff 关税的作用

There are two functions for levying tariff:

First, The tariff is levied to increase a country's revenue, with which function the tariff is called revenue tariff.

Revenue tariff is usually levied on the commodities which are imported and consumed in large quantities. A revenue tariff rate is usually moderate as a too high rate will discourage import and fail to increase revenue. Currently, in developing countries, tariff income occupies a large share in the total government income. However, the revenue of developed countries seldom depends on tariff income, for instance, the tariff income of the United States and Japan only share 1% or so in the total government income.

Second, the tariff is levied for the purpose of protecting the country's industry and domestic market, and the tariff with the function is called protection tariff.

With a high tariff, the foreign commodities are restricted from being imported to a country, further protecting the domestic market and industry. With a high tariff, the cost of imported commodity is raised, being less competitive and decreased in market, as a result the home industry and market are protected. The protection tariff is also used to control the quantity of imported and exported goods through adjusting tariff rate, then to influence the price in domestic market to protect the market balance.

征收关税的作用主要有两个方面。

第一，增加本国财政收入，以此为目的征收的关税称为财政关税。

财政关税的征收对象一般是针对国内有大量消费、进口数量大的商品，而且税率要适中，如果税率过高，会阻碍进口，达不到增加财政收入的目的。目前，发展中国家的关税收入则占政府收入的较大比例。但发达国家的财政预算很少来自关税的收入，美国和日本的关税收入只占到其政府收入的 1%左右。

第二，保护本国的产业和国内市场，以此为目的征收的关税称为保护关税。

各国利用高关税限制外国商品进口，保护国内生产和国内市场。保护关税的税率越高，保护作用越强，因为进口关税税率提高可以提高进口商品的成本，从而削弱其竞争力，使其进口数量减少，以达到保护国内工农业生产的目的。保护关税的另一个目的是可以通过调整关税税率的高低来控制进出口商品的数量，以此调节国内的价格，保证国内市场供求平衡。

3. Classification of Tariff 关税的种类

3.1 In Accordance with the Levy Object and Flow Direction of Commodities, Tariff May Be Classified into Import Duty, Export Duty, and Transit Duty 按照征收的对象和商品流向分类：进口税、出口税和过境税

3.1.1 Import Duty 进口税

Import duty is levied by the import country according to the relative tariff regulations on the commodities imported from other countries or free ports, export processing zones and bonded warehouses to the import country's market. Import duty is also named normal tariff or import tariff.

In international trade, the so-called tariff barrier is import tariff which is an important measure to implement protective trade policy. Governments need to take many factors into consideration during the establishment of import duty rate regulations. A variety of duty rates are set on different commodities for the purpose of efficient protection and development of economy.

Import duty may be classified into general tariff rate, MFN (Most Favored Nation) tariff rate, preferential tariff rate, GSP (Generalized System Preference) tariff rate.

进口税是进口商品进入一国关境时或者从自由港、出口加工区及保税仓库进入进口国市场时，由进口国家的海关根据海关税则对本国进口商所征收的关税，又称为正常关

税或进口关税。

在国际贸易中，通常所说的关税壁垒就是指进口关税，关税壁垒是一国推行保护贸易政策所实施的一项重要措施。各国制定进口税税率要考虑多方面的因素。从有效保护和发展经济的角度出发，应对不同商品制定不同的税率。

进口税的种类主要有普通税率、最惠国税率、特惠税率、普惠制税率。

1) General duties 普通税率

In case that the import country is not in any tariff reciprocal treatment agreement with the origin country of the imported commodities, general tariff will be levied on the commodities. The general tariff rate is the highest rate, higher than the preferential tariff rate by 1 to 5 times, even 10 times, 20 times for a few kinds of commodities. Currently, only very few countries levy general tariff on the commodities from the specific countries (generally without diplomatic relations), and mostly the general tariff rate is taken as the reduction basis for the preferential rate. Therefore, the general tariff rate is not implemented at large.

如果进口国未与该进口商品的来源国签订任何关税互惠贸易条约，则对该进口商品按普通税率征税。普通税率是一国税率中的最高税率，一般比优惠税率高 1—5 倍，少数商品甚至高达 10 倍、20 倍。目前，仅有个别国家对极少数（一般是未建交）国家的出口商品实行这种税率，大多数只是将其作为优惠税率减税的基础。因此，普通税率并不是普遍实施的税率。

2) MFN duties 最惠国税率

It is a kind of preferential rate which is applied on the countries which are under the agreement of the MFN (Most Favored Nation) treatment. MFN treatment means that the members under the MFN treatment treaty must implement reciprocal treatment on each other, and any privilege, benefit and exemption granted to any third party must be granted to the MFN agreement members. The MFN treatment covers a large scope, but is mainly on preferential tariff. The MFN tariff rate is reciprocal, lower than the general tariff rate, sometimes even a big difference.

For instance, in the United States, the general duty rate levied on the imported toys is 70% and the MFN duty rate is 6.8%. Since most countries worldwide have joined GATT (now followed by WTO) with MFN treatment treaties, the MFN tariff rate has come to be the normal tariff rate.

MFN tariff is not the lowest duty. There are also some exceptions in a MFN treatment treaty, under which the MFN treatment is not applicable, such as tariff union, free trade zone, or more favorable tariff treatment between the countries in special relations.

最惠国税率是一种优惠税率，往往和双边或多边最惠国待遇相关。最惠国待遇是指缔约国各方实行互惠，凡缔约国一方现在和将来给予任何第三方的一切特权、优惠和豁免，也同样给予对方。最惠国待遇的内容很广，但主要是关税待遇。最惠国税率是互惠的，且比普通税率低，有时甚至差别很大。

例如，美国对进口玩具征税的普通税率为70%，而最惠国税率仅为6.8%。由于世界上大多数国家都通过签订多边最惠国待遇条约加入关贸总协定（现由世界贸易组织继承其协定），因而这种关税税率实际上已成为正常的关税税率。

最惠国税率并非是最低税率。在最惠国待遇中往往规定有例外条款，如在缔结关税同盟、自由贸易区或有特殊关系的国家之间规定更优惠的关税待遇时，最惠国待遇并不适用。

3) Preferential duties 特惠税

① Conception 概念

The special low duties or duty free treatment are granted to some even all commodities from a specific country or region. The preferential duties are applied for the purpose of the enhancement of the trade relationship with the beneficiary countries. Preferential duties are divided into mutual beneficial duty and non-mutual beneficial duty, with the rate lower than the MFN rate and the accorded rate.

特惠税指对从某个国家或地区进口的全部商品或部分商品给予特别优惠的低关税或免税待遇。使用特惠税的目的是增进与受惠国之间的友好贸易往来。特惠税有互惠与非互惠之分，税率一般低于最惠国税率和协定税率。

② Varieties 种类

The origin of preferential tariff is from the trade relation between imperial nation and his colonial vassal states. For the time being, the most influential preferential tariff is that of LOME convention [which is an trade and aid agreement between the European Community (EC) and 46 African, Caribbean, and Pacific (ACP) countries, first signed in February 1975 in Lomé, Togo]. According to the accord, during 8 years of transitional period, 96% of the agricultural products and all industrial products from the developing countries under the agreement have access to EU market with zero duty, and beneficiary countries of preferential duty are not required to grant reverse preference.

特惠税始于宗主国与殖民地附属国之间的贸易往来，目前国际上最有影响的是洛美协定（1975 年 2 月欧共体与非洲、加勒比海沿岸和太平洋地区 46 个发展中国家首次签署于多哥首都洛美）国家之间的特惠税。根据协定，在协定的八年过渡期中，这些发展中国家 96%的农产品和全部工业产品可免税进入欧盟市场，而不要求受惠国给予反向优惠。

4) Duties under GSP (Generalized System of Preference) 普惠制关税

Generalized system of preference is a preferential tariff system, under which, the developed countries grant a generalized, non-discriminatory, and non-reciprocal tariff preferential treatment to developing countries. It is a duty reduction and duty exemption on the basis of MFN tariff.

The three principles of GSP program are generalized, non-discriminatory, and non-reciprocal. Generalized, means developed countries under the system grant a general tariff preferential treatment to the manufactured products and semi-manufactured products of all less developed countries; non-discriminatory, means that all less developed countries enjoy the preferential treatment under GSP without any exception; non-reciprocal, means the preferential treatment is granted to less developed countries by developed countries laterally, without requiring the less developed countries to grant the reciprocal treatment to the developed countries.

普惠制是普遍优惠制的简称，是发达国家给予发展中国家出口的制成品和半制成品（包括某些初级产品）普遍的、非歧视的且非互惠的一种关税优惠制度。它是在最惠国税率的基础上进行减税和免税，按最惠国税率的一定百分比征收。

普遍性、非歧视性和非互惠性是普惠制的三项基本原则。普遍性是指发达国家对所有发展中国家出口的制成品和半制成品给予普遍的关税优惠待遇；非歧视性是指应使所有发展中国家都无歧视、无例外地享受普惠制待遇；非互惠性是指普惠制不是对等的关税优惠，发达国家应单方面给予发展中国家特殊的关税减让，而不要求发展中国家对发达国家给予对等待遇。

3.1.2 Export Duty 出口税

Export duty is levied on the exported commodities by the export country. Currently, most countries don't levy export duty on the exported commodities in general. Export duty will raise the cost of exported commodities and its price in foreign market, weakening its competition in the market abroad, and discouraging the expansion of export. Yet there are few countries (especially the less developed countries) levying export duty.

Usually, our country are always taking policy to stimulate export. However, in order to control the export quantity of some specific commodities, we have levied export duty on a very few kinds of commodities. The commodities with export duty levied are including raw silk, non-ferrous metal, ferroalloy and silk products etc.

出口税是出口国的海关对本国输往国外的商品所征收的关税。目前，大多数国家对绝大部分出口商品都不征收出口税。征收出口税会抬高出口商品的成本和国外售价，削弱其在国外市场的竞争力，不利于扩大出口。但目前世界上仍有少数国家（特别是经济落后的发展中国家）征收出口税。

我国历来采用鼓励出口的政策，但为了控制一些商品的出口流量，采用了对极少数商品征收出口税的办法。被征收出口税的商品主要有生丝、有色金属、铁合金和绸缎等。

3.1.3 Transit Duty 过境税

Transit duty is the duty levied by a country on the foreign goods going through its customs boundary. After World War II, GATT stipulated the principle of free transit. Therefore, most countries currently purely levy little visa charges, stamping taxes, registration fees, statistic charges and the like on the transit goods.

过境税又称通过税或转口税，是一国海关对通过其关境的外国货物所征收的关税。第二次世界大战后，关贸总协定规定了“自由过境”的原则。目前，大多数国家对过境货物只征收少量的签证费、印花费、登记费和统计费等。

3.2 In Accordance with Different Treatment and Special Measures, Tariff May Be Classified into Import Surtax, Variable Duty, Preferential Duty and GSP Duty 按照差别待遇和特定的实施情况分为进口附加税、差价税、特惠税和普惠制关税

3.2.1 Import Surtax 进口附加税

Import surtax, means the extra duty levied on the imported commodities for a special purpose in addition to general customs duty. It is an important measure to restrict import of a specific commodity, including anti-dumping duty and anti-subsidy duty.

进口附加税是指对进口商品除征收一般关税外，出于某种特定的目的再增加额外的关税。它是限制商品进口的重要手段，主要包括反倾销税和反补贴税。

1) Anti-dumping duty 反倾销税

① Conception 概念

Dumping: It happens when commodities of one country are input into the other country at the price much lower than the normal price. In the import country, the imported commodities dumped at cheap price have attacked the home industry in the same variety, thus threatening the survival of the industry of the import country.

There are three standards to confirm normal price: domestic market price, the third country's price, and constitution price, the details of which are as follows.

Domestic market price, means the price of the same commodity consumed in domestic market of the export country under the normal condition; a third country's price, the price of the same commodity exported to the third country under the normal trade relationship; constitution price is worked out based on the production cost plus reasonable promotion charges and profit.

Anti-dumping duty: Anti-dumping duty is an additional duty, levied temporarily on the imported commodities, in order to protect home industry and market against the import of foreign commodities in large quantities at cheap price.

倾销：一国商品以低于正常价格的价格输入另一国市场的行为。进行倾销的进口商品以价格优势打击进口国的同类产业，因此对该国领土内已建立的某种工业造成重大损害或产生重大威胁。

确定正常价格有三个标准：国内价格、第三国价格、构成价格。

国内价格是指相同商品在出口国用于国内消费时在正常情况下的可比价格；第三国价格，即相同产品在正常贸易情况下向第三国出口的最高可比价格；构成价格是指该产品在原产国的生产成本加合理的推销费用和利润。

反倾销税：对实行倾销的进口货物所征收的一种临时性进口附加税。其目的是抵制外国商品大量低价进口，保护国内产业与市场。

② Levy conditions: the existence of dumping, severe damage, the causality between dumping and damage 征收条件：倾销存在、重大损害、倾销与损害之间存在因果关系

Dumping: The sale lower than the cost is regarded as dumping. So it is key to confirming what is the normal price.

Great damage: Dumping has caused substantial damage or damage threat to the same industry of the import country; the surging quantity of the imported commodities has an impact on the price of the same products of the import country and has influenced the relevant producers.

Causality: The above mentioned damage must be resulted from dumping. If the damage is due to other factors (such as demand shrinking or consumption change etc.), the dumping shall not be responsible for the damage.

However, there are some disagreement on the confirmation of dumping, the definition of normal value and the implementary ways of anti-dumping in different countries. In some developed countries, anti-dumping measures are often adopted to restrict the import from less developed countries with low production cost, coming to be one of the non-tariff barriers with the expansion of anti-dumping.

倾销存在：关键是对正常价格的界定，低于成本的销售是倾销。

重大损害：倾销对进口国同类产业的造成实质性的损害或实质性的损害威胁；进口商品的激增对进口国同类产品产生了价格影响，对同类产品的生产者产生了影响。

因果关系：上述损害须为倾销所致，若由于其他因素（如需求萎缩或消费模式改变等）造成的损害则不应归咎于倾销性进口。

但是，对于倾销的认定、“正常价值”的含义、反倾销的实施方式等，各个国家之间存在着一定的分歧。一些发达国家则利用反倾销手段对来自低成本的发展中国家的产品进口加以限制，反倾销扩大化趋势明显，成为非关税壁垒的手段之一。

2) Countervailing duty 反补贴税

① Conception 概念

Subsidy: It's a financial donation to the exporter or an income or price support for the exported commodities, which is supplied by the export country's government or any other public institution in order to enhance the competition of the exported commodities.

Countervailing duty: Also known as anti-subsidy duty, it is an additional duty imposed on the imported commodities which have received prize or subsidy directly or indirectly in order to weaken its competition in the domestic market, usually levied in the amount equivalent to subsidy.

补贴：为了提高出口商品的价格竞争力，出口国政府或任何其他公共机构向企业提供财政捐款或收入或价格支持。

反补贴税：又称抵消税或补偿税，是对于直接或间接地接受过奖金或补贴的外国商品所征收的一种进口附加税，一般按照“补贴数额”征收。征收反补贴税的作用是削弱接受出口补贴的进口商品的价格竞争力。

② Levy conditions: existence of subsidy, damage, causality between subsidy and damage.征收的条件：存在补贴、损害，且补贴与损害之间存在因果关系。

③ Levy basis 征税的依据

The amount of the countervailing duty levied is no more than the net amount of the subsidy received for the commodity; the levy term is subject to the elimination of the damage caused by the export subsidy; the countervailing duty shall be cancelled after the export country's government agrees to cancel or limit the relevant subsidy.

Remark: Anti-dumping duty and countervailing duty must not be levied at the same time.

反补贴税的税额不得超过该商品接受补贴的净额；以消除出口补贴造成的损害为征收反补贴税的期限；出口国政府同意取消或限制补贴后，应取消反补贴税。

注意：反倾销税与反补贴税不能同时征收。

3.2.2 Variable Duty 差价税

Variable duty is levied on the imported commodities when the domestic price of the commodities produced by the import country is higher than the imported ones. The levy amount is variable subject to the difference between the domestic price and import price.

当某种国内生产的产品国内价格高于同类进口商品的价格时，为削弱进口商品的竞争力，按国内价格与进口价格之间的差额征收的关税即为差价税。差价税随着国内外价格差额的变化而变动，因此是一种滑动税。

3.3 In Accordance with Levy Standard, Tariff May Be Divided into Specific Duty, Ad Valorem Duty, Mixed Duty, and Alternative Duty 按照征税标准，关税可分为从量税、从价税、混合税和选择税

3.3.1 Specific Duty 从量税

1) Conception 概念

Specific duty is levied according to the quantity, volume, weight and the like of the imported commodities. Weight is mostly adopted to calculate duty amount in the levy of specific duty. For instance, the United Stated levy specific duty on the import of menthol, the general duty rate is 50 cents per pound, and the MFN duty rate is 17 cents.

从量税是以进口商品的数量、体积、重量等计量单位为标准的一种计征关税的方法。重量单位是最常用的从量税计量单位。例如，美国对薄荷脑的进口征收从量税，普通税率为每磅 50 美分，最惠国税率为每磅 17 美分。

Amount of specific duty = Quantity of imported goods × Specific duty rate

从量税税额=货物计量单位数×从量税税率

2) Characteristics 特点

The calculation method is simple with rapid customs clearance, discouraging the import of cheap goods or the commodities sold at low or fake price on purpose. Since the unit duty amount of the specific duty is fixed, the duty amount cannot be variable with the fluctuation of market price, and the control function of the specific duty is weakened when the price is rising.

这种计税方法简便，通关手续快捷，能抑制低廉商品或故意瞒报价格商品的进口。每一种进口商品的单位税额是固定的，物价涨落时，税额不能相应变化。因而，在物价上涨时，关税的调节作用相对减弱。

3) Application 应用

Specific duty is applied to the commodities which are in simple specifications and varieties, easy to compute, with little difference in prices of the same sort, imported in large quantities. The commodities on which specific duty is levied are mostly corn, cotton and the like and standard products. For the import of the valuable commodities of high quality, the duty levied is so little that the function of tariff protection and revenue income is weakened.

从量税适用于规格品种简单、计量容易、同一种商品规格价差比较少且经常性大宗进口的商品，征收对象一般是谷物、棉花等大宗产品和标准产品。对于质优价高的商品而言，税负相对减轻，关税的保护与财政收入作用相对减弱。

3.3.2 Ad Valorem Duty 从价税

1) Conception 概念

Ad valorem duty is levied based on the price of the goods. The duty rate is indicated in a percentage of the price.

Amount of ad valorem duty = Duty paid price × Import ad valorem duty rate

The duty paid price is determined by customs to calculate the duty.

从价税是以货物价格作为征税标准来征收的关税。税率表现为商品价格的一定百分比。

从价税税额=完税价格×进口从价税率

进口货物的完税价格是指经海关审定的作为计征关税依据的商品价格。

2) Characteristics 特点

The duty on the quality and valuable commodities is high and the duty on the cheap commodities is much lower; the duty on the highly processed products and luxury items are high, and the protection function is apparent.

优质价高的商品税高，质劣价低的商品税低；加工程度高的商品和奢侈品价高，税额较高，保护作用较大。

3) Application 应用

For instance, in the United States, it is stipulated that the general duty rate is 60% and MFN duty rate is 4.7% for the import of feather products. The calculation formula: import duty amount = total import amount × ad valorem duty rate. In 2006, the duty rate for cars in China is 25%. If an imported car values 20,000 US dollars, then the import duty is 5,000 US dollars.

例如，美国规定，针对羽毛制品的进口，普通税率为 60%，最惠国税率为 4.7%。计算公式：进口关税税额=进口商品总额×从价税率。2006年，中国的汽车关税率为25%，如果进口一辆价值20 000美元的汽车，关税税额为5 000美元。

3.3.3 Mixed Duty 混合税

It is also known as compound duty, a combination of specific duty and ad valorem duty levied on imported commodities. Compound duty may restrain the import of goods at low price as well as be levied on the imported goods at a reasonable and stable rate.

混合税也称复合税，是对某种进口商品混合使用从价税和从量税的一种计征关税的方法。混合税既发挥从量税抑制低价进口商品的优点，又可发挥从价税税负合理、稳定的优点。

3.3.4 Alternative Duty 选择税

In tariff regulation, some commodities are listed with both specific duty rate and ad valorem duty rate. Customs may adopt one of them as the duty rate for levy and may usually select the higher one. When the market price is rising, the ad valorem duty is adopted; when the market price is down, the specific duty is used. In this way both duty amount and protection function are ensured.

在税则中，对某种进口商品同时规定从价和从量两种税率，征税时由海关选择其中一种计税，一般是选择税额较高的一种征收。在物价上涨时，使用从价税；在物价下跌时，使用从量税，这样既可保证税收数量，又可发挥保护作用。

4. Customs Tariff 海关税则

Customs Tariff, a regulation book about the duty levied on the imported and exported commodities and the systematic classification of the levy, reduction and exemption of the duties and taxes. Customs tariff is the basis for customs to levy, and an important part of customs tariff system, expressing a country's tariff policy in detail.

There are two parts in *Customs Tariff*: one part is about the regulations and illustrations of customs duty levy; the other part is a table of tariff duty rates.

Tariff duty rate table includes three parts, which are as follows: tariff number, description of goods and rate of duty.

It's very important to make a systematic classification of items in customs tariff for the convenience of taxation, rate paying, statistics and search. In order to harmonize the different classifications of items in customs tariffs of various countries, *The Harmonized Commodity Description and Coding System* (H.S. for short) has been established and come into force on 1st Jan.1988, which is a new systematic and multifunctional classification system about the commodities in international trade.

The classification is principally on the basis of raw materials of the items, in combination of process degree, manufacture phase, and the final uses of the items.

The data of the *Harmonized System* is taken as the basis of customs duty reduction in GATT (General Agreement on Tariffs and Trade). Since 1st Jan. 1992, our country has compiled and implemented a new edition of customs tariff, named *Customs Import and*

Export Tariff of the Peoples' Republic of China and *Commodities Classification on China Customs Statistics*, adopting 8-digit H.S. codes.

For the items listed in Customs Tariff, some of them are levied at one kind of duty rate, or at two or more kinds of duty rates.

海关税则又称关税税则，是一国对进出口商品计征关税的规章和对进出口应税与免税商品加以系统分类的一览表。海关税则是各国征收关税的依据，是关税制度的重要内容，是国家关税政策的具体体现。

海关税则一般包括两个部分：一部分是海关课征关税的规章条例及说明；另一部分是关税税率表。

关税税率表主要包括三个部分：税则号列、商品分类目录及税率。

如何对海关税则中的商品进行系统分类，是海关税则制定中的重要问题。系统分类的目的是便于征税、纳税、统计和查找。为了协调各国在海关税则商品分类方法上的差异，《商品名称及编码协调制度》，简称《协调制度》，于 1988 年 1 月 1 日正式生效实施。这是一套新型的、系统的和多用途的国际贸易商品分类体系。

商品分类目录的分类原则是以商品的原料组成为主，结合商品的加工程度、制造阶段和商品的最终用途来划分。

关税及贸易总协定是按《协调制度》目录统计的数据作为关税减让谈判的基础。我国自 1992 年 1 月 1 日起也正式实施了以《协调制度》为基础编制的新的《海关进出口税则》和《海关统计商品目录》，采用 8 位数字编码。

海关税则中的同一种商品，可以采用一种税率征税，也可以采用两种或两种以上税率征税。

Lesson 2　Non-tariff Barriers 非关税壁垒

1. General Introduction to Non-tariff Barriers 非关税壁垒概述

Non-tariff barriers, mean all kinds of measures to restrict import without using tariff. Under WTO system, non-tariff barriers include anti-dumping, countervailing, import quota, auto export restriction, technical trade barrier and protection etc.

Non-tariff barriers and tariff barriers both have the function of restraining import. However, compared with tariff barriers, non-tariff barriers have the characteristics as follows.

非关税壁垒（NTBs）是指关税以外的一切限制进口的各种措施。它是与关税壁垒相对而言的。在 WTO 规则体系中，非关税壁垒主要包括反倾销、反补贴、进口配额、自动出口限制、技术性贸易壁垒和保障措施等。

非关税壁垒与关税壁垒都有限制进口的作用。但是，与关税壁垒相比，非关税壁垒具有以下特点。

1.1 Being More Flexible and Well-targeted 灵活性和针对性

Generally speaking, the establishment, adjustment and revision of tariffs need to get through some complicated legal procedures, being required to be in continuity, as well as being restricted with MFN treatment clauses, so it is not so easy and free to make changes and adjustments on tariff rates.

Comparatively, the measures of non-tariff barriers may be adopted and implemented more rapidly. With more simple administrative procedures, the measures to restrict the import of commodities from a country can be taken and adjusted more rapidly.

一般来说，各国关税税率制定、调整或更改必须通过较为烦琐的法律程序和手续，并要求具有一定的连续性，所以调整或更改税率的随意性有限。因此，在需要紧急限制进口时往往难以适应。同时，关税税率的调整还受到最惠国待遇条款的约束，因而较难在税率上进行灵活性的调整。

非关税壁垒措施的制定手续比较迅速，通常采用行政程序，程序简便，能随时针对某国的某种商品采取或更换相应的限制进口措施，较快地达到限制进口的目的。

1.2 Being More Effective 有效性

Tariffs are usually implemented in order to raise the costs and prices of imported commodities and weaken their competitiveness, accomplishing the restriction on import indirectly. However, tariff hardly restrains the import in case that export country cuts down the costs and prices of commodities by means of export subsidy, dumping etc.

But some non-tariff barriers such as import quota, import license can restrict import definitely, which cannot be by passed by exporters.

关税的实施旨在提高进口商品的成本和价格，削弱其竞争能力，间接地达到限制进口的目的。如果出口国采用出口贴补、商品倾销等办法降低出口商品成本和价格，关税往往较难起到限制商品进口的作用。

但一些非关税措施如进口配额制、进口许可证等对进口的限制作用是绝对的，出口商无论如何都无法绕过这种壁垒。

1.3 Being More Concealing and Discriminatory 隐蔽性和歧视性

Generally, tariff rates will be promulgated in legal form after being determined, and implemented legally. On the contrary, some non-tariff barriers will not be publicized or complicated standards and procedures are set so that exporters hardly deal with it. As far as the technical standard is concerned, some countries have set so strict, complicated and special standards and inspection procedures on some commodities in terms of quality, specification, performance or safety which the foreign commodities cannot meet and adapt to. In addition, some countries will implement a non-tariff barrier on a specific country, which strengthen the discrimination from non-tariff barriers.

一般说来，关税税率确定后，往往以法律形式公之于众，依法执行。但是，一些非关税壁垒措施往往不公开，或者规定极为烦琐复杂的标准和手续，使出口商难以适应。就技术标准而论，一些国家对某些商品的质量、规格、性能和安全等规定了极为严格、烦琐和特殊的标准，检验手续烦琐复杂，而且经常变化，使外国商品难以对付和适应，因而往往由于不符合某一规定而不能进入对方的市场销售。同时，一些国家经常针对某个国家实施某种限制性的非关税壁垒措施，结果大大加强了非关税壁垒的差别性和歧视性。

2. Classification of Non-tariff Barriers 非关税壁垒的主要种类

In so many kinds of non-tariff barriers, the following are the most common ones.

非关税壁垒名目繁多，下面介绍最常见的几种。

2.1 Import Quota 进口配额制

Quota is set by a country's government to restrict the import or export quantity of a kind of commodity or service and control the trade with other countries. Import Quota is set by a country's government to restrict the import quantity or amount of some commodities within a specific period, that is, usually one year. Within the specified period, the goods in the quota have access to the import country and the goods out of quota are prohibited or allowed to enter after paying higher duty or penalty. Import quota is one of the most important measures to limit import quantity. For instance, in the year of 2005, the import quota of cotton in China is 89.4 tons and granted to the relevant enterprises by the end of 2004.

For import quota, there are two sorts including absolute quota and tariff quota.

配额是一国政府为了控制本国与其他国家之间的贸易而施加的对商品或服务进出口量的限制。进口配额又称进口限额，是一国政府在一定时期（通常为一年）以内，对某些商品的进口数量或金额加以直接限制。在规定的期限内，配额以内的货物可以进口，超过配额不准进口，或者征收更高的关税或罚款后才能进口。进口配额制是实行进口数量限制的重要手段之一。例如：2005 年中国的棉花进口配额为 89.4 万吨，并于 2004 年年底前发放到相关企业。

进口配额制主要有绝对配额和关税配额两种。

2.1.1 Absolute Quota 绝对配额

It means that the highest limitation to quantity or amount of some commodities is specified within a period, reaching which the goods cannot be imported. In the implementation of absolute quota, there are three kinds which are global quota, country quota and importer quota.

绝对配额是在一定时期内，对某些商品的进口数量或金额规定一个最高限额，达到这个限额后，便不准进口。这种进口配额在实施中，又有全球配额、国别配额和进口商配额三种方式。

2.1.2 Tariff Quota 关税配额

Tariff quota means that the import amount of a kind of commodity is not restricted absolutely, but granting low duty, duty reduction or free duty on the commodities imported within the specified quota; higher duty, additional tax or penalty will be levied on commodities with the quantity over the quota.

The main difference between absolute quota and tariff quota is as follows: absolute quota means setting the highest limit on the import quantity or amount and the items over the quota are prohibited to be imported; the tariff quota means that the items are permitted to enter even when they surpass the quota, but higher duty will be levied on the excess.

关税配额是对商品进口的绝对数额不加限制，而对规定配额以内的进口商品给予低税、减税或免税待遇；对超过配额的进口商品则征收较高的关税、附加税或罚款。

绝对配额与关税配额的主要区别在于：绝对配额规定一个最高进口额度，超过就不准进口；而关税配额在商品进口超过规定的最高额度后，仍允许进口，只是超过部分被课以较高关税。

2.2 "Voluntary" Export Quota “自动”出口配额制

"Voluntary" export quota, also known as "voluntary" restriction of export, means that export countries or regions "voluntarily" restrict the export of some commodities to an import country within a period (generally 3–5 years) under the pressure of the import country, controlling the export within the quota and banning the export of the excess.

The main differences in forms between "voluntary" export quota and absolute import quota are as follows: absolute import quota means that import countries control the import quota to restrict the import of a commodity, and that the "voluntary" export quota is implemented by export country to control the export to the specific import country.

"Voluntary" export quota is compulsory. An import country may require the concerning export country to restrict the export voluntarily and have a well-ordered increase on export, taking the excuse that the import in large quantity of some commodities have damaged the relevant home industries and caused the so-called "market mess". In this case, some export countries are forced to implement "voluntary" restriction of export.

“自动”出口配额制又称“自动”限制出口，是指出口国家或地区在进口国的要求或压力下，“自动”规定某一时期内（一般为3～5年）对该国某些商品实施出口限制，在限定的配额内自行控制出口，超过配额即禁止出口。

“自动”出口配额制与绝对进口配额制在形式上的主要区别是：绝对进口配额制是由进口国家直接控制进口配额来限制商品的进口；“自动”出口限额制是由出口国家直接控制这些商品对指定进口国家的出口。但是，就进口国家来说，“自动”出口配额制与绝对进口配额制一样，均起着限制商品进口的作用。

“自动”出口配额制带有明显的强制性。进口国家往往以商品大量进口使其有关工业部门受到严重损害并造成所谓“市场混乱”为理由，要求有关国家的出口实行“有秩序的增长”，“自动”限制商品出口，否则就单方面强制限制进口。在这种情况下，一些出口国家被迫实行“自动”出口限制。

2.3 Import License System 进口许可证制

Import license system means that the import country requires the importers of some commodities to apply for import license before importing the items.

Import license may be classified into two sorts depending on if there is a limit on the countries or regions of origin.

One sort of license is named as Open General License. Without any limit on the countries or regions from which the goods are imported, the items listed for open general license may get the access to the import country after the importer filling the form of the open general license. Therefore, these commodities are imported freely.

The other sort of license is known as Specific License, an importer must apply for the specific license and get the permit from the import county's government before importing the items listed for specific license. The specific license is usually made for the specified countries and regions. In order to distinguish the commodities respectively for the two sorts of licenses, the concerning authority will promulgate the items listed for each sort of license and make adjustment from time to time when necessary.

进口许可证制是指进口国为了管制对外贸易，规定进口某些商品必须事先领取许可证才可进口，否则一律不准进口。

从进口商品有无限制上看，进口许可证又可分为两种。

一种为公开一般许可证，又称公开进口许可证或一般许可证和自动进口许可证。它对进口国别或地区没有限制，凡列明属于公开一般许可证的商品，进口商只要填写公开一般许可证后，即可获准进口。因此，属于这类许可证的商品实际上是自由进口的商品。

另一种为特种进口许可证，又称非自动进口许可证，进口商必须向政府有关当局提出申请，经政府有关部门逐笔审查批准后才能进口。这种进口许可证，多数都指定进口国别或地区。为了区分这两种许可证所进口的商品，有关部门通常定期分别公布有关的商品项目并根据需要随时调整。

2.4 Foreign Exchange Control 外汇管制

Foreign exchange control is a kind of system taken by a country's government to keep the balance of the international payment and stabilize the foreign exchange rate through restricting international settlement and foreign exchange business with legal rules.

Under foreign exchange control, exporters must sell the foreign exchange they received as the payment for the exports to the concerning foreign exchange administration at a specified official exchange rate; importers also must purchase foreign exchange at the official rate from the foreign exchange administration, and the home currencies are also restricted to move out or into the home country. In this way, through fixing official exchange rate, collecting the foreign exchange of international payment and permitting the purchase of foreign exchange, the government can control the supply of foreign exchange and restrict the varieties, quantity and original countries of the imported commodities.

外汇管制是指一国政府通过法令对国际结算和外汇买卖实行限制，以平衡国际收支和维持本国货币汇价的一种制度。

在外汇管制下，出口商必须把他们出口所得的外汇收入按官定汇率卖给外汇管制机关；进口商也必须在外汇管制机关按官定汇价申请购买外汇，本国货币出入国境也受到严格的限制等。这样，国家的有关政府机构就可以通过确定官定汇价、集中外汇收入和批汇的办法，控制外汇供应数量，以达到限制进口商品品种、数量和进口国别的目的。

2.5 State Monopoly on Import and Export 进口和出口的国家垄断

State monopoly on import and export means that the government of a nation controls the import and export of some specific commodities directly, or grants the monopoly right of some commodities to some monopoly organizations.

For most countries, the state monopoly is mainly focused on the following four sorts of items. Firstly, cigarettes and wines, usually a government may obtain a great amount of revenue income from the monopoly on import and export of cigarettes and wines. Secondly, farm produce, the monopoly of farm produce on foreign sales are taken as a part of national agricultural policies. For instance, Commodity Credit Corporation of the United State purchased the "overplus" farm produce in domestic market at a high price, and then dumped it abroad at a cheap price or sent it to the countries in short of grain as an "aid". Thirdly, weapon, which accounts for so much of national safety and world peace, monopolized by government certainly. Fourthly, oil, which is vital to a nation. In most countries which export or import oil in large, national oil companies are established to monopolize the oil business.

进口和出口的国家垄断，是指在对外贸易中，对某些商品的进出口规定由国家机构直接经营，或者是把某些商品进口或出口的专营权授予某些垄断组织。

各国主要对四类商品进行进口和出口的垄断。第一类是烟和酒。政府可以从烟和酒的进出口垄断中取得巨大的财政收入。第二类是农产品。把对农产品的对外垄断销售作为国内农业政策措施的一部分。例如美国的农产品信贷公司，高价收购国内的“剩余”农产品，然后以低价向国外倾销，或者“援助”给缺粮国家。第三类是武器。它关系国家安全与世界和平，自然要受到国家专控。第四类是石油，它是一国的经济命脉，主要的石油出口国和进口国都设立了国营石油公司，对石油贸易进行垄断经营。

2.6 Discriminatory Governmental Purchase Policy 歧视性政府采购政策

Discriminatory governmental purchase policy refers to the legal rules and articles set by the government, stipulating that home products must be purchased prior to the foreign products in the same variety, consequently leading to the discrimination against the foreign products and restriction on import.

For instance, in some regions of Japan, it is stipulated legally that as for official equipment, cars, computers, cables, wires, machine tools and the like home products must be purchased. In Britain, the communication equipment and computers are required to be purchased from home enterprises.

歧视性政府采购政策是指国家制定法令，规定政府机构在采购时要优先购买本国产品，从而导致对国外产品的歧视，起到了限制进口的作用。

例如，日本有几个省规定，政府机构使用的办公设备、汽车、计算机、电缆、导线、机床等不得采购外国产品。英国限定通信设备和电子计算机要向本国公司采购。

2.7 Internal Tax 国内税

Internal tax means the taxation on the products and commodities produced, distributed, used or consumed within a country. Internal taxation will be adopted in some countries to restrict the export of some specific commodities directly or indirectly. It is more flexible and disguisable than tariff as internal taxation is not restrained by trade agreements or multi-lateral accords.

For example, French government had levied highway maintenance tax of USD 12.15 on cars with engine of 5 hp, USD 30 on cars with engine of 16hp. At that time, the cars with the most powerful engine produced in France is 12 hp. So, the taxation was aimed at the restriction of the import of cars.

Taking another example, the consumption taxes on imported liquor in the United States, Switzerland and Japan are higher than their home products.

For the time being, EU members adopt Value Added Tax, that is to say, the taxation on the value added between sales value and purchase value, to be levied on commodities in domestic market. The VAT is applicable to each section from production to distribution. VAT Exported commodities are exempted from VAT and VAT is levied on the imported commodities.

国内税是指在一国的国境内，对生产、销售、使用或消费的商品所应支付的捐税，一些国家往往采用国内税制度直接或间接地限制进口某些商品。这是一种比关税更灵活、更易于伪装的贸易政策手段，因为国内税通常是不受贸易条约或多边协定限制的。

例如，法国曾对引擎为 5 匹马力的汽车每年征收养路税 12.15 美元，对引擎为 16 匹马力的汽车每年征收养路税 30 美元，当时法国生产的动力最强劲的引擎为 12 匹马力。因此，实行这种税率的目的在于抵制进口汽车。

例如，美国、瑞士和日本进口酒精饮料的消费税都高于本国制品。

目前，欧盟国家采用增值税，即按销货值大于进货值的增值部分，对国内产品征收一定比例的税金。它适用于生产和销售的每一个环节。增值税对出口商品实行免税或退税，而对进口商品则如数征收。

2.8 Minimum Price and Prohibitive Import 最低限价制和禁止进口

2.8.1 Minimum Price 最低限价制

Minimum price is the lowest price stipulated by the government for an imported commodity. For a kind of commodity imported at the price lower than the fixed minimum price, the import surtax or prohibitive import is adopted to restrain the import at a cheap price. For instance, in 1985, Chile stipulated that the minimum price of silk cloth imported should be 52 dollars per ton; the surtax was to be levied for the goods at a lower price than it.

最低限价就是一国政府规定某种进口商品的最低价格，凡进口货价低于规定最低价格的，则征收进口附加税或禁止进口，以达到限制低价商品进口的目的。例如，1985 年智利对绸坯布进口规定每千克的最低限价为 52 美元，低于此价格，将征收进口附加税。

2.8.2 Prohibitive Import 禁止进口

Prohibitive Import is a kind of extreme measure to restrict import. In some countries, in case that the government finds that import quantity restriction cannot rescue the domestic market from the impacts and troubles brought by the imported products, the government may promulgate decrees and rules to prohibit the import. For instance, in March of 1975, EU made a decision that the canned beef below 3 tons were prohibited to be imported from the foreign markets other than EU since March 15, 1975.

禁止进口是进口限制的极端措施，当一些国家感到实行进口数量限制已不足以解救国内市场受冲击的困境时，往往颁布法令公布禁止某些商品的进口。例如，1975 年 3 月，欧共体决定自 1975 年 3 月 15 日起，禁止从欧共体以外市场进口 3 千克以下的牛肉罐头。

2.9 Import Advanced Deposit System 进口押金制

Import Advanced Deposit System means that an importer is required to make non-interest deposit in the amount of a certain percentage of the import amount into the specified bank within the specified time before import. Increasing the capital burden of the importer and influencing the capital running, advanced deposit system plays a role of restricting import. For instance, Italian government had implemented the system on over 400 sorts of imported commodities, stipulating the non-interest deposit in the amount equal to half of the import value should be paid to Italian central bank and be frozen for 6 months before the import from whatever country. The force of the measure is equal to the levy of import surtax at 5%.

Import Advanced Deposit System is adopted in Finland, New Zealand and Brazil etc. In Brazil, it's stipulated in the Advanced Deposit System that the importer should make deposit for 360 days in the amount equal to the contract value at FOB price before the import.

进口押金制又称进口存款制或进口担保金制，是指进口商在进口商品时，必须预先按进口金额的一定比率和规定的时间在指定的银行无息存入一笔现金。这样就增加了进口商的资金负担，影响了资金的流转，起到了限制进口的作用。例如，意大利政府曾对 400 多种进口商品实行这种制度，规定无论从哪一国进口，都必须先向中央银行缴纳相当于进口货值半数的现款押金，无息冻结 6 个月，这项措施相当于征收 5%以上的进口附加税。

芬兰、新西兰、巴西等国也实行这种措施。巴西的进口押金制规定，进口商必须按进口商品船上交货价格交纳与合同金额相等的为期360天的存款方能进口。

2.10 Customs Evaluation System 海关估价制

Customs evaluation system is a system established by the government to levy duty and fix the price of imported commodities. In some countries, in accordance with some special regulation, the custom evaluation price of the imported commodities is raised to increase the duty born by the imported commodities to discourage the import.

The United States often adopts the customs evaluation system to restrain import. For a long time, the customs of the United States takes the higher one of the two prices which are the export country's market price and export price to levy duty.

海关估价制是指海关为了征收关税而确定进口商品价格的制度。有些国家根据某些特殊规定而提高进口商品的海关估价，以增加进口商品的关税负担，阻碍商品的进口，就成为专断的海关估价。

用专断的海关估价限制商品的进口，以美国最为典型。长期以来，美国海关按照进口商品的外国价格（在出口国国内销售市场的批发价）或出口价格（在出口国市场供出口用的售价）两者之间较高的一种进行征税。这实际上提高了关税的税额。

2.11 Technical Barriers to Trade 技术性贸易壁垒

Technical barriers to trade are usually made to restrict import. In some countries, the governments have set a variety of complicated and rigorous technical standards, health quarantine regulations, package and label requirements in excuse of production maintenance, consumer safety and health. These regulations and requirements are so complicated and variable that foreign products cannot adapt to them; the imports are limited.

技术性贸易壁垒是指为了限制进口，一国对进口商品所规定的复杂苛刻的技术标准、卫生检疫规定以及商品包装和标签规定，这些标准和规定往往以维护生产、消费者安全和人民健康的理由而制定。有些规定十分复杂且经常变化，往往使外国产品难以适应，从而起到限制进口的作用。

2.11.1 Multifarious Technical Standards 繁杂的技术标准

Many developed countries have set rigorous and complex technical standards for the manufactured products to be imported. The importers have to import the goods meeting the standards with some of which are just aimed at some specific countries. For instance, former Federal Republic of Germany prohibited importing cars whose the doors are opened from the front. This kind of cars was Italian Fiat No.500. France prohibited the import of juice containing glucose aiming to restrict products from the US as the juice produced in the US was often with the additive.

These technical standards not only restrict the sales of foreign products in text but also set various barriers during the sales of foreign products. Taking the disputes of car business between Britain and Japan as an example, it was stipulated in Britain that the cars imported to Britain from

Japan should be inspected in Japan by an inspector from Britain and be repaired or replaced with accessories in Japan in case of failure to meet the British technical safety regulations. However, for the cars imported to Japan from Britain, it was stipulated in Japan that the cars imported be inspected by Japan and repaired in Japan by an exporter of Britain, which may take more time and more labour. Moreover, the Japanese technical standards had been put off, which brought more troubles to the export of British cars to Japan market.

发达国家对于许多制成品规定了极为严格、烦琐的技术标准。进口货物必须符合这些标准才能进口，其中有些规定往往是针对某些国家的。例如，当年联邦德国禁止在国内使用车门从前往后开的汽车，这种汽车正是意大利菲亚特 500 型汽车的式样。法国禁止进口含有葡萄糖的果汁，这些规定意在抵制美国的货物，因为在美国，这类产品是经常加上这种附加物的。

这些技术标准不仅在条文上限制了外国产品的销售，而且在实施过程中也为外国产品的销售设置了重重障碍。以英国、日本汽车争端为例，英国方面规定，日本输往英国的轿车可由英国派人到日本进行检验，如发现有不符合英国技术安全规定的地方，可在日本检修或更换零件，比较方便。但日本方面规定，英国输往日本的轿车在运到日本后，必须由日本人检验，如不符合规定，则要由英方在日本检修，这要耗费更多的时间和人工，加上日本有关技术标准推迟公布，给英国轿车出口日本造成了更大的困难。

2.11.2 Strict Health Quarantine Regulations 严格的卫生检疫规定

Developed countries have more widely made use of health quarantine regulations to restrict the import, requiring more and more commodities to go through the inspection of health quarantine with much more strict health quarantine rules. For example, it is stipulated in the United States that the foods, beverages, drugs and cosmetic products imported to the US meet the standards of *Federal Food，Drug and Cosmetic Act*.

In Japan, Canada and Britain, it is stipulated that the aflatoxin contained in peanuts not be over 20 ppm, and the aflatoxin in peanut jam not be over 10 ppm, otherwise the products are not permitted to enter their markets. Japan requires the pesticide remnant in tea be no more than 0.2 ppm to 0.5 ppm. The US and Canada require the lead content be no more than 7 ppm, and Australia requires be no more than 20 ppm.

发达国家更加广泛地利用卫生检疫的规定限制商品进口。它们要求需接受卫生检疫的商品种类越来越多，卫生检疫规定越来越严。例如，美国规定，其他国家或地区输往美国的食品、饮料、药品及化妆品必须符合美国的《联邦食品、药品及化妆品法》，否则不准进口。

日本、加拿大、英国等要求花生黄曲霉素含量不超过百万分之二十，花生酱不超过百万分之十，超过者不准进口。日本对茶叶农药残留量规定不超过百万分之零点二至零点五。美国、加拿大规定含铅量不得超过百万分之七；澳大利亚规定的含铅量不得超过百万分之二十。

2.12 Corporate Social Responsibility and Social Accountability 8000 企业社会责任和社会责任标准认证 SA8000

There are some multi-lateral organizations about "Corporate Social Responsibility" in western countries coming up with some evaluation and authentication systems, in which SA8000 (Social Accountability 8000) is the most influential one. SA8000 certification is an independent auditable certification standard that encourages organizations to develop, maintain, and apply socially acceptable practices in the workplace. SA8000 is a management system standard based on the principles of international human rights norms as described in International Labour Organization Conventions, the United Nations Convention on the Rights of the Child and the Universal Declaration of Human Rights. It measures the performances of companies in eight areas important to social accountability in the workplace: child labour, forced labour, health and safety, free association and collective bargaining, discrimination, disciplinary practices, working hours and compensation. Since May 2004, some developed countries in the US and the EU began to implement SA8000, integrating the enterprise's ethnic into the enterprise management system, requiring suppliers to gain orders after accepting and going through the verification of social responsibility.

SA8000 is also taken by developed countries as a labor trade barrier. As a new trade barrier, social responsibility system standard is quite covert and complex, hardly can be judged as reasonable or not. At the same time, social responsibility system involves technology, law and administration etc. So home enterprises and administrations shall pay attention to it and strengthen competitiveness of export enterprises to overcome new barriers.

欧美先后出现了一些关于企业社会责任（简称 CSR）的多边组织，逐步形成了一些评价体系和认证制度，企业社会责任标准认证 SA8000 是其中最有影响的一种。SA8000 是根据国际劳工组织公约、世界人权宣言及联合国儿童权益公约制定的一套可被第三方认证机构独立审核、认证的标准体系，其宗旨是确保生产商及供应商所提供的产品符合社会责任的要求，主要包括童工、强迫劳工、安全卫生、结社自由和集体谈判权、歧视、惩罚性措施、工作时间、工资报酬及管理体系九方面内容。2004 年 5 月，欧美一些发达国家开始强制推行 SA8000，将企业道德规范纳入企业经营管理体系，要求供应商必须接受并通过社会责任审核才能获得订单。

作为全球第一个用于第三方认证的社会责任管理体系标准，社会责任标准认证 SA8000 既是责任也是工具，它绝不仅仅是一道门槛，社会责任的推行将成为发达国家实施“劳工贸易壁垒”的又一借口。社会责任标准这类新贸易壁垒具有合理和不合理的双重性，非常隐蔽和复杂。同时，新贸易壁垒涉及技术、法律以及行政管理等各个方面和各个部门，国内企业和政府部门须及早应对，提高企业综合竞争力，突破新贸易壁垒。

2.13 Green Trade Barrier 绿色贸易壁垒

Green trade barrier is also known as environmental protection barrier, which is a new kind of trade protection measure made with a variety of strict environmental standards in excuse of environmental protection, natural resource reservation, and human health.

Green trade barrier is a new kind of non-tariff barrier arising in last years. With the intensifying industrialization, the global environmental pollution is increasingly serious and even threatening the survival and sustainable development of human itself. With people's awareness of environmental protection and acknowledgement of sustainable development, various international environmental protection accords and agreements have been concluded, bringing a considerable influence on international trade.

However, trade protectionists made a confusion of environmental protection and trade protection, setting up various green trade barriers. The trade barrier is more effective and hidden, even more justifiable. For the time being, more and more green trade barriers are abused as the environmental standards of developed countries are higher than those of developing countries. In particular, a few developed countries adopted different standards for the imported products and home products, making the products of developing countries more difficult to enter developed countries.

For instance, the United States prohibited the entry of gasoline from Venezuela due to the contained Pb over the US standard; the EU forbade the import of leather products from Canada as the Canadian hunter captured lots of wild animals with traps. Since the 1990s, the EU countries have forbidden the import of refrigerators with Freon, leading to the export drop of refrigerators from China by 59%. All of these were caused by green trade barrier.

Green trade barriers are classified into four kinds in forms as follows.

绿色贸易壁垒也就是环境壁垒，它是一种以保护环境、自然资源和人类健康为借口而制定的一系列严格的环境标准，是一种贸易保护主义新措施。

绿色贸易壁垒是近几年兴起的一种新的非关税壁垒。随着工业化的加强，全球环境污染日益严重，甚至威胁到人类自身的生存和发展。人们的环保意识逐渐增强，可持续发展的观念日益为各国接受，各种类型的国际环保公约和协议也越来越多，因而对国际贸易产生了明显的影响。

但贸易保护主义者混淆了环境保护与贸易保护的关系，乘机设置各种绿色贸易壁垒，这种贸易壁垒比其他壁垒更有效、更隐蔽，甚至更加“名正言顺”。当前，绿色贸易壁垒被滥用的情况越来越严重。由于发达国家的环境标准普遍高于发展中国家，特别是少数发达国家对进口产品和本国产品采取不同的标准，发展中国家的产品因此更难进入发达国家市场。

例如，美国拒绝进口委内瑞拉的汽油，因为含铅（Pb）量超过了本国规定；欧盟禁止进口加拿大的皮革制品，因为加拿大猎人使用捕猎器捕获了大量野生动物；从 20 世纪 90 年代开始，欧洲国家严禁进口含氟利昂的冰箱，导致中国的冰箱出口由此下降了 59%

等。这些都是由于绿色贸易壁垒而产生的一系列事件。

绿色贸易壁垒的表现形式主要有以下四种。

2.13.1 Green Duty and Market Admittance 绿色关税和市场准入

In the name of environmental protection, some developed countries levy import surtax or make restriction or prohibit the import of some commodities which are regarded as polluting environment or ecological influence, and even implement trade sanction. For example, in 1990, the United States made announcement to prohibit the import of tunnies from Mexico owing to the fishing net used in Mexico bigger than the US standard one which may capture the dolphins supposed to be protected during the capture of tunnies.

绿色关税和市场准入是发达国家以保护环境为名，对一些污染环境和影响生态环境的进口商品征收进口附加税或者限制、禁止其进口，甚至实施贸易制裁。如 1991 年，美国宣布禁止从墨西哥进口金枪鱼，理由是墨西哥使用超过美国标准的大型渔网，在捕获金枪鱼时，也捕杀了应受保护的海豚。

2.13.2 Green Environment Identification Symbol 绿色环境标志

It's a special symbol granted by government administration indicating that the production, operation, consumption and recycling of the products are in compliance with ecological protection requirement. In China, environment symbol system has been established and linked up with ISO14000 in order to make sure of the authority of environment standard.

绿色环境标志是由政府部门颁布，表明该产品在生产、使用、消费和回收处理整个过程中符合生态环境保护要求的一种特殊标志。我国已经建立了环境标志制度，并逐步与 ISO14000 相衔接，以确立环境标准的权威性。

2.13.3 Green Health Quarantine System 绿色卫生检疫制度

With the designated strict health quarantine standard, the foreign products are restricted or forbidden to enter home market. In China, lots of farm products have been refused due to failing to meet health quarantine standards of import countries.

通过制定严格的卫生检疫标准，外国产品的进口被限制或禁止。如中国出口的许多农产品由于不符合进口国的卫生检疫标准而屡遭拒绝。

2.13.4 Green Environment Subsidy System 绿色补贴制度

It is established in aid of the corporations settling pollution problems and investing in new ecological protection technology and equipment. The government helps enterprises to develop cleaning technologies in form of green environment subsidy.

当由于治理污染费用高昂，一些企业没有足够资金投资于新的环保技术、设备或无力开发清洁技术产品时，政府便采用绿色补贴制度予以帮助。

Lesson 3 Measures to Encourage Export
鼓励出口的措施

In many countries, international trade policies are made for the restriction of import as well as the encouragement of export. Except for tariff and non-tariff barriers adopted to restrict import, many countries also take a variety of measures to encourage export. Generally, export countries' governments take economical, administrative measures to stimulate the export of home products and expand foreign markets.

限制进口和鼓励出口是国际贸易政策相辅相成的两个方面，许多国家除了利用关税和非关税措施限制进口外，还采取各种鼓励出口的措施。鼓励出口的措施是指出口国家的政府通过经济、行政和组织等方面的措施，促进本国商品的出口，并扩大国外市场。

1. Export Credit 出口信贷

1.1 Conception of Export Credit 出口信贷的概念

Export credit is the loan offered by banks of an export country to home exporters or foreign importers in order to stimulate exports and increase the ability of competition of the exported commodities. Export credit is an important means by which the export country may make use of the loans of banks to expand the export of commodities, especially items in large amount and items with long contract period like whole set equipment and ships. With export credit, the capital shortage during the production and export of large machines and whole set equipment can be solved.

出口信贷是一个国家为了鼓励商品出口、增强商品的竞争能力，通过银行对本国出口厂商或国外进口厂商提供的贷款。它是一国的出口商利用本国银行的贷款扩大商品出口，特别是金额较大、期限较长的商品，如成套设备、船舶等出口的一种重要手段，目的是解决出口企业在经营大型机器装备和成套设备出口过程中由于进口商不能立即付款而造成的资金短缺的难题。

1.2 In Accordance with the Relationship between Debit and Credit, Export Credit May Be Divided into the Following Two Kinds 出口信贷按借贷关系可分为两类

1.2.1 Supplier's Credit 卖方信贷

Supplier's credit is the loan offered by an export country's bank to an exporter (a seller). A credit agreement is signed by an exporter and a bank, usually applied to the export of machinery and ships. Due to the large amount of capital and long period needed in the production and export of these items, importers usually require payment by installments.

Then, to keep the faster running of capital, exporters will need loans from banks.

An exporter will take interest on the loan and costs into the export price to transfer the costs of the loan to the importer. Therefore, the supplier's credit is actually a commercial credit in which the exporter gets a loan from an export bank and offers payment by installments to the importer.

卖方信贷是出口方银行向本国出口厂商（即卖方）提供的贷款。这种贷款协议由出口厂商与银行签订。卖方信贷通常用于机器设备、船舶等的出口。由于这些商品出口所需的资金较多、时间较长，进口厂商一般都要求采用延期付款的方式。出口厂商为了加速资金周转，往往需要取得银行的贷款。

出口商一般将利息等资金成本费用计入出口货价中，将贷款成本转移给进口商。所以，卖方信贷实际上是出口商从供款银行取得贷款后，再向进口商提供延期付款的一种商业信用。

1.2.2 Buyer's Credit 买方信贷

Buyer's credit is the loan offer by an export bank to an importer (a buyer) or an importer's bank with the condition that the loan must be used for the purchase of the export country's commodities to boost the export, which is also a tied loan.

买方信贷是出口商所在地银行直接向外国的进口商（即买方）或进口商的银行提供的贷款。其附带条件就是贷款必须用于购买债权国的商品，因而起到促进商品出口的作用，这就是所谓的约束性贷款。

2. Export Subsidy 出口补贴

Export subsidy is a cash subsidy or favorable fiscal treatment granted by the government to reduce the export price and enhance the competition ability in international market.

出口补贴又称出口津贴，是一国政府为了降低出口商品的价格，增强其在国际市场上的竞争能力，在出口某种商品时给予出口厂商的现金补贴或财政上的优惠待遇。

2.1 Forms of Export Subsidy 出口补贴的方式

There are two kinds of export subsidies as follows.

出口补贴的方式有直接补贴和间接补贴两种。

2.1.1 Direct Subsidy 直接补贴

Direct subsidy means that the subsidy in cash paid by government when the commodities are imported. After World War II, some developed countries like the United States and the EU adopted this way to encourage their agricultural products.

直接补贴是指政府在商品出口时，直接付给出口厂商的现金补贴。第二次世界大战后美国和欧洲一些发达的工业国家对某些农产品的出口就采用这种形式。

2.1.2 Indirect Subsidy 间接补贴

Indirect subsidy means the favorable fiscal treatment granted by the government to the export of some commodities, such as, the tax refund or tax reduction on some exported commodities, import duty exemption or refund on the re-export of some products produced with imported raw materials or semi-manufactured products, freight reduction of some exported commodities etc. The government adopts the above-mentioned measurements to reduce export cost and expand export.

间接补贴是指政府对某些商品的出口给予财政上的优惠。如政府退还或减免出口商品缴纳的税、对进口原料或半成品加工再出口给予免征或退还已交的进口税、对出口商品减低运费等。这些方法都是为了减少出口成本，扩大销路。

2.2 Classification of Subsidies 补贴的分类

According to the *Agreement on Subsidies and Countervailing Measures* signed in Uruguay Round negotiation, there are three kinds of subsidies as follows:

Prohibited Subsidies are divided into export subsidies and import substitute subsidies, which are the subsidies adopted to make domestic products over the import products or upon the export performance.

Actionable Subsidies refer to the subsidies permitted to be adopted. It is allowed to be consulted or applied to dispute settlement procedure or countervailing measures in the event of adverse effects brought about to the WTO members.

Non Actionable Subsidies mean the subsidies are legitimate and free of countervailing sanctions, which include all non-specific subsidies, not specific to an enterprise, industry or group of enterprises or industries.

乌拉圭回合谈判中达成的《补贴与反补贴协议》将补贴分为三类。

禁止使用补贴：分为出口补贴和进口替代补贴两类，主要指出口补贴，是形式上或实际上依出口情况而定或用于使本国货物压倒进口货物的补贴。

可申诉的补贴：指允许使用的补贴，但若该补贴对 WTO 成员产生了不利影响，则可对其采取磋商手段，或动用争议解决程序或对其采取反补贴措施。

不可申诉补贴：是合法的补贴，不能受到反补贴制裁，它包括所有非专门补贴，即那些不是主要使某个企业、某个产业或某个产业集团受益的补贴。

3. Dumping 商品倾销

3.1 Conception of Dumping 商品倾销的概念

Dumping means that the producer or exporter of a country or region makes a sale of a product in the market abroad at the price lower than that usually charged in the country or even lower than the production cost in order to defeat the competitors to occupy the market.

For instance, the American government set the Commodity Credit Company, which bought the farm produce at a high price and sold them it at half the price to foreign countries.

Dumping is regarded as an unfair competition act in international trade, violating the principles of fair competition and fair trade.

商品倾销是指一国（地区）的生产商或出口商以低于国内市场的价格，甚至低于商品生产成本的价格，在国外市场抛售商品，以打击竞争者进而占领市场。

例如，美国政府设立商品信贷公司，以高价在国内收购农产品，然后按照比国内低一半的价格在国外倾销农产品。

倾销被认为是国际贸易中违反公平竞争与公平贸易规则的不正当的商业竞争行为，是一种不公平的竞争。

3.2 Classification of Dumping 商品倾销的分类

In accordance with the specific purpose and time of dumping, dumping may be divided into the following three kinds.

按照倾销的具体目的和时间的不同，商品倾销可分为以下三种。

3.2.1 Sporadic Dumping 偶然性倾销

Due to the end of boom season or the transition of business, being incapable of selling the remanent products in domestic market, an enterprise may dump the products in a foreign market at a lower price even than the production cost to dispose the stock products. The kind of dumping may bring about adverse effect on the same kind of products of the import nation. However, because of short time of dumping, the import nation seldom adopts anti-dumping measures.

偶然性倾销是指因为销售旺季已过，或因公司改营其他业务，需要处理库存商品，在国内市场上不能出售“剩余货物”，而以低于成本或较低价格在国外市场抛售。这种倾销对进口国的同类生产必然造成不利的影响，但由于持续时间短暂，进口国通常较少采用反倾销措施。

3.2.2 Predatory Dumping 掠夺性倾销

Predatory dumping means that the export nation dumps commodities in a foreign market, defeating all or most of rivals, to monopolize the market and then raise the price. The dumping is aimed at occupying, monopolizing and depriving the foreign market in order to obtain high profits. The dumping damages the benefit of import country, and therefore many countries adopt anti-dumping measures to reject it.

掠夺性倾销是指一国在国外市场上倾销商品，在打垮或摧毁了所有或大部分竞争对手并垄断了这个市场之后，再提高价格。这种倾销的目的是占领、垄断和掠夺国外市场，获取高额利润。这种倾销严重损害了进口国的利益，因而许多国家都采取反倾销税等措施进行抵制。

3.2.3 Long-run Dumping 长期性倾销

The kind of dumping is to sell products in a foreign market at a price lower than the domestic market’s price continually without time limit. The dumping is long term with the export price higher than marginal cost, and otherwise the export will cause long-term loss. Therefore, the dumper usually expands production scale to reduce production cost. Some exporters will keep dumping through obtaining export subsidies from home government.

这种倾销是无限期地、持续地以低于国内市场的价格在国外市场出售商品。这种倾销具有长期性，其出口价格至少应高于边际成本，否则货物出口将长期亏损。因此，倾销者往往通过扩大生产规模来降低成本。有的出口厂商还可通过获取本国政府的出口补贴来进行这种倾销。

4. Exchange Dumping 外汇倾销

Exchange dumping is that a country manipulates its exchange rates to lower the selling prices of its products when calculated in terms of the foreign currency. The depreciation of home currency will benefit export and be unfavorable to import, so exchange dumping is taken as a special means to seize international markets.

外汇倾销是一国降低本国货币对外国货币的汇价，使本国的货币贬值（本国货币贬值有利于出口，不利于进口），从而争夺国外市场的特殊手段。当一国货币贬值后，以外国货币表示出口商品的价格降低，提高了该商品的竞争能力，从而扩大出口，限制进口。

Lesson 4 Measures on Export Control 出口管制方面的措施

1. Conception of Export Control 出口管制的概念

Export control means that some nations adopt some laws and administrative measures to restrict or prohibit the export of some commodities especially strategic materials and advanced technical information for political, military or economic purposes.

出口管制是指一些国家为了达到一定的政治、军事和经济目的，通过法令和行政措施，对某些商品，特别是战略物资与先进技术资料，实行限制出口或禁止出口。

2. Items under Export Control 出口管制的商品

Items under export control may be classified into the following six kinds.

- Strategic materials and related top technologies, such as arms, military equipment, military airplanes, warships, advanced computers and the relative technologies etc.
- Materials in shortage in home country, for instance, mineral products, fertilizers, and some specific foodstuffs which are in shortage for Japan.
- The commodities under "voluntary" restrictions on export, such as the textiles under the *Arrangement regarding International Trade in Textiles*.
- The commodities occupying the leading positions in international market, such as the oil output of members controlled by OPEC to stabilize the oil price.
- The animals and plants under the protection to maintain ecological balance.

- Historical cultural relics and valuable artworks.

出口管制的商品主要可分为以下六类：

- 战略物资以及有关的尖端技术和先进技术资料，如武器、军事设备、军用飞机、军舰、先进的电子计算机及有关技术资料等。各国对这类商品与技术资料都严格控制出口。
- 国内的紧缺物资，如日本的矿产品、肥料、某些食品。
- 需要“自动”限制出口的商品，如发展中国家根据纺织品“自限协定”自行控制出口的商品。
- 本国在国际市场占主导地位的重要商品，如石油输出国组织（OPEC）对成员国的石油产量和出口量进行控制，以稳定石油价格。
- 为保持生态平衡而得到保护的某些动植物。
- 历史文物和艺术珍品。

Case Study 本章案例

Case 1 “Battle of Poitiers”

【案例 1】普瓦蒂埃海关效应

In 1982, in the face of the storming success of the Japanese consumer electronics industry, the French government decreed that all VCRs imported into France had to go through the customs office in Poitiers, which is a small town located several hundreds miles away from north port of France, where they had a few staff in a small house. The result is that more than sixty thousand of VCRs monthly cleared by French customs had been cut down to less than 10 thousand monthly.

1982 年法国规定，所有从日本进口的录像机都必须通过普瓦蒂埃海关，它位于距法国北部港口数百英里的小镇上。海关人员不多，屋子非常窄小。结果进入法国的日本录像机从每月 60 000 多台骤减到每月不足 10 000 台。

Italy’s “Pasta Purity” Law 意大利的通心粉纯度法

It is ruled in Italy that the pasta shall be made only with durum wheat, and the kind of wheat is mainly produced in the south of Italy. The pasta of most other European countries is made of mixed wheat, unable to meet the purity law of Italy. Thus they hardly enter Italian market.

在意大利有一个“通心粉纯度法”，要求空心粉的制作原料必须是硬质小麦，而这种硬质小麦主要产于意大利南部。欧洲其他国家的空心粉大多由混合种类的小麦制成，不符合“通心粉纯度法”，很难进入意大利市场。

The Adjustment of Commodities Classification 商品归类调整

The customs of the United States made adjustment to the classification of cabs and chassis of truck imported from Japan, classifying the parts of vehicles as the knock-down cars, so that the import duty rate was raised to 25% from 4%.

For example, the US don’t impose tax on printer, but if it is classified as toy printer, 35%

custom duty will be imposed on it.

美国海关曾把日本出口到美国的卡车司机室和底盘重新归为“组装车辆”，使原来只有 4%的税率升至 25%。

例如，美国对一般进口打字机不征收关税，但如归为玩具打字机，则要征收 35%的进口关税。

The EU's Package Standard of the Porcelain Imported from China 欧盟进口中国瓷器的包装标准

The EU requires that the straw used for packing Jingdezhen porcelain imported from China should go through the fumigation process of 200 degrees centigrade.

欧盟要求从中国进口的景德镇瓷器的包装稻草必须经过 200 摄氏度高温熏蒸消毒处理。

Case 2 Two EU Laws Pushed China Household Appliance Suppliers to Take on Challenge in a Hurry

【案例 2】欧盟两项环保指令促使中国家电企业急忙备战

On 13th Feb. 2003, The Waste Electrical and Electronic Equipment Directive (WEEE Directive) together with the ROHS Directive 2002/95/EC became European Law, which set collection, recycling and recovery targets for all types of electrical goods and set restrictions on the six kinds of harmful content like lead and Hg of new electronic equipment placed on the market.

The two EU Directives which came into force on 13th August 2005 and 1st July 2006 were regarded as a vital barrier to restricting the export of the mechanical and electronic products of China.

The two Directives involved nearly 200 thousand of products, almost covering all electronic products and the allied industries in China. The export volume of the concerned products from Guangdong Province of China, where the export of mechanical and electronic products to the EU accounted for one third of the total export volume of China, was over ten billion dollars.

Shunde, a small town famed for the production base of household electronic appliances in China, became the most severe “disaster area”. It is required in WEEE directive that the manufacturers have to reserve the recycling charges for electronic waste in the sales price of the products, and the recycling charges are different depending on different countries and products, so, the production costs of enterprises will rise largely. Taking the example of microwave ovens, it was informed that the EU planned to levy “electronic waste charges” of 1–20 euros per set, on the basis of 10 euros per set, and 8.2 million euros would be paid by Galanz, a famous Chinese manufacturer of microwave ovens, as a result the production cost of which will increase by 10 percent.

2003 年 2 月 13 日，欧盟出台《报废电子电气设备指令》（WEEE）和《关于在电子电气设备中限制使用某些有害物质的指令》（ROHS），规定了废旧电子电气产品的回收、处理、再利用以及禁止在电子电气产品中使用铅、汞等六种有害物质。

这两项欧盟指令分别于 2005 年 8 月 13 日和 2006 年 7 月 1 日实施，被国内机电出口企业称为“生死坎”的这两项指令限制了我国机电产品的出口。

这两项指令涉及的产品包括近 20 万种，几乎涵盖我国所有的出口电子产品及其上下游行业。对欧出口贸易量占全国 1/3 的广东机电产品直接受两项指令影响的相关产品出口额超过百亿美元。

素有“家电王国”之称的顺德无疑将成为受其影响最大的“重灾区”。WEEE 规定，制造商必须在其电子产品销售价格中预留电子垃圾回收费用，费用多少因国家不同、产品不同而有较大差异，为此企业成本将大幅增加。以微波炉为例，据悉，欧盟目前计划征收“电子垃圾费”的幅度为每台 1～20 欧元，如果按 10 欧元一台计算，光格兰仕每年就需为此增加 8 200 多万欧元的支出，产品成本将增加一成多。

（资料来源：《国际商报》，2005–06–14）

Case 3 The Green Barrier War between the US, Japan and the EU

【案例 3】美、日、欧围绕汽车的“绿色壁垒”展开论争

Recently, the new war on trade barriers to automobiles between the US, West European countries and Japan has started again, indicating the trade conflicts have intensified. The cars made in Japan occupied much bigger shares in the US and the EU markets than the shares of the US and the EU cars in Japanese market; therefore, the EU tried to establish and implement new automobile emissions standards to restrain the growth of Japanese autos in the EU market.

According to the new environment protection standard, the emissions of carbon dioxide of all the cars in the EU market have to be reduced by 25% compared with 1995 by 2008, it was obvious that the regulation was aimed at Japan and Korea. Facing the regulation, the automobile companies of Korea opposed to it, arguing technology hardly reaches it; Japan Auto Parts Industries Association were not sure if they could reach the standard on time though they declared to work hard together with the EU corporations.

The EU were scheduled to force the auto companies of Japan and Korea to reach the standard before the new emissions standard would be passed by all the EU members, otherwise the autos were not permitted to enter the EU market.

Depending on the analysis, the average level of carbon dioxide emissions of the cars imported from Japan was 10% higher than the EU local automobiles as the cars from Japan were mainly top-grade leisure cars. To meet the standard, the Japanese cars have to reduce the emissions of carbon dioxide by 31%.

After the collapse of negotiation on the automobile emissions standard, Japan government also took corresponding measures against the EU restriction and implemented the new discriminatory law on 19th March 1999.

According to the act coming into force on 1st April 1999, the automobiles for Japanese market have to meet the relative energy-saving standard to reduce the exhaust emissions of

Autos.

The detailed regulations are as follows: the gasoline cars of less than 1,000 kg for two persons in 2010 shall save 17.7% energy more than 1995; the cars of 1,000–1,249 kg in the same period shall save 25.7% energy; the cars of 1,250–1,499 kg shall reach more than 30% energy saving; the cars of 1,500–1,749 kg and the above shall save 24% and 9.7% energy in 2010 more than 1995.

Consequently, almost all the cars from the US and the EU have to go through a more restrict energy saving standard in Japanese market as nearly 90% of the cars from the US and the EU are above 1,250 kg; whereas the cars of Japan for domestic market are mainly of light and mini types, so little influenced by the regulation. Therefore, the US government submitted a position paper to the WTO, in which it was said that Japan enhanced the automobile energy saving standard to discourage the automobile import from abroad, requiring the WTO to take an investigation into the matter.

最近，在美国、西欧主要国家以及日本之间，又展开了建立汽车贸易壁垒的新较量，这标志着世界汽车三大市场之间的贸易摩擦又将升级。由于日本轿车在美欧市场的份额是美欧车企在日本市场份额的几倍，欧盟试图通过建立和实施新的汽车排放标准来限制日本汽车在欧洲市场的增长。

按照新的环境保护标准要求，到 2008 年，欧洲市场销售的所有轿车的二氧化碳排放量要比 1995 年下降 25%，这无疑是冲着日本和韩国企业而来的。对此，韩国的汽车企业认为“在技术上难以达到”而表示反对；日本汽车配件工业协会则表示“与欧盟企业共同努力”，但是不能保证届时达标。

欧盟准备在各成员国一致通过新的排放标准之前，先拿日本和韩国企业开刀，即首先强制要求日韩企业先达标，否则不能向欧洲市场出口汽车。

据分析，由于在欧洲市场上，从日本进口的轿车以高级休闲车为主，其平均二氧化碳排放水平比欧洲当地生产的车要高出近 10%。若要达标，日本车就要平均减少 31%以上的二氧化碳排放量。

日本政府与欧盟的汽车废气排放标准谈判破裂后，日本针对欧盟的限制采取了针锋相对的策略——在 1999 年 3 月 19 日开始实施“歧视性”的新法案。

1999 年 4 月 1 日实施的该法案规定，在日本市场上销售的汽车必须达到相应的节能标准，以减少汽车的废气排放。

具体规定是：两人乘坐时总质量在 1 000 千克以下的汽油轿车，到 2010 年要比 1995 年的相当车型节能 17.7%；同期 1 000～1 249 千克的轿车，要节能 25.7%；1 250～1 499 千克的轿车要实现 30%以上的节能；1 500～1 749 千克及以上的轿车，到 2010 年要比 1995 年分别实现节能 24%和 9.7%。

由于在日本市场上的美国和欧洲生产的轿车的 90%属于 1 250 千克以上的范围，即几乎所有的美欧轿车都要在日本市场上受到更加严格的节能要求的限制；而日本车在国内市场由于主要是轻型车和微型车，因此受此修正法案的影响较小。为此，美国政府向世界贸易组织提交了一份意见书，该意见书指出，日本单方面提高汽车节能标准直接阻碍了国外汽车进口，要求世界贸易组织调查。

（资料来源：吉林省质量信息网，http://www.jlqi.gov.cn/wto/anli/）

Case 4 The 1st Winning Case in Responding to the Antidumping Charges after China Joining the WTO

【案例 4】中国加入 WTO 后钢铁行业反倾销胜诉第一案

On 21st May 2002, the US Department of Commerce made the final arbitrament for the steel tubes of Shanghai Alison Co. with the judgment that the ERW steel tubes exported by Alison CO. did not cause substantial damage to the similar enterprises in the US domestic market. It means that the antidumping charges against the Chinese steel tubes in the US for nearly one year has come to an end with the winning of Shanghai Alison Co., which is the first enterprise winning the antidumping charges in the steel & iron industry after China joined the WTO.

Shanghai Alison Steel Tube Co., Ltd. was established in 1995 with an annual output of 3000 thousand tons of ERW steel tubes, 50% of which are for export and mostly exported to the US. After receiving the notification that the antidumping duty will be levied on the exported steel tubes to the US, the company faced two choices: one is to accept the levy of heavy duty and then give up the US market share which they have paid great effort to get; the other choice is to respond to the antidumping charge and get through the complicated and redundant investigation procedure for expense in large amount. For the interest in a long run, Alison decided to respond to the antidumping charges and fight to the end. The company has set up an institution especially for the lawsuit and paid a high salary to employ senior lawyers with rich experiences in the field to get engaged in the long and complex procedures. The company has to cope with trivial investigation into details from the US Department of Commerce involving the purchase of raw materials, whole production process, marketing, fiscal records, after-sale service etc., even facing the strict on-spot investigation.

On 20th Dec. 2001, the US Department of Commerce made the initial arbitrament that the duty for the steel tubes exported by Alison from China was zero on the basis of the investigation result. With the first win, Alison got down to working for the next phase to face the local verification of the US Department of Commerce. On 18th–19th Jan. 2002, Alison company met officials from the US Department of Commerce for their spot verification. After the local investigation and discussion, the US Department of Commerce recognized the steel tube price of Alison was the real price without dumping. On 21st May 2002, the US Department of Commerce publicized the final result: the duty of the steel tubes exported by Alison to the US was zero then Alison obtained the final win.

The Alison's win over the antidumping charges has brought significant reference to other Chinese exporters. At first, the company has presented a lively case for Chinese enterprises after China's entry into the WTO, indicating that Chinese exporters shall be aware of self-protection and take reasonable measures against the unfair antidumping charges.

Secondly, the winning of Alison has enhanced the fame of the company in the United States and expanded its market share in the US with a more favorable position in international competition. Thirdly, Chinese enterprises shall be more familiar with the international market and master the rules and regulations of the WTO to better protect the benefit of themselves.

2002 年 5 月 21 日，美国商务部对中国上海埃力生公司的钢管做出了最终裁决，认定埃力生出口到美国的 ERW 钢管没有给美国国内的同类企业造成实质性危害。这标志着历时近一年的美国对中国钢管实施的反倾销诉讼以埃力生的胜诉而告终，埃力生成为中国加入世界贸易组织后在钢铁行业国外反倾销案中胜诉的第一家企业。

成立于 1995 年的上海埃力生钢管有限公司，年产 ERW 钢管 30 万吨，50%以上的产品出口，其中大部分出口到美国。在得到美国对中国钢管征收反倾销税的消息后，公司面临着两种选择：不应诉，将接受沉重的反倾销税，从而自动退出好不容易占领的美国市场；应诉，就要面对令人望而生畏的复杂冗长的调查程序和巨额的应诉费用。为了长远的利益，埃力生决定应诉，将美国的反倾销官司进行到底。公司组建了专门的应诉机构，出巨资聘请国内外的资深律师，开始了漫长、复杂的反倾销应诉过程。美国商务部的调查琐碎、详细，范围涉及公司两年以上的原材料采购至产品到客户的整个生产、销售、财务、服务过程，而且其实地调查近乎苛刻。

2001 年 12 月 20 日，美国商务部初步裁定公司出口到美国的钢管的税率为零。初战告捷，埃力生公司转入了更加周密细致的下一步工作，迎接美国商务部官员的现场核实。2002 年 1 月 18—19 日，埃力生迎来了美国商务部官员的现场核实工作。经过实地考察论证，美国商务部官员认定埃力生的钢管价格是实际的，初步裁定不存在倾销问题。2002 年 5 月 21 日，美国商务部公布了终裁结果：埃力生出口到美国的钢管税率为零，埃力生赢得了最后的胜利。

埃力生公司对美反倾销案的胜诉对国内企业有着重要的借鉴意义。首先，它为中国加入世界贸易组织后，国内企业走向国际市场上了生动的一课，说明企业要有自我保护意识，在受到不公正的反倾销诉讼时，一定要据理力争。其次，埃力生的胜诉提高了公司在美国的知名度，巩固并将扩大了在美国的市场，在国际竞争中将处于更加有利的地位。最后，企业一定要熟悉国际市场，尽快掌握世贸组织的有关法规，这样才能有效维护企业自身利益。

（资料来源：《人民日报》，2002–01–03；WTO 法律咨询司）

Questions 思考题

1. Please give an introduction in brief to non-tariff barriers.
   简述非关税壁垒主要有哪些。

2. Please clarify the different functions between non-tariff barriers and tariff in international trade.
   试比较非关税壁垒与关税在国际贸易中对限制进口的作用。

3. What is import quota and import license system?

什么是进口配额制和进口许可证制？

4. What is the classification of import licenses?

进口许可证可分为哪几种？

5. What are the major differences between absolute quota, tariff quota, and "voluntary" export quota?

绝对进口配额与关税配额、"自动"出口配额的主要区别是什么？

6. What are the characteristics of non-tariff barrier measures?

非关税壁垒措施有何特点？

7. What is export credit? Please make comparison between the two kinds of export credit.

什么是出口信贷？试比较两种出口信贷的异同。

8. What is anti-dumping duty?

什么是反倾销税？

9. What is export subsidy?

什么是出口补贴？

10. Please try to make an explanation of the functions of currency devaluation in import and export.

试述一国的货币贬值对进出口的作用。

Chapter 3

International Capital Movement and Transnational Corporations 国际资本移动与跨国公司

Lesson 1 International Capital Movement 国际资本移动

1. Fundamental Connotation and Basic Types 国际资本移动的基本内涵和基本类型

International Capital Movement refers to the international manufacturing, marketing and financial service activities that transfer capital from one country or region across borders to others. International Capital Movement is mainly represented by direct or indirect international movement of factors of production. The capital account on a country's balance-of-payment sheet embodies a concentrated reflection of the country's capital movement, including capital output and capital input in a certain period. International capital movement can make up for deficit of current account for some countries. Capital moving from capital-abundant countries to capital-short countries could facilitate the resource exploitation and import of advanced technologies and managerial expertise in the capital-short countries, and at the same time, find a way to make profit of excessive capital for the capital-abundant countries. International Capital Movement involves capital exporting country and capital importing country; the former is also called the home country, and the latter is called the host country.

Depending on ways of investment, International Capital Movement is mainly classified into foreign direct investment and foreign indirect investment.

Both foreign direct investment and foreign indirect investment can take the form of purchasing foreign enterprise stocks. The difference is that foreign direct investment means the amount of purchased stocks reaches certain ratio so that the investors obtain the rights of operation and management, while foreign indirect investment means the investors can only receive dividends and bonuses but no rights of operation and management.

国际资本移动是指从事国际生产、营销或金融服务方面的投资活动，具体指资本从一个国家或地区跨越国界向其他国家或地区移动。国际资本移动主要体现为生产要素在国家间的直接或间接移动。一国国际收支平衡表中的资本项目集中反映了该国在一定时期内资本移动（包括资本输出和资本输入）的概况。国际资本移动可以弥补一些国家国际收支经常项目的逆差。资本从资本充裕国家流至资本短缺国家，有利于资本短缺国家开发资源、引进先进的技术和管理知识，同时也为资本充裕国家的过剩资本获利找到出路。国际资本移动涉及资本输出国和资本输入国，前者也叫母国，后者则称为东道国。

依据投资方式的不同，国际资本移动主要分为对外直接投资和对外间接投资两种基本类型。

对外直接投资和对外间接投资都可以以购买外国企业股票的形式出现。其区别在于：对外直接投资指凡购买外国企业股票达到一定比例即可取得经营和管理权；而对外间接投资是指投资者只能取得股息和红利，对企业不具有经营权和管理权。

2. Foreign Direct Investment 对外直接投资

Foreign Direct Investment is the main form of international capital movement. It refers to the investment activities that foreign investors conduct to found enterprises in foreign countries. The core of these activities is to control the enterprises operation and management, and the purpose is to obtain profit. It involves direct investment of production factors and features investors using those factors and directly controlling the management of the production process.

对外直接投资（FDI）是指外国投资者以控制企业经营管理为核心，以获取利润为目的在国外创立企业的投资行为，它是国际资本移动的主要形式。它涉及生产要素的直接投入，其特点是投资者对所投入的生产要素的使用和对生产过程的管理有直接的控制力。

2.1 Sole Proprietorship vs. Joint Venture 独资经营与合资经营

Depending on the stake ratio that investors hold in the investing enterprise, foreign direct investment falls into two categories: sole proprietorship and joint venture.

对外直接投资根据投资者对投资企业拥有的股权比例，可分为独资经营和合资经营。

2.1.1 Sole Proprietorship 独资经营

Sole proprietorship refers to the type of investment that foreign investors establish enterprises in host country with approval according to the laws of host country, and own all the capital of the enterprises. Investor of sole proprietorship enterprise owns entire equity of the enterprise and is entitled to all of its ownership and right of control and bears all the responsibilities and risks. There are mainly three forms of international sole proprietorship: foreign branch, foreign subsidiary and international tax haven.

独资经营是指由外国投资者根据投资所在国的法律，经批准在东道国建立、全部资本为外国投资者所有的企业的经营形式。独资经营企业的投资者拥有企业的全部股权，因此享有企业的全部所有权和控制权，并对企业承担全部责任和风险。国际独资企业的形式主要包括国外分公司、国外子公司和国际避税地公司三种。

2.1.2 Joint Venture 合资经营

A joint venture is an equity company formed on contract between transnational company and company in host country, according to the laws of host country. The parties invest, manage and share profits and risks together at certain equity ratio. Joint venture is the most common investment form in modern international economy cooperation. There are two categories of international joint ventures: equity joint venture and contractual joint venture.

合资经营是指跨国公司与东道国企业根据投资所在国的法律，在一国境内通过签订合同，按一定比例或股份共同投资、共同管理、分享利润、分担亏损和风险的股权式企业。合资经营企业是当代国际经济合作中最普遍的投资方式，国际合资企业又可分为国际股权合资企业和国际契约合资企业两种。

1) International equity joint venture 国际股权合资企业

International Equity Joint Venture means all kinds of investments from all parties will be converted into equity ratio at which the parties share risks and profits. This is the most common international joint venture.

国际股权合资企业是指投资各方无论以何种形式出资都将被折算成一定的股权比例，投资各方按股权比例分担风险，分享利益，是国际上最为普遍的合资企业形式。

2) Contractual joint venture 国际契约合资企业

Contractual joint venture, also called co-operative joint venture, is based on cooperation contract with or without legal entity created. In contractual joint ventures, partners are allowed to share rights and obligations, such as forms of investment, enterprise structure and distribution of profits, risks and debts, according to contract stipulation, not necessarily in proportion to capital contribution.

国际契约合资企业，亦称为合作经营企业，它是建立在合作契约基础上的合资形式，可以组成法律实体，也可以不组成法律实体。在国际契约合资企业中，签约各方可不按出资比例而按合同条款的规定，确定出资方式、组织形式、利润分配、风险分担和债务清偿等权利和义务。

2.2 Greenfields vs. Mergers and Acquisitions 新建与并购

Depending on the way in which foreign direct investment enters oversea market, foreign direct investment has two forms: greenfield and acquisition.

Greenfield investment is the investment of building new companies or new factories to establish new manufacturing forces or operation units in host country. It occurs when it is the first time for the investment to enter the host country.

International mergers and acquisitions refer to the acts of companies in home country to fully or partly obtain ownership, by buying or combining, of target companies in host country through legal procedures and channels. The greatest advantage of international M&A for manufacturing companies is the time saved from building new factories so that they are able to enter target country's market at the fastest speed. Merger companies or acquirers can take advantage of the existing production organization and management system of merging companies to establish production and marketing network rapidly, which can help to seize market opportunities.

Since the early 1990s, the wave of international M&A rose again and reached its summit in 2000 in which year the volume of transaction achieved $1.1438 trillion, accounting for 82% of the international FDI of $1.393 trillion in the same year.

按直接投资进入海外市场的方式，对外直接投资可分为新建与并购两种类型。

新建投资是指在投资目标国建立新企业或新工厂，形成新的生产能力或经营单位。如果是第一次进入目标国投资，则称为“绿地投资”。

跨国并购是指资本输出国企业按照东道国的法律，通过一定的程序和渠道依法收购与兼并，取得东道国目标企业全部或部分所有权的行为。对于制造业企业来说，跨国并购最大的优点就是可以省掉建设新厂的时间，从而以最快的速度进入目标国市场。并购企业可以利用被并购企业现成的生产组织体系和管理体系，迅速建立在东道国市场的产销网络，有利于抓住市场机会。

从 20 世纪 90 年代初开始，国际并购浪潮又一次兴起，到 2000 年达到高潮。该年跨国并购交易额达 11 438 亿美元，占当年国际直接投资额 13 930 亿美元的 82%。

3. Foreign Indirect Investment 对外间接投资

Foreign Indirect Investment is realized in the forms of loan capital output and portfolio investment. It features that investors are not directly involved in the operations and management of investing companies.

对外间接投资包括借贷资本输出和证券投资，其特点是投资者不直接参与这些接受投资企业的经营和管理。

3.1 Loan Capital Output 借贷资本输出

Loan Capital Output is the way in which investors lend capital to host country governments or companies in the forms of loans or export credit. It has the following types。

借贷资本输出是投资方以贷款或出口信贷的形式把资本借给东道国政府或企业。一般有以下方式。

3.1.1 Government Aid Loans 政府援助贷款

Government Aid Loans happen in the lending activities between country governments or government agencies. Such loans are usually with aid nature, provided by the developed countries to the developing countries and regions.

Government aid loans have generally low interest (about 3%–5%) or even no interest in some instances, and the repayment periods can be as long as 20–30 years. Those loans are usually issued with specific usage, such as importing goods from lending countries or developing aid projects. The aid loan for Guangde Sewage Treatment Plant in Anhui Province, for example, was approved by the Danish government, and the $7.5 million loan from the government was mainly used in the construction of the plant.

政府援助贷款是各国政府或政府机构之间的借贷活动。这种贷款通常带有援助性质，一般是发达国家对发展中国家或地区提供的贷款。

政府援助贷款一般利息较低（3%～5%），有时甚至是无息贷款，还款期较长，可达20～30年。这种贷款一般有的指定用途，如用于支付从贷款国进口各种货物或用于某些开发援助项目。如安徽广德污水处理厂项目获批丹麦政府援助贷款，得到丹麦政府750万美元的援助贷款，贷款主要用于污水处理厂的建设。

1) International financial institution loans 国际金融机构贷款

International Financial Institutions refers to the International Monetary Fund, the World Bank, the International Development Association, the International Finance Corporation, the Development Bank of each continent and the United Nations aid agencies. Loans from international financial institutions are generally favorable, but not unlimited.

国际金融机构一般包括国际货币基金组织、世界银行、国际开发协会、国际金融公司及各洲的开发银行和联合国的援助机构等。来自国际金融机构的贷款条件一般比较优惠，但并不是无限制的。

① International Monetary Fund 国际货币基金组织

The IMF provides loans to its members, and the loan purpose is limited to correcting the short-term imbalances by payments of trade or non-trade current accounts. Borrower members are required to pay the loan in foreign currency with corresponding amount of local currency, and buy back local currency with currency that is specified by the IMF when repaying the loan. The IMF loans have very low interest rate and small amount of fee.

国际货币基金组织的贷款对象是成员国政府，贷款用途只限于解决短期性国际收支不平衡问题，用于贸易和非贸易经常项目的支付。国际货币基金组织在贷款时要求借款国以相应数量的本币购买外币，偿还贷款时再用国际货币基金组织指定的货币购回本币。国际货币基金组织的这种贷款利率较低，此外还需支付少量的手续费。

② The World Bank (the International Bank for Reconstruction and Development) 世界银行（国际复兴开发银行）

The World Bank only issues loans to its member governments or public organizations and private companies that are guaranteed by member governments. The loans are mainly for developing countries to invest in energy, agriculture, transportation, education, etc. The maturity of loans ranges from 3–5 years in the short term, to 20 years in the long term, with a grace period of 5 years.

世界银行只对成员国政府或经成员国政府担保的公共机构和私人企业提供贷款，主要面向发展中国家，贷款重点用于能源、农业、交通运输、教育等方面。贷款期限短则3～5年，长则20年，宽限期为5年。

③ International Development Association（IDA）国际开发协会

The International Development Association is a subordinate organization of the World Bank, also called the Second World Bank, which specializes in lending interest-free loans to the world's poorest developing countries. All the members of the World Bank are also members of the IDA. The IDA offers loans after the same strict censorship as the World Bank, but with more favorable terms. The IDA offers interest-free loans with very little issue fee (normally 0.75%), and charges commitment fee of 0.5% for the part of loan that is committed but not expended yet. The length of maturity ranges from 35 to 40 years, with an average grace period of 10 years. The loans can be fully or partly repaid by the local currency.

国际开发协会属于世界银行的下设机构，又称第二世界银行，专门从事对最不发达国家提供无息贷款的业务。世界银行的成员国均为国际开发协会的成员国。与世界银行的贷款相同，国际开发协会的贷款也要经过严格的审查，但它的贷款条件更为优惠。国际开发协会的贷款为无息贷款，只收取少量的手续费（一般为0.75%），并对已承诺未支用的贷款收取0.5%的承诺费。贷款期限一般为35～40年，宽限期平均为10年。贷款可部分或全部用本国货币偿还。

④ International Finance Corporation（IFC）国际金融公司

International Finance Corporation is another subordinate of the World Bank, focusing on the loan business for private sectors of members. Offering medium to long-term loans to those sectors is the main task of the IFC. The corporation has two kinds of investment activities: lending loans and stake participation.

国际金融公司是世界银行的另一个附属机构，专门从事对成员国私营部门的贷款业务。向发展中国家的私营部门提供中、长期贷款是国际金融公司的主要任务。公司的投资活动分为两种形式：一是贷款；二是参股。

2) Loans in international financial markets 国际金融市场贷款

International financial markets include money markets and capital markets. The former are the markets in which short-term loans are traded, and the latter are long-term loans. The length of maturity is no longer than one year in money markets, while longer than one year in capital markets so that they are medium-to-long term. Maturity of medium-term loans is usually 1 to 5 years, and that of long-term loans is usually longer than 5 years, up to 10 years. Generally, the interest rates of loans in international financial markets are higher, but the borrowings can be used for any need of borrower countries without any limit.

国际金融市场分为货币市场和资本市场。前者是经营短期资金借贷的市场，后者是经营长期资金借贷的市场。货币市场的贷款期限在一年以内，资本市场的贷款期限在一年以上，属中、长期贷款。中期贷款一般为1～5年，长期贷款一般期限在5年以上，最长可达10年。一般来讲，国际金融市场贷款利率较高，但可用于借款国任何需要，对贷款的用途没有限定。

3.1.2 Export Credit 出口信贷

Export Credit refers to the loans that national governments issue through banks to domestic exporters or foreign importers or importer's banks, with the purpose of facilitating commodity export and strengthening the product competitiveness.

出口信贷是指一个国家为了鼓励商品出口，提升商品的竞争能力，通过银行对本国出口商或国外进口商或进口方的银行所提供的贷款。

3.2 Portfolio Investment 证券投资

Portfolio investment is investment that investors make by purchasing medium-to-long term debts of foreign enterprises and governments in international securities markets, or stocks of listing foreign enterprises in stock markets. Investors of portfolio investment are only entitled to dividends and bonuses from the debts and stocks, but no control of operations and management of the investing enterprises.

证券投资指投资者在国际证券市场上购买外国企业和政府的中长期债券，或在股票市场上购买上市的外国企业股票的一种投资活动。证券投资者一般只能取得债券和股票的股息和红利，对投资企业并无经营和管理的直接控制权力。

Lesson 2 Overview of Transnational Companies 跨国公司概述

1. Definition and Nature（跨国公司的）定义与性质

1.1 Definition 跨国公司的定义

A transnational corporation, is also called a multi-national enterprise, an international firm, a supernational enterprise or a cosmo-corporation.

A transnational corporation refers to a large international enterprise consisting of entities in two or more countries, that operates manufacturing, sales and other business. Transnational Corporation is a new type of international monopoly organization which results from sophisticated monopoly capitalism. It first emerged in the late 19th century. Some large enterprises in developed capitalist countries, through foreign direct investment, started to set up factories and companies abroad and run business internationally at that time. They became the pioneers of modern large multinational enterprises. Transnational corporations, since the

1970s have further grown to be an important role and main force of world economy globalization.

跨国公司，又称多国公司、国际公司、超国家公司和宇宙公司等。

跨国公司指由两个或两个以上国家的经济实体所组成，并从事生产、销售和其他经营活动的国际性大型企业。跨国公司是一种新型的国际垄断组织，是垄断资本主义高度发展的产物。它最早出现于19世纪末。当时，在发达资本主义国家中，一些大型企业通过对外直接投资，在国外设厂、设企业，开展跨国经营，成为现代大型跨国公司的先驱。跨国公司成长于19世纪70年代之后，已经成为世界经济国际化和全球化发展的重要内容和主要推动力。

1.2 Differences between a Transnational Corporation and a Domestic Enterprise 跨国公司与国内企业的区别

The strategy of a transnational corporation is global market-oriented, aiming at the optimization of global profits, while that of a domestic enterprise is domestic market-oriented.

A transnational corporation controls foreign companies by shareholding, while a domestic enterprise controls its fewer foreign business activities in a contractual way.

A transnational corporation conducts activities worldwide in a comprehensive range of aspects, such as capital, commodities, talents, technologies, management and information. The package activities must accord with overall strategy and under the control of parent company. Therefore, a multinational enterprise must implement highly centralized and unified management to its branches. The relationship between foreign business activities by a domestic company is yet loose and occasional. The foreign business activities often terminate as soon as the transaction is completed with no involvement in reproduction process afterwards.

There are more forms of global production and operations in a transnational corporation, including importing and exporting, licensing, technology transfers, co-operation, managerial contracts and setting up oversea subsidiaries. In particular, setting up oversea subsidiaries is the main way to extend business globally. But a domestic enterprise lacks diversity of business operations.

跨国公司的战略目标是以国际市场为导向，目的是实现全球利润最大化；而国内企业是以国内市场为导向。

跨国公司通过控股的方式对国外的企业实行控制；而国内企业对其较少的涉外经济活动大多是以契约的方式实行控制的。

跨国公司在世界范围内的各个领域全面开展资本、商品、人才、技术、管理和信息等交易活动。这种一揽子活动必须符合公司总体战略目标并且处于母公司控制之下。所以，跨国公司对其分支机构必然实行高度集中的统一管理。而国内企业的对外经济活动的关系是松散的，有较大偶然性，其涉外经济活动往往在交易完成后就立即终止，不再参与以后的再生产过程。

跨国公司的全球性生产经营方式较多，包括进出口、许可证、技术转让、合作经营、管理合同和在海外设立子公司等。其中，尤以在海外设立子公司为主要形式开展和扩大其全球性业务。而国内企业生产经营方式则比较单一。

2. Features of Transnational Corporations 跨国公司的特点

A transnational corporation sets a base in home country and distributes entities in various countries and regions to implement multinational investments. A certain large company in one country serves as the controlling, managing and directing center.

跨国公司以母国为基地，将其实体分布于不同的国家或地区，在多国从事投资活动，由一国的某一大型企业作为其控制、管理和指挥中心。

2.1 Global Strategies and Centralized Management by Transnational Corporations 跨国公司推行全球性战略和集中性管理

Transnational Corporations aim at global market and arrange business activities under their global strategies. They search for markets and sound production patterns around the world and allocate specialized production and sales to achieve profit optimization. Parent companies control and manage the major decisions of investment, production, price system, marketing distribution, profit allocation and R&D in a highly centralized and unified way.

The relationship between entities within a transnational corporation is very close. Numerous oversea subsidiaries are in control by parent company and make operation plans and measures according to parent company's global strategies. The internal entities share resources and responsibilities with other peers based on cooperation in an organic whole.

跨国公司的战略以整个世界市场为目标，从全球战略出发安排自己的经营活动，在世界范围内寻求市场和合理的生产布局，定点专业生产，定点销售产品，以谋取最大的利润。母（总）公司对整个公司的投资计划、生产安排、价格体系、市场分布、利润分配、研制方向等重大决策实行高度集中统一的管理。

跨国公司内部各实体之间具有密切的联系，在海外设立的大量子公司受制于母公司，并根据母公司的全球战略制定各自的经营计划及措施。在分工协作的基础上，公司内部的各个实体与其他实体分享资源和分担责任，成为一个有机的整体。

2.2 Transnational Corporations Capture Global Market by Direct Investment 跨国公司利用直接投资争夺世界市场

There are two ways in which multinational enterprises expand business overseas, commodity exporting, and oversea investment and production. To expand commodity output, multinational enterprises set up sales companies in foreign companies, as the simplest type of ownership investment. There are three functions: to promote the products of parent company or parent country; to understand local market and collect information of economy and business in local country; to enhance the influence of parent company for further investment.

Along with the more intensive competition, exporting is no longer enough to achieve the goals of market capture. Multinational Enterprises therefore increasingly utilize FDI to set up oversea manufacturing facilities, which better optimizes profits through direct production.

跨国公司对外扩张有两条途径：一是商品出口；二是海外投资和海外生产。为了扩大商品输出而在国外建立销售公司，这种销售公司是最简单的所有权式的投资，其作用有三：推销母公司或母国的产品；了解当地市场行情并收集所在国的经济和商业情报；扩大母公司的影响以作为进一步投资的跳板。

随着竞争的加剧，以向外输出商品为主的做法已满足不了争夺市场的需要，跨国公司已越来越多地利用海外直接投资建立工业企业，海外直接生产更能最大限度地扩大盈利。

Case Study 本章案例

Case: Manufacturing: China Is Just a "Workshop", Far Away from a "World Factory"

【案例】制造业：中国是“车间”，远非“世界工厂”

"China is a significant part of world manufacturing industry; however, it's just a 'workshop', far away from a 'factory'." This was the most representative opinion of the entrepreneurs and scholars who participated in the annual meeting of the 2004 Boao Forum for Asia.

Long Yongtu, the President of Boao Forum for Asia, considered China to be in the low end of global manufacturing chain; in view of that there is still noticeable distance between China and the so-called "world factory" countries in world economic history, such as Britain, America and Japan, in particular with respects to comprehensive national strength and manufacturing competency.

Modern manufacturing is operated in an interactive industrial chain, which China is a part of. World factories have actually linked countries around the world through transnational corporations. China has been a component of world manufacturing base, the more well-developed China's manufacturing becomes, the more raw materials it imports from other countries. This is a kind of process of mutual fusion and mutual influence.

China's manufacturing industry has been greatly developed in recent years, and occupied the fourth place by volume in the world. The number of goods produced by multinational companies in China has been ranked No.1 in the world. As Japan's Ministry of International Trade and Industry (MITI) published white paper claiming that China has become "World Factory", this argument has come out of nowhere.

The president of China Reform Forum thought that Chinese companies have grabbed the opportunities in the world-wide large-scale industrial transfer, when multinational companies have been moving manufacturing bases to the low-cost areas, to foster and develop the domestic manufacturing industry. It is the first time that the Chinese companies found their definite position in global cooperation.

But he also argued that China is still away from a manufacturing powerhouse, although there have been three world-class manufacturing bases in the Pearl River Delta, Yangtze River Delta and Bohai Bay. In the aspect of volume, China only contributes 5% of production in the global market, whereas the figures are 15% and 20% for Japan and America respectively. The high-tech made-in-China goods are far away from becoming the mainstream.

He proposed to fully develop and utilize the comparative advantage of Chinese manufacturing, to establish fundamentally overall competency, and to promote the rise of Chinese manufacturing comprehensively. The key at current stage is to create an independent, complete, multi-level and coordinative system of manufacturing, base on our comparative advantage. This is, on the one hand, to absorb more FDI companies into this system, and on the other hand, to develop advanced manufacturing technologies thus creating our own brands and independent intellectual property.

Carlos Magarinos, Director General, UNIDO, said that China has gradually become an important production and supply base of industrial goods. However, to further develop from a large manufacturer to a strong one, there is still a difficult process ahead. It is a large systematical project to redress the layouts and positions of industries around China, including correctly balancing the relationship between developing high technologies and manufacturing as well as striving to develop high-tech manufacturing.

The "Made-in-China", which has been fostered for more than ten years, has come through two upgrades and been deemed as the sustenance of China's economy. After discussing the comparative advantage for many years, Chinese companies are now focusing on the development of "core technology" and spurting to make its way to the global supply chain.

To strengthen the "Made-in-China", attracting more international capital to invest in R&D organizations in China is a helpful way to promote the upgrade of Chinese manufacturing industries. So far, over 200 multinational companies, including Panasonic, LG, GE and Intel, have established their R&D centers in China one after another. Some experts believe that attractiveness of R&D in China will further rise as China has the second largest number of R&D persons, more doctors than Japan, and almost the same number of science and engineering graduates as the US.

To push up its manufacturing industries to the high end, the Chinese Government is fueling a R&D boom with a 100 billion investment which accounts for up to 1% of GDP. Meanwhile, the manufacturing that had once promoted the development of the Pearl River Delta and Yangtze River Delta has begun to spread into the areas of Beijing-Tianjin-Hebei, Liaodong Peninsula, Jiaodong Penisula and Xiamen-Zhangzhou-Quanzhou. The governments in those areas have exploited the comparative advantage according to local environment.

Experts, scholars and CEOs at the conference deemed that the concept of "World Factory" has been much different from before, that it is no longer a single country but several countries together to make a "World Factory". Different from that in the industrial era, "World Factory" doesn't mean that a country's overall manufacturing capability is improved comprehensively, but that it is able to play the role of a workshop in "World Factory" as a production base that features global network of manufacturing and procurement.

China's entry into the WTO implies its full acceptance of rules of market economy, which is beneficial for Chinese manufacturing industries to participate in competition in a fair and open world market. Viewed from the external circumstances, currently, multinational companies are rearranging their global presence, going to move many manufacturing bases to China. This is the optimal chance for Chinese manufacturing to integrate with the world and to enhance international competency.

"中国制造业是世界制造生产链中的重要一环，但中国只是一个'车间'，还远未成为'世界工厂'"，这是参加博鳌亚洲论坛2004年年会的企业家、专家学者中最具有代表性的看法。

博鳌亚洲论坛秘书长龙永图表示，在全球制造业的生产链上，中国企业只处在中低端，从中国的综合国力和制造业的素质和能力来看，与世界经济史上被称为"世界工厂"的英国、美国和日本相比，还有很大差距。

现代制造业是一个相互作用的产业链，中国是这个链条的一环。实际上，世界工厂已经通过跨国公司的全球生产链把世界各国联结起来。中国已经成为世界制造基地的一个组成部分，中国的制造业越发达，从其他国家进口的原料就越多。这是一个相互融合而又相互影响的过程。

中国制造业近年来得到长足发展，总量已升至世界第四位。包括跨国公司在华生产的产品在内的百余种产品的数量已位居世界第一。日本通产省发表的白皮书称中国已成为"世界工厂"之后，中国是"世界工厂"的说法便不胫而走。

中国改革开放论坛理事长认为，当跨国公司将制造基地转移到具有低成本优势的地区以培育和发展自身的制造业时，中国企业成功地抓住了世界范围内正在进行的大规模产业转移的时机，这可以说是中国企业第一次在全球分工当中找到明确的位置。

但他表示，尽管中国已形成珠江三角洲、长江三角洲、环渤海湾三大世界级制造基地，但中国仍称不上制造业强国。从总量上来看，中国的制造业产值仅占全球市场的5%，而日本所占的比重是15%，美国是20%。技术含量高的"中国制造"产品在全球市场上远未形成主流。

他提出，要充分开发、利用和发挥中国加工制造业的比较优势，并在此基础上形成多方面的综合竞争优势，促进中国制造业的全面提升。现在的关键在于围绕自身的比较优势创造并形成独立、完整、多层次、协调发展的加工制造体系。一方面吸引更多的外商投资企业融入这一体系；另一方面开发先进的制造技术，创造中国自己的品牌和自主知识产权。

联合国工业发展组织总干事卡洛斯·马加里尼奥斯说，中国已经日渐成为世界重要的工业品生产和供应基地。但中国由“制造大国”向“制造强国”转变，仍需经历一段艰苦过程。这是庞大的系统工程，各地各行业需要重新调整自己的工业布局和定位，包括正确处理发展高科技与制造业的关系，大力发展高科技制造业等。

十多年前就开始孕育的“中国制造”已经历了两次升级，并被认为是中国经济发展的“支撑”。在讨论了多年“比较优势”后，中国企业正关注“核心技术”的发展，正为全面打进“全球供应链”而冲刺。

要使“中国制造”做大做强，大力吸引越来越多的跨国资本在中国投资研发机构，将有效带动中国制造业的升级。迄今为止，包括松下、LG、GE、英特尔等在内的200多家跨国公司纷纷在中国设立了研发中心。有专家认为，中国的研发吸引力还将持续上升，因为它拥有数量位列世界第二的研发人员，拥有比日本还多的博士，以及和美国数量接近的理工科毕业生。

中国政府为使中国制造业向高端努力，正在推动“研发热潮”，政府的研发投入已经占到GDP总量的1%，约1 000亿元。与此同时，曾经带动珠三角和长三角兴起的制造业，开始向京津冀、辽东半岛、胶东半岛和厦漳泉地带扩散。各地政府因地制宜地发挥了比较优势。

与会的专家学者及企业总裁认为，“世界工厂”概念与以往已大不相同，不再是一个国家孤军奋战，而是许多国家一起共同打造。与工业化时代的“世界工厂”不同，信息化时代的“世界工厂”并不意味着一个国家整体制造能力的全面提高，而是更多地充当“世界工厂的一个车间”的角色，是以全球性的网络化生产、网络化采购为特征的制造基地。

中国加入世界贸易组织意味着全方位接受市场经济的规则，这样一种公平、公开的市场竞争有利于中国制造业参与世界竞争。从外部条件看，目前跨国公司正在进行全球调整，将把许多生产制造基地从国外转向中国。这是中国制造业与世界接轨提升国际竞争力的绝好机会。

（资料来源：制造业：中国是“车间”远非“世界工厂”，新华网，2004–04–25）

Questions 思考题

1. What are the forms of international capital movement?
   国际资本移动形式有哪些？
2. What is a transnational corporation? What are its features?
   什么是跨国公司？它具有哪些特点？
3. Discuss the influence of transnational corporations on international trade.
   讨论跨国公司对国际贸易的影响。

Chapter 4

International Trade in Services

国际服务贸易

Lesson 1 Concepts of International Trade in Services 国际服务贸易概念

1. Service and Service Sector 服务与服务业

Service, alternatively called “labor service”, refers to those activities in which someone’s need is fulfilled not by substance but by living labor.

People’s awareness of services originates from daily life. When suffering from illnesses, we need services from doctors; when we have tires punctured on the road, we need services from fixers; when kids are at school age, parents begin to pay attention to services from teachers and schools. So it is proved that in a society with normal development, needs for all types of services are equal in both quantity and quality with those for commodities.

The differences between service sector and tertiary sector are as follows:

- Tertiary sector is defined on a residual basis. There are fewer business included in service sector than in tertiary sector.
- The starting point of the three divisions of sectors is the supply classification of economic system, while service sector is based on the demand classification.
- The economical meaning of tertiary sector is concerned with domestic economy, while that of service sector is concerned with marketplace, looking at both domestic and international marketplaces.

服务，也称劳务，是指不以实物形式而以提供活劳动的形式满足他人某种需要的活动。人们对于服务概念的认识起源于日常生活。身体为病痛所困扰时，我们需要医生的服务；路上自行车爆胎了，我们需要修车师傅的服务；孩子到了上学的年龄，家长便开始关注教师和学校提供的服务。可见，一个正常发展的社会对于各种类型服务的需求，在数量上和质量上同对商品的需要是完全一样的。

服务业与第三产业的区别如下：

● 第三产业的界定采用的是剩余法。服务业所包含的行业要少于第三产业。

● 三次产业划分的出发点是按经济体系的供给分类，而服务业则是以经济系统的需求分类为基础。

● 第三产业概念的经济结构含义主要是就国内经济而言，而服务业概念的经济结构含义主要是以市场为基础，面向国内和国际两个市场。

2. Concepts of International Service Trade 国际服务贸易的概念

The General Agreement on Trade in Services (GATS) at the Uruguay Round of Trade Negotiations groups services into twelve sectors:

① Business services.

● Professional services (including consulting);

Such as legal, engineering design, tourism, city planning and environment protection, public relationship and consulting service of those projects.

● Research and development services.

● Computer and relevant services.

● Real property services.

● Equipment rental services.

② Communication services.

③ Construction services.

④ Sales services.

⑤ Education services.

⑥ Environmental services.

⑦ Financial services.

⑧ Health and society services.

⑨ Tourism and relevant services.

⑩ Culture, entertainment and sports services.

⑪ Transportation services.

⑫ Others.

乌拉圭回合协议把服务贸易分为 12 大类：

① 商业服务类。

● 专业性服务（包括咨询服务）；

如法律服务、工程设计服务、旅游服务、城市规划与环保服务、公共关系服务等，还包括这些项目的咨询服务。

- 计算机及相关服务。
- 研究与开发服务。
- 不动产服务。
- 设备租赁服务。

② 通信服务。
③ 建筑服务。
④ 销售服务。
⑤ 教育服务。
⑥ 环境服务。
⑦ 金融服务。
⑧ 健康及社会服务。
⑨ 旅游及相关服务。
⑩ 文化、娱乐及体育服务。
⑪ 交通运输服务。
⑫ 其他。

Lesson 2 The Relationship between Service Trade and Goods Trade
服务贸易与货物贸易的关系

Generally speaking, international service trade and goods trade complement and promote each other. On the one hand, the development of international goods trade can stimulate the development of related international service trade. And on the other hand, the development of traditional international service trade and emergence of new ones can also promote the goods trade. International service trade normally neither goes through customs nor is shown on customs statistics.

国际服务贸易与国际货物贸易的关系从总体上说是一种相辅相成、相互促进的关系。一方面，国际货物贸易的发展可刺激与之有关的国际服务贸易的发展；另一方面，传统国际服务贸易的发展以及新型服务贸易的出现也可以促进国际货物贸易的发展。国际服务贸易一般不经过海关，也不显示在海关统计上。

Complementarity between Service Trade and Goods Trade 服务贸易和货物贸易的互补性：

1) International goods trade can promote related international service trade

国际货物贸易可推动与之有关的国际服务贸易的发展

The growth of international goods trade has led to the internationalization of related sectors, such as finance, insurance, transportation and communication. In particular, along with the increasing intensity of goods service and gradual shift of global competition from sole tangible substance to composition of tangible substance and intangible added service, service trade has followed to develop rapidly.

国际货物贸易的增长带动了与之相关的金融、保险、运输、通信等服务行业的国际化。特别是随着货物服务密集程度的提高以及世界竞争逐步由有形的单一物质实体竞争转向有形的物质实体竞争和无形的各种附加服务的复合商品的竞争，服务贸易跟随货物贸易实现同步快速发展。

2) Development of traditional service trade and emergence of new service trades have also advanced the growth of goods trade

传统服务贸易的发展和新型服务贸易的出现也促进了货物贸易的发展

The growth of transportation has increased demand for vehicles, like cars, ships, airplanes, etc. The growth of data processing and communication service has increased demand for computers, routers, PC telephone exchange facilities and communication satellites, etc.

运输的增长增加了对汽车、轮船、飞机等交通工具的需求。数据处理和通信服务贸易的增长促进了对计算机、路由器、程控电话交换设备、通信卫星等商品的需求。

3) The interpenetrating of service production and goods production has also enhanced their complementarity

服务生产和商品生产的相互渗透也大大增强了两者的互补性

The development of technologies has brought the materialization trend of service production. For example, intangible software can be solidified on tangible disks. At the same time, there has also been virtualization phenomenon in goods production. Goods trades are engaging more and more service elements, such as technology, management and marketing, so that services and goods are interpenetrated to form composition products thus enhancing their complementarity.

伴随着科学技术的进步，服务生产出现了服务硬件化趋势。比如，无形的软件程序可以固化到有形光盘中，同时商品生产出现了商品软化的现象，货物商品贸易越来越密集地使用科学技术、管理、营销等服务要素，服务和实体货物相互渗透形成复合产品，从而两者互补性增强。

Questions 思考题

Summarize the reasons for the rapid development of international service trade.

简述国际服务贸易迅速发展的原因。

Chapter 5

Regional Economic Integration

区域经济一体化

In recent years, the momentum of regional economic integration has been growing rapidly, which become a highlighted phenomenon in global economy. At present, various types of regional economic integration unions are spreading around the whole world, which exerts a multi-level influence on world political and economic setup.

近年来，区域经济一体化发展很快，势头迅猛，成为国际经济领域里十分突出的现象。目前，各种类型的区域经济一体化组织遍布世界各地，对世界政治经济格局产生了多方面、多层次的影响。

Lesson 1 Summary of Regional Economic Integration

区域经济一体化概述

1. The Meaning and Development of Regional Economic Integration 区域经济一体化的含义

Regional economic integration is two or more countries and regions in the same geographic area to integrate into a supranational entirety with highly coordinative economy and trade. To safeguard their common economic and political interests, those countries pursue long-term and steady supranational economical regulation in the ways of signing certain treaties or agreements between governments, taking common economy and trade policies and even founding joint organizations under each government's authorization.

区域经济一体化是指一个地理区域内的两个或两个以上的国家和地区，为了维护共同的经济和政治利益，通过签订某种政府间条约或协定，制定共同的经济贸易政策等措施，甚至通过建立起各国政府授权的共同机构，实行长期而稳定的超国家经济调节，形成一个超国家的、经济贸易高度协调统一的整体。

2. Main Forms and Features of Regional Economic Integration 区域经济一体化的主要形式及特征

2.1 Divided by Scope of Integration 按一体化区域的范围大小划分

2.1.1 Departmental Integration 部门一体化

It refers to the integration of one or several departments of member countries in the union, such as European Coal and Steel Community formed on 25th July, 1952 and European Atomic Energy Community formed on 1st Jan, 1958.

部门一体化是指区域内各成员国的一个或几个部门（或商品）的一体化。如 1952 年 7 月 25 日建立的欧洲煤钢共同体和 1958 年 1 月 1 日建立的欧洲原子能共同体。

2.1.2 Overall Integration 全盘一体化

It implies that all the economic departments of members are integrated, such as CMEA (Council of Mutual Economic Assistance) founded by the Soviet Union and Eastern European countries and disbanded in 1991.

全盘一体化是指区域成员的所有经济部门实现一体化。如 1991 年解散的由苏联与东欧一些国家组成的经济互助委员会。

2.2 Divided by Economic Development Level of Members 按成员的经济发展水平划分

2.2.1 Horizontal Integration 水平一体化

It refers to the integration of countries and regions with similar or close level of economic development. Out of the practice and development of regional economic integration, most of existing unions are in such a form, such as European Union and ASEAN Free Trade Area.

水平一体化是指由经济发展水平大致相同或接近的国家和地区共同组成的一体化。从区域经济一体化的发展实践来看，现存的一体化大多属于这种形式，如欧盟和东盟自由贸易区。

2.2.2 Vertical Integration 垂直一体化

It refers to the integration of countries and regions with different levels of economic development, such as North American Free Trade Agreement.

垂直一体化是指经济发展水平不同的国家和地区组成的一体化，如北美自由贸易区。

2.3 Divided by Degrees of Regional Economic Integration and Removal of Trade Barriers 按照区域内经济一体化程度或贸易壁垒取消的程度划分

2.3.1 Preferential Trade Arrangement 优惠贸易安排

It is to stipulate especially preferential tariffs on all or part of the goods by signing agreements between members or other methods. This is the most low-level and loose form of economic integration. There are examples such as African Timber Organization, Canada-United States Automotive Products Agreement, and Association of Southeast Asian Nations.

优惠贸易安排指成员间通过协定或其他形式对全部或部分商品规定特别优惠的关税。这是经济一体化中最低级和最松散的形式，例如非洲木材组织、美加汽车产品协定、东南亚国家联盟。

2.3.2 Free Trade Area 自由贸易区

It refers to the trade area that consists of countries and regions who have signed free trade agreements. Member countries have mutually eliminated tariffs for each other and removed the non-tariff trade barriers so that goods can flow freely between the countries. But there is no common external tariff and member countries charge respective tariff on non-member countries.

Examples include European Free Trade Association, Latin American Free Trade Association and North American Free Trade Area.

自由贸易区指签订了自由贸易协定的国家或地区组成的贸易区。成员国之间相互取消了商品贸易关税和非关税的贸易障碍，商品可在成员国间完全自由移动，但成员国之间没有统一的对外关税，按照各自的标准对非成员国征收关税。

例如欧洲自由贸易联盟、拉丁美洲自由贸易联盟和北美自由贸易区。

2.3.3 Tariff Association 关税同盟

Participating members in tariff association entirely remove all the tariffs and non-tariff trade barriers between each other and charge common tariffs on non-member countries. Tariff association has initial supranational nature, such as Benelux.

关税同盟指成员之间完全取消关税和其他贸易壁垒，并对非成员实行统一的关税税率的同盟。关税同盟一开始带有超国家的性质，例如比荷卢关税同盟。

1) Common market 共同市场

Common market means that all members eliminate all the barriers of tariffs and quotas, charge common tariffs on non-members, and allow factors of production to move freely among members. European Economic Community (EEC) had been close to this form in 1970.

共同市场是指在成员内完全废除关税与配额限制，建立统一的对非成员的关税，而且允许生产要素在成员间可以完全自由移动。欧洲经济共同体在 1970 年已接近这一形式。

2) Economic union 经济同盟

Besides freedom of movement of products and factors of production and common external tariffs, economic unions also enable members to formulate common economic and social policies to gradually eliminate divergence and promote integration to a level of holistic economy.

For example, European Economic Community in 1991 and Council of Mutual Economic Assistance founded by the Soviet Union and Eastern European countries and disbanded in 1991.

经济同盟指成员之间不仅商品和生产要素可以完全自由流动，建立统一对外关税，而且成员还制定并执行某些共同的经济政策和社会政策，逐步消除各成员在政策方面的差异，使一体化的程度扩展到整个国民经济。

例如，1991 年的欧洲经济共同体，1991 年解散的由苏联与东欧一些国家组成的经济互助委员会。

3) Complete economic integration 完全经济一体化

Based upon the realization of economic union's mission, complete economic integration is the highest stage of economic integration. The integrated units have unified all the major economic policies, such as fiscal policy, monetary policy, welfare policy, agriculture policy and policy that related to trade and movement of factors of production, and have corresponding organizations, e.g. unified central bank, to execute common external economic policies.

The six forms of regional economic integration can also be seen as the six developing stages of integration; however, it doesn't have to be inevitable process within stages. For example, European Economic Community started from tariff association without developing from preferential trade arrangement and free trade area; and European Free Trade Association doesn't necessarily need to evolve into a tariff association.

完全经济一体化指在实现了经济联盟目标的基础上，还统一了所有的重大经济政策（如财政政策、货币政策、福利政策、农业政策，以及有关贸易及生产要素流动的政策）和相应的机构（如统一的中央银行，执行共同的对外经济政策）。它是经济一体化的最高级阶段。

区域经济一体化的六种形式也可以看成是一体化发展的六个阶段，但阶段之间不一定是必经过程。例如，欧洲经济共同体是从关税同盟开始的，并未经过优惠贸易安排和自由贸易区阶段；而欧洲自由贸易联盟也未必要向关税同盟方向发展。

Lesson 2 Major Regional Economic Integration Unions 主要区域经济一体化组织

1. The European Union (EU) 欧洲联盟

In terms of the number of members, the EU is the largest free trade area in the world, and is also a regional economic and political union with the highest level of regional integration. The EU is not only a common market, but is also an economic and political union having unified monetary and social policies.

欧洲联盟简称欧盟，按照成员国的数目来算，是世界上最大的自由贸易区，也是目前世界上一体化程度最高的区域政治经济集团组织。欧盟不仅是一个共同市场，更是一个具有统一的货币政策和社会政策的经济和政治联盟。

The Unified Economic Policy of the EU 欧盟的统一经济政策：

1) Establish customs union, eliminate internal tariffs 建立关税同盟，取消内部关税

At the same time of eliminating internal tariffs, member states apply a common external tariffs on industrial and agricultural products from non-member states.

在取消内部关税的同时，成员国对非成员国的工农业产品实行统一关税税率。

2) Common agricultural policy 共同农业政策

The Common Agricultural Policy's price controlling system ensures the prices of agricultural products fluctuating within "target price" and "intervention price" by means of the EU's purchasing and delivery. The policy involves application of Variable Levy on some imported agricultural products and subsidies on exports. European Agriculture Guide and Guarantee Funds were established to promote the mechanization and modernization of agriculture.

实行统一的农业产品价格管理制度。农产品价格通过欧洲共同体的收购或投放，保证其在“目标价格”和“干预价格”之间波动；对部分农产品进口征收差价税，实行农产品出口补贴制度；设立“欧洲农业指导和保证基金”，促进农业的机械化和现代化。

3) Common market 统一大市场

Since 1993, the EU has been running an internal market covering a non-boundary area, where the goods, people, services and capital can move freely.

1993 年初开始运行统一大市场，内部市场由一个没有内部边界的区域构成，在内部，商品、人员、服务和资本可以自由流动。

4) European Monetary union 欧洲货币体系

A European single currency was launched. National currencies of member states were exchanged at fixed rate internally and at joint floating rate externally so that a relatively stable exchange-rate system was formed. The European Monetary Fund was founded to provide short and medium term loans to member countries with the objectives of foreign exchange market intervention, stabilization of exchange rate and adjustment of international payment. On 1st Jan, 1999, the European single currency, the Euro, started to be used in domestic trade followed by euro notes and coins issued in 2002.

设立欧洲货币单位，成员国之间实行固定汇率，对外实行联合浮动，从而形成一个相对稳定的汇率制度，建立欧洲货币基金，向成员国提供中短期贷款，借以干预外汇市场、稳定汇率、调节国际收支。1999 年 1 月 1 日，欧洲单一货币——欧元开始在其内部经济贸易活动中使用，2002 年欧元纸币和辅币正式流通。

5) European Economic Area 欧洲经济区

On 1st January, 1994, the European Economic Area was officially established to allow free movement of goods, services, capital and people.

1994 年 1 月 1 日，欧洲经济区正式启动，旨在建成一个能保证货物、服务、资本和人员自由流动的贸易集团。

2. North American Free Trade Area (NAFTA) 北美自由贸易区

On 1st Jan, 1989, with the United State-Canada Free Trade Agreement coming into effect, the United States-Canada Free Trade Area was established.

The United States-Canada Free Trade Area comprises two countries, the United States and Canada. Its goals were to eliminate all barriers to trade of goods and services, investment, commerce and travel, to provide code of conduct for both governments so as to regulate the behavior of private enterprises and general economic policy of government.

On 1st Jan, 1994, with the North American Free Trade Agreements coming into effect, the North American Free Trade Area was established.

The core of the agreement was to reduce and eliminate all the tariffs of bilateral trade in ten years from 1989 to 1998.

The North American Free Trade Agreements supersede the United States-Canada Free Trade Agreement with the addition of Mexico. The North American Free Trade Area was a regional trade group established by the United States allying itself with Canada and Mexico, serving its purpose of countering against the EU.

The main content of the agreement included: the elimination of tariffs and non-tariff barriers on over 9,000 kinds of goods by stages within 15 years and the elimination of import quota and export license; the opening of telecommunication, finance and insurance industries in Mexico to the US and Canadian merchants to allow them to participate in competition and investment by establishing wholly owned subsidiaries. The three countries agreed to grant national treatment to the finance enterprises in North America. To prevent tariff evasion by countries outside of the area, the three countries agreed on more strict regulations on the rules of origin. And there were also laws in the area of intellectual property and issues of labor protection and environment protection.

The establishment of the North American Free Trade Area represented a fresh try of vertical international division of labor in a regional economic union by both developed and developing countries, and was also a new attempt of South-North cooperation.

Based on the North American Free Trade Area, the US sought to establish Free Trade Area of America to embrace South American countries. The idea was brought to the 1st Summit of the Americas including 34 countries, with the goal of establishing the Free Trade Area of America in January 2005 with the biggest area of the world and the GDP amounting to 14 trillion dollars as well as the population of 0.8 billion. In November of 2003, the frame agreement on FTAA has been reached in the eighth ministerial meeting, reiterating FTAA would be started on January 2005.

However, the negotiation on FTAA has been going along slowly, staying on the agenda and framework, and no agreement has been reached substantially on the key subjects like agricultural subsidy, tariff reduction, market access, etc.

1989 年 1 月 1 日，《美加自由贸易协定》生效，美加自由贸易区成立。

美加自由贸易区由美国、加拿大两国组成。其目标是消除商品贸易、服务贸易和投资、商业、旅行方面的一切障碍，提供双方政府的行为准则，以规范私人企业的行为和政府的总体经济政策。

1994 年 1 月 1 日，《北美自由贸易协定》正式生效，北美自由贸易区宣布成立。

协定的核心内容是从 1989 年起到 1998 年的 10 年内，逐步削减并取消双边贸易的全部关税。

《北美自由贸易协定》是在《美加自由贸易协定》的基础上，吸收墨西哥参加之后形成的。北美自由贸易区是美国为了与欧盟相抗衡而联合加拿大和墨西哥组成的区域贸易集团。

协定的主要内容包括：三国将在 15 年内分阶段逐步取消 9 000 多种商品的关税和非关税壁垒，取消进口配额和进口许可证；开放墨西哥的电信、金融和保险业；允许美国和加拿大商人进入竞争和投资，包括建立独资子公司，三国同意对北美地区的金融公司给予国民待遇；为防止区外第三国利用自由贸易区逃避关税，三国就原产地规则达成了更加严格的规定；保护知识产权的规定，以及有关劳工和环境保护问题的补充规定等。

北美自由贸易区的建立是发达国家和发展中国家在区域经济一体化组织内实行垂直型国际分工的一种新的尝试，是南北合作的一种新尝试。

在北美自由贸易区的基础上，美国还力图建立包括南美洲各国在内的美洲自由贸易区。这一设想在 1994 年的美洲 34 国首脑会议上提出，目标是在 2005 年 1 月建立世界上面积最大、国民生产总值达 14 万亿美元、拥有 8 亿人口的美洲自由贸易区。2003 年 11 月，美洲自由贸易区第 8 次部长级会议《美洲自由贸易框架协议》取得共识，并重申最迟于 2005 年 1 月启动美洲自由贸易区。

但有关美洲自由贸易区的谈判进展缓慢，在农业补贴、降低关税、市场准入等关键问题上尚未达成实质性的协议，谈判一直停留在议程和框架层面上，无法深入。

3. Asia-Pacific Economic Corporation 亚太经济合作组织（APEC）

APEC (Asia-Pacific Economic Corporation) is an important international organization aiming to strengthen regional economic corporation of Asia-Pacific countries and regions. APEC is a regional economic integration organization in vastness of area and various economic situations with members including the developed economies, newly industrialized economies, and developing economies which are in different social and political systems.

In the proposal of Australia, APEC was established in 1990. Up to the year of 2021, there are 21 member.

亚太经济合作组织（简称亚太经合组织、APEC）是亚太国家和地区加强区域经济合作的重要国际组织之一。亚太经合组织是幅员广阔、情况复杂的区域经济一体化组织，其成员既有发达经济体、新兴工业化经济体，也有发展中经济体，社会经济制度差异很大。

在澳大利亚的倡议下，亚太经合组织于1990年成立。截至2021年，亚太经合组织共有21个正式成员。

4. Association of Southeast Asian Nations (ASEAN) 东南亚国家联盟，简称“东盟”（ASEAN）

ASEAN is an organization consisting of developing countries.

In August 8th 1967, the five countries including Indonesia, Malaysia, the Philippines, Singapore, and Thailand singed ASEAN declaration namely Bangkok Declaration, founding the organization known as ASEAN.

From the 1980s to the 1990s, with Brunei, Vietnam, Myanmar, Laos, Cambodia joining the organization, there are 10 members for the time being.

ASEAN free trade area was established and took effect on January 2002 with goal of realizing zero duty for the trade within the region. Up to the year of 2010, the six members including Malaysia, the Philippines, Thailand, Singapore, Indonesia, Brunei agreed to eliminate duty. By the year of 2015, it is scheduled to realize trade liberalization for all members.

东盟是一个全部由发展中国家组成的南南合作的典型。

1967年8月8日，马来西亚、菲律宾、泰国、新加坡、印度尼西亚五国发表《东南亚国家联盟宣言》即《曼谷宣言》，正式组建东盟。

20世纪80年代至90年代，又有文莱、越南、缅甸、老挝和柬埔寨相继加入，目前共有十个成员国。

东盟自由贸易区自2002年1月正式启动，目标是实现区域内贸易的零关税。2010年，东盟六个成员国（马来西亚、菲律宾、泰国、新加坡、印度尼西亚、文莱）率先实现关税互免，而到2015年，东盟所有成员国实现贸易自由化。

5. Regional Economic Integration and China 区域经济一体化和中国的参与情况

5.1 CAFTA (China-ASEAN Free Trade Area) 中国—东盟自由贸易区（CAFTA）

In November 2002, Chinese leaders and the leaders of 10 ASEAN member countries signed the Framework Agreement on China-ASEAN Comprehensive Economic Co-operation Area. China-ASEAN Free Trade Area is covering goods trade, service trade, investment and economic cooperation etc., of which the goods trade is the core content. It is stipulated in the Framework Agreement on China–ASEAN Comprehensive Economic Co-operation Area that China and ASEAN members shall start to reduce tariffs on the normal goods since 2005.

During the 8th leaders meeting of China-ASEAN Free Trade Area in November of 2004, the minister of commerce of China and the ministers of ASEAN signed the

Agreement on Trade in Goods and the Agreement on Dispute Settlement Mechanism, which are both under the Framework Agreement on China-ASEAN Comprehensive Economic Co-operation Area.

In the Agreement on Trade in Goods, it is stipulated that China and the six founder members of ASEAN shall cut down the duty of most normal commodities to zero.

The Agreement on Dispute Settlement Mechanism is the legal file to regulate the dispute settlement between China and ASEAN members under the the Framework Agreement.

2002 年 11 月，中国国家领导人与东盟十国领导人共同签署了《中国东盟全面经济合作框架协议》，中国—东盟自由贸易区将包括货物贸易、服务贸易、投资和经济合作等内容，其中货物贸易是自由贸易区的核心内容。《中国东盟全面经济合作框架协议》规定中国和东盟双方从 2005 年开始正常产品的降税。

2004 年 11 月，在第八次中国—东盟领导人会议期间，中国商务部部长与东盟十国经贸部长分别代表各自政府签署了中国—东盟自由贸易区《货物贸易协议》和《争端解决机制协议》。

《货物贸易协议》规定中国和东盟中的六个老成员将在 2010 年把绝大多数正常产品的关税降为零。

《争端解决机制协议》是规范中国与东盟双方在自由贸易区框架下处理有关贸易争端的法律文件。

5.2 The Economic Cooperation between China and Northeast Asian Countries—Aiming to Establish the Free Trade Area of China, Japan and Republic of Korea 中国与东北亚国家的经济贸易合作——努力建立中日韩自由贸易区

The idea of the free trade area of China, Japan and Republic of Korea was initially put forward by the former president of Republic of Korea Kim Dae-jung in the "10+3" meeting in Manila in 1998. The proposal was getting on slowly due to some reasons though it received positive responses from China and Japan.

中日韩自由贸易区的概念最早是由韩国前总统金大中在 1998 年马尼拉"10+3"会议上提出的，虽得到了中日两国的积极回应，但由于各种原因进展缓慢。

5.3 New Zealand-China Free Trade Area 中新自由贸易区

In recent years, the relationship between China and New Zealand has been going on well. The exported products to New Zealand to China are covering electronic machines and equipment, mechanical equipment, dress, furniture, toys and steel products etc., and the exported products from New Zealand to China are primarily diary products, timber, paper pulp and other paper products as well as wool products etc.

On 7th April 2008, China and New Zealand signed the Free Trade Agreement between the Government of the People's Republic of China and the Government of New Zealand, which is the first free trade agreement signed with any developed country covering various fields from trade of goods, trade of services to investment and so on.

The agreement reached has brought a great favor of tariff reduction to the Chinese enterprises in the trade with New Zealand. A large quantity of products have been granted tariff-free since the agreement come into force. Furthermore, the tariffs on more and more goods have been reduced gradually in phases to tariff-free up to 2012. The great tariff reduction has brought more opportunities to enterprises in trade. In accordance with the agreement, about 60% of the Chinese products exported to New Zealand are tariff-free since the agreement coming into force including mechanical and electronic products, wooden products, textiles and clothes, plastic products, mineral products etc. At the same time, 24% of New Zealand products exported China is also tariff free.

From 1st October 2008, with the New Zealand-China Free Trade Agreement taking effect, the goods exported from China to New Zealand may enjoy tariff-free by the Certificate of Origin Form for the Free Trade Agreement between the Government of the People's Republic of China and the Government of New Zealand.

近年来，中国和新西兰两国经贸关系保持良好发展势头。中国出口新西兰的主要产品包括电子机器和设备、机械设备、服装、家具、玩具、钢铁产品等，新西兰出口中国的主要产品则为乳制品、木材、纸浆及其他纸制品和羊毛等。

2008 年 4 月 7 日，中国与新西兰在北京签署了《中华人民共和国政府和新西兰政府自由贸易协定》，这是中国与发达国家签订的第一个自由贸易协定，涵盖了货物贸易、服务贸易、投资等诸多领域。

自由贸易协定的签订，给中国从事中新双边贸易的企业带来的最大优惠是大幅减让关税。大量产品从协议公布之日起实行零关税。还有更多的货物关税开始逐步减让，到 2012 年成为零关税产品。关税的大幅度减让，给企业带来难得的机会。根据协定，中国出口到新西兰的产品中约有超过 60%从协定生效时起实行零关税，产品主要包括机电产品、木制品、纺织品、塑料制品、矿产品等。同时，24%的自新西兰进口的产品从协定生效时起也实行零关税。

自 2008 年 10 月 1 日起，中国—新西兰双边自由贸易协定开始生效，中国出口到新西兰的部分货物凭中—新自由贸易区优惠原产地证书可享受零关税待遇。

Case Study 本章案例

Case: NAFTA Push Mexico into Being Manufacturing Center of North America

【案例】北美自由贸易协定使墨西哥成为北美制造中心

In Tijuana, a small town on the frontier of Mexico with the population of one million, you can see blue high advertising billboards standing in the broad new industrial zone of

Samsung, looking not in harmony with the gloomy and dirty town. Since the 70 inches high steel building were erected for a few months, it has become an informal monument and the beacon of the poor in Mexico as well as the symbol of north America free trade power. Boosted by the power, the opportunities of working in manufacturing industry are flowing into Mexico from the United States.

Since North American Free Trade Area was established in 1992, the United States and Mexico have eliminated the trade barriers between each other so that the commodities manufactured by the two countries may be traded freely within the area without duty and restriction measures like quotas. Whereas for the economies outside the area such as Korea, Japan, there are still trade barriers resulting in "trade creation" and "trade transfer". The products from Korea and Japan encounter price discrimination and may be squeezed out of the US market, which lowers the utilization efficiency of global resource.

In confrontation with the situation, the developed economies like Korea and Japan are not ready to be defeated but resort to new strategy. Upon that, more and more branch companies of Samsung, Sony, Hitach, and Panasonic are established in the border towns like Tijuana. In the town, about 24.6 thousand of workers are employed by these multinational companies. Cheap labour of Mexico also have attracted many American companies in consumption commodities with little technology like apparel and hand tools as the scale production cost is just part of the cost in the US. For the Asian companies in hi-tech, the elimination of trade barriers puts the towns like Tijuana to be the first stop for their expansion drive in north America. In addition, the long beach port nearby Silicon Valley and California makes the transfer easier to other places of world.

在墨西哥人口约 100 万的边境小镇蒂华纳，一眼望去，高耸入云的蓝色广告牌照亮夜空，耸立在三星集团开阔的新工业区中，这一切与这个灰暗、肮脏的边境小镇似乎显得不太协调。自从这个 70 英尺（约合 21.35 米）高的钢筋建筑物竖起几个月以来，它已经成了一个非正式的纪念碑，成了墨西哥穷人的指路灯。它也是北美自由贸易力量的象征。由于这种力量的作用，制造业工作机会从美国源源不断流往墨西哥。

自 1992 年北美自由贸易区建立后，美国和墨西哥取消了相互之间的贸易壁垒，两国制造的商品可以在区内自由流通，相互间没有什么关税、配额保护措施。而对于区外国家，如韩国、日本等国家，仍然维持贸易壁垒，因此会产生"贸易创造"和"贸易转移"的双重结果。韩国、日本的产品会受到价格歧视，很可能被挤出美国市场，就全球资源利用角度看，这也是一种效率的降低。

针对这种情况，韩国、日本等国也不愿坐以待毙，转而采取新的战略。于是就有了三星公司、索尼公司、日立公司和松下电器在诸如蒂华纳这样的边境小镇开的子公司。在该镇，受雇于这些跨国公司的墨西哥人已达 2.46 万人。由于墨西哥有廉价的劳动力，从而也吸引了众多生产诸如成衣和手工工具之类低技术消费品的美国公司，因为这里成批生产的成本只有在美国生产的几分之一。对于生产高技术产品的亚洲公司而言，由于贸易壁垒取消，蒂华纳成了它们在北美的第一站。而且由于接近硅谷和加利福尼亚的长潍港，产品再转运到世界各地也比以前容易了。

（资料来源：《参考消息》，1996-07-06）

Questions 思考题

1. What are the forms of regional integration?
   区域经济一体化有哪些形式？
2. Please give an introduction in brief to the static effect of Tariff Association.
   简述关税同盟的静态效果。

Chapter 6

WTO and China

世界贸易组织与中国

The predecessor of WTO (World Trade Organization) is GATT (General Agreement on Tariff and Trade, GATT), entering into force on 1 January, 1948, signed by 23 countries on 30 October, 1947 in Geneva, which is a multilateral accord dealing with the regulation of the foreign policies and the mutual rights and obligations of international trade relations of members, replaced by WTO on 1 January, 1995.

世界贸易组织的前身是关税及贸易总协定，关税及贸易总协定简称关贸总协定或 GATT，GATT 订立于 1948 年 1 月 1 日，是由 23 个国家于 1947 年 10 月 30 日在日内瓦签订，并于 1948 年正式生效，是关于调整缔约方对外贸易政策和国际贸易关系方面的相互权利、义务的国际多边协定。1995 年 1 月 1 日被世界贸易组织所取代。

Lesson 1　General Introduction to GATT

关税及贸易总协定概述

1. The Origin and Development of GATT 关税及贸易总协定的产生和发展

After World War II, being on the leading economic position, the United States engaged in political, economic, financial, and trade expansion, advocating trade liberation. In 1945, Bretton Woods Institution sponsored by United States with 23 members was convened in New Hampshire, in which three international organizations dedicated in trade liberation were established including International Monetary Fund (IMF), World Bank, and GATT.

With the advocation of the United States, the draft of "Charter of International Trade Organization" was passed by Trade Economic and Social Council of the UN in the preparatory committee held in Geneva. In the meeting, in order to go into tariff reduction negotiation earlier, based on the articles about tariff in the draft, the representatives of the committee compiled a file named General Agreement on Tariff and Trade and reached a "temporary applicable protocol" through negotiation as the integral part of GATT, singed by 23 members in Geneva on 30th October, 1947 and went into effect on 1st January, 1948.

The top power body of GATT is general conference of members, usually held annually for discussion and decision of important events, and the council between the two general councils is in charge of routines and emergencies, under which are all kinds of committees. The GATT also set secretariat in Geneva dealing with the arrangement, recording, and drafting of reports as well as the researches necessary for GATT and contacting work with members etc.

The goal of GATT is "Governments of contracting parties, recognizing that their relations in the field of trade and economic endeavour should be conducted with a view to raising standards of living, ensuring full employment and a large and steadily growing volume of real income and effective demand, developing the full use of the resources of the world and expanding the production and exchange of goods. Being desirous of contributing to these objectives by entering into reciprocal and mutually advantageous arrangements directed to the substantial reduction of tariffs and other barriers to trade and to the elimination of discriminatory treatment in international commerce, contributes to the above-mentioned goals."

From the commence in 1948 to the end in 1995, over the 47 years with the expansion of GATT contents and activities as well as the increasing members, GATT had played an increasingly important role in international trade as follows:

GATT promoted trade liberation and development of international trade. After 8 rounds of trade negotiations under GATT, tariff reduction was fulfilled substantially, covering over 60 thousands of items for the former 6 rounds involving half of commodities of international trade. During the 7th round negotiation, the commodities with tariff reduction have occupied one fifth. In addition, during the negotiation, some agreements on non-tariff barriers were also reached.

GATT advanced the standardization of international trade. The members under GATT are required to follow the principles and accords of GATT when they are whatever involved in foreign trade, making and revising their foreign trade measures and dealing with the economic and trade relations with other members, to assure international trade going on with an ordered and fair regulation. The principles and accords are the main legal basis for the members under GATT to make and revise foreign policies and measures as well as get engaged into foreign trade.

GATT granted favorable treatment to developing countries to benefit the development of their foreign trade through the following ways: offering tariff reduction to the manufactured products and semi-manufactured products produced by developing countries; offering the negotiation occasion for trade for developing countries and developed countries; helping developing countries to protect their benefits and encourage the development of foreign trade.

第二次世界大战后，美国在世界经济中处于领先地位，在战后的政治、经济、金融、贸易领域进行对外扩张，并提出贸易自由化的口号，率先举起了贸易自由的大旗。1945年，在美国的新罕布尔州召开了由美国发起、23个国家参加的布雷顿森林会议。这次会议决定成立三个以实现贸易自由化为目标的国际组织，即国际货币基金组织、世界银行、关税及贸易总协定。

在美国的积极倡导下，联合国经济和社会理事会于1947年4月在日内瓦举行的筹备会议上通过了“国际贸易组织宪章”草案。在这次会议上，为了尽快进行关税减让谈判，参加会议的代表根据这项草案的有关关税的条文汇编成一个文件，即称为关税及贸易总协定，并经过谈判达成一项“临时适用议定书”，作为总协定的组成部分，于1947年10月30日在日内瓦由23个国家签署，并于1948年1月1日正式生效。

关贸总协定的最高权力机构是缔约方大会，一般每年召开一次，讨论和决定有关重大事项，在两届缔约方大会期间由理事会处理日常和紧急事务。在理事会下还设立各种委员会，关贸总协定还在日内瓦设立秘书处，除处理有关上述各项会议的准备、记录和编写报告外，还进行关贸总协定的各项必要调查，负责各缔约方之间的联络工作等。

关贸总协定的宗旨是“各缔约方政府，认为在处理它们的贸易和经济事业的关系方面，应以提高生活水平、保证充分就业、保证实际收入和有效需求的巨大持续增长、扩大世界资源的充分利用以及发展商品生产与交换为目的。切望达成互惠互利协议，大幅度地削减关税和其他贸易障碍，取消国际贸易中的歧视待遇，以对上述目的做出贡献”。

关贸总协定从1948年开始至1995年正式结束的47年内，其内容及其活动所涉及的范围不断扩大，关贸总协定的正式成员不断增加，它在国际贸易领域内的作用日益加强，主要表现在以下几个方面：

关贸总协定促进贸易自由化和国际贸易的发展。在关贸总协定的主持下，经过8轮贸易谈判，大幅度削减了关税税率，在前6轮谈判中，降低税率的范围达60 000个税目以上，涉及的商品占世界商品贸易的一半以上。在第7轮谈判中，减税的商品占世界商品贸易的1/5。此外，这次谈判还就减缓非关税壁垒达成某些协议。

关贸总协定促进了国际贸易的规范化。关贸总协定要求有关成员在从事对外贸易活动和在制定或修改它们的对外贸易措施以及处理成员之间的经济贸易关系方面均应遵循GATT的原则与协议，保证国际贸易在一个有序、公正的规则下进行。这些原则和协议成为关贸总协定各成员制定和修改对外贸易政策和措施及从事对外贸易活动的主要法律依据。

关贸总协定给予发展中国家优惠待遇，有利于发展中国家发展对外贸易。对发展中国家的工业制成品和半制成品给予减税优惠，为发展中国家与发达资本主义国家开展贸易对话提供了场所，并为发展中国家维护自身利益和促进对外贸易发展发挥了一定的作用。

2. Uruguay Round Multilateral Negotiation 乌拉圭回合多边贸易谈判的议题

Conducted within the framework of GATT, seven rounds of multilateral trade negotiations have been fulfilled from 1947 to the end of 1979. The eighth round of negotiation was launched in Punta del Este, Uruguay on 15th September, 1986, named Uruguay Round. With the participation of 123 members, the round of negotiation was finished in Geneva until 15th December, 1993. The negotiators participating in Uruguay Round held a meeting in Marrakesh of Morocco and signed the Final Act of Uruguay Round as well as the agreements on the establishment of World Trade Organization, declaring the close of the round. On 1st January 1995, World Trade Organization came into being to replace GATT system.

在关贸总协定主导下，从 1947 年到 1979 年完成了 7 轮多边贸易谈判。第 8 轮谈判于 1986 年 9 月 15 日在乌拉圭首都埃斯特角开始举行，称为“乌拉圭回合”。这次谈判有 123 个成员参加，至 1993 年 12 月 15 日在日内瓦完成。参加乌拉圭回合的谈判方于 1994 年 4 月 15 日在摩洛哥马拉喀什城举行会议，草签了乌拉圭回合最后文件和建立世界贸易组织协议，宣告正式结束“乌拉圭回合”。1995 年 1 月 1 日，世界贸易组织正式成立，原 1947 年的关贸总协定失效。

Lesson 2　World Trade Organization (WTO) 世界贸易组织

1. The Creation of World Trade Organization 世界贸易组织的产生

World Trade Organization, namely WTO for short, was established on 1st January 1995 in accordance with the Agreement Establishing the World Trade Organization which was reached in Uruguay Round of Multilateral Trade Negotiations to replace GATT, and with a full set of accords and agreements formed upon the Final Act reached in Uruguay Round as the international trade regulations in law, in supervision, management and fulfillment of the rights and obligations of the economic and trade relations between members.

In the later phase of Uruguay Round, with many substantial negotiation subjects coming to an agreement, members paid more and more attention to how to conduct Uruguay Round agreements and what kind of framework to be adopted for WTO. Since 1990, members including the EU, Canada, Switzerland and the United States have brought out schemes and took a formal proposal to establish “multilateral trade organization” (MTO) in Uruguay Round negotiation on 20th December 1991 after negotiations over and over. With the Final Act and the Agreement Establishing the World Trade Organization signed in Marrakesh, Morocco, taking the agreements of the Final Act as the annex of WTO, WTO was created and entered into force on 1st January 1995.

世界贸易组织简称 WTO，是根据乌拉圭回合多边贸易谈判达成的《建立世界贸易组织协定》于 1995 年 1 月 1 日建立的，它取代了之前的关贸总协定，并将乌拉圭回合多边谈判达成的最后文件所形成的一整套协定和协议的条款作为国际法律规则，对各成员之间经济贸易关系的权利和义务进行监督、管理和履行。

到了乌拉圭回合谈判的后期，在对许多实质性重要议题基本上达成协议后，如何执行乌拉圭回合协议及世界贸易组织采取何种组织框架等问题日益受到各成员的关注。1990 年，欧洲共同体、加拿大、瑞士和美国先后提出方案，经过多次谈判，1991 年 12 月 20 日在乌拉圭回合谈判中正式提出建立“多边贸易组织”（MTO）的决定。1994 年 4 月，在摩洛哥马拉喀什会议签署了乌拉圭回合最后文件和《建立世界贸易组织协定》，于 1995 年 1 月 1 日正式建立世贸组织，并将最后文件中的其他协定和协议列为世界贸易组织的附件。世界贸易组织就这样诞生了。

2. The Key Points about the Agreement Establishing World Trade Organization《建立世界贸易组织协定》的主要内容

The agreement consists of 16 articles and 4 annex with the annex list, stipulating the objectives, functions, structure, membership accession, the way of decision-making as well as non-application multilateral trade agreement between particular members.

《建立世界贸易组织协定》（以下简称《协定》）由 16 个条款、4 个附件及附件目录组成，主要规定了世界贸易组织的宗旨和目标、职能、组织机构、成员资格、决策方式，以及特定成员之间互不适用多边贸易协议等内容。

2.1 Objectives 宗旨与目标

In the prologue, it is said that “Recognizing that their relations in the field of trade and economic endeavour should be conducted with a view to raising standards of living, ensuring full employment and a large and steadily growing volume of real income and effective demand, and expanding the production of and trade in goods and services, while allowing for the optimal use of the world’s resources in accordance with the objective of sustainable development, seeking both to protect and preserve the environment and to enhance the means of doing so in a manner consistent with their respective need and concern at different levels of economic development”.

序言指出，其宗旨和目标是世界贸易组织成员在处理其贸易和经济领域的关系时，应力求提高生活水平，保证充分就业和大幅度稳定提高实际收入及有效需求，拓展货物和服务的生产和贸易，持久地开发和合理地利用世界资源，保护和维护环境，并以符合各国在不同经济发展水平下各自需要的方式采取相应措施来加强环保。

2.2 Functions 职能

In accordance with the agreement, the functions of WTO are as follows:

Supervision and administration. To advance the realization of WTO objectives, WTO shall supervise and administer the implementation of the multilateral trade agreements under the WTO framework.

Settlement of Trade Dispute. To facilitate the implementation of plurilateral trade agreements, WTO shall provide forum for multilateral trade negotiations, and administer the understanding of rules and procedures governing the settlement of disputes.

Review of trade system and policies. WTO shall review the trade systems and domestic economic policies of country members.

Cooperation. With a view to achieving greater coherence in global economic policy-making, the WTO shall cooperate, as appropriate, with the International Monetary Fund and with the International Bank for Reconstruction and Development and its affiliated agencies.

Providing developing countries and economy-transferring countries with technology aid.

根据《协定》及相关文件，世界贸易组织的职能为：

监督和管理——促进世界贸易组织目标的实现，监督和管理其统辖范围内的各项协议的贯彻实施；

解决贸易纠纷——组织实施各项多边贸易协议，为各成员方提供多边贸易谈判的场所，按一体化的争端解决规则与程序，主持解决各成员方之间的贸易纠纷；

审议贸易制度和政策——按照有关贸易政策审议机制，负责定期审议各成员方的贸易制度和与贸易相关的国内经济政策；

协调——协调与国际货币基金组织和世界银行及其分支机构的关系，以保障全球经济决策的一致性；

提供技术援助——向发展中国家和转型经济国家提供必要的技术援助。

3. Basic Principles of WTO 世界贸易组织的基本原则

3.1 Non-discrimination 非歧视原则

Non-discrimination is the most important principle of the WTO agreement, which is given concrete form in the "most-favored-nation" (MFN) and "national treatment" rules, mostly aiming at imported and exported commodities and the relevant issues.

非歧视原则是《协定》中最为重要的原则，这个原则是通过最惠国待遇条款和国民待遇条款体现的，主要针对进出口商品与有关事项。

3.1.1 Most-Favored-Nation Treatment (MFN) 最惠国待遇条款

The clause means that the contracting parties were bound to grant to the products of other contracting parties treatment no less favorable than that accorded to products of any other country. As it is stipulated in GATT, "any advantage, favor, privilege or immunity granted by any member to any product originating in or destined for any other country shall be accorded immediately and unconditionally to the like product originating in or destined for the territories of all other members."

For instance, a contracting party can enjoy all favorable treatments including tariff reduction provided in any trade agreement between other contracting parties through negotiation upon MFN clause. Thus, MFN treatment is expanded to multilateral benefit from mutual benefit though there are also some exceptions to which MFN is not applicable, such as the preferential duty treatment tariff, tariff union and other favorable treatment accords on border trade between neighbor countries exited before signing GATT.

这一条款是指每一个缔约方应该在进出口方面以相等的方式对待所有其他缔约方，而不应采取歧视待遇。关贸总协定规定："一成员对来自或运往其他国家的产品所给予的利益、优待、特权或豁免，应当立即无条件地给予来自或运往所有其他成员的相同产品。"

例如，一缔约方可根据最惠国待遇条款，享受任何缔约方通过谈判达成的所有关税减让和其他贸易上的优惠待遇。这样，最惠国待遇就从双边互惠推广到多边互惠。但这项条款有若干例外，例如，最惠国待遇条款不适用于总协定签订时已经存在的特惠关税、关税同盟、自由贸易区以及毗邻国家之间对边境贸易所给予的优惠待遇。

3.1.2 National Treatment 国民待遇条款

The national treatment requires that each contracting party shall grant the same treatment to the goods entering into domestic market from any other contract party as the home products in terms of taxation and other commercial regulations without discrimination.

As it is provided in national treatment articles, "The products of one contracting country entering into the other contracting country shall not be charged higher tax or other domestic charges than charged on the local-produced products directly or indirectly." The principle is to make sure that the imported goods have the equal competition as the local produced goods in domestic market and avoid the protection measures including domestic taxation and charging taken by the import country to set off the tariff reduction effect.

The difference between MFN clause and the national treatment clause are as follows:

The intent of MFN clause is to make the imported goods from various contracting parties be treated equally without discrimination, and the national treatment clause is to make the imported goods be treated as equally as the home-made products; MFN clause emphasizes the import country shall not grant discriminatory treatment on the products from different countries while the national treatment clause stresses the import country shall not give discriminatory treatment between the imported products and local-produced products.

这一条款要求每一缔约方对任何缔约方的产品进入本国国内市场时，在国内税或其他国内商业规章等方面应给予与本国产品同等的待遇，不应歧视。

根据相关规定："一缔约方领土的产品输入到另一缔约方领土时，不应对它直接或间接征收高于相同的国内产品所直接或间接征收的国内税或其他国内费用。"其目的在于保证进口产品与国内产品在国内市场上以同等的条件进行竞争，避免缔约方利用征收国内税及费用的办法保护国内生产，抵消关税减让效果。

最惠国待遇条款和国民待遇条款的区别如下：

最惠国待遇条款的目的是使来自不同国家的进口商品在一缔约方的市场上处于同等地位，不受歧视，而国民待遇条款的目的是使进口商品在一缔约方的国内市场与其本国商品处于同等竞争地位，不受歧视；最惠国待遇条款强调一缔约方不得针对不同出口方的商品实行歧视待遇，而国民待遇条款强调一缔约方不得在进口国与本国商品之间实行歧视待遇。

3.2 Free Trade Principle 自由贸易原则

Free trade principle is set to restrict and eliminate all the obstacles in international trade, cutting down tariff substantially and reducing non-tariff barriers through multilateral negotiation, further expanding trade relations in goods and services between members.

The principle is fulfilled through the following provisions including protection through tariff, tariff reduction and prohibition of quantitative restrictions.

自由贸易原则就是限制和取消一切妨碍和阻止国际贸易开展与进行的障碍，通过多边贸易谈判，实质性削减关税和减少其他非关税贸易壁垒，扩大成员方之间的货物和服务贸易。

自由贸易原则主要有关税保护和关税减让规则以及一般取消数量限制规则。

3.2.1 Protection through Tariff and Tariff Reduction 关税保护和关税减让规则

Tariff shall be the only measure adopted to protect domestic industry, and tariff reduction is fulfilled through multilateral negotiation. Tariff reduction means that contracting parties cut down tariff, making concessions on tariff reduction level on the basis of mutual benefit and equality, and reach agreement on tariff reduction schedule. It is provided in GATT that contracting parties have obligation to make tariff reduction and only protect domestic industry with tariff.

关税保护规则是指以关税作为唯一保护手段的规则，多边贸易谈判是实现关税减让的主要途径。关税减让规则是指缔约方之间相互约束关税减让水平，即各缔约方彼此作出互惠与平等的让步，达成关税减让表协议。GATT 规定只能通过关税来保护本国工业，缔约方有义务实行关税减让。

3.2.2 Prohibition of Quantitative Restriction 一般取消数量限制规则

Contracting parties are required to eliminate quantitative restriction on trade, prohibited to adopt non-tariff barriers especially quota and license. In the fields of agriculture and textiles, there are some exceptions though the quantitative restrictions have been removed after passing the Agreement on Textiles and Clothing to realize the trade liberalization finally.

在非关税方面，要求各缔约方应坚持一般取消数量限制原则，禁止使用非关税壁垒，尤其是以配额和许可证作为主要的数量限制。但是在农产品、纺织品领域还存在不少例外，但已通过《纺织品与服装协议》逐步取消纺织品与服装贸易中的数量限制，最后实现这类商品的贸易自由化。

3.3 Market Access 市场准入原则

It is referred to how much one member permits the other member's goods and services as well as capital to enter into the local market. Market access is an advancing process for the purpose of supplying a favorable commercial environment encouraging trade, investment and employment.

There are so many factors which influence market access.

In goods trade, the details are as follows: 1) The degree and scope of tariff restriction; 2) The implementation of non-tariff barriers, including quantitative restriction, licensing procedures, customs valuation methods and procedures, the rules of technology barriers of trade, regulations on origin, regulations on pre-shipment inspection, implementation of anti-dumping and counter-vailing; 3) transparency of national policies and acts and administrative regulations; 4) the implementation of the national treatment on the imported products etc.

In service trade, market access degree is indicated with the channels and barriers established for the services and service suppliers of other contracting parties. The market access is also the focus of negotiators in the negotiation of international trade. The market access degree is also taken by the contracting parties as the negotiation terms to exchange benefit and keep balance of the whole benefit.

The variety of agreements and accords under WTO are requiring members to realize trade liberalization gradually in phases in order to enhance market access level and promote the reasonable competition and appropriate protection of market.

市场准入原则是指一方成员允许另一方成员的货物、劳务与资本进入本方市场的程度。市场准入原则要求缔约方开放本国（地区）市场。市场准入是一个渐进的过程，其目的是向外国商人提供一个有益于贸易、投资和创造就业的商业环境。

影响市场准入的因素很多。

具体来说，在货物贸易方面，主要有以下因素：（1）关税约束的程度及范围大小；（2）非关税壁垒的实施情况，包括对进口产品实施数量限制的措施，进口许可制程序的繁简，海关估价的方法、手续及程序，实行贸易技术壁垒的规定，原产地规则，装船前检验的规则，反倾销反补贴的实施情况等；（3）国家政策法令、法规、行政命令等透明度的大小；（4）对进口产品实行国民待遇的情况等。

在服务贸易方面，市场准入程度则体现在一缔约方为其他缔约方的服务与服务供应者能够进入其市场提供什么样的渠道，设置哪些障碍。市场准入的程度也是谈判各方关心的热点，在国际贸易谈判中，市场准入的程度也是谈判准入条件，往往被缔约方利用，作为一种交换利益的筹码，以保持其在谈判中总体利益的平衡。

WTO 一系列协定或协议都要求成员分阶段逐步实行贸易自由化，以扩大市场准入水平，促进市场的合理竞争和适度保护。

3.4 Transparency 透明度原则

Transparency means that the members shall promulgate all the trade policies and measures and the change of them, and at the same time notify WTO in time of the implementation and changes of the measures.

Transparency principle is made to prevent members from carrying out the unpublicized trade management which is not in compliance with WTO agreement then leading to trade discrimination and trade barriers.

透明度原则是指成员方应公布所制定和实施的贸易措施及其变化情况，同时还应将这些贸易措施及其变化情况及时通知 WTO。

透明度原则的目的是使成员方的贸易管理具有透明度，防止成员之间进行不公开的、与 WTO 协定不相适应的贸易管理，从而造成贸易歧视和贸易壁垒。

3.5 Fair Competition 公平竞争原则

Whatever member government or enterprise shall avoid the adoption of the measures distorting market competition and correct the unfair trade practices between members in order to create a fairly competitive market environment.

WTO takes the dumping and export subsidy as the unfair trade measures, permitting contracting parties to take measures to set off the damage brought to the import country.

公平竞争原则是指无论是成员方政府还是企业都应避免采取扭曲市场竞争的措施，纠正在各个贸易领域、在成员方之间、本方和其他成员之间的不公平贸易行为，创造公平竞争的市场环境。

WTO 认为倾销和出口补贴是不公平的贸易手段，允许缔约方采取措施来抵消倾销行为和出口补贴对进口国造成的损害。

3.6 Grant Favorable Treatment to Developing Countries and Less-developed Countries 对发展中国家和最不发达国家给予优惠待遇原则

With a view to promoting the economic growth and reform of developing members, the special aid and trade concessions are provided to them. For instance, the developing members may enjoy the GSP system treatment of the developed members; the developing members may take export subsidy to some extent.

In accordance with the concerning regulations, the developed contracting parties cannot expect reciprocal benefit from the obligation they promised to the developing members about the reduction or elimination of tariffs and other barriers in trade.

对发展中成员给予提供特别的援助和贸易减让，以促进其发展和经济改革。比如，发展中成员可享受发达成员提供的普惠制待遇；发展中成员在一定限度内可对其出口实行补贴等。

根据规定，发达缔约方对其在贸易谈判中对发展中缔约方的贸易所承诺的减少或撤除关税和其他壁垒的义务不能希望得到互惠。

4. Primary Characteristics of WTO 世界贸易组织的主要特点

World Trade Organization is established on the basis of GATT, forming a full set of international laws and regulations, with the following characteristics.

世界贸易组织是在关贸总协定的基础上建立的，并形成了一整套较为完备的国际法律规则。它主要具有以下特点。

4.1 WTO is a Formal Organization 组织机构正式

WTO changed the temporary and informal form of GATT. According to the agreement, a full set of institutions have been established coming into being a formal international economic organization with legal status. In law, WTO is the subject of international law taking an status as equal as IMF and World Bank, with the organization and staff enjoying diplomatic privileges and exemptions.

世界贸易组织的成立改变了关贸总协定临时适用和非正式性的状况。根据其协定建立起来的一整套的组织机构成为具有法人地位的正式国际经济组织。从法律地位上看，它与国际货币基金组织、世界银行具有同等地位，都是国际法主体，其组织机构及有关人员均享有外交特权和豁免权。

4.2 WTO Agreement is with Legal Authority 法律权威

The Agreement Establishing World Trade Organization can but come into force under the approval of the legislation institutions of contracting countries getting through the legal procedures after the initial signing of the representatives of contracting parties. In Marrakesh meeting dated on 15th April of 1994, seven members including the USA, and Japan couldn't sign the agreement because of the limitation of domestic legislation procedures, and the Agreement could not come into force until the parliaments of the members approved it.

世界贸易组织协定要求各成员代表在草签后，还须通过立法程序，经本国立法机构批准才能生效。1994 年 4 月 15 日，在马拉喀什会议上包括美国、日本在内的七个国家因国内立法程序的限制不能当场草签。直到 1994 年年底，美国等国家的议会才予以通过和生效，因而使世界贸易组织协定更具完整性和权威性。

4.3 WTO is Covering a Wider Scope 管辖内容广泛

In the GATT system, the accords and agreements are only involved in the trade of goods.

WTO system is covering the goods trade regulations of GATT as well as the rules of service trade, international regulations of intellectual property protection in trade, and international investment regulations in trade. The full set of international rules are relative to various fields including goods trade, service trade, intellectual property protection and investment measures etc.

关贸总协定的多边贸易体制及其所制定的一整套国际贸易规则只涉及货物贸易。

世界贸易组织体制不仅包括关贸总协定已有的货物贸易规则，还包括服务贸易的国际规则、与贸易有关的知识产权保护的国际规则、与贸易有关的国际投资规则，这一整套国际规则涉及货物贸易、服务贸易、知识产权保护和投资措施等领域，表明世界贸易组织所管辖的内容更为广泛。

4.4 WTO Is with an Unifying System 体制统一

The contracting parties under WTO system must sign and participate in the full set of agreements and accords under WTO except for Agreement on Trade in Civil Aircraft, Agreement on Government Procurement, International Dairy Agreement, International Bovine Meat Agreement. The balance between rights and obligations are reached on the basis of all the accords, thus strengthening the unification and restriction of member's rights and obligations, in order to make sure of WTO's being integrated, non-selective and inseparable.

世界贸易组织体制所管理的协议，除政府采购协议、牛肉协议、民用航空器贸易协议、国际奶制品协议等东京回合的四个协议外，成员方必须无选择地以“一揽子”方式签署参加，权利和义务的平衡是在所有协议的基础上达成的，从而加强了成员方权利和义务的统一性和约束性，以确保世界贸易组织体制是完整的、不可选择的、不可分割的统一体。

4.5 WTO Is with a More Perfect System to Settle Disputes 争端解决机制的完善

The Dispute Settlement Body (DSB) of WTO is in charge of the settlement of the disputes between members.

世界贸易组织所实施的综合争端解决机制是一套较为完善的机制。解决争端由世界贸易组织的争端解决机构（Dispute Settlement Body，DSB）负责。

5. China's History of Entering WTO 中国加入 WTO 的历程

China is one of the 23 contracting parties of GATT of 1947.

In July 1986, China made an application to GATT for resuming its status as a GATT contracting party.

In 1995, WTO was established and came into force and China's application for resuming status had come to be applying for the accession to WTO.

In 10th November 2001, in the meeting of the 4th minister conference of WTO which was held in Doha of Qatar, WTO approved by consensus the agreement for China's entry into WTO. On 11th November 2001, the representative of China government signed the protocol on the accession of the People's Republic of China and submitted the WTO approval to WTO secretariat. 30 days later, China became one of the WTO members.

中国是 1947 年 GATT 的 23 个签约国之一。

1986 年 7 月，中国正式向 GATT 提交“复关”申请。

1995 年，WTO 正式成立，中国“复关”演变成“入世”。

2001 年 11 月 10 日，世界贸易组织第四届部长级会议在卡塔尔首都多哈以全体协商一致的方式，审议并通过了中国加入世贸组织的决定。2001 年 11 月 11 日，中国政府代表签署中国加入世贸组织议定书，并向世贸组织秘书处递交中国加入世贸组织批准书。30 天后，即 2001 年 12 月 11 日，中国正式成为 WTO 成员。

Case Study 本章案例

Case: The US Initiate Retaliation Sanction on the Imported Autos from Japan upon "Section 301"

【案例】美国依据“301 条款”对日本汽车进口进行报复的单边性制裁纠纷案

Brief of Case 案由

On 16th May 1995, the United States government made a unilateral declaration to impose 100% duty on the imported luxury cars from Japan in accordance with the Section 301 of Trade Act of 1974.

The US market share of the cars of Japan was one forth whereas American cars occupied only 1.5% in Japan market. In the trade of automobile parts between both sides, the United States had trade deficit of 12.8 billion dollars. In July 1993, Japan agreed to take negotiation to settle the problems of opening automobile market, whereas rejected to go into the substantial negotiation procedures with the United States. Therefore, the US decided to take the measure to require Japan to open its domestic market to auto manufacturers worldwide with the appropriate transparency and competition.

The measure involved the principle problem in world trade: Whether the unilateral retaliation based on "section 301" was consistent with the multilateral negotiation of WTO? In brief, whether it was justifiable for the United States to make decision and take sanction measures without the authorization of WTO?

Owing to the opposition to the unilateral retaliation system of the US, on 25th November,1998, the EU made charge against the US according to WTO regulation, claiming that the EU benefits had been lost or damaged as well as did harm to the target of GATT and WTO due to the "section 301" in unconformity with the rules of WTO.

1995 年 5 月 16 日，美国政府单方面宣布，根据美国 1974 年贸易法 301 节、304 节（即单边报复制度的“301 条款”），对来自日本的豪华轿车征收 100%的关税。

日本车占有美国市场 1/4 的份额，而美国车仅占有日本市场 1.5%的份额。在双方的汽车零部件贸易中，美国则有 128 亿美元的逆差。1993 年 7 月，日本虽然同意通过谈判解决汽车市场的开放问题，但实际上却拒绝与美国进入实质性的谈判程序。因此，美国采用这样的措施，要求日本向世界汽车商开放市场，而且要求日本市场应该具有相应的透明度和竞争性。

这涉及世界贸易中的一个原则问题：美国依据“301 条款”进行报复的单边性与世界贸易组织争端解决制度的多边性是否相容？简言之，美国在世界贸易组织争端解决机构做出决定之前，是否有权单方面做出制裁决定并实施制裁措施？

出于对美国单边报复制度的不满，1998 年 11 月 25 日，欧盟根据 WTO 规定起诉了美国，认为“301 条款”与 WTO 的相应规定不符，造成了欧盟利益丧失或受损，也损害了关税及贸易总协定和世界贸易组织的目标。

Arbitrament 裁决

The final arbitrament of the experts group was that, the United States was not permitted to take unilateral measure before the authorization of WTO, while “section 301” was not in violation of the relative regulation of WTO and GATT. As a result, the arbitrament did not prevent the US from the unilateral adoption of “section 301” to make sanctions and threats to other countries especially the non-WTO members.

专家组最终裁决，美国不可以在世贸组织争端解决机构做出决定之前单方面确定制裁措施，但“301 条款”并不违反世界贸易组织和关税及贸易总协定的有关规定。这一裁决，使得美国事实上仍然可以运用“301 条款”对其他国家实行贸易制裁和威胁，尤其是对非世贸组织成员进行单方的制裁。

Remarks 点评

After China’s entry into WTO, although the trade disputes can be settled under the multilateral framework of WTO, we shall pay attention to the influence of the unilateral sanction like the “section 301” the US brought to us. In this case, we shall take reasonable measures and make claim together with other members to protect our benefits through the multilateral dispute settlement system of WTO.

中国加入世贸组织后，虽然将来面对的贸易争端可以在世界贸易组织的多边框架下获得相应的解决，但也要注意诸如美国实施“301 条款”这样的单边制裁行为对我们的危害。在遇到这样的情况时，应据理力争，联合其他受损者共同提出申诉，根据世界贸易组织解决争端的多边机制维护中国的利益。

（资料来源：http://www.hecom.gov.cn/wtofadian/wen/wtoal/al119.htm）

Questions 思考题

1. What is WTO? What are its characteristics?
   什么是世界贸易组织？它具有哪些特点？
2. What are the basic principles of WTO?
   世界贸易组织有哪些基本原则？
3. What are the advantages and disadvantages of China’s entry into WTO?
   我国加入世界贸易组织有何利弊？

Part Two

Chapter 7

International Trade Terms and Customs
国际贸易术语与国际贸易惯例

Lesson 1 Trade Terms and Customs
国际贸易术语与国际贸易惯例

1. Definitions and Functions of International Trade Terms 国际贸易术语的定义及作用

International commodity prices consist of not only unit price and amount but also related liabilities, costs and risks between the seller and buyer.

国际贸易商品价格构成中，除了要表明每一计量单位的价格、金额外，还要表明买卖双方在货物交接过程中有关责任、费用、风险的划分问题。

1.1 Definitions 定义

Trade terms, also called price terms or price conditions, are abbreviations of letters or words specifying certain liabilities, costs and risks between the seller and the buyer.

It covers two basic elements: 1) trade terms indicate commodity price composition, for instance, whether the seller's quotation includes freight, insurance premium or discharge. FOB excludes freight and insurance premium which are paid by the buyer. while CIF is the opposite with freight and insurance premium included in the goods price, paid by the seller. 2) Trade terms are specified terms concerning place of delivery, risks, obligations and costs during delivery of goods between the seller and the buyer.

国际贸易术语，也称为价格术语、价格条件，它是指用短语或英文缩写来说明商品的价格构成及买卖双方在货物的交接过程中有关的风险、责任和费用划分问题的专门用语。

这一定义包含两层意思。第一层含义：贸易术语说明了商品的价格构成，卖方所报价格是否包含运费、保费，装卸费是离岸价还是到目的港的价格。如用 FOB，不包含运费、保费，称离岸价，运费、保费要由买方出。CIF 则相反，运费、保费都已包含在货价中，由卖方承担。第二层含义：国际贸易术语是买卖双方在货物交接过程中，关于交货地点以及风险、责任、费用如何划分的专门用语。

1.2 Functions 国际贸易术语的作用

Trade terms, which are used as united and specific language for worldwide merchants, take shape gradually in international practice and greatly simplify dealing procedures, improving efficiency and play significant roles in international trade.

国际贸易术语是在长期的国际贸易实践中逐渐发展形成的，作为全世界国际贸易商人的统一专门用语，大大简化了交易程序，提高了交易效率，降低了交易成本，有力地促进了国际贸易的发展，在国际贸易中具有重要的作用。

2. International Trade Customs 有关国际贸易术语的国际贸易惯例

2.1 Definition 国际贸易惯例的概念

International trade customs are universally recognized as customary ways of doing business and explanation evolving in the long process of trade development and have been compiled by relative international organizations into rules and regulations which are acquainted, recognized and adopted by many trading organizations in most countries.

国际贸易惯例是在国际贸易的长期实践中逐步发展、形成的具有普遍意义的一些习惯做法和解释，经过有关国际组织的编纂与解释成为规则、条文，并为较多的国家或贸易团体所熟悉、承认和采用。

2.2 Nature 国际贸易惯例的性质

International trade customs are not compulsory since they are not legislations or laws for all countries, neither legislation nor laws of a certain country.

When both parties cite one international custom, it becomes legally valid and both parties are subject to it.

Even if the contract does not indicate which custom the contract is subject to, the custom still has binding force.

When disputes arise during the contract execution, courts of justice or arbitration agencies usually make rulings according to the customs, thus the customs are influential to some extent. Especially lately, some international conventions and laws endow the customs with legality. China's laws indicating what the laws fail to cover are subject to international trade customs. CISG stipulates that the commonly used and universally known customs which are not excluded from the contract are binding on both parties.

United Nations Convention on Contracts for The International Sale of Goods (1980) [CISG] Article 9:

1) The parties are bound by any usage to which they have agreed and by any practices which they have established between themselves.

2) The parties are considered, unless otherwise agreed, to have impliedly made applicable to their contract or its formation a usage of customs which the parties knew or ought to have known and which in international trade are widely known to, and regularly observed by, parties to contracts of the type involved in the particular trade concerned.

Therefore, it is of great significance to get familiar with the customs and carry out trade practices.

If the contract clauses conflict with customs, the contract is to be followed as a basic principle.

Both parties could make out some clause different from customs when signing a contract on the principle of contract first and contract freedom.

它不是各国的共同立法，也不是某一国的法律，不具有法律的强制性。

当买卖双方在合同中援引某项惯例时，则该惯例即具有法律效力，对双方均有约束力，有法律强制性。

即使合同中未引入某项惯例，惯例也有约束力。

在合同执行中发生争议时，法院判决、仲裁机构仲裁往往以惯例作为准则，因此这些惯例在某种程度上有一定的影响力，目前新的趋势是，某些国际公约或某些国家以立法的形式直接赋予惯例以法律效力。如我国的法律规定，凡中国法律没有规定的，适用国际贸易惯例。《公约》规定，合同没有排除的惯例，已经知道或应当知道的惯例和经常使用反复遵守的惯例对双方当事人均有约束力。

（《联合国国际货物销售合同公约》第 9 条：

（1）双方当事人已同意的任何惯例和他们之间确立的任何习惯做法，对双方当事人均有约束力。

（2）除非另有协议，双方当事人应视为已默示地同意对他们的合同或合同的订立使用双方当事人已知道或理应知道的惯例，而这种惯例在国际贸易上已为有关特定贸易所涉同类合同的当事人所广泛知道并为他们所经常遵守。

因此，熟悉并掌握有关的国际贸易惯例并按照惯例来进行国际贸易业务的操作，具有非常重要的意义。

如果合同的条款与惯例有冲突，将遵循合同优先的原则。

遵循契约至上、契约自由的原则，合同双方当事人在签订合同时也可以做出与惯例不同的规定。

3. Three Main International Rules on Trade Terms 三个主要国际贸易惯例

3.1 Warsaw-Oxford Rules 1932《1932 年华沙—牛津规则》

They are rules for CIF contracts drafted at a conference of the international law association in Warsaw. In the mid-19th century, CIF is widely applied in international trade and however, there are no unified explanations or rules on each party's obligations, misunderstandings and disputes that frequently arise. International law association drafted and adopted rules for CIF contracts in the capital of Poland, Warsaw in 1928. After that, this rule is combined into 21 provisions in Oxford Conference in 1932 and renamed as Warsaw-Oxford rules 1932 used till now.

Warsaw-Oxford Rules states that this rule is not legally binding and is up to both parties' option; once this rule is explicitly adopted, both parties shall be subject to it. In sales contract, the clauses could be different from the rules and each rule could be altered or added according to both parities' agreement. If conflicts arise between the clauses and the rules, refer to the clauses. If the contract contains no relating clauses, refer to the rules.

这是国际法协会制定的，专门用来解释 CIF 这一贸易术语。19 世纪中叶起，CIF 贸易术语在国际贸易中得以广泛应用，由于这一贸易术语中买卖双方各自承担的义务没有统一的规定和解释，因而在交易中经常发生争议和纠纷。国际法协会于 1928 年在波兰首都华沙起草并制定 CIF 统一规则。其后，于 1932 年牛津会议上，将此规则定为 21 条，更名为《1932 年华沙—牛津规则》，沿用至今。

《华沙—牛津规则》在总则中说明，这一规则并无法律约束力，仅供双方自愿使用。凡明示采用本规则的，合同当事人应按照本规则的规定办理。在买卖合同中，经双方当事人协议，也可以做出与该规则不同的规定，也可以对本规则的任何一条进行变更、修改或增添。如本规则与合同发生冲突，以合同为准。但合同中没有规定的事项，应按本规则办理。

3.2 Revised American Foreign Trade Definition 1990《1990 年美国对外贸易定义修订本》

The constitutors are nine trade organizations, including Chamber of Commerce of the United States of America, American Importers Association (AIA) and National Foreign Trade Council, etc.

It includes 6 terms, namely, EX (Point of Origin), FOB (Free on Board), FAS, C&F, CIF and EX DOCK and is used in some North American and Latin American countries.

制定人由美国商会、美国进口商协会、美国对外贸易协会等九个贸易团体组成。

内容包括六种术语：EX 产地交货；FOB 在运输工具上交货；FAS 在运输工具旁边交货；C&F 成本加运费；CIF 成本加保险费、运费；EX DOCK 目的港码头交货。该惯例适用地区：一些北美及拉丁美洲国家。

3.3 Incoterms® 2020《国际贸易术语解释通则 2020》

"International rules for the interpretation of trade terms" is short for Incoterms, are the most widely used, most influential and most important international practices published by ICC and all trade terms in this textbook are subject to it. Incoterms was first created in 1936 by ICC (International Chamber of Commerce) and has been regularly updated to keep pace of the development of the international trade. The latest version, Incoterms® 2020 came into force on 1st January, 2020.

When it was revised in 1990, it mainly contained 13 trade terms. Incoterms® 2010, 11 trade terms were changed, DAF, DES, DEQ and DDU in group D were deleted, and DAT and DAP were added. Incoterms ® 2020, 11 trade terms will remain, DAT of group D will be deleted and DPU will be added. Incoterms ® 2020, the 11 trade terms will be divided into two groups.

One of the main features of the Incoterms® 2020 is that they are available for application to both international and domestic sale contracts. The forming of various trade blocs, like the European Union, has made it a must for the rules to be applicable for both international and domestic trade.

《国际贸易术语解释通则》，简称 Incoterms，是目前使用最广泛、影响最大、最重要的一个国际贸易惯例，本书所提到的贸易术语的解释都以该通则为准。《国际贸易术语解释通则》由国际商会最早发布于 1936 年，后经多次修订，最新的一次修订成果就是 2020 年 1 月 1 日生效的《国际贸易术语解释通则 2020》。

1990 年修订时，主要内容包含 13 个贸易术语。Incoterms® 2010 改为 11 个贸易术语，删去了原来 D 组的 DAF、DES、DEQ 和 DDU，新增加了 DAT 和 DAP。Incoterms ® 2020 仍然保持 11 个贸易术语，删去了原来 D 组的 DAT，新增加了 DPU。Incoterms® 2020 把这 11 个贸易术语分成两组。一组是可以适用于任何运输方式或多种运输方式的术语——EXW、FCA、CPT、CIP、DAP、DPU 与 DDP；另一组为适用于海运及内河水运的术语——FAS、FOB、CFR 与 CIF。

Incoterms® 2020 一个很重要的特点是其中所涉及的国际贸易术语对国际和国内货物买卖合同均可适用。像欧盟这样的区域性贸易组织的出现，使国际贸易术语必须在适用于国际贸易的同时也能适用于国内贸易。

Lesson 2 FOB, CFR and CIF
装运港交货的贸易术语

Among the 11 trade terms, FOB, CFR and CIF are the most commonly used terms, with the longest usage in international trade history. Nowadays, they are used as trade terms for symbolic delivery, which means documents sales replace goods sales, and the seller delivers the documents instead of the goods while the buyer pays according to the documents. Symbolic delivery creates a new epoch of international trade. And symbolic delivery is basic to understanding modern international settlement and credit dealings.

FOB, CFR and CIF are classified into one group as they are alike in characters from the below 6 aspects:

1) They are used for port-to-port waterway transportation;

2) Place of delivery of the seller is on board a ship in the export country;

3) Risks are borne by the seller until the goods are on board the vessel;

4) Symbolic trade terms of symbolic delivery, or, delivery of documents instead of goods dealing is the core of selling and buying;

5) The risks are transferred to the buyer once the seller delivers the goods on board the vessel;

6) Contracts signed under the 3 terms refer to shipment contracts, in other words, the seller is only responsible for punctual shipment and disregards when it arrives.

在国际贸易中，我们使用最多的贸易术语是 FOB、CFR、CIF。这三个贸易术语是国际贸易史上渊源最久远的贸易术语。在现代的国际贸易中，它们已经升华为象征性交货的贸易术语。所谓象征性交货，也就是以单据的买卖代替了货物的买卖，卖方以交单代替了交货，买方凭单付款。象征性交货开创了国际贸易的新纪元。理解什么是象征性交货才能理解现代的国际结算、信用证交易。

我们把 FOB、CFR、CIF 作为一组来论述，是因为这三个贸易术语在性质上是一样的，有着它们共同的规律，可以从以下六个方面来看：

（1）这三个贸易术语都适用于港到港的海洋运输；

（2）卖方的交货地点都是在出口国的装运港船上；

（3）风险的划分都是在出口国装运港以货物装上船为界；

（4）都是象征性交货的贸易术语，也就是说是以单据的买卖为核心，以交单代替了交货；

（5）都是属于装运港交货条件的术语，也就是说卖方只要在装运港把货物装上船就完成了交货义务，风险就转移给了买方；

（6）以这三个贸易术语签订的买卖合同都属于装运合同，也就是卖方只管按时装运，不管何时到达。

1. FOB

Free on Board（named port of shipment）

It shall be followed by the name of port of shipping, like FOB FUZHOU.

中译名：“装运港船上交货”“离岸价”“船上交货”（加注装运港名称）

采用此术语时，后面一定要加注装运港名称，如 FOB FUZHOU。

1.1 Definition 定义

The seller is responsible for shipping the contracted goods on board the ship designated by the buyer at the port of shipment within specific period and bearing all costs and risks before the goods are on board the ship.

The buyer is responsible for the freight and insurance premium from port of shipment to port of destination. The risks of loss of or damage to the goods passes from the seller to the buyer when the goods are on board the ship.

The seller should notify the buyer promptly as the buyer shall cover the risks under FOB terms. If the buyer fails to cover the risks as a result of deferred notice by the seller and once accidents happen, the seller is responsible.

卖方在合同规定的装运港和期限内把合同规定的货物装到买方指定的船上，并负担货物装上船为止的一切费用和风险。

到目的港的运输和投保由买方自行安排，承担运费和保费。风险划分是在货物装上船时，风险即由卖方转移至买方。

装船后卖方应及时通知买方，因为 FOB 贸易术语是由买方自己投保的。如果卖方装船后没有及时通知买方，致使买方没有投保，一旦发生风险或事故，由卖方承担责任事故。

1.2 Obligations 买卖双方义务

1.2.1 The Seller's Obligations 卖方义务

a. Ship the goods on board at port of shipment within due time and notify the buyer promptly.

b. All costs and risks before the goods are loaded on board the ship.

c. Clear export customs and provide related documents and certificates.

d. Provide related shipping documents or EDI electronic information.

- 负责在合同规定的装运港和规定的期限内（日期内），将货物装上买方指定的船只并及时通知买方。
- 负担货物装上船前的一切费用和风险。
- 负责办理出口报关手续，提供出口国政府或有关方面签署的证件。
- 负责提供有关货运单据或 EDI 电子信息。

1.2.2 The Buyer's Obligations 买方义务

a. Book space and pay the freight and notify the seller of sailing date and name of sailing vessel.

b. Bear all costs and risks after the goods are loaded on board the ship.

c. Accept related documents provided by the seller and pay duly according to the contract.

- 负责租船或订舱，支付运费，并将船期、船名及时通知卖方。
- 负责货物装上船后的一切费用和风险。
- 接受卖方提供的有关货运单据，并按合同规定支付货款。

1.3 Some Points for Attention about FOB 关于 FOB 要注意的问题

It is a historic practice before Incoterms® 2020 to regard the rail as the boundary. However, some defects were found in practical application. Moreover, the meaning of it is obscure. "Revised American Foreign Trade Definition 1990" has stipulated that the risk transfers when the goods are on board the ship. Incoterms® 2020 specified that the risk of loss of and damage to the goods passes when the goods are on board the vessel, and the buyer bears all costs from that moment onwards. It could be an engagement that both parties agree to regard boarding ship as the boundary. The concept of "cross the rail" was cancelled thereafter.

以船舷作为风险划分的界限是《2020 通则》以前长期沿用的一种惯例，但是在实际应用中有很多缺陷，不是很确切。《1990 年美国对外贸易定义修订本》是以货物装上船作为风险划分的界限，有它的科学性。Incoterms® 2020 在 FOB 风险划分方面做了重新规定——取消了以船舷为界划分风险的概念，明确规定以货物装上船作为风险划分的界限。

2. CIF

Cost Insurance and Freight (Named Port of Destination)

It shall be followed by the name of port of destination, like CIF London.

CIF is a typical symbolic delivery term and contracts under this term are shipment contracts. As the same with FOB, place of delivery of CIF is port of shipment in export country but not port of destination.

中译名：成本、保费加运费（指定目的港）

这个贸易术语在后面要加注目的港名称，如 CIF London。

CIF 是典型的象征性交货术语，以 CIF 术语签订的买卖合同为装运港交货条件，属于“装运合同”。CIF 贸易术语和 FOB 贸易术语一样，卖方的交货地点是在出口国装运港，并不是在目的港。

2.1 Definition 定义

The seller is responsible for booking space and delivering the goods on board the ship sailing for the destination in due time according to the contract and covering the risks and expenses during carriage. The risks of loss or damage to the goods pass when the goods are on board the ship.

Notably, the boundary for risk transfer is the same for FOB, CIF and CFR.

卖方负责租船订舱，并按照合同规定的装运期或在期限内将合同规定的货物装上运往约定目的港的船上，办理保险手续，负责支付运费和保险费并负担货物在装运港装上船前的一切费用和风险。货物灭失或损坏的风险在货物交到船上时转移。

需要注意的是：FOB、CIF 与 CFR 三个贸易术语风险转移的界限是一样的。

2.2 Obligations 买卖双方义务

2.2.1 The Seller's Obligations 卖方义务

a. Book shipping space and sign shipment contracts from designated port of shipment to destination; load the goods on board the ship in contracted time and port and pay the freight; notify the buyer after shipment promptly.

b. Bear all expenses and risks before the goods are on board the vessel at port of shipment.

c. Cover the insurance and pay insurance premium as the contract stipulates.

d. Clear export customs and bear all relating risks and expenses; get export license or other official permission documents.

e. Provide relating shipping documents, commercial invoices or equivalent eclectic information or e-documents.

- 负责租船订舱，签订从指定装运港承运货物的合同。在合同规定的时间和港口，将合同要求的货物装上船并支付至目的港的运费；装船后须及时通知买方。
- 负担货物在装运港装上船前的一切费用和风险。
- 按照买卖合同的规定，负责办理运输保险，支付保费。
- 负责办理出口报关手续，并自负风险和费用，取得出口许可证或其他官方批准文件，负责办理货物出口所需的一切海关手续。
- 提供有关货运单据、商业发票，或相等的电子信息或电子单据。

2.2.2 The Buyer's Obligations 买方义务

a. All expenses and risks after the goods delivered on board at port of shipment.

b. Accept related documents provided by the seller and take delivery of the goods and pay for them.

c. Clear import customs at port of destination; bear all expenses and risks; get import license or other official permissions.

- 负担货物装上船后的一切费用和风险。
- 接受卖方提供的有关单据，受领货物，并按合同规定支付货款。
- 办理目的港货物进口报关手续；（按通则规定由买方办）自负风险和费用；取得进口许可证或其他官方许可。

2.3 Some Points for Attention about CIF 关于 CIF 要注意的问题

2.3.1 Insurance Coverage 保险险别问题

As explained by Incoterms® 2020, the seller acts for the buyer to cover insurance. If there is no stipulation on the contract, the lowest level of insurance could be covered, and however, a higher level may be covered at the buyer's requirement. Revised American Foreign Trade Definition 1941 states both parties agree to cover WPA or FPA while Warsaw-Oxford rules 1932 states "Insurance shall be covered according to practices of specific industry".

按《2020 通则》解释：卖方还要为买方在运输途中货物的灭失或损坏风险办理保险。买方应注意到，在 CIF 下卖方仅需投保最低险别。如买方需要更多保险保护的话，则需与卖方达成明确协议，或者自行做出额外的保险安排。如买方有要求，由买方付费，可加保较高险别。根据《1990 年美国对外贸易定义修订本》的解释，对于保险险别双方共同明确是投保水渍险或平安险。《1932 年华沙—牛津规则》规定，卖方“应按照特定行业惯例或在规定航线上应投保的一切风险，办理投保手续”。

2.3.2 Symbolic delivery 象征性交货问题

CIF is a typical term for symbolic delivery, in comparison with physical delivery. Symbolic delivery refers to that the seller fulfills obligation on condition that the seller ships the goods on board the ship as the contract stipulates at port of shipment within due time and delivers related entitled documents as stipulated in the contract. The risks are transferred when the goods are on board the ship. The seller is liable for loading the goods in due time and has no guarantee for the arrival of goods. The core of symbolic delivery is the buying and selling of related documents instead of physical goods. In other words, delivering the documents is delivering goods by the seller to the buyer. The seller delivers the goods against documents and the buyer pays for the goods against the documents. As long as the seller provides all sets of qualified documents in due time and even if the goods are damaged or lost during shipment, the buyer shall pay. Reversely, if the seller provides wrong documents and even if the goods are in good shape, the buyer may refuse to pay.

Physical delivery refers to that the seller delivers the goods to the buyer in due time and at due place as agreed in the contract. The seller fulfills obligation on condition that the seller ships the goods on board the vessel as the contract stipulates at port of shipment within due time and has no guarantee for the arrival of goods. The seller delivers the goods against documents and the buyer pays for the goods against the documents.

CIF 贸易术语是一个典型的象征性交货的贸易术语。象征性交货是针对实际交货而言的。它是指卖方只要按照合同规定的时间在装运港把货物装上船并向买方提交了合同规定的代表货物所有权凭证的有关单据，就算完成了交货义务。风险在货物装上船时由卖方转移给买方，卖方只负责按时装运，无须负责保证到货。象征性交货的核心是单据的买卖，双方交易的是单据而不是货物，也就是说卖方只要向买方交单就是向买方交货。卖方是凭单交货，买方是凭单付款。只要卖方如期向买方提交了全套合格单据，即使货物在运输途中损坏或灭失，买方也必须履行付款义务。相反，如果卖方提交的单据不符合要求，即使货物完好无损地到达目的地，买方仍有权拒绝付款。

实际交货是指卖方要在合同规定的时间和地点，将符合合同规定的货物提交给买方或其指定的人，而不能以交单代替交货。按期在约定装运港船上装运，并向买方提交合同规定的包括物权凭证在内的有关单据，就算完成了交货义务，无须保证到货。卖方凭单据交货，买方凭单据付款。

3. CFR

Cost and Freight (Named Port of Destination)

It shall be followed by the name of port of destination, like CFR London.

中译名：成本加运费（指定目的港）

采用此术语后加注目的港，如 CFR London。

3.1 Definition 定义

The seller is responsible for booking space and delivering the goods on board the vessel sailing for the destination in due time according to the contract and covering the risks and expenses during carriage (the risks are transferred when goods are delivered on board).

卖方负责租船订舱，在合同规定的装运港和期限内，将合同规定的货物装上运往指定目的港的船只，支付运费并负担风险（货物在装运港装上船后风险即由卖方转移至买方）。

3.2 Obligations 买卖双方义务

Except that the insurance is covered by the buyer, both parties' obligations are basically the same as that of CIF.

除了保险是由买方自己投保，CFR 买卖双方义务基本上和 CIF 一样。

3.3 Some Points for Attention 注意事项

The seller shall dispatch shipping notice promptly to facilitate the buyer's insurance covering and if the buyer fails to cover insurance and suffers losses as a result of the seller's late notice, the seller is responsible for the loss.

Contracts under CFR belong to shipment contracts.

卖方要及时发出装船通知以便买方办理保险，如卖方未及时发出装船通知，买方因此未办理保险，如造成损失，由卖方承担。

CFR 贸易术语也是装运港交货术语，以该贸易术语签订的买卖合同属于装运合同。

Lesson 3 FCA, CPT and CIP
向承运人交货的贸易术语

The above three trade terms are used when the exporter delivers the goods to the carrier and share the following characters.

1) They are suitable for any means of transport including marine cargo transportation.

2) Place of shipment is in the exporting country.

3) Risk is transferred at port of shipment.

4) Contracts under these terms are shipment contracts.

5) Contracts signed as per these three rules are all shipping contracts.

The nature of these three terms is the same as that of FOB, CFR and CIF. The difference between the two classifications is the mode of transport. FCA, CPT and CIP are applicable to all modes of transportation includes marine cargo transportation.

向承运人交货的贸易术语是 FCA、CPT、CIP。这三种贸易术语都是在出口国货交承运人时使用，在性质上有以下共同点。

（1）都适合于包括海洋运输在内的任何一种运输方式。

（2）卖方交货的地点都是在出口国装运地货交承运人。

（3）风险划分都是以出口国装运地货交承运人。

（4）都是出口国装运地交货条件。

（5）签订的买卖合同都是装运合同。

这三种贸易术语与 FOB、CFR、CIF 在性质上是相近的，只不过适用的运输方式有所不同。FCA、CPT、CIP 适用于包括海洋运输在内的任何一种运输方式。

1. FCA

Free Carrier (Named Place)

FCA is similar to FOB and place of delivery could be any place in the exporting country. Free Carrier refers to the free carriers of the export country.

中译名：货交承运人（指定地点）

FCA 后加注指定地点。

出口国装运地为什么用 place 而不用 port，是因为 FCA 贸易术语不限于码头、船上交货，可以在出口国任何地点交货，但性质上类似于 FOB。

另一个要注意的是货交承运人所指的是在出口国货交承运人，而不是在进口国。

1.1 Definition 定义

The seller delivers the goods, cleared for export, to the carrier nominated by the buyer at the named place and the buyer concludes shipping contract on his own expense and notifies the seller promptly.

买方自费订立从指定地点起运的运输合同，并及时通知卖方。卖方在规定的时间、地点把货物交给买方指定的承运人并办理出口手续后就完成了交货。

1.2 Characteristics 特点

This rule is suitable for all modes of transportation including sea waterway transport.

a. Place of delivery: the exporting country or port where the goods are delivered to the carrier.

b. Risk transfer: the buyer bears all risks and any costs occurring after the goods have been delivered to the carrier.

c. Carrier: any one actually fulfills the obligation of shipment or the shipping agent.

该术语适用于包括海洋运输在内的各种运输方式。

特点：

- 交货地点：出口国内地或港口货交承运人。
- 风险转移：货交承运人时卖方转移至买方。
- 承运人：指两种人，实际履行运输义务的承运人和运输代理人。

1.3 Differences between FCA and FOB FCA 与 FOB 的异同点

1.3.1 Similarities 相同点

1) The buyer is responsible for shipment and covering insurance and the contracted price does not include shipping charges or insurance premium.

2) Port of loading is the place of delivery.

3) Contracts under these two terms are shipment contracts but not arrival contracts.

（1）都由买方负责运输，买方负责保险，在价格构成上都不包含运费和保费。

（2）都属于出口国装运港（地）交货条件。

（3）签订的买卖合同都是装运合同，而不是到达合同。

1.3.2 Differences 不同点

1) FOB is used in port-to-port marine shipment; FCA could be used in all means of transport including marine shipment.

2) Places of delivery for FOB are on board the ship at port of loading; FCA is free carrier to a named place.

3) Risks transfer when the goods are on board the ship for FOB and when the goods are delivered to the carrier for FCA.

4) FOB is a symbolic delivery trade term.

（1）适用的运输方式不同：FOB 只适用于港到港的海洋运输；FCA 适用于包括海洋运输方式在内的一切运输方式。

（2）交货地点不同：FOB 装运港船上交货；FCA 在出口国装运地货交承运人。

（3）风险划分的地点不同：FOB 装运港以装上船为界；FCA 在出口国装运地货交承运人。

（4）FOB 是象征性交货的贸易术语。

2. CPT

Carriage Paid To (Named Place of Destination)

The seller delivers the goods to the carrier nominated by him and the seller shall in addition pay the cost of carriage necessary to bring the goods to the named destination and notify the buyer promptly. The risks are transferred to the buyer when the goods are delivered to the carrier. The place of delivery could be inland in the exporting country, port or railway station. In other words, the seller is obliged to arrange the goods to be transported to the destination, but the place of delivery is still in the exporting country.

中译名：运费付至（指定目的地）

CPT 后加注目的地。

卖方要自负费用订立货物运往目的地指定地点的运输契约，并负责按合同规定的时间将货物交给承运人（在多式联运的情况下，交给第一承运人）处置，即完成交货。交货后及时通知买方。货交承运人处置后风险转移至买方，与 FCA、CPT、CIP 相同。交货地点为出口国的内陆、港口或车站。采用 CPT，卖方要负责安排将货物运到目的地，但卖方交货的地点还是在出口国内。

3. CIP

Carriage Insurance Paid to (Named Place of Destination)
中译名：运费、保险费付至（指定目的地）
CIP 后要加注进口国目的地的名称。

3.1 Definition 定义

The seller contracts for insurance and pays the insurance premium for the carriage of the goods in addition to whatever should be covered and the transfer of risk happens when the seller delivers the goods to the carrier he chooses.

卖方要负责订立运输契约并支付将货物运达指定目的地的运费，还要办理货运保险、支付保险费。卖方在合同规定的装运期内将货物交给承运人，在第一承运人的处置之下即完成交货义务。交货后及时通知买方，风险于交货时转移给买方。

3.2 Comparison of CIF and CIP　CIF 与 CIP 的区别

3.2.1 Similarities 相同点

1) The contract price includes shipping charges and insurance premium and the seller arranges for transportation to port of destination and pays for related shipping charges and insurance premium.

2) Place of delivery is port of shipment in the exporting country.

3) Contracts under both terms are shipment contracts.

（1）二者的价格构成中都包含了通常的运费和保费，卖方都要安排到目的港（地）运输，负责投保，支付有关运费和保费。

（2）二者交货地点都是出口国装运港或装运地，也可称为装运港或装运地交货条件。

（3）两种术语签订的买卖合同均为装运合同。

3.2.2 Differences 不同点

1) CIF is typically used in symbolic delivery.

2) CIF is especially suitable for ocean marine transport; CIP is used in multi-modal transport.

3) Place of deliver for CIF is on board the ship in port of shipment and for CIP is to the carrier in the exporting country.

4) Risks transfer when goods are on board the ship for CIF and for CIP risks transfer when the goods are delivered to the carrier.

5) Insurance under CIF is purely ocean transport insurance; insurance under CIP may not only involve transport insurance but also inland or airway insurance.

（1）CIF 为典型的象征性交货。

（2）适用运输方式不同：CIF 专门适用于海洋运输；CIP 适用于国际多式联运包括各种运输。

（3）交货地点不同：CIF 交货地点为出口国装运港船上；CIP 为出口国装运地（包括装运港）货交承运人。

（4）风险划分不同：CIF 以装运港货物装上船为界；CIP 出口国货交承运人。

（5）二者的保险不一样：CIF 单纯为海洋运输保险；CIP 可能牵涉陆运或航空险，如果用海洋运输还包括海运险。

Lesson 4 EXW and FAS
出口国交货的贸易术语

1. EXW

EX Works (named place)

This term imposes on the seller the minimum obligations, costs and risks. It is frequently used in coastal areas in mainland, Hong Kong and Macao.

Incoterms® 2020 stipulates: The seller delivers when he places the goods at the disposal of the buyer at the seller's premises or at another named place (i.e. works, factory, warehouse, etc.). The seller does not need to load the goods on any collecting vehicles, nor does he need to clear the goods for export, where such clearance is applicable.

Thus the buyer has to bear all costs and risks, and handle all necessary procedures from the moment he agrees to accept the goods or to take delivery of the goods. This term imposes on the seller the minimum obligations, costs and risks.

中译名：工厂交货（指定地点）

EXW 后加注指定地点。

这一术语是 11 个贸易术语中卖方义务最小的一个，在我国沿海开放地区和靠近港澳的地区经常使用这一术语。

《2020 通则》规定，卖方在其所在地或其他指定的地点（如工场、工厂或仓库等）将货物交给买方处置时即完成交货，卖方不办理出口清关手续，亦不将货物装上任何前来接收货物的运输工具。

需要注意的是，买方应承担自卖方所在地将货物运至预期目的地的全部费用和风险。因此，工厂交货是卖方承担责任、费用和风险最小的一种贸易术语。

2. FAS

Free Alongside Ship (named place of shipment)

中译名：装运港船边交货（指定装运港）

FAS 后加注指定装运港。

2.1 Definition 定义

The seller places the goods alongside the ship nominated by the buyer at the named port of shipment to fulfill his delivery obligation under this term.

卖方将货物运到指定的装运港码头船边，即船舶吊钩所及之处，以履行其交货义务。

2.2 Allocation of Risks and Costs 风险与费用划分

The seller bears all costs (including shipping charges, charges for transshipment and losses or damages of the goods) and risks of transporting the goods alongside the ship. When the goods are alongside the ship, costs and risks are transferred to the buyer.

货物运至装运港船边前的一切费用和风险（包括驳船费用和改运过程中发生的货物风险和损失）由卖方负责。当货物交到船边后，费用和风险转移给买方。

Lesson 5 DAP, DPU and DDP 目的地交货的贸易术语

There are 3 terms in D group, namely DAP, DPU and DDP.

D 组贸易术语共三个，即 DAP、DPU 和 DDP。

The common points of the above 3 terms：

a. The seller shall deliver the goods to the buyer in the importing country.

b. They are used in physical delivery.

c. Risks are transferred when the buyer takes hold of the goods in the importing country.

d. Contracts under the terms are arrival contracts.

e. The seller shall bear shipping charges and insurance premiums which are both included in the contract price.

这三个贸易术语的共同点是：

- 三个贸易术语都是在进口国目的地交货的贸易术语，卖方都是要把货物运到进口国并实际交到买方手上。
- 相对于象征性交货，这三个贸易术语都是实际交货。
- 这三个贸易术语风险都是在进口国货物处于买方处置之下时转移。
- 以这三个贸易术语签订的买卖合同都是到达合同。
- 这三个贸易术语下的运输和保险都由卖方来承担，在价格构成中都包含了运费和保费。

1. DAP

Delivered at Place（Named Place of Destination）

This rule may be used irrespective of the mode of transport selected and may also be used where more than one mode of transport is employed.

"Delivered at Place" means the seller must sign a transportation contract or arrange the transportation of the goods, deliver the goods to the designated destination within the agreed date or time limit, and deliver the goods to the buyer from the time when the goods placed on the means of transportation at the destination are disposed of by the buyer. At this time, the seller only needs to be ready for unloading and does not need to be responsible for unloading.

中译名：目的地交货（指定目的地）

该术语可适用于任何运输方式，也可适用于多种运输方式。

"目的地交货（……指定目的地）"是指卖方必须签订运输合同或安排货物运输，在约定日期或期限内将货物运至指定目的地，在将置于目的地运输工具上的货物交给买方处置时起即完成交货，此时卖方只需做好卸货准备而无须负责卸货。

2. DPU

Delivered at Place Unloaded (Named Place of Destination)

This rule may be used irrespective of the mode of transport selected and may also be used where more than one mode of transport is employed.

Delivered at Place Unloaded (...Named Place of Destination) means that the seller must sign a transportation contract or arrange the transportation of the goods, and deliver the goods to the designated destination within the agreed date or time limit, and then deliver them to the buyer for disposal. The Seller shall bear all risks and expenses after unloading the goods at the designated destination and before handing them over to the buyer for disposal. The difference between DPU and DAP lies in the unloading fee. The former is borne by the buyer, while the latter is borne by the seller.

中译名：目的地卸货后交货（指定目的地）。

该术语可适用于任何运输方式，也可适用于多种运输方式。

"目的地卸货后交货（指定目的地）"是指卖方必须签订运输合同或安排货物运输，在约定的日期或期限内将货物运至指定目的地卸货后交给买方处置即完成交货。卖方承担在指定目的地卸货后交给买方处置之前的一切风险和费用。DPU 与 DAP 的区别在于卸货费，前者的卸货费由买方负担，后者的卸货费由卖方承担。

3. DDP

Delivered Duty Paid (named place of destination)

This rule may be used irrespective of the mode of transport selected and may also be used where more than one mode of transport is employed.

"Delivered Duty Paid" means that the seller delivers the goods when the goods are placed at the disposal of the buyer, cleared for import on the arriving means of transport ready for unloading at the named place of destination. The seller bears all the costs and risks involved in bringing the goods to the place of destination and has an obligation to clear the goods not only for export but also for import, to pay any duty for both export and import and to carry out all customs formalities.

DDP represents the maximum obligation for the seller.

中译名：完税后交货（指定目的地）

DDP 后加注指定目的地

该术语可适用于任何运输方式，也可适用于多种运输方式。

"完税后交货"是指当卖方在指定目的地将仍处于抵达的运输工具上、但已完成进口清关且可供卸载的货物交由买方处置时，即为交货。卖方承担将货物运至目的地的一切风险和费用，并且有义务完成货物出口和进口清关，支付所有出口和进口的关税和办理所有海关手续。

DDP 术语代表卖方的最大责任。

Case Study 本章案例

Case: An exporter in Beijing contracts an English customer to export a lot of goods. After negotiating the price, the exporter insists on "FCA Beijing" while the English customer insists on "FOB Tianjin". Please explain the reasons.

【案例】北京某外贸公司与英商商订出口一批货物。在价格商谈好后，北京公司坚持用"FCA 北京"贸易术语，英商坚持用"FOB 天津"贸易术语，试分析原因。

Case Analysis: 1) The seller insists on "FCA Beijing" as he fulfills obligation once he delivers the goods to the carrier in Beijing and risks are transferred to the buyer. However, if "FOB Tianjin" is adopted, the seller has to bear shipping charges and risks from Beijing to Tianjin. 2) The seller shall get documents for negotiation after he delivers the goods to the carrier under "FCA Beijing". However, the seller shall load the goods on board the ship to get documents for negotiation under "FOB Tianjin".

In conclusion, the exporter insists on "FCA Beijing" while the English customer insists on "FOB Tianjin".

【案例分析】（1）卖方坚持用"FCA 北京"，卖方在北京货交承运人，卖方的交货义务就算完成，风险也就转移给了买方。如果采用"FOB 天津"，卖方还要多承担北京到天津的运输和风险。（2）采用"FCA 北京"，卖方货交承运人后，即可取得单据，交单议付。而采用"FOB 天津"，卖方要到天津装船后才能取得单据并议付货款。所以，买方坚持要用"FOB 天津"，卖方坚持用"FCA 北京"。

Questions 思考题

1. What are trade terms? What are international trade conventions?
   什么是贸易术语？什么是国际贸易惯例？
2. What are the similarities and differences among FOB, CFR and CIF?
   FOB、CFR、CIF 的共同点和不同点是什么？
3. What are the differences between FOB and FCA?
   FOB 与 FCA 的区别是什么？
4. What are the differences between CIP and CIF?
   CIP 与 CIF 的区别是什么？
5. What are the differences between DAP and DPU?
   DAP 与 DPU 的区别是什么？
6. What is symbolic delivery?
   什么是象征性交货？
7. What are the characteristics of F group of trade terms?
   F 组贸易术语有哪些特点？
8. What are the characteristics of C group of trade terms?
   C 组贸易术语有哪些特点？

Appendix: Incoterms® 2020 Rules

First Group

Trade Term	Full Name	Chinese Name	Place of Delivery	Risks Transfer	Foreign Freight	Insurance Premium	Export Duty	Import Duty	Means of Transport
EXW	Ex Works	工厂交货	Works of exporting countries	Works of exporting country deliver goods to buyer	Buyer	Buyer	Buyer	Buyer	All modes
FCA	Free Carrier	货交承运人	Free carrier…named place	Delivered to the carrier	Buyer	Buyer	Seller	Buyer	All modes
CPT	Carriage Paid To	运费付至	To the carrier in export country	To the carrier	Seller	Buyer	Seller	Buyer	All modes
CIP	Carriage and Insurance Paid To	运费，保险费付至	To the carrier in export country	To the carrier	Seller	Seller	Seller	Buyer	All modes
DAP	Delivered At Place	目的地交货	To deliver at place of destination	Delivered to buyer at place of destination	Seller	Seller	Seller	Buyer	All modes
DPU	Delivered at Place Unloaded	目的地卸货后交货	Specify destination approximate point	After unloading at the designated destination and handing over the goods to the buyer for disposal	Seller	Seller	Seller	Buyer	All modes
DDP	Delivered Duty Paid	完税后交货	To deliver at named place of destination	Delivered to buyer at named place of destination	Seller	Seller	Seller	Seller	All modes

Second Group

Trade Term	Full Name	Chinese Name	Place of Delivery	Risks Transfer	Foreign Freight	Insurance Premium	Export Duty	Import Duty	Means of Transport
FAS	Free Alongside Ship	装运港船边交货	Alongside ship at the port of shipment	Alongside ship at the port of shipment	Buyer	Buyer	Seller	Buyer	Sea and inland waterway
FOB	Free on Board	装运港船上交货	On board at the port of shipment	On board at the port of shipment	Buyer	Buyer	Seller	Buyer	Sea and inland waterway
CFR	Cost and Freight	成本加运费	On board at the port of shipment	On board at the port of shipment	Seller	Buyer	Seller	Buyer	Sea and inland waterway
CIF	Cost, Insurance and Freight	成本加保险费，运费	On board at the port of shipment	On board at the port of shipment	Seller	Buyer	Seller	Buyer	Sea and inland waterway

附：《2020通则》国际贸易术语一览表

第一组

贸易术语	全称	中译名	交货地点	风险转移	运费	保险费	出口报关	进口报关	运输方式
EXW	Ex Works	工厂交货	出口国工厂	出口国工厂货交买方	买方	买方	买方	买方	任何方式
FCA	Free Carrier	货交承运人	出口国内地（港口）货交承运人	出口国货交承运人	买方	买方	卖方	买方	任何方式
CPT	Carriage Paid To	运费付至	出口国内地（港口）货交承运人	出口国货交承运人	卖方	买方	卖方	买方	任何方式
CIP	Carriage and Insurance Paid To	运费，保险费付至	出口国内地（港口）货交承运人	出口国货交承运人	卖方	卖方	卖方	买方	任何方式
DAP	Delivered At Place	目的地交货	指定目的地约定点	指定目的地尚未卸货交买方处置货物后	卖方	卖方	卖方	买方	任何方式
DPU	Delivered at Place Unloaded	目的地卸货后交货	指定目的地约定点	指定目的地卸货交买方处置货物后	卖方	卖方	卖方	买方	任何方式
DDP	Delivered Duty Paid	完税后交货	进口国内地	买方在指定地点收货后	卖方	卖方	卖方	卖方	任何方式

第二组

贸易术语	全称	中译名	交货地点	风险转移	运费	保险费	出口报关	进口报关	运输方式
FAS	Free Alongside Ship	装运港船边交货	装运港船边	装运港货交船边	买方	买方	卖方	买方	海洋运输
FOB	Free on Board	装运港船上交货	装运港船上	以货物装上船为界	买方	买方	卖方	买方	海洋运输
CFR	Cost and Freight	成本加运费	装运港船上	以货物装上船为界	卖方	买方	卖方	买方	海洋运输
CIF	Cost, Insurance and Freight	成本加保险费，运费	装运港船上	以货物装上船为界	卖方	买方	卖方	买方	海洋运输

Chapter 8

Quality, Quantity and Packaging of Commodity

商品的品质、数量和包装

In the trade practice, the quality, quantity, packaging, price, delivery and payment terms are the subject terms of the contract. An international trade sales contract is dealing with the transfer of ownership of the subject matter. There are thousands of types of the subject matters. A transaction is firstly described by the name, quantity and quality (including packaging) of the subject matter, and these terms and conditions must be explicitly stipulated during the business negotiation.

外贸实践中，合同中货物的品质、数量、包装、价格、交货和支付条件为主要交易条件。国际贸易的买卖合同是转移标的物所有权的合同，商品种类达上千种，一项交易首先表现为交易标的物的品名、一定的数量和质量（包括包装），在交易磋商时要先对这些条件做出明确具体的规定。

Lesson 1 Quality of Commodity

商品的品质

When signing an international sales contract, the description of commodity is the first term to be stipulated concerning the quality of commodity.

在签订国际贸易的买卖合同时，有关商品的描述，首先要列明的是商品名称（品名）。

1. Description of Commodity and Its Significance 商品的名称及其意义

1.1 Significance of Stipulating the Description of Commodity 列明品名的意义

In international trade, symbolic delivery is adopted, so buyers and sellers may not necessarily meet in the transaction. The description of commodity is actually a legal definition of the subject matter in the transaction. Therefore, the description of commodity must be first specified when both parties sign the contract.

According to the precedents over the years, terms of quality, quantity and the delivery time are defined as the terms and conditions in Anglo-American Contract Law. The consequence of breach of the conditions would be very serious. However, the description of commodity is included in terms of quality, which is part of the quality clause. It is the description of goods and an important component of trade description and is a fundamental basis for the buyers and sellers to deliver and receive goods, which also relates to the rights and obligations of both parties.

In accordance with the Anglo-American Contract Law, breach of contract is divided into breach of conditions and breach of warranty, which have different legal consequences. The consequence of breach of the former is particularly serious. As to breach of conditions, the non-breaching party (the buyer) has the right to cancel the contract, return and reject the goods, and claim damages. While breach of warranty is different, the buyer can't require the cancellation of the contract and reject the goods, but can only claim damages.

在国际贸易中，采用象征性交货方式时，买卖双方并不一定见面。在合同中，列明品名实际上是对交易的标的物的性质进行法律上的界定。所以，买卖双方商订合同时必须首先列明商品名称。

根据历年的判例，英美法把合同中的品质条款、数量条款、交货期作为条件条款。如违反条款，后果将十分严重。而品名是包括在品质条款中的，是品质条款的一部分。品名涉及对商品的描述，是构成商品说明的一个重要组成部分，是买卖双方交接货物的一项基本依据，还关系到买卖双方的权利和义务。

按照英美法，违约分为违反条件与违反担保两种，二者的法律后果不同。前者的违约后果特别严重。违反条件，守约方（买方）有权撤销合同、退货、拒收货物，同时要求损害赔偿。而违反担保则不同，买方不能要求撤销合同、拒收货物，只能要求损害赔偿。

1.2 Points for Attention in Stipulating Description of Commodity Clause 规定品名条款的注意事项

In the description of commodity clause of the sales contract, the stipulation of the commodity must be precise and specific. As the basis of buyers and sellers' delivery, it relates to the definition of the properties of the subject matter.

Make a realistic stipulation based on the goods, avoid exaggeration about the commodity.

Adopt international common terms as practical as possible.

Pay attention to the appropriate choice of commodity name. If the stipulation of the description has little influence on the properties of the subject matter, we should choose and utilize appropriate commodity names in terms of lowering costs and reducing tariffs.

在商订买卖合同的品名条款时，对品名的规定必须明确、具体。这关系到标的物性质的界定，可作为买卖双方交货的依据。

针对实际做出实事求是的规定，对商品的品名不要夸大宣传。

尽可能使用国际通用名称。

注意选用合适的品名。如果对于品名的规定对标的物的性质没有太大的影响，那么注意选择和利用可以降低成本、适用于较低关税的商品名称。

2. Quality of Goods 商品的品质

2.1 Definition of Quality of Goods 品质的定义

The quality of goods is the integration of the intrinsic attributes and the outer forms or shapes of goods. The former includes the physical, mechanical, biological and natural properties and chemical compositions of goods, while the later includes shape, color, transparency, or style of the goods.

商品品质指商品的内在本质和外观形态的综合。前者包括商品的物理性能、机械性能、化学成分和生物的特性与自然属性，后者包括商品的外形、色泽、透明度或款式。

2.2 Significance of Quality of Goods 品质的重要性

Quality of goods not only refers to the value of use and the value of the commodity, but also affects the market price and marketability of the commodity, involving the relevant corporate and even a country's reputation.

To change the old pattern of dumping, our export strategy should win success through quality, and improve product quality so as to enhance export competitiveness and expand market.

货物品质优劣不仅关系到商品的使用价值和价值，还影响商品的市场价格和商品的销路，涉及有关企业甚至国家的声誉。

我们的出口战略要改变过去的低价倾销的格局，必须以质取胜，提高商品的质量，这样才能增强出口竞争能力，扩大销路。

2.3 Quality Requirements 对品质的要求

The quality of goods relates to the vital interests of the buyers and sellers, and the stipulation of quality is also an important clause in a sales contract. How do we define commodity quality?

商品的品质关系到买卖双方的切身利益，在买卖合同中对品质的规定也是合同的要件条款。那么，我们如何来界定商品的质量？

ISO 9000 standard is the quality standard of manufacturing enterprises established by International Organization for Standardization in 1987. With the certificate of ISO 9000, export products will obtain permits to enter international market.

The release of ISO 9000 series of standards has unified the concepts, principles, methods and procedures of quality management and quality certification to an international standard, marking a new height of quality management and quality certification. Since ISO 9000 series of standards were issued, they have been adopted by 60 countries and regions, including China, as the national standards and regarded as the technical basis of mutual recognition and confirming quality assurance capacity in international economic and technological cooperation.

ISO 9000 标准是国际标准化组织在 1987 年制定的产品生产企业的质量标准。出口产品如果能得到 ISO 9000 的质量认定，就取得了进入国际市场的通行证。

ISO 9000 系列标准的发布，使主要发达国家的质量管理和质量认证概念原则、方法和程序统一在国际标准的基础上，它标志着质量管理和质量保证走向规范化、程序化的新高度。自发布以来，已有包括我国在内的 60 个国家和地区采纳为国家标准，并在国际经济技术合作中被视作相互认可的技术基础和确认质量保证能力的依据。

3. Methods of Stipulating Quality of Goods 表示品质的方法

Commodities traded in international trade have various types and characteristics, so are the methods of stipulating quality of goods. Generally, there are two ways to indicate quality of goods either by description or by actual commodity.

在国际贸易中所交易的商品，种类繁多，特点各异。所以，表示品质的方法也多种多样。但归纳起来，一般可分为凭实物表示和凭文字说明表示两大类。

3.1 Sale by Actual Commodity 凭实物表示品质

3.1.1 Sale by Inspection 看货买卖

Trading under this term, the buyer inspects the goods on the spot, for instance, various trade fairs, transaction and consignment of bulk agricultural products and heavy machinery, auction, exhibition, etc.

买方到现场实际看货并成交，如各种展销会以及大宗农副产品、大型机器设备的交易和寄售、拍卖、展卖等贸易方式都属于看货买卖。

3.1.2 Sale by Sample 凭样品买卖

1）Concept 概念

The transaction that is concluded on the basis of the sample representing the quality of the whole lot can be called sale by sample.

In international trade, most of the transactions adopt sale by sample. The sample refers to the article which can be used to represent the quality of the whole lot. The so-called sample is a small quantity of a product, often taken out from a whole lot or specially designed and processed by the production or user department.

凡以样品表示商品的品质并以此作为交货依据的就叫凭样品买卖。

国际贸易中大多数的交易采用凭样品买卖。所谓样品就是指从一批商品中抽出来的，或由生产、使用部门设计、加工出来的，足以反映和代表整批商品品质的少量实物。

2）Two Basic Requirements for Sale by Sample 凭样品买卖的两个基本要求

The sample is the only legal basis of confirming whether the whole consignment is in conformity with the contract.

The seller must deliver goods in conformity with the sample. This is an implied warranty of the seller. Though not expressed clearly in the contract, the seller must do as this.

样品是作为交货品质的唯一依据。交货时大货品质是否与样品一致关系交货是否符合合同的规定，所以样品是一种法律依据。

卖方所交货物必须与样品一致，这是卖方的一项默示担保。合同无须明示，但是卖方必须做到。

3）Types 种类

① Sale by Seller's Sample 凭卖方样品买卖

Sample provided by the seller is seller's sample. When a sale is made based on the sample provided by the seller, it's called a sale by seller's sample.

由卖方提供的样品称为“卖方样品”，凡凭卖方样品作为交货的品质依据者，称为“凭卖方样品买卖”。

② Sale by Buyer's Sample 凭买方样品买卖

Sample provided by the buyer is buyer's sample. When a sale is made based on the sample provided by the seller, it's called a sale by seller's sample.

From the standpoint of the seller, generally the seller would like to adopt sale by seller's sample rather than sale by buyer's sample in order to avoid risks.

以买方样品作为交货的品质依据的，称为“凭买方样品买卖”。

以卖方立场说，卖方为避免风险，一般不采用“凭买方样品买卖”而是尽量采用“凭卖方样品买卖”。

③ Counter Sample (Return Sample or Confirming Sample) 对等样品，也称回样，确认样

A counter sample is a duplicate made by the seller according to the sample provided by the buyer. After the confirmation of the buyer, the sample will serve as the basis of the transaction and delivery. A counter sample is also called a return sample.

Actually, counter sample is a transfer from sale by buyer's sample to sale by seller's sample.

When a transaction is made based on the sample, the seller should keep one or more equivalent samples for file, which are called duplicate samples.

In addition, there are reference samples, pattern samples (shipping samples), etc.

卖方根据买方提供的样品，加工自制一个类似的样品交买方确认。在买方确认后，这一样品就作为成交和交货的依据，我们称为对等样品，也叫回样。

对等样品实际上是把凭买方样品买卖转化为凭卖方样品买卖。

复样：一个样品做成一式多份。

此外，还有参考样和船头版/装船样品等。

4）Points for Attention in Sale by Sample 凭样品买卖应注意的事项

① The quality of sample should be neither too high nor too low in comparison with the whole consignment. It should represent the average quality of the whole lot. Otherwise, high quality will add difficulties to a seller in terms of production and delivery and increase costs. If too low, the seller will suffer losses in price and also it may affect the deal.

样品质量与大货相比不能太高也不能太低，应该代表整批货的平均水平。否则，样品质量高于大货，之后交货、生产会有困难，还会增加成本。样品质量太低，价格上吃亏，影响成交。

② When a sale is based on sale by sample, the quality of delivery from the seller must be in strict accordance with the sample. The buyer has reasonable opportunity to make comparison with the sample and the delivery. There should not be any flaws leading to sale-failure of the delivery; otherwise the buyer is entitled to reject the goods or claim for compensation.

凭样品买卖，卖方交货品质必须与样品完全一致。买方应有合理机会对卖方交付的货物与样品进行比较，卖方所交货物不存在在合理检查时不易发现的会导致不适合商品销售的瑕疵，否则买方有权拒收，或提出赔偿。

③ Not all the commodities can be transacted using sale by sample. It's inadvisable to adopt sale by sample when it is difficult to keep the goods in strict accordance with the sample, such as bulk agricultural products, mining products, some of the crafts, etc. When the quality of goods can be described by the scientific indicators, sale by sample is not suitable.

并不是所有的商品都可以采用凭样品买卖。凡大货不易做到与样品完全一致的，不宜采用凭样品买卖，如大宗农副产品、工矿产品、某些工艺品等。凡能用科学的指标表示商品品质的，不宜采用凭样品买卖。

④ One method is better than more to stipulate the quality of goods.

可以用一种方法表示商品的品质就不要用两种。

⑤ When the seller sends out the sample, it is better that the seller will keep the duplicate sample and hand it to an independent third party, such as surveyor, commodity inspection department to be sealed for further check in case of dispute.

寄样时要留有复样，交由独立的第三方如公证行、商检部门封存，以便日后备查。一旦发生纠纷，则以第三方手中的样品作为法律依据。

⑥ If the buyer insists on sale by sample or can only provide buyer's sample, the seller can adopt sale by counter sample to transfer from sale by buyer's sample to sale by seller's sample, so as to avoid risks.

当买方坚持用买方样品，或仅能提供买方样品，卖方可采用对等样品的方法，将凭买方样品的买卖转化为凭卖方样品的买卖，以避免风险。

⑦ The absolute stipulation like "the whole consignment must be in complete accordance with the sample" should be avoided, allowing for some flexibility.

签合同时，尽量避免用样品与大货"完全一致"的绝对说法，要留有余地。

⑧ In order to avoid future disputes, a reference sample should carry the mark clearly showing "For Reference Only". It is not considered as the basis of delivery.

如是参考样品，在寄样时则要明确表明是参考样品，不作为交货的依据，以免日后发生纠纷。

3.2 Sale by Description 凭文字说明表示品质

3.2.1 Sale by Specification 凭规格的买卖

The specification of the goods refers to certain main indicators which are sufficient to reflect the quality of the goods, such as chemical composition, content, purity, length, etc.

When buyers and sellers use the specification to determine the quality of goods, it is called sale by specification.

商品的规格是指一些足以反映商品品质的主要指标——化学成分、含量、纯度、长度等。

凡买卖双方用商品的规格来确定品质的，即称为凭规格的买卖。

3.2.2 Sale by Grade 凭等级的买卖

The grade of goods refers to the classification of commodities of the same kind. The commodities are graded as low or high quality by differences in specification. Since different grades of goods embody different specifications, when stipulating the grades of goods in quality clause, the specific specifications of each grade should also be stipulated.

When the grade is used to determine the quality of goods, the sale is called sale by grade.

商品的等级是指同一类商品，按其规格上的差异，分为品质优劣各不相同的若干等级。由于不同等级商品具有不同规格，品质条款在列明等级的同时，应一并规定每一等级的具体规格。

以等级来确定商品的品质，称为凭等级买卖。

3.2.3 Sale by Standard 凭标准的买卖

Goods standard is the standardization of the specification and grade.

Standards are formulated either by government authorities or by the trade associations, exchanges or commercial organizations. Some commodities are used to sale by standards.

商品的标准是指将商品的规格和等级予以标准化。

商品的标准有的由国家或政府主管部门规定，有的由同业公会、交易所或工商组织规定。有些商品习惯于凭标准买卖。

3.2.4 Sale by Specifications and Illustrations 凭说明书和图样的买卖

In case of sale by specifications and illustrations, the delivery must be in conformity with all the indicators stipulated in the illustrations. Some machines, electric equipment and instrumentation technology products have complicated structures. These commodities are described by the specifications accompanied by pictures, design drawings, analytic tables and various data, so as to indicate their specific properties and structural features.

凭说明书和图样买卖时，要求所交的货物必须符合说明书规定的各项指标。某些机器、电器和仪表技术产品结构复杂，通常是以说明书并附以图样照片、设计图纸、分析表及各种数据来说明其具体性能和结构特点，此类方式成交称为凭说明书和图纸的买卖。

3.2.5 Sale by Brand Name or Trade Mark 凭品牌或商标的买卖

Trade mark is a mark used by the producers or merchants to identify the commodity they produce or sell. It is composed of one or a few distinctive words, letters, numbers, graphics or pictures.

Brand name is the particular name of business enterprise and the product they produce and sell to differentiate the product from other competitor offerings.

The quality of goods is the physical basis of the trade mark and brand name. Some well-known trademarks or brand names (a symbol of quality for itself) represent the quality of the commodities. When we use the trade mark and brand name to indicate the quality of goods, it's called sale by brand name or trade mark. That is to say, people transact only on the basis of trade mark or brand, without detailed requirements for quality.

商标是指生产者或商家用来识别其所生产或出售的商品的标志，可由一个或几个具有特色的单词、字母、数字、图形、图片组成。

品牌是指工商企业及其制造或销售的商品名称，以便与其他企业的同类产品区别开来。

商品的品质是商标或品牌的物质基础。某些著名的商标或品牌（本身是一种品质象征）代表、象征某一商品的品质。我们以商标或品牌来表示商品的品质就称为凭商标或品牌的买卖。也就是说，人们在交易中只凭商标或品牌进行买卖，不需对品质提出详细要求。

3.2.6 Sale by Product Origin 凭产地名称的买卖

Owing to some special factors like natural conditions and traditional production techniques in certain areas, the native products are renowned for their unique specialty in quality. So we can take the origin of the goods as characteristic of the commodity when stipulating the quality of goods such as Beijing Roast Duck, Zhangzhou Narcissus, Zhangzhou Mandarin Orange, Kweichow Moutai Liquor, etc.

某些商品由于产地的自然条件等特殊因素和产地的传统工艺，具有与众不同的特殊品质。那么，我们在规定产品的品质时，就以商品的产地作为商品品质的特点，如北京烤鸭、漳州水仙花、漳州芦柑和贵州茅台酒等。

4. Points for Attention When Signing Commodity Quality Clause 签订品质条款的注意事项

Because quality clause is one of the essential terms and conditions in a contract, a breach of contract by the seller will lead to a very serious consequence. In order to facilitate the seller's performance of the contract, certain tolerance is allowed in commodity quality. In the quality clause concerning agricultural byproducts, quality latitude is stipulated, and as to manufactured goods, the concept of quality tolerance is applied.

因为品质条款是合同的要件条款，如果卖方违约，将产生十分严重的后果。为了便于卖方履约，要给予其在品质掌握上一定的宽容度。我们在品质条款中对于农副产品规定了品质机动幅度，对于工业制成品我们采用品质公差的概念。

4.1 Quality Tolerance 品质公差

Errors are inevitable in the process of producing industrial products. Some are due to the limit of technological level and production level. These errors are allowed by the same industry. This is quality tolerance given to the seller's delivery. Within the range of tolerance, seller's delivery of goods are qualified; the buyer shall neither reject the goods nor require adjustment to the price.

对于工业制成品，在生产制作的过程中产生一定的误差是不可避免的。有些误差是因为科技水平、生产水平所限，是同行业公认允许的误差，这是给卖方的交货品质的宽容度。只要在品质公差范围内，卖方的交货都是合法的，买方不得拒绝接受，也不得要求调整价格。

4.1.1 Definition 定义

Quality tolerance is the tolerance that is recognized internationally such as manufactured goods like watch which is allowed a quality tolerance within 60 seconds per day.

品质公差是国际上公认的产品品质的允许误差，工业制成品，如手表，允许每天快慢误差在 60 秒内。

4.1.2 Points for Attention 注意事项

The buyer should not require returning goods and compensation within the range of quality tolerance.

Within the range of quality tolerance, price adjustment is not allowed.

The quality tolerance is used in terms of industrial manufactured goods.

在品质公差范围内，买方不得要求退货和赔偿。

在品质公差范围内，不得调整价格。

品质公差是针对工业制成品而言的。

4.2 Quality Latitude—In Terms of Bulk Agricultural Byproducts, Metals and Minerals 品质机动幅度——针对大宗农副产品、五金矿产品

A certain deviation is allowed in the quality clause to allow some flexibility in the quality indicators within a certain range.

对品质的规定，允许有一定差异，允许卖方所交货物的品质指标具有一定的灵活度。

4.2.1 Method of Stipulating Quality Latitude 规定品质机动幅度的方法

To stipulate a certain scope, e.g. cotton cloth 35–36 inches wide.

To stipulate “max” or “min”, e.g. soybean moisture: 14% max; starch: 18% min.

To stipulate more or less allowance, e.g. down content of down garment: 16%±1%.

规定一定的范围，如棉布幅阔 35～36 英寸。

规定极限，如大豆水分最高 14%，淀粉含量最低 18%。

规定上下差异，羽绒含绒量 16%±1%。

4.2.2 Commodity Price Can be Adjusted Within the Range of Quality Latitude 品质机动幅度范围内价格可以调整

Fix the price according to the quality and stipulate “Price Adjustment Clause Relating to Quality”. Some commodities’ prices can be adjusted based on the actual delivery performance.

Adopt discount price when the quality is below the stipulation of the contract. E.g. long-shaped rice: crushed grain 35% max, moisture 15% max, admixture 17% max.

体现按质议价，有些商品也可根据实际交货品质情况调整价格，规定“品质增减价条款”。

当品质低于合同的规定时采用折扣价，如籼米合同规定品质要求为碎粒最大 35%、水分最大 15%、杂质最大 17%。

Lesson 2 Quantity of Goods 商品的数量

1. Significance of Stipulating Quantity of Goods 约定商品数量的意义

Quantity clause is also one of the essential terms and conditions in a contract. It is required that the seller’s delivery of quantity must be identical to that stipulated in the contract; otherwise, the buyer reserves the right to claim for compensation and even reject the goods.

British Sale of Goods Act 1893 (1993 Revision) provides, "If the quantity delivered by the seller is greater than the amount stipulated in the contract, the buyer is entitled to reject the goods excessive in quantity, or he may reject the whole lot."

United Nations Convention on Contracts of International Sale of Goods also states: To deliver goods by the agreed amount is a fundamental obligation of the seller. If the delivery quantity is more than quantity agreed upon, the buyer may reject delivery of the excess quantity, or he may take delivery of all or part of the excess quantity, but he must pay for it at the contract rate.

Since the quantity agreed by both parties is the basis of delivery, it is of great significance to command quantity and conclude quantity clause in the transaction correctly. The main content of quantity clause includes measurement units, systems of calculating units, methods of calculating weight, etc. If the delivery is less than the agreed quantity, the seller should make up for the shortage within the time limit, but even so, the buyer reserves the right to lodge a claim.

商品的数量也是国际贸易货物买卖合同中的要件，卖方的交货数量必须与合同规定相符。否则，买方有权索赔甚至拒收货物。

英国《1893 年货物买卖法》（1993 年修订）中规定："卖方交货的数量如果大于合同规定的数量，买方除了可以拒收超额部分外，也可以全部拒收。"

《联合国国际货物销售合同公约》也规定，按约定的数量交付货物是卖方的一项义务。如卖方交货的数量大于约定的数量，买方可以拒收多交的部分，也可以收取多交部分中的一部分或全部，但应按合同价格付款。

由于交易双方约定的数量是交货的依据，因此，正确掌握成交数量、订立数量条款意义十分重大。数量条款的主要内容包括计量单位、度量衡、计算重量的方法等。如卖方交货的数量少于约定的数量，卖方应在规定的期限内补交。但即使如此，买方也保留要求损害赔偿的权利。

2. Measurement Units 计量单位

There are a great diversity of measurement units because of different categories and characteristics of commodities and different systems of calculating units in each country.

计量单位因商品种类特性和各国度量衡的不同而多种多样。

2.1 To Calculate by Weight 按重量计量

This is the most frequently used method in international trade at present. Most of the agricultural byproducts, metals and minerals are measured by weight. The following units are measurement units by weight: metric tons, long tons, short tons, and ounces.

这是当今国际贸易中使用最多的一种方法，大部分的农副产品、五金矿产品都是按重量计量。按重量计量的单位有公吨、长吨、短吨、盎司。

1 metric ton (metric system) = 1,000 kg　　　公吨（metric ton）公制=1 000 千克

1 long ton (British system) = 1,016 kg　　长吨（long ton）英制=1 016 千克
1 short ton (U.S. system) = 907 kg　　短吨（short ton）美制=907 千克

2.2 To Calculate by Number 按数量计算

It is constantly used for measurement of industrial manufactured goods, e.g. piece, pair, set, dozen, roll, ream, gross, bag, bale.

这种方法主要用于工业制成品，例如件、双、套、打、卷、令、罗、袋、包。

2.3 To Calculate by Length 按长度计算

This method is mainly used for cloth, rope, etc., e.g. meter, foot, yard.

这种方法主要用于布匹、绳索等，例如米、英尺、码。

2.4 To Calculate by Area 按面积计算

It is often used in trade of glass, carpets, leather, etc., e.g. square meter, square foot, square yard.

这种方法主要用于玻璃、地毯、皮革等，例如平方米、平方英尺、平方码。

2.5 To Calculate by Volume 按体积计算

It is generally used for woods, natural gas, chemical gas, etc, e.g. cubic meter, cubic foot.

这种方法主要用于木材、天然气、化学气体等，例如立方米、立方尺。

2.6 To Calculate by Cubage 按容积计算

It is generally used for grains, liquid cargo, alcohol, oils, etc., e.g. liter, gallon.

这种方法主要用于谷物、液体货物、酒类、油类等，例如公升、加仑。

3. Methods of Calculating Weight 计算重量的方法

The main methods of calculating weight include gross weight and net weight. In addition, there are methods such as conditioned weight, theoretical weight and legal weight.

计算重量的方法主要有毛重和净重，此外还有公量、理论重量和法定重量。

3.1 Gross Weight 毛重

Gross weight is the sum of total weight of the commodity itself and the package weight.

毛重是商品本身的重量加包装的重量。

3.2 Net Weight 净重

Net weight is the actual weight of the commodity itself without the addition of the tare.

商品本身的实际重量，不包括包装的重量。

3.2.1 Gross for Net 以毛作净

As to some commodities of relatively low value such as agricultural byproducts, the weight of its packaging can be negligible, taking gross weight for net weight.

对某些价值比较低的商品如农副产品，对包装物的重量可以忽略不计，以毛重当作净重计价。

3.2.2 Net Net Weight 净净重

Subtracting outer packaging weight from the gross weight is net weight, and then subtracting inner packaging in direct contact with the commodity is "net net weight".

In international trade, it is customary to calculate the weight by net weight if a contract does not stipulate definitely by gross weight or by net weight.

从毛重中减去外包装的重量为净重，再从净重中减去直接接触商品包装的重量即为"净净重"。

在国际贸易中，如合同未规定按净重还是毛重计价，按惯例即视为按净重计价。

4. Points for Attention in Stipulating Quantity Clause in Import and Export Contracts 进出口合同中规定数量条款的注意事项

Quantity clause includes quantity and measurement of the traded commodities. If the quantity is calculated by weight, the clause should also contain the method of calculating weight such as gross weight, net weight, conditioned weight, etc.

As to some commodities like agricultural byproducts and industrial and mineral products, it is hard for the actual delivery quantity to conform to the contracted quantity, owing to the characteristics of the commodity itself or the impacts of natural conditions or restrictions subject to packaging and transportation. For the sake of facilitating the processing of contract by the seller, the buyer will stipulate quantity difference when stipulating the quantity clause. Quantity difference is usually referred to as "more or less clause".

According to the convention, when the numbers or items of some commodities (such as automobiles, color televisions and other manufactured goods) can be accurately calculated, it is not suitable to adopt more or less clause. (*UCP600 Article 30*)

数量条款包括成交商品的数量和计量单位。如果按重量计量，还包括计算重量的方法，如毛重、净重、公量等。

有些商品，如农副产品和工矿产品，由于商品本身特性或受自然条件影响，或受包装和运输工具限制，实际交货数量往往不易符合原定的交货数量。为使卖方能够顺利地履行合同，买卖双方在规定合同数量条款的同时还规定数量机动幅度。我们通常也将数量机动幅度称为溢短装条款。

按惯例，对于某些个数、件数可以精确计数的商品（如汽车、彩电等工业制成品）不适用溢短装条款。（UCP600 第 30 条）

4.1 Concept of More or Less Clause 溢短装条款的概念

The buyer and seller stipulate in a sales contract that the seller is allowed to deliver the goods within a certain percentage of more or less than the contracted quantity.

E.g. Zinc ingot: 1,000 metric tons, with 5% more or less (namely, between 9,500 metric tons and 10,500 metric tons)

买卖双方在合同中规定卖方的实际交货数量可以比合同规定的数量多交或少交百分之几，但不超过一定的范围。

如：10 000 公吨锌锭，5%溢短装（数量为 9 500～10 500 公吨）

4.2 Content of More or Less Clause 溢短装条款的内容

4.2.1 Right of Choice Relating to Quantity Difference 机动幅度的选择权

Who should determine how much more or less would be allowed? Generally, the seller is to decide the quantity difference in practice. As stipulated in a contract, it is also practical to allow the shipper or the party in charge of shipment to decide the quantity according to the capacity of cabin. For example, under the FOB terms, it is the buyer who charters a liner to carry the goods, so in the contract we can stipulate that the shipper or the buyer determine the quantity difference.

溢短装多装还是少装在实践中一般由卖方来决定，也可按合同的规定，根据舱容的大小由船方或负责安排运输的一方来决定。如用 FOB 术语由买方负责派船，也可在合同中规定由买方或船方来决定机动幅度的大小。

4.2.2 Pricing Approach 作价办法

Under the more or less clause, the payment for the over-load or under-load portion will be made either according to contract price or at the international market price at the time of shipment or arrival so that when international market price fluctuates, the seller cannot take advantage of the more or less clause to load more or less on purpose and harm the interests of the buyer.

溢短装部分的价格既可按照合同的价格来规定，也可不按合同的价格，而根据装船或到达时国际市场的价格另定，以免卖方利用溢短装条款在国际市场价格波动时有意多装或少装，给买方带来不利。

Lesson 3 Packaging of Goods 商品的包装

1. Significance of Packaging 包装的重要意义

Packaging is a continuation of the commodity production. The vast majority of goods can only go into circulation to realize its use value and value after packaged. In the export trade, packaging is of great importance to protect, glorify, promote commodities and plays a significant role in storage, transportation, sale and the use of the goods. Apart from a few products which do not need to be packaged and adopt nude pack or conveyance in bulk, most of the commodities require appropriate packaging.

From a legal point of view, packaging is a part of the commodity instructions. Packaging clause is the continuation of the commodity terms, a component of the quality clause, and also an essential term of a sales contract. By law in some countries, the buyer is entitled to reject the goods if the seller's delivered goods fail to be packaged in accordance with the agreed terms.

包装是商品生产的继续，绝大多数商品只有进行了包装才能进入流通领域，从而实现其使用价值与价值。在出口贸易中，包装对保护商品、美化商品、宣传商品以及对商品的贮藏、运输、销售和使用都起着重要作用。除少数商品不需要包装而采用裸装或散装外，绝大多数的商品都需要适当的包装。

从法律上来说，包装是商品说明的一部分，包装条款是商品品质条款的延续，是品质条款的组成部分，同样也是买卖合同中的一项要件条款。按某些国家的法律规定，如卖方所交的货物未按约定的条件包装，买方有权拒收。

2. Transport Packaging 运输包装

Transport packaging is also called giant packing or outer packing. It is used mainly to keep the goods safe, facilitate the transportation, storage, identification and count, reduce freight and cut costs.

In order to facilitate the goods' transportation, storage, handover and identification, the transport packaging can be printed with three kinds of marks: shipping marks, indicative marks, and warning marks.

Shipping marks are the most important one among these marks. All of the three kinds of marks can be printed on the transport packaging. But all of the transport documents including business receipts must embody shipping marks, while the other two marks do not need to be reflected in the documents.

It is customary to stipulate shipping marks in a contract; otherwise, generally the seller will stipulate the shipping marks.

运输包装又称大包装、外包装。它的作用主要是保护商品，便于运输、储存，便于识别计数、减少运费、降低成本。

为了方便运输、储存、货物的交接和识别，在运输包装上可刷印三种标志，即运输标志、指示性标志和警告性标志。

其中，运输标志是最重要的一种标志。在商品的包装上，可以刷制这三种标志，但是在所有的运输单据（包括商业单据）上都必须体现运输标志，而其他两种标志不需要在单据上体现。

运输标志的制定，按惯例一般在合同中规定。如合同中未作规定，一般由卖方规定。

2.1 The Legal Sense of Shipping Marks 运输标志的法律意义

In accordance with the laws in some countries, the shipping marks agreed by both parties in the contract are part of the commodity instructions. The seller must deliver goods in accordance with the instructions; otherwise, it will lead to a breach of contract.

Invoices, insurance policies, Bs/L and other documents are marked only with shipping marks; other marks are unnecessary.

按照一些国家的法律，双方在合同中规定的运输标志是商品说明的一部分，卖方必须切实照办，否则构成违约。

在发票、保单、提单和其他单据上只标出运输标志，其他标志不显示。

2.2 Indicative Marks 指示性标志

Indicative marks are remarkable diagrams and words printed on the outer packing of the commodity which is fragile, delicate or perishable, for example, "HANDLE WITH CARE", "THIS SIDE UP", and "GUARD AGAINST DAMP".

The relevant transport documents are marked only with shipping marks. There is no need to print the indicative marks on the documents (It only needs to be printed on the outer packing).

指示性标志指用在易碎、易坏、易变质的一类商品外包装上的醒目的图形和文字，如"小心轻放""此端向上""防止潮湿"。

在有关运输单据上，只打上运输标志，而无须打出指示性标志（只印刷在外包装上）。

2.3 Warning Marks 警示性标志

Warning marks, also called hazardous marks, refer to noticeable diagrams and words printed on the outer packing of dangerous goods that are flammable, explosive, toxic, radioactive and so on. They must be printed on the remarkable position of the outer packing.

警示性标志又称危险性标志，是指易燃、易爆、有毒、放射性等危险品的外包装上醒目的图形和文字，必须印在运输包装上的明显位置。

2.4 Sales Packaging 销售包装

Sales packaging, also called inner packaging, or small packaging, is in direct contact with the commodity and will get into sales outlets with the products to meet the consumers.

销售包装又称内包装、小包装，是指直接接触商品并随商品进入销售网点和消费者直接见面的包装。

2.5 Requirements for Sales Packaging 销售包装的要求

Easy to display 便于陈列

Easy to identify 便于识别

Easy to carry and use 便于携带和使用

Artistically attractive 有艺术的吸引力

With the intensifying competition in international market, supermarkets and chain stores are developing rapidly. Supermarkets in many countries are using barcode technology to automatically scan and settle accounts. Commodities without barcode on the packaging have no permission to enter supermarkets.

随着国际市场竞争的日益加剧，超级市场和连锁商店迅速发展。许多国家的超市都使用条形码技术进行自动扫描和结算，如商品包装上没有条形码，即使是名优商品也不能进入超市。

Case Study 本章案例

Case 1: A trade company of China exported a batch of cannabis to Germany. It is specified in the contract that: moisture, 15% max; admixtures, 3% max. But we have sent the sample to the buyer before the transaction is concluded. We also telephoned the buyer that the delivered goods are similar to the sample after contracting. After the goods arrived in Germany, the buyer provided an inspection certificate stating that the quality of the goods is lower than that of the sample by 7%, and according to this, they also claimed for 600 pounds as the compensation against the losses.

【案例 1】我国某外贸公司向德国出口一批大麻。合同规定水分最高为 15%，杂质不得超过 3%，但在成交前我方曾向买方寄过样品，订约后我方又电告对方成交货物与样品相似。货到德国后，买方提出货物的质量比样品低 7%的检验证明，并据此要求赔偿 600 英镑的损失。

Question: Could we ignore the claim for the reason that the deal was not conducted based on sale by sample?

问题：我方可否以该批业务并非凭样买卖而不予理睬？

Case Analysis: In this case, it was a sale both by sample and by description, so that the seller was in a very passive situation. If we can use one method to indicate the quality of goods, we do not adopt two. Originally, the delivered goods are up to standard, but it also requires the quality should be equal to the sample, which leads to the breach of contract.

Case revelation: As to agricultural products such as ginseng, cannabis and so on, it is advisable to illustrate the quality of goods by scientific indicators rather than sale by sample.

【案例分析】本案实际上是既凭样品又凭文字说明的买卖，卖方因此处于非常被动的局面。我们能用一种方法表示商品的品质，就不用两种方法来表示。本来凭文字说明表示品质，我方的交货是合格的。但又规定大货和样品一致，导致我方违约。

本案启示：农副产品如大麻、人参等，只适用以科学的指标来说明商品的品质，而不适用于凭样品买卖。

Case 2: A trade company of China exported several batches of wool textiles to a country in the Middle East. When the goods arrived, the buyer received them one by one, without raising any objections. But a few months later, the buyer sent a set of clothing made by the wool textiles, claiming that there was an obvious color shading of the clothing made by our products and it was difficult to put into the market, thus filing a claim for compensation.

【案例 2】我国某外贸公司先后向中东某国家出口纯毛纺织品数批。货到国外后买方一一收货，从未提出异议。但数月之后，买方寄来制成的服装一套，声称用我方毛料制成的服装色差严重，难以投入市场销售，因而要求赔偿。

Question: How to solve this problem?

问题：对此问题应如何解决？

Case Analysis: (1) According to international practice, once the textiles are cut, the buyer cannot return the goods. In this case, the importer has sold the goods to garment factories, and the textiles have already been made into the clothing, indicating that the importers have accepted our goods. Since the form of the goods has been changed, it is unreasonable for the importer to return the goods and lodge a claim. (2) In the Article 82 of "United Nations Convention on Contracts for the International Sale of Goods", it stipulates that the buyer loses the right to declare the contract void or to require the seller to deliver substitute goods if it is impossible for him to make restitution of the goods substantially in the condition in which he received them.

【案例分析】（1）按照国际惯例，纺织品一经开剪，不得退货。本案进口商已经把货卖给了服装厂，制成了成衣，说明了进口商已经接受了我们的货物，货物的形态已经发生了变化，进口商不得退货和要求索赔。（2）《联合国国际货物销售合同公约》第 82 条规定，买方如果不可能按实际收到的货物的原状归还货物，其就失去了宣告合同无效或要求卖方赔偿的权利。

Case 3: A trade company of China exported 1,000 fans to America. Partial shipments are not allowed according to the credit. However, when the seller made the shipment, he found 40 fans with broken package, some of the fan covers deformed and some switches off. The replacement was already too late. To ensure the quality of the goods, the shipper regarded that, according to UCP600, even if partial shipments were not allowed, there was a tolerance of 5% of the quantity. He thought 40 fans were within the range of 5% of the whole quantity, so he shipped 960 fans actually. When the seller went to the bank with the documents for negotiating, the bank refused to negotiate. Question: What is the reason?

【案例 3】我国某外贸公司向美国出口电扇 1 000 台，国外来证规定不允许分运。但在出口装船时才发现有 40 台的包装破裂，有的风罩变形，有的开关按钮脱落。临时更换已来不及。为保证质量起见，发货人员认为根据 UCP600 规定即使不准分运，在数量上也可有5%的伸缩幅度，如甩下40台并未超过5%，结果实装960台。当该外贸公司持单到银行议付时，银行则不予议付，问原因是什么？

Case Analysis: As stipulated in the UCP600, if the numbers or items of goods can be accounted accurately, the more or less clause is not applicable. In this case, fan is just this kind of commodity, so it does not apply to the 5% more or less clause. The documents with an amount of 960 fans the exporter submitted were not in conformity with credit, so the bank had the right to refuse the payment.

【案例分析】按照UCP600的规定，个数、件数可以精确计数的商品不适用于溢短装条款。本案电扇属于个数、件数可以精确计数的商品，不适用于数量可以5%增减的条款。我方提交960台的提单，与信用证不符，银行有权拒付。

Questions 思考题

1. What is more or less clause?
   什么是溢短装条款？
2. What is the concept of shipping marks?
   运输标志的概念是什么？
3. What is sale by sample? Why should exporters strive for sale by sellers' sample for the sake of their own interests?
   什么是凭样品买卖？为什么出口方争取凭卖方样品买卖较为有利？
4. What is counter sample? When a sale is made by buyer's sample, how should the seller avoid risks?
   什么是对等样品？如凭买方提供的样品买卖，卖方如何避免风险？
5. Does sale by sample apply to all commodities?
   是否所有的商品都可以凭样品买卖？
6. What should be concerned when a transaction is made by sample?
   凭样品买卖要注意哪些问题？
7. What are the basic requirements for sale by sample?
   凭样品买卖有哪些基本的要求？
8. What is the quality tolerance? What is quality latitude? What's the difference between them?
   什么是品质公差？什么是品质机动幅度？二者有何区别？

Chapter 9

International Cargo Transportation

国际货物运输

In international trade, the seller delivers the goods in exchange for the buyer's payment. It is the seller's basic duty to deliver the goods to the buyer or the specified carrier in due time, place and transport means according to the contract after signing it.

In common law, according to the cases over the past years, common law countries regard quality clauses, quantity clauses and time of delivery as the fundamentals of the contract. The consequences could be very serious once the rules are broken. In this chapter, time of delivery is the priority of shipment clauses. Time of shipment and time of delivery are totally different concepts. But under FOB, CFR and CIF terms, the seller delivers the documents instead of the goods, which means, once the goods are sent to the ship or shipping conveyance in the shipping port, the seller's duty to deliver the goods is accomplished. The date indicated by the carrier on the shipping documents is the time of delivery and the place of shipment is rightly the place of delivery. That is to say, under CIF, FOB and CFR trade terms which indicate symbolic delivery, shipment just means delivery and time of shipment is rightly time of delivery.

在国际贸易中，卖方交付货物与买方支付货款是对流条件。买卖合同签订后，按照合同规定的时间、地点和方式将货物运交买方或装上指定的承运工具，是卖方所承担的基本义务。

在英美法中，根据历年的判例，采用英美法的国家把品质条款、数量条款、交货期作为合同的要件条款。如果违反了要件条款，后果十分严重。在本章中，装运条款首先要讲到装运期。装运期和交货期是两个不同的概念，但是在 FOB、CFR、CIF 条件下，卖方以交单代替了交货，也就是说，只要把货交到装运港的船上或运输工具上，卖方的交货义务就算完成，承运人在运输单据上所注明的日期即作为交货日期，货物的装运地点即作为交货地点。也就是说，在 CIF、FOB、CFR 象征性交货的贸易术语下，“装运”

就意味着交货，成为同一个概念，交货期等于装运期。

Lesson 1 Means of Transportation
运 输 方 式

In international trade, there are various kinds of modes of transportation: ocean transportation, rail transportation, air transportation, river transportation, road transportation, channel transportation, container transportation, international multimodal transportation and continental-bridge transportation, etc., of which ocean transportation is the most important, traditional and time-honored means of transport. Currently, as the most preferred mode of transport, ocean transportation accounts for 80% of the total capacity. We'll introduce a few significant means of transportation in international trade hereinafter.

在国际贸易中，运输方式有许多种，如海洋运输、铁路运输、航空运输、内河运输、公路运输、管道运输、集装箱运输、国际多式联运、大陆桥运输（重点在海洋运输）等。其中，最重要的方式是海洋运输，海洋运输是国际贸易中历史最悠久的一种传统的运输方式。目前，在国际货物运输总量中，海洋运输占80%以上，是目前国际贸易中最重要的一种运输方式。以下我们主要介绍国际贸易中比较重要的几种运输方式。

1. Ocean Transport 海洋运输

Ocean transport is mostly preferred due to its large capacity, low cost, massive passing ability and freedom from road and railway limitations, while it's comparatively slow, risky and vulnerable to bad weather.

There are two main types of ocean transportation: liner transportation and charter transportation.

海洋运输有通过运量大、运费低、不受道路和轨道限制等优点，缺点是受自然条件影响较大，航行速度较慢，风险较大。

海洋运输的船舶运输方式主要有两种：班轮运输和租船运输。

1.1 Liner Transport 班轮运输

1.1.1 Definition 定义

A liner is vessel with regular sailings and arrivals and sails on a fixed (regular) sailing route and calls at fixed (regular) base ports. It adopts a comparatively fixed timetable and charges at comparatively fixed rates. Liner transport is suitable for goods in small lots and high frequency. Most goods are transported through liner transport in international trade.

班轮运输又称定期船运输，简称班轮，指船舶按照预定的航行时间表，在固定的航线和港口往返航行，从事客货运输业务并按事先公布的费率收取运费。班轮运输适合批量小、次数多的商品。国际贸易中大部分的货物还是采用班轮运输。

1.1.2 Characteristics 特点

Fixity, namely fixed routes, fixed ports of call, fixed dates and fixed rates.

Responsibility: goods are subject to the loading and unloading by the liners and handling charges are already included in the freight. Liners and the consignor are free from handling charges, demurrage charges and dispatch money.

Liabilities, obligations and exemptions of liners and the shipper are all on the basis of the bill of lading issued by liners. In terms of goods with large transport volume and low value like grains, beans, mines and coals, the price is negotiated by both parties.

“四固定”，即固定的航线、固定的停靠港、固定的船期、固定运费率。

责任：货物由班轮公司负责配载和装卸，装卸费已包含在运费内，班轮公司和托运人双方不计装卸费、滞期费和速遣费。

班轮公司和货主双方的权利、义务和责任豁免均以班轮公司签发的提单条款为依据。某些运量大、货价低的货物，如粮食、豆类、矿石、煤炭，由船货双方协商定价。

1.2 Shipping by Charter 租船运输

Charter transport refers to a cargo ship not operating on regular routes and schedules. A ship or just some shipping space may be hired for transportation.

Contrary to a liner, a charter vessel does not follow a fixed route, freight rate or timetable and has no fixed ports of call. Charter vessels fall into three types: voyage charter, time charter and bare boat charter. This chapter focuses on voyage charter here because of its high relativity with export enterprises.

租船运输又称不定期船运输，指包租整船或部分舱位进行运输。

与班轮运输相反，租船运输具有“四不固定”的特点：航线不固定、停靠港不固定、船期不固定和运费不固定。租船运输又分为期租船、程租船和光船运输。与出口企业关系较为密切的是程租船运输。下面着重讲述程租船运输。

1.2.1 Voyage Charter 程租船

Voyage charter is also named irregular charter, divided into one-way charter, round-way charter and consecutive voyage charter according to the way of financing leasing.

程租船又称为不定期船、航次租船。程租船按租赁方式可分为单程租船、来回航次租船、连续航次租船。

1）Definition 定义

A voyage charter is the hire of a ship for the carriage of goods from one specified port to another, or for a round trip and is characterized by shipping low-value and bulk commodities like grains, coals, wood, and mines.

由船舶所有人负责提供船舶，在指定港口之间进行一个航次或数个航次承运指定货物的租船运输。特点是以运输价值较低廉的粮食、煤炭、木材、矿石等大宗货物为主。

2）Stipulations of Loading and Unloading Cost 程租船装卸费的规定

Loading and unloading costs are stipulated in the contract after negotiation and five methods are usually used to divide the expenses of loading and unloading:

程租船的装卸费由租方和船方共同协商后在合同中做出规定，可由船方负担，也可由货方负担。规定如下。

- liner terms/gross terms/berth terms 班轮条件

  The ship-owner bears loading and unloading cost.

  船方负担装卸费。

- free in and out (FIO) 船方不管装卸

  The ship-owner does not bear loading and unloading cost.

  船方不负担装卸费。

- free in (FI) 船方管卸不管装

  The ship-owner is only responsible for unloading cost.

  船方不负担装船费。

- free out (FO) 船方管装不管卸

  The ship-owner is only responsible for loading cost.

  船方不负担卸货费。

- free in and out, stowed and trimmed (FIOST) 船方不管装卸、理舱、平舱。

  The ship-owner does not bear loading and unloading cost, not even bear the expenses of stowing and trimming.

  船方不负担装卸费，也不负担理舱和平舱。

3）Lay Time 装卸时间

In voyage charter transport, the lay time is directly related to the operating cycles and benefits of the ship-owner, so lay time should be stipulated in detail when both parties enter into a contract. If the charterer fails to finish loading the goods within the limited time resulting in extended staying time and trip time, it would increase expenses as well as decrease cycling rates for the ship-owner. So lay time stipulations are closely related to the benefits of both parties.

采用程租船运输方式，货物在装卸港口的装卸时间长短直接关系船舶的使用周期和船方的利益。租方在和船方签订租船合同时，要就船舶在港装卸的时间做出具体的规定。如租船人未能在约定的装卸时间内将货物装完或卸完而延长了船舶在港停留时间，从而延长了航次时间，这对船舶所有人来说，既可能因增加船舶在港口停泊时间而增加港口费用开支，又因航次时间延长而降低了船舶的周转率。装卸时间规定直接关系船方和租方的切身利益。

1.2.2 The Difference between Voyage Charter and Time Charter 程租船运输与期租船的区别

Ship-owner of a voyage charter is responsible for hiring the crew and providing fuel while the charterer is in the latter case.

Ship-owner of a voyage charter takes on sailing and maintaining of the ship while the charterer does in the latter case.

前者船员、燃料配备都由船方负责，后者由租方负责。

船舶经营调度，前者都由船方负责，后者由租方自己负责。

2. Rail Transport 铁路运输

In international transportation, the importance of rail transport is only secondary to the maritime transportation; moreover the cargoes imported or exported by ship are mostly distributed or collected overland by rail.

For China with a vast territory, the cargoes imported by ships are usually transported by rail to the consumers across the country, and most of cargoes for export are pooled to the ports by rail. Therefore, railway plays an important role in the distribution or collection of goods in China for international trade. The movement of the raw materials, semi-final products, and packing materials for international trade throughout the country are mainly by rail too. Generally speaking, the railway is one of the necessary parts in international transport chains.

With the characteristics of large carrying load, high speed, and low risk, the carrying capacity of railway is the largest other than the maritime transportation.

在国际货物运输中，铁路运输是一种仅次于海洋运输的主要运输方式。海洋运输的进出口货物，也大多是靠铁路运输进行货物的集中和分散。

由于我国幅员辽阔，海运进口货物大部分利用铁路运往消费者所在国，海运出口货物也多是通过铁路向港区集中。因此，铁路运输是我国国际贸易货物集散的重要工具。国内各省和地区调运外贸物资、各种原料、半成品和包装物料，也主要是依靠铁路运输来完成。我国国际贸易进出口货物运输一般都要通过铁路这一环节，铁路运输在国际货物运输中发挥着重要作用。

铁路运输具有运量大、速度快、风险小的特点。在国际货运总量中，铁路货运量仅次于海洋货运量。

International Carriage of Goods by Rail 国际铁路货物联运

With one set of uniform transportation documents, the goods are moved through two or more countries by rail as a whole, without the involvement of the consigner and consignee when the goods are delivered from one country to the other country.

For the transport mode, the goods are free from the check-in again at the frontier office, and carried over the frontier by train. It benefits the international trade and transaction, urging the development of the integrative economy.

凡是使用一份统一的国际联运票据由铁路负责经过两国或两国以上铁路的全程运送，并在一国铁路向另一国铁路移交货物时不需要发货人和收货人参加的运输被称为国际铁路货物联运。

国际铁路货物联运免除了货物在国境站重新办理托运的手续，火车可以直接过轨运输。这种方式有利于各国之间的国际贸易和经济交往，加速了经济一体化的发展。

3. Air Transport 航空运输

As a modern transportation mode, air transport has developed rapidly with the advantages of being speedy, exact, safe and convenient. At the same time, the drastic growth of the goods adapted to air transport also pushes the development of air industry. More and more modern and big airplanes, big airports with perfect facilities and modern telecommunication facilities are produced and constructed to meet the demand of air transportation in international trade. In this way, international trade and air industry boost each other with the advancement of air technology and air transportation. For the time being, the proportion of air transportation occupied in the whole international transportation is increasing with the growing quantity of cargoes transported by air.

The goods which are the most adapted to air transport are including urgent cargoes, fresh and living products, precise appliances, valuables, putrescible and seasonal items etc.

China joined International Civil Aviation Organization (ICAO) in 1974.

Classifications of Air Transport Modes are as follows.

航空运输是一种现代化的运输方式。由于航空运输具有速度快、准确、安全、方便等优点，航空货物运输在世界范围内得到迅速发展。同时，国际贸易中适合于航空运输的货物大量增加，促进了航空事业的发展。航空事业的发展又给航空运输提供了现代化、大型化的飞机，机场规模宏大、设施完善，航空公司不断增加，通信手段日益现代化。这些都为国际贸易货物的空运提供了更为便利的条件，同时也促进了国际贸易的发展。国际贸易与航空业务互相促进，航空技术与航运共同发展。目前，在整个国际贸易运输中，航空货物运输所占的比重不断增加，货运量也越来越大。

航空运输最适合运输急需物品、鲜活产品、精密仪器、贵重物品和易腐、鲜活、季节性强的物品。

我国于 1974 年加入国际民航组织。

航空运输主要采用以下几种运输方式。

3.1 Scheduled Airline 班机运输

Scheduled airlines refer to the airlines that transport regularly by fixed route, between fixed departure and destination at fixed time schedule. Usually this kind of flights uses passenger-cargo airplanes, and some bigger air companies have opened up regular full air cargo flight. With the advantage of its fixed time, route and stop station, the scheduled airline is more suitable for the transport of emergency items, fresh and live produce or seasonal commodities.

班机是指在固定时间、固定航线、固定始发站和目的站运输的飞机，通常班机使用客货混合型飞机，也有一些大的航空公司开辟定期全货机航班。班机因有定时、定航线、定站等特点，因此适用于运送急需物品、鲜活商品以及节令性商品。

3.2 Chartered Carrier 包机运输

Chartered carrier refers to the airplane that is hired by one consigner or share-hired by several consigners (or air-freight service agency). Thus, chartered carrier could be divided into two kinds: whole-hired and share-hired. The former kind is suitable for transporting goods in large quantity, and the latter one is suitable for goods to be delivered to the same destination by different consigners.

包机是指包租整架飞机或由几个发货人（或航空货运代理公司）联合包租一架飞机运送货物。因此，包机又分为整包机和部分包机两种形式，前者适用于运送数量较多的商品，后者适用于多个发货人且货物到达站是同一地点的货物运输。

3.3 Consolidation 集中托运

Consolidation is usually utilized by air-freight service agency, who combines scattered goods into one batch, with the airway bills for each shipment issued respectively for each consignor, and then makes delivery of the whole batch of goods to the scheduled destination with one set of chief airway bill. After the arrival, the goods are cleared, sorted out and dispatched to the actual consignees respectively by the local agency of air-freight carrier. The price of consolidation flight is usually 7%–10% lower than that of scheduled airliner fixed by International Air Transportation Association. For this reason, the consigners are more willing to commit the goods to air-freight agency for delivery.

集中托运是指航空货运公司把若干单独发运的货物（每一个货主的货物都要出具一份航空运单）组成一整批货物，用一批总运单（附分运单）整批发运到预定目的地，由航空公司在那里的代理人收货、报关、分拨后交给实际收货人。集中托运的运价比国际空运协会公布的班机运价低 7%～10%。因此，发货人更愿意将货物交给航空货运公司安排。

3.4 Air Express Service 航空特快专递

Air Express is the fastest one in the current international air transportation modes. Different from air par avion and air freight, air express service is operated by the organizations specializing in this business field, who is in close cooperation with airline companies, with urgent mails transferred by specially-assigned persons, between consigner, airport and consignee at the fastest speed. It is most suitable for delivery of medicines and medical equipment in urgent needs, valuables, blue print documents and other goods and documents, therefore it is called “Desk to Desk Service”.

航空特快专递是目前国际航空运输中最快捷的运输方式。它不同于航空邮寄和航空货运，而是由一个专门经营此项业务的机构运营。该机构与航空公司密切合作，设专人用最快的速度在货主、机场、收件人之间传送急件，特别适用于急需的药品、医疗器械、贵重物品、图纸资料、货及单证等的传送，被称为“桌到桌运输”。

4. Container Transport 集装箱运输

4.1 Definition 定义

Container, in a literal sense, it is a kind of tremendous holder with sort of intensity (most containers are made of steel now) for cycling and easy to be mechanically operated.

The concept of container transport is a modern transport method which puts a certain number of single items into the container and transports it as the basis unit. Container transport is a method of distributing merchandise in a unitized form adopting an inter-modal system which provides a possible combination of sea, road and other modes of transportation.

集装箱又称“货箱”“货柜”。按字面的含义，它是一种容器，必须具有一定的强度（现在集装箱多为钢制），是专供周转使用、便于机械操作的大型货物容器。

集装箱运输就是将一定数量的单件货物装入按标准规格特制的集装箱内，并以该箱作为运送单位的一种现代化的运输方式。它可适用于各种运输方式的单独运输和不同运输方式的联合运输。

4.2 Types and Specifications of Containers 集装箱的种类、规格

The most widely adopted sizes are twenty-foot equivalent unit (TEU) and forty-foot equivalent unit (FEU). But recently, containers are becoming lager and lager. For instance, American President Lines adopt 53-foot container. The generally adopted sizes in China are:

8′8′20′　twenty-foot equivalent unit (TEU)

8′8′40′　forty-foot equivalent unit (FEU)

目前，在国际航运上使用的集装箱多为 20 英尺和 40 英尺集装箱。但近年来，集装箱的发展向大型化方向发展，如美国总统轮船公司采用 53 英尺型集装箱。我国通常采用的规格为：

8′×8′×20′　20 英尺集装箱

8′×8′×40′　40 英尺集装箱

4.3 Goods Handing Over of Container Transportation 集装箱运输货物的交接

1）Full Container Load (FCL) 整箱货

The FCL consignments are packed into the container as one unit by the consigner for shipment. This means is adopted when the goods are of a container load or many containers load. Except that some consigners have containers, others generally lease a few to send to the production side or the warehouse, and then under the customs officials' supervision, the consigner packs the goods into the container, after locking and sealing up the container, getting the dock receipt (D/R) in exchange for bills of lading or shipping documents.

这种装箱方式是指货主自行将货物装满整箱后，以箱为单位向承运人进行托运。这种情况是货主有足以装满一个或几个整箱的货源时所采用的装箱方式。除有些较大的货主自己备有集装箱外，一般都是货主向承运人或集装箱租赁公司租用一定数量的集装箱。当空箱运到货主的工厂或仓库后，在海关人员的监督下，由货主把货物装入箱内，加锁铅封后交给承运人并取得场站收据，凭场站收据换取提单或运单。

2）Less than Container Load (LCL) 拼箱货

LCL stands for less than container load or partial container load as opposite to FCL. LCL consignments are first sent to the container freight station or inland container depot where the carrier can consolidate and pack the goods into containers according to the nature, destination, and weight and so on and then send the containers to the container yard for shipment. This method is used when a consigner's goods are not enough to fill one container. Classification, sorting, concentration, packing and delivery of LCL are done by consigner in pier container freight station or inland container station.

这种装箱方式是指承运人（或其代理人）接受货主托运的数量不足装满整箱的小票货运后，根据货物性质和目的地进行分类整理，把去同一目的地的货物集中到一定数量后拼装入箱。由于箱内不同货主的货物拼装在一起，所以叫拼箱货。这种方式是在一个货主的货物不足以装满整箱的情况下采用的。拼箱货的分类、整理、集中、装箱（拆箱）、交货等均由承运人在码头集装箱货运站或内陆集装箱转运站进行。

5. International Multi-modal Transport 国际多式联运

It involves the transportation of freight in an international container or vehicle, using multiple modes of transportation (rail, ship and truck), without any handling of the freight itself when changing modes.

The practice is the MTO (Multi-modal Transport Operator) taking the cargo from the place of sellers in one country to the site of the buyers in another country by at least two modes of transportation on the basis of a multi-modal transportation contract.

The characteristics is that only one carriage contract, one freight rate and one combined transport document are required however long the distance is and however complex the procedures are. The only one shipper is responsible for the entire journey in case that the goods are lost or damaged. However, the combined bill of lading in ocean transport is only responsible for the first part of the journey.

国际多式联运是在集装箱运输的基础上发展起来的一种综合性的连贯运输方式，它将过去的那种海、陆、空、公路、江河等互不关联的单一运输方式有机地结合起来，以完成一票进口或出口货物在国际之间的运输。

具体做法：由多式联运经营人根据多式联运合同以至少两种不同的运输方式将货物从一国境内的接管地运至另一国境内指定交货地点。

特点：不管路途多么远、手续多复杂，货主只办理一次托运、支付一笔运费、取得一张联运单据。如货物在途中发生灭失、货损之类的问题，只找一个对全程负责的经营人解决。注意：海运中联运提单只对第一程负责。

6. Land Bridge Transport 大陆桥运输

The means of container transport which takes the cross-land railway (road) transporting system as a bridge to connect two sides of oceans is referred to as land bridge transport. The main land bridges all over the world are as follows.

使用横贯大陆的铁路（公路）运输系统作为中间桥梁，把大陆两端的海洋连接起来的集装箱连贯运输方式就称为大陆桥运输。世界上主要的大陆桥有以下几个。

6.1 Siberian Land Bridge Transport 西伯利亚大陆桥

The Siberian railway runs through Europe and Asia, all the way through the Baltic ports, and finally reaches Rotterdam, connecting the Atlantic Ocean and the Pacific Ocean. As the longest land bridge now in the world, it is commonly used as a short-cut by China, Japan and the Philippines.

利用贯穿欧洲、亚洲东西的西伯利亚大铁路，沿途经过波罗的海的港口，最终到达荷兰鹿特丹。它连接了大西洋和太平洋，是中国、日本、菲律宾的一条捷径，利用率很高，是世界上目前最长的一条大陆桥。

6.2 Asia Europe Land Bridge Transport 亚欧大陆桥

It was established in 1992, east from Lianyungang, all the way through Longhai Line, Lanzhou-Xinjiang Line, and Northern Xinjiang Railway and finally reaching Rotterdam.

亚欧大陆桥建成于 1992 年，东起我国连云港，经陇海线、兰新线、北疆铁路，最终到达荷兰鹿特丹。

6.3 North American Land Bridge 北美大陆桥

It takes advantage of the rail and road systems across North America to connect western Pacific ports with eastern Atlantic ports.

北美大陆桥利用横贯北美的铁路和公路运输系统，连接西部太平洋口岸至东部大西洋口岸。

7. OCP 内陆公共点

Overland Common Points are bounded on the east by Rocky Mountains in western America and with the east regions as the inland area. The destination of OCP transport is the inland area. If agreed on OCP shipping clauses, the exporter could enjoy not only favored inland freight rate but also favored ocean freight rate.

OCP，即“内陆公共点”，以美国西部的洛基山脉为界，以东地区为内陆地区范围。海运到达美国太平洋西岸港口，最终目的地在内陆地区，如果采用 OCP 运输条款达成交易，出口商不仅可享受美国内陆运输的优惠费率，而且可以享受 OCP 海运的优惠费率。

The Conditions of OCP Shipping Clauses

1) The destinations must be within OCP areas.

2) The cargo must be transferred in American western coasts, so the port of destination must be American western ports under CFR and CIF contracts.

3) Bills of lading must indicate OCP typeface and the name of American western ports as well as the name of the inland city, like CIF San Francisco OCP New York.

采用 OCP 运输条款必须具备以下条件：

（1）货物最终目的地必须属于 OCP 地区范围。

（2）货物必须经由美国西海岸港口中转。因此，签订 CFR 和 CIF 出口合同时，目的港必须是美国西海岸港口。

（3）提单上必须标明“OCP”字样，并且在提单目的港一栏中除填明美国西部海岸港口名称外，还要加注内陆地区的城市名称，如 CIF San Francisco OCP New York。

Lesson 2 Clause of Shipment
装 运 条 款

Shipment clauses include time of shipment, port of shipment and port of destination, partial shipment and transshipment, demurrage, dispatch and so on.

装运条款包括装运时间、装运港和目的港、分批装运、转运、滞期、速遣条款等内容。

1. Time of Shipment 装运时间

Time of shipment is the deadline by which the seller makes shipment of the contracted goods or delivers them to the carrier.

装运时间也称装运期，指卖方将合同规定的货物装上运输工具或交给承运人。

2. Shipment and Delivery 装期与交货期

Shipment and delivery are totally different concepts, but under CIF, CFR, CIP, CPT, FCA and FOB trade terms, the two have the same meaning. As we often refer shipment to delivering and most contracts are under CIF, CFR and FOB terms, we tend to regard these two concepts as one.

Quality clauses, quantity clauses and time of shipment are fundamentals of the sales contract in Common Law. The consequences could be so serious that the buyer has the right to reject the goods, terminate the contract and claim for compensation if the seller breaks any one of the three clauses. As a result, the seller should deliver the goods strictly according to the contract.

装期与交货期是两个截然不同的概念，但在 CIF、CFR、FOB 象征性交货的贸易术语下（也包括 CIP、CPT、FCA），二者是一致的。我们所说的装期也就是指交货期，又由于买卖合同大部分是用这三个贸易术语，习惯上人们已经把二者视为一体。

英美法把品质条款、数量条款和交货期作为合同的要件。如卖方违反三者之一，买方有权拒收货物、解除合同，如果同时要求损害赔偿，后果将十分严重。因此，卖方一定要严格按照合同规定的时间交货，也就是装船。

3. Port of Shipment and Port of Destination 装运港和目的港

Port of shipment and port of destination should be clearly specified in the contract when both parties come into agreement. Generally, port of shipment is put forward by the seller for the buyer's confirmation while port of destination is put forward by the buyer for the seller's confirmation.

凡涉及运输的合同均需规定装运港和目的港，必须在磋商交易时就达成一致。一般来说，装运港由卖方提出，经买方同意后确认。目的港由买方提出，卖方确认。

3.1 Port of Shipment 装运港

It is the port where the goods are shipped and depart from. In the case of FOB, CIF and CFR, the delivery of the goods is fulfilled when the goods are loaded on board the ship or to the carrier nominated by the buyer and at the same time the seller submits the shipping documents. Hence, port of shipment should be clearly stated in the contract so that the seller could deliver the goods to the carrier.

装运港是货物开始装运的港口。在 FOB、CIF、CFR 条件下，卖方按合同规定在装运港将货物装上开往目的港的船舶并提交运输单据，就算完成了交货义务，因此，在买卖合同中必须明确规定装运港，以便货交承运人。

3.2 Port of Destination 目的港

It is the port at which goods are ultimately discharged. Port of destination should closely follow CIF and CFR terms and CIP and CPT should indicate the final destination after delivery.

目的港是最终卸货的港口。CIF、CFR 都必须在贸易术语后规定目的港，CIP、CPT 需规定发货后最终运达的目的地。

4. Partial Shipment and Transshipment 分批装运和转运

One of the most important issues in the contract is whether partial shipment and transshipment are allowed as it directly affects the benefits of both parties. The buyer hopes to receive the goods at one time to decrease the cost and keep safety while the seller hopes that partial shipment and transshipment are allowed in consideration of production cycle and convenient conveyance.

能否分批装运和转运直接关系到买卖双方的切身利益，是买卖合同中的重要内容。买方希望直运并一次性交货，以降低成本和保护货物安全。卖方考虑到生产周期、运输方便，希望最好是“允许分批，允许转船”。

4.1 Partial Shipment 分批装运

It means the commodities are to be shipped in more than one lot. The reason for allowing partial shipment may be: the lack of means of conveyance or shipping space; the limitations of loading and unloading facilities; the restriction of market capacity and production ability. However, the buyer may require shipment in one lot in consideration of decreasing costs and expenses. Generally, “partial shipment allowed” is beneficial to the seller.

According to the contract law of some countries, if there is no stipulations about partial shipment and both parties have no conventions or customs, partial shipment shall not be deemed allowed.

UCP600 states:

(1) Unless otherwise stipulated, partial shipment is allowed.

(2) Paragraph B, Article 31 in UCP600 states, “...Transportation documents, which appear on their face to indicate that shipment commencing on the same means of conveyance and for the same journey, provided they indicate the same destination, will not be regarded as covering a partial shipment, even if they indicate different dates of shipment, different ports of loading, or places of dispatch.” That is to say, the goods under the same one contract and loaded on the same vessel will not be regarded as covering a partial shipment.

(3) Article 32 in UCP600 states, “if a drawing or shipment by installments within given periods is stipulated in the credit and any installment is not drawn or shipped within the period allowed for that installment, the credit ceases to be available for that and any subsequent installment.”

E.g. If shipment during May/June/July, with first shipment 100mt, second shipment 200mt, and third shipment 300mt, the beneficiary should strictly deliver 100mt in May, 200mt in June and 300mt in July. Once one lot failed to be shipped punctually, this lot and the rest lots are of no avail and the bank is entitled to dishonor.

分批装运又称分期装运，是指一个合同项下的货物分若干批或若干期装运。凡数量较大，受货源、运输、销售、资金等条件限制，有必要分期分批发货的，通常在买卖合同中规定“允许分批”。买方为了减少提货手续、节省费用开支，在进出口业务中往往要求出口人一次装运货物，并在合同中规定“不准分批装运”。一般来说，规定“允许分批装运”对卖方比较有利。

按某些国家的合同法规定，如合同中未对分批装运做出规定，买卖双方事先也没有特别约定或习惯做法，则卖方不得分批装运。

国际商会制定的《跟单信用证统一惯例》（UCP600）规定：

（1）除非信用证另有规定，允许分批装运。

（2）UCP600 第 31 条 b 款规定："表明使用同一运输工具并经由同次航程运输的数套运输单据在同一次提交时，只要显示相同目的地，将不视为部分发运，即使运输单据上表明的发运日期不同或装运港、接管地或发送地点不同。"也就是说，装于同一航次、同一条船上的同一合同项下的货物，即使装运的地点、时间不同，只要运往同一目的地，也不视为分批装运。

（3）UCP600 第 32 条规定："信用证规定在指定的时间段内分期付款或分期发运，任何一期未按信用证规定期限支取或发运时，信用证对该期及以后各期均告失效。"也就是说，限期限量分批装运的货物只要其中有一批未按时装运，该批和以后各批均告无效。

例如：信用证规定：船期为 5 月/6 月/7 月；第一批为 100 公吨；第二批为 200 公吨；第三批为 300 公吨。受益人交货必须严格按照 5 月份 100 公吨、6 月份 200 公吨、7 月份 300 公吨装出。其中，只要有一批未按时装运，则该批及以后各批均告无效。银行有权拒付货款。

4.2 Transshipment 转运/转船

Transshipment is adopted when ships sailing directly to the port of destination are not available or direct sailings to the destinations are few and far between. Transshipment is allowed in UCP600 unless otherwise stipulated in the credit.

Goods are subject to loss or damage during the journey in case of transshipment, which would increase costs and expenses and extend the time of arrival. But transshipment is inevitable when there is no direct sailing to the destination. Therefore, it is essential for both parties to make it clear in the contract.

With the development of means of transportation such as super vessels, container vessels, ro-ro ship and barge carrier, and especially the increasing use of multi-modal transportation, transshipment is widely used in international trade practice. UCP600 states, "transshipment means a transfer and reloading during the course of carriage from one conveyance or vessel to another conveyance or vessel, with the same mode of transport or from one mode of transport to another."

"A bill of lading may indicate that goods will or may be transshipped provided that the entire carriage is covered by one and the same bill of lading."

"A transport document indicating that transshipment will or may take place is acceptable provided that the goods are transported by container, trailer or barge carrier, even if the credit prohibits transshipment."

In brief, transshipment is prohibited in case of port-to-port ocean transportation and the non-container transportation.

如果没有直达船驶往目的港或航班间隔太长，则在合同中应订明“允许转船”。根据UCP600，除非信用证另有规定，否则准许转运。

货物在运输途中转运容易受损或散失，而且会增加费用和支出，会延迟到达目的地的时间。但在无直达运输工具的情况下转运就不可避免。是否允许转运关系买卖双方切身利益，有必要在买卖合同中明确规定。

但是，随着运输工具的不断改进和大型化、集装箱化，集装箱船、滚装船、母子船的涌现和推广使用，以及各种新的运输方式，尤其是多式联运方式的日益广泛运用，转运在实际业务中几乎已成为经常发生，甚至不可避免的事。UCP600 对转运做出新的规定:“转运是指在信用证规定的装货港到卸货港之间的运输过程中将货物从一船卸下并再装上另一船的行为。”

“提单可以表明货物将要或可能被转运，只要全程运输由同一提单涵盖。”

“即使信用证禁止转运，注明将要或可能发生转运的提单仍可接受，只要其表明货物由集装箱、拖车或母子船运输。”

简言之，真正被禁止的转运，仅指海运中港至港、非集装箱货物运输的转运。

Lesson 3 Shipping Documents
运 输 单 据

Shipping documents refer to the evidence of the cargo on board the ship or under the supervision of the carrier after getting receipt of it. The shipping documents are of great significance as they are proof of receiving the cargo, dealing with claims and making settlements.

运输单据是指承运人收到货物后证明货物已装上运输工具、已发运或已由承运人接收监管的单据。它是交接货物、处理索赔与理赔及向银行结算货款的重要凭据。

1. Ocean Bill of Lading (B/L) 海运提单

A bill of lading, most commonly used in international trade, is a document issued by a carrier to a shipper, signed by the captain, agent, or owner of a vessel, stating the conditions in which the goods are to be transported to the specified port of destination to the lawful holder of the bill of lading. It is also a document of title to the goods, enabling the consignor to get receipt of the goods from shipping company or its agent at the port of destination.

海运提单简称提单，是目前海运业务使用最为广泛和主要的运输单据。它是由船长或船公司或其代理人签发，证明已收到特定货物，允诺将货物运至指定目的港，并交付给收货人的凭证。海运提单也是收货人在目的港据以向船公司或其代理提取货物的凭证。

1.1 Nature and Functions of Bill of Lading 海运提单的性质和作用

It is a receipt issued by a carrier evidencing that a consignment of goods has been received at his disposal for shipment.

It is a document of title to the goods; that is, the legal owner of a bill of lading holds legal possession of the goods described in it. The legal holder is given the right to obtain delivery of the goods. Because of this, it can be transferred, pledged or negotiated by banks before the arrival at the destination.

It is an evidence of a contract of carriage between the consignor and consignee. Clauses printed overleaf stipulate both parties' rights and liabilities and are regarded as proof of treatment of disputes.

A bill of lading functions as evidence of loading, unloading, transferring, dispatching, claiming, and freight collecting by the carrier.

海运提单是承运人或其代理人签发的货物收据，证明承运人已按提单所列内容收到货物。

海运提单是物权凭证。海运提单是代表货物所有权的凭证。收货人是提单的合法持有人，有权凭提单向承运人提取货物。由于提单是一种物权凭证，因而在国际市场上，提单可以在载货船舶到达目的港交货之前办理转让，或凭以向银行办理押汇、议付或抵押贷款。

海运提单是托运人和承运人之间运输契约的证明。提单的背面条款规定了双方的权利、义务和责任，作为双方处理纠纷的依据。

提单的作用：海运提单作为承运人收取运费的证明，是在运输过程中办理货物装卸、转船、发运、交接以及最后索赔的依据。

1.2 Types of Bills of Lading 海运提单的种类

1.2.1 According to Whether the Goods Are Loaded on Board the Vessel 根据是否装船

According to whether the goods are loaded on board the vessel, B/L can be classified as follows:

根据是否装船可分为：

1）On Board B/L; Shipped B/L 已装船提单

On board B/L refers to the one that shall be issued after the cargo has been actually shipped on board the vessel. It is issued by the shipping company or its agent, on which both the loading date and the name of the vessel shall be indicated in detail.

已装船提单是指承运人已将货物装上指定船舶后所签发的提单，其特点是提单上必须以文字表明货物已经装至某船上，并载明装船日期，同时还应由船长或其代理人签字。

2）Received for Shipment B/L 备运提单，又称收讫待运提单

Received for shipment B/L is the one that acknowledges that goods have been received for shipment but not been loaded on board the carrying vessel yet. The consignor could exchange it for on board B/L, or turn it into on board B/L on condition that the carrier or agent adds an on board notation on received for shipment B/L indicating the name of the vessel and shipping date, and signs his or her name.

备运提单是指承运人已收到托运货物等待装运期间所签发的提单。在签发备运提单的情况下，发货人可在货物装船后凭备运提单调换已装船提单；也可经承运人或其代理人在备运提单上批注货物已装上某具名船舶及装船日期，签署后使之成为已装船提单。

1.2.2 According to the Apparent Condition of the Received Cargo 根据提单上有无不良批注

According to the Apparent Condition of the Received Cargo, B/L Can Be Classified as follows:

根据提单上有无不良批注可分为：

1）Clean B/L 清洁提单

A clean bill of lading refers to the one that does not contain any notation declaring a defective condition of the exterior packing of goods. UCP600 states, "banks favor only clean bills of lading, and a clean bill of lading refers to the one that does not contain any notation declaring a defective condition of the exterior packing of goods."

清洁提单是指货物在装船时表面状况良好，船公司在提单上未加任何有关货物受损或包装不良等批注的提单。UCP600 规定："银行只接受清洁运输单据。清洁运输单据指未载有明确宣称货物或包装有缺陷的条款或批注的运输单据。"

2）Unclean B/L; Foul B/L 不清洁提单

Unclean B/L or Foul B/L is the one that contains unfavorable notation about the apparent condition of the cargo, e.g. "packages in damaged condition", "iron strap loose or missing". An unclean B/L is not acceptable to banks.

不清洁提单是指船公司在提单上对货物表面状况或包装加有不良或存在缺陷等批注的提单。例如，提单上批注"包装损坏""铁条松散"等。银行不接受不清洁提单。

1.2.3 According to the Title 根据提单抬头

The title of the bill refers to the consignee who is entitled to take delivery of the goods. Different title means different means of transferring title of goods. It is of great importance to learn about different types of bills according to the title and choose different means of transaction and payment in order to get the goods safely exchanged and obtain bank financing.

According to the title, B/L can be classified as follows:

提单的抬头是指提单的收货人，是有权凭提单向承运人提货的人。因为提单的抬头做法不同，关系到物权和物权转移的方法问题，为了使货物安全交接、卖方安全收汇，必须了解各种不同抬头提单的做法和本身的意义以及如何转让提单的所有权，并根据不同交易方式和付款方式选用不同做法的提单。

根据提单抬头的不同可分为：

1）Straight B/L 记名提单

It is the one that is made out to a designated consignee. Only the named consignee at the destination is entitled to take delivery of the goods under the bill, not to any other party through endorsement. A straight B/L is non-negotiable.

记名提单指在提单的收货人栏内（抬头人）直接打出收货人的名称。这就表明该提单项下的货物只能由该特定收货人提取，不能用背书的方式转让给第三者。因此，记名提单不能流通转让。

2）Blank B/L; Bearer B/L; Open B/L 不记名提单

It means that there is no definite consignee of the goods. Any one who holds the bill is entitled to the goods. No endorsement is needed for the transfer of the blank bill. Due to the exceedingly high risk involved, this bill is rarely used. If it is lost or stolen, the goods will be picked up by others, so it is highly risky.

不记名提单是指在提单的收货人栏内完全空白，不写收货人的名称。这种提单的特点：提单的持有人即收货人。不需要通过背书手续就可任意转让。提单的物权属于持有人，转手就意味着物权转移。所以，这种提单不安全，如遗失或被盗，货物也就被人提走。因此，同样也较少使用。

3）Order Bill 指示提单

It is a title document to the goods, issued "to the order of" a party in the box of consignee. The consignee is for the consigner's ratification. Order bills, widely used in international trade, are transferable and the transfer or the shipper should endorse the bill overleaf to transfer the title to the goods.

Order bill with blank endorsement is the most common requirement for bills of lading in terms of payment by letters of credit. Endorsement is a legal process during which the holder of the documents transfers the title to another party. In detail, the documents holder, the endorser signs or stamps the endorsee's name on the back of the bill, and this is also called special endorsement. The blank endorsement carries only the signature of the endorser and does not specify in whose favor it is made. In practice, to facilitate the transfer of bills in each stage, for instance, bills are firstly transferred to the negotiation bank; the blank endorsement is usually used.

Order B/L refers to the bill in which the name of a definite consignee is not mentioned and marked "to order". The seller keeps in possession of the goods before the buyer dominates a consignee, but after blank endorsement by the consignor, the bona fide holder is entitled to take delivery of the goods from the shipping company. Bills under collection should stick to order bills endorsed by the seller.

指示提单是指提单的收货人栏内不写收货人的名称，只写“凭指示”字样。这种提单的特点是收货人尚待提单所有人（发货人）确定。发货人（出口人）可以通过背书转让提单的所有权，也就是转让提单的提货权。所以，这种提单又称可转让提单，在国际贸易中广泛使用。

“空白抬头、空白背书”是在信用证方式下对提单的形式要求，是最普遍、使用最广泛的一种。背书是单据（或票据）的所有人转让单据所有权的一种法律手续。具体说，就是单据所有人在提单的背面签名或盖章，他就被称为背书人，再写上受让人的名字，受让人称为被背书人。通过这种方式就把提单的所有权（具体地说是提货权）从背书人手中转移给被背书人（受让人），这也叫记名背书。如果只有背书人在提单背面签名，而不写受让人的名字，就称为“空白背书”。在国际贸易中为了方便在各个环节转让提单，比如提单先转让给议付行，通常采用“空白背书”。

“空白抬头”，也就是“凭指示”的指示提单，再加上“空白背书”，习惯上就把这种提单称为“空白抬头、空白背书”的提单。在发货人（出口人）未指定收货人之前，卖方凭指定提单仍保持货物的所有权。如经发货人在提单上空白背书后，即成为凭单提货的单据，合法持有这种提单的人就有权向船公司提货。凡是以托收方式出口的提单必须坚持使用卖方背书的指示提单。

1.2.4 According to the Validity 根据提单的效力

According to the validity, B/L can be classified as follows:

根据提单的效力，提单可分为以下几类：

1）Original B/L 正本提单

It is legally valid and signed and dated by either the shipping company or by a duly authorized agent. Original bills of lading should be marked “original” on their faces. Bills of lading are usually made out in 2 copies or 3 copies and when one of the originals is used for taking delivery of the goods, the others automatically become null and void.

正本提单是指提单上有承运人、船长或其代理人签名盖章并注明签发日期的提单。这种提单在法律上是有效的单据。正本提单上必须标明“正本”字样。正本提单一般签发一式两份或三份，凭其中的任何一份提货后，其余的即作废。

2）Copy B/L 副本提单

A copy B/L, without Carriers’ signatures or stamps, is just the opposite of an original bill and only for reference. For easy distinction, a copy bill of lading is marked “Copy”, “Duplicate” or “Non-negotiable”.

副本提单是指与正本提单相对的提单，即提单上没有承运人签字盖章，只供参考使用。副本提单上一般都印有“Copy”（副本）、“Duplicate”（副本）、“Non-negotiable”（不可转让）字样，以示与正本提单的区别。

1.2.5 According to Means of Transportation 根据运输方式

According to means of transportation, B/L can be classified as follows:

提单根据运输方式，可分为以下几类：

1）Direct B/L 直达提单

Direct B/L means the B/L in which the goods are shipped directly from the port of loading to the port of destination without involving transshipment.

轮船从装运港装货后，中途不经过换船而直接驶往目的港卸货称为直达。签发这种情况的提单叫直达提单。

2）Transshipment B/L 转船提单

Transshipment B/L indicates the goods need to be transshipped at an intermediate port as there is no direct service between the shipment port and the destination port. It is sometimes necessary to employ two or more carriers to get the goods to the final destination.

转船提单是指货运全程由至少两艘轮船承运。也就是说，从装运港装货的轮船不直接驶往目的港，需要在中途港换装另一只船运往目的港，甚至有时换船不止一次。在这种情况下，就要签发转船提单。

3）Stale B/L 过期提单

Bills presented to the consignee or buyer after the stipulated expiry date of presentation or after the goods are at the port of destination are described as "stale B/L". In the former case, the seller presents the bills for negotiation 21 days after the issue date. In the latter case, the bill fails to arrive before the arrival of the goods. According to UCP600, banks would decline shipping documents presented more than 21 days after the issue date. The latter case often appear in short sea voyages, so it is necessary to add a clause of "stale B/L acceptable" in short sea voyages.

过期提单是指错过规定的交单日期或者晚于货物到达目的港日期的提单。前者是指卖方超过提单签发日期后 21 天才交到银行议付的提单，后者是指货已到但提单未到。根据《跟单信用证统一惯例》规定，如信用证无特殊规定，银行将拒绝接受在运输单据签发日后超过 21 天才提交的单据。后者是在短途海上运输时容易出现情况，故在短途海上运输贸易合同中，一般都订有“过期提单可以接受”的条款。

2. Railway Consignment Note 铁路运单

2.1 International Railway Through Transport Bill 国际铁路联运运单

It does not represent the title of the goods, and is non-transferable. International railway through transport bill and its copies are shipping contracts between the railway and the consignor and are of legally binding force to the railway, the consignor and the consignee. When the consignor submits all goods to the starting station, and the starting station dates and stamps the transport bill and its copies to testify all goods are received by the shipper; that is to say, transporting contract comes into effect.

国际铁路联运运单，不是代表货物所有权的凭证，不可转让。铁路运单和运单副本是国际联运中铁路与货主之间的运输契约，对收货人、发货人和铁路都具有法律约束力。当发货人向始发站提交全部货物时，始发站在运单和运单副本上加盖注明日期的印章证明货物已被接受承运，即认为运输契约已经生效。

2.2 Cargo Receipt 承运货物收据

It is the shipping contract between the carrier and the consignor which is issued by the carrier and is used under special circumstances. The cargo transported by road from mainland to Hong Kong and Macao is usually entrusted to Chinese foreign trade transportation corporations. When cargo is loaded and dispatched, Chinese foreign trade transportation corporations immediately issue a copy of cargo receipt to the consignor as evidence to deal with settlement of exchange. Cargo receipt is also a certificate for the consignee to take delivery of the cargo.

承运货物收据是在特定运输方式下所使用的一种运输单据，它是承运人出具的货物收据，也是承运人与托运人签订的运输契约。我国内地通过铁路运往港澳地区的出口货物，一般多委托中国对外贸易运输公司承办。当出口货物装车发运后，对外贸易运输公司即签发一份承运货物收据给托运人，以作为对外办理结汇的凭证。货物收据还是收货人凭以提货的凭证。

3. Airway Bill 航空运单

It does not represent the title of the goods and is non-transferable. It is cargo receipt issued by the carrier after receiving the goods. The carrier sends out an arrival notice and the consignee takes delivery of the goods by virtue of arrival notice and identification. So, airway bill is not title of goods and shall not be transferred or financed. However, it is a formal proof evidencing the consignor has already taken delivery of the goods, with which the consignor could make a settlement with the consignee.

航空运单不是代表货物所有权的凭证，不可转让。航空货运单是承运人收取货物后签发的货物收据。货抵目的地后，承运人向收货人发出到货通知，收货人凭到货通知和身份证明提取货物。所以，航空货运单并非物权凭证，也不能转让和借以向银行融通资金。但航空货运单是证明发货人业已交运货物的正式凭证，发货人可凭航空货运单向收货人结算货款。

4. Non-negotiable Seaway Bill 不可转让海运单

It is a non-negotiable seaway bill popular in European, Scandinavian Peninsula, North America, and the Far East and the Middle East areas in recent years. It is also a receipt signed by the captain, the shipping company or its agent, evidencing that the goods have been received and would be sent to a designated consignee. Non-negotiable seaway bill and seaway bill are both receipts of goods and proofs of seaway transportation. But non-negotiable seaway bill is not the title of the goods, which is not supposed to be presented when the consignee takes delivery of the goods. The consignee shall prove that it is the designated one indicated on the bill to take delivery of the goods. Therefore, non-negotiable seaway bill facilitates the importer's prompt delivery of the goods, simplifies the procedures, cuts down expenses and decreases the possibility of fraud. In addition, with the development of EDI, non-negotiable seaway bill is perfect in international trade.

不可转让海运单是近些年来欧洲、斯堪的纳维亚半岛、北美和某些远东、中东地区开始通行的一种不可流通转让的海运单据。它也是由船长或船公司或其代理人签发的证明已收到特定货物（已接管或已装船）并保证将货物运至目的地交付给指定收货人的一种凭证。不可转让海运单与海运提单同样也是船方出具的货物收据，也是海上货物运输契约的证明。但它不是货物所有权的凭证，收货人提货时无须出示海运单，承运人仅凭收货人提交的证明其为海运单上指定收货人的凭条交付货物。所以，使用不可转让海运单有利于进口商及时提货、简化手续、节省费用，并有助于减少欺诈现象。另外，由于EDI在国际贸易中的广泛运用，更适宜使用不可转让海运单。

5. Multimodal Transport Documents, MTD 多式联运单据

Multimodal transport documents come into being to adapt to the widely used means of containerization and multimodal transportation.

According to *Uniform Rules on Combined Transport Documents* (ICC NO. 298 Publication) and *United Nations Convention on International Multimodal Transport of Goods* passed in May 1984, multimodal transport documents are either negotiable (made out to order or bearer) or non-negotiable (clearly indicating the name of the consignee).

Currently in the field of ocean shipping, some companies like China Ocean Shipping Company establish “combined transport bill of lading” (CTB/L) which can be used both in port-to-port transportation and inter-modal transportation between ocean transportation and other kinds of transportation.

多式联运单据是适应广泛开展集装箱运输的需要而产生的，在使用多种运输方式联合运送货物时使用。

《联合运输单据统一规则》（国际商会第298号出版物）和1984年5月通过的《联合国国际货物多式联运公约》规定，国际多式联运所使用的多式联运单据既可以是可转让的（作成“凭指示”或“凭来人”抬头，即列明按指示或向持单人交付货物），也可以是不可转让的（表面注明“不可转让”并做成记名抬头，即指明记名的收货人）。

目前在航运界，一些船公司如中国远洋运输公司制定了一种“联合运输提单”，既可以用于一般港到港的运输，也可用于海运与其他运输方式的联运。

Case Study 本章案例

Case 1: A Chinese foreign trade exporter contracted with a Canadian importer to export 1,000 pairs of sneakers in CIF terms, time of shipment is between July to August in the contract and letters of credit, 5,000 pairs of sneakers each month, and transshipment is allowed. Our exporter loaded 5,000 pairs of sneakers on board the ship “Wuyi” on 31st, July and got bill of lading for July, and loaded the rest of sneakers on board the ship “Triumph” on 10th, August and got bill of lading for August. Both ships transshipped in Hong Kong and both lots of goods are transported to the final destination by “Noble” of Maersk INC.

Questions: 1) Was it transshipment? Why?

2) Could the seller safely get financed? Why?

【案例 1】我国某外贸公司与加拿大客商按 CIF 纽约出口运动鞋 1 000 双，合同与信用证装期为 7—8 月份，每月装运 5 000 双，允许转船。我公司于 7 月 31 日将 5 000 双运动鞋装上“武夷号”轮，取得 7 月份的提单，又于 8 月 10 日将余下的 5 000 双装上“胜利号”轮，取得 8 月份的提单。两船均在香港转船，两批货均由马士基公司“贵族号”轮运至目的地。

请问：（1）这种做法，是否属于分批装运？为什么？

（2）卖方能否安全收汇？为什么？

Case Analysis: (1) It is transshipment. According to UCP600: “Transshipment means unloading form one means of conveyance and reloading to another means of conveyance (whether or not in different modes of transport) during the carriage from the place of dispatch, taking in charge or shipment to the place of final destination stated in the credit.” While in this case, the goods were shipped by “Wuyi” on 31st, July and shipped by “Triumph” on 15th, August. Both ships were totally different, so it was transshipment. (2) The seller could safely get payment for goods as a result of conformity with the letter of credit clauses.

【案例分析】（1）本例做法属于分批装运。因为《跟单信用证统一惯例》（UCP600）规定：“同一船只同一航次中多次装运货物，即使提单表示不同的装船日期或表明不同的装船港口，只要运输单据注明的目的地相同也不视为分批装运。”但本例中，7 月 31 日货装“武夷号”轮，8 月 15 日货装“胜利号”轮，即非同一船只，所以应视作分批装运。（2）卖方能安全收汇，因为符合信用证装运条款的要求。

Case 2: A Chinese foreign trade exporter exported 30,000 boxes of goods, contracting to ship the goods in each lot during March to August, 5,000 boxes each month, payment by confirmed irrevocable letter of credit. The customer duly sent letter of credit on which the total amount is in conformity with the contract, but the shipping clauses indicated “the latest date of shipment is 31st, August, by partial shipment.” Our exporter dispatched 5,000 boxes in March, 6,000 boxes in April, 10,000 boxes in May and 9,000 boxes in June. The customer raised an objection to this. Is it right to do so? Why?

【案例 2】我国某外贸公司向英国出口商品 30 000 箱，合同规定 3—8 月按月等量装运，每月装运 5 000 箱，凭不可撤销信用证付款，客户按时开来信用证，证上总金额与总数量均与合同相符，但装运条款规定“最迟装运期为 8 月 31 日，分批装运”。我方 3 月份装出 5 000 箱，4 月份装出 6 000 箱，5 月份装出 10 000 箱，6 月份装出 9 000 箱。客户发现后向我方提出异议。我们这样做是否可以？为什么？

Case Analysis: In order to get payment in due time, we were supposed to do this. As credit is independent of the contract and once the credit and the relating documents are in conformity, the exporter can get payment. The Letter of credit generally indicates that “the latest date of shipment is 31st, August, in partial shipments”. So our exporter was right, but in case of trouble in the following days, we shall adopt partial shipment in equal lots, which is corresponding to the contact and letter of credit.

【案例分析】从信用证项下我方能否如期收回货款考虑，这样做是可以的。因为信用证一经开立就成为独立于合同之外的法律文件，只要单证一致，即可收取货款。信用证中笼统规定“最迟装运日期为 8 月 31 日，分批装运”，所以我方的做法是可以的。但为防日后麻烦，我方应争取等量分批的做法，这样既符合合同规定，又满足了信用证的要求。

Questions 思考题

1. What is multimodal transport? What are the necessary conditions of multimodal transport?
   什么叫国际多式联运？构成国际多式联运应具备什么条件？
2. What are the stipulations for port of shipment and port of destination in the sales contract?
   销售合同中的装运港和目的港有哪些规定方法？
3. What are the provisions for partial shipment according to UCP600?
   《跟单信用证统一惯例》对分批装运有何规定？
4. What are shipped bill of lading and received for shipment B/L?
   什么叫已装船提单和备运提单？
5. What are clean B/L and received B/L?
   什么叫清洁提单和不清洁提单？
6. What is order B/L?
   什么叫指示提单？

Chapter 10

Cargo Transportation Insurance

国际货物运输保险

Insurance is a kind of economic compensation system, which collects insurance premium from most units and individuals. It is the practice of sharing among many persons, risks of life or property that would otherwise be suffered by only a few. This is affected by each person paying a sum of money called a premium, which is put into a "pool" or insurance fund, out of which money is paid to those who suffer loss.

With insurance, the applicant not only assists others who need help, but also safeguards his or her own economic benefits. This fully embodies the sprit of "all for one and one for all", that is, getting from the mass and utilizing for one man.

Legally speaking, it is a compensational contract, that is, the insurant pays a sum of consideration (premium) to the insurance company and the insurance company will, according to the terms indicated in the insurance contract, indemnify the insurant of any loss that occurs within the scope of the coverage.

保险是一种经济补偿制度，它集中多数单位和个人的保险金建立保险基金，利用分散危险、分摊损失的办法，对参加保险的少数被保险人由于特定灾害事故所遭受的损害或责任给予经济补偿或对人身伤亡给付保险金。

保险是一种组织经济补偿的互助行为。通过参加保险，投保人既帮助了他人，也保障了自己的经济利益，充分体现了"一人为众，众人为一"的精神，即"取之于面，用之于点"。

从法律角度看，它是一种补偿性契约行为，即被保险人向保险人提供一定的对价（保险费），保险人则对被保险人将来可能遭受的承保责任范围内的损失负赔偿责任。

Lesson 1 Coverage of Marine Cargo Insurance 海上货物运输保险承保范围

The insurance company covers three aspects, i.e. risks, losses, and expenses and compensates for the losses according to different risks. Risks, losses and expenses are closely related to one another. Risks lead to losses and the insurance company makes indemnity on the basis of different coverage, that is, the insurance company does not hold responsibility to all risks and all losses.

保险公司保障的范围包括三个方面：风险、损失及发生的费用。保险公司按照不同险别风险所造成的损失承担赔偿责任。风险、损失和险别三者有着紧密的联系。风险引起损失，险别则是保险公司对风险和损失的承保责任范围。也就是说，保险公司并不是对所有的风险、所有的损失都承担赔偿责任，而是根据险别不同，决定保险公司责任的大小。

1. Perils and Risks 风险

Risks include two kinds: perils of the sea and extraneous risks. Perils of the sea include natural calamities and fortuitous accidents.

Risks	Perils of the Sea	Natural Calamities: bad weather, thunder and lightening, earthquake, flood, tsunami, etc.
		Fortuitous Accidents: grounding, stranding, sunk, collision, fire, explosion, missing, etc.
	Extraneous Risks	General Extraneous Risks: theft, breakage, leakage, contamination, etc.
		Special Extraneous Risks: military affairs, war, strike, failure to delivery, rejection, etc.

风险包括两大类：海上风险和外来风险。海上风险又分为自然灾害和意外事故两类。如下图所示：

风险	海上风险	自然灾害：恶劣气候、雷电、海啸、地震、洪水等
		意外事故：搁浅、触礁、沉没、互撞、失火、爆炸、失踪等
	外来风险	一般原因：偷窃、雨淋、短量、渗漏等
		特殊原因：战争、罢工、交货不到、拒收等

Fortuitous accidents refer to the accidents caused by unexpected haphazard. Marine insurance business covers not only marine accidents, but also road accidents as well.

Extraneous risks are the unexpected risks resulting in losses other than perils of the sea, including general extraneous risks and special extraneous risks.

意外事故指由于偶然的非意料之中的原因造成的事故。海上保险业务中的意外事故，并不局限于发生在海上，也包括发生在陆地上的意外事故。

外来风险是指海上风险以外的其他外来原因所造成的风险。外来原因是指事先难以预料的、致使货物受损的某些外部因素。外来风险分为一般外来风险和特殊外来风险。

1.1 General Extraneous Risks 一般外来风险

- Theft/Pilferage 偷窃险；
- Contamination 沾污险；
- Leakage 渗漏险；
- Breakage 破碎险；
- Sweating and/or Heating 受热受潮险；
- Taint of Odor 串味险；
- Rusting 生锈险；
- Hook Damage 钩损险；
- Fresh and/or Rain Water Damage 淡水雨淋险；
- Shortage in Weight 短量险；
- Clashing 碰损险。

1.2 Special Extraneous Risks 特殊外来风险

- War Risk 战争险；
- Strikes Risk 罢工险；
- Rejection Risk 拒收险；
- Failure to Delivery Risk 交货不到险；
- Aflatoxin Risk 黄曲霉菌险；
- On Deck Risk 舱面险。

2. Loss 损失

Marine losses refer to any loss or damage due to natural calamities and fortuitous accidents and the related costs incurred in the process of transit, both on ocean-connected inland and in the river.

<table>
<tr><td rowspan="2">Marine Losses</td><td>Total Loss</td><td>Actual Total Loss
Constructive Total Loss</td></tr>
<tr><td>Partial Loss</td><td>General Average
Particular Average</td></tr>
</table>

海上损失指被保险货物在海洋运输途中，因遭遇海上自然灾害和意外事故所引起的损坏或灭失，还包括与海运连接的陆上运输和内河运输过程中遭受的损坏或灭失。

海上损失	全部损失（按程度分）	实际全损
		推定全损
	部分损失（按性质分）	共同海损
		单独海损

2.1 Total Loss 全部损失

It refers to the loss of the entire value of the subject matter to the insured, normally involving the maximum amount for which a policy is liable. Total Loss can be actual or constructive.

全部损失简称全损，是指被保险货物由于承保风险造成的全部灭失或完全变质、或不可能归还被保险人的损害。全损分为实际全损和推定全损两种。

2.1.1 Actual Total Loss 实际全损

It means that the cargo has been totally lost or has been damaged to the extent that it has lost its original usage.

货物完全灭失或变质而失去原有用途，即货物的全部损失已经发生或不可避免。

2.1.2 Constructive Total Loss 推定全损

It means the cargo is not totally lost, but the actual total loss shall be unavoidable or the restoration fees together with other miscellaneous expenses will exceed the anticipated amount of profit when the cargo is delivered to the destination. In other words, when a ship or a cargo is so badly damaged, the cost of repair or the effort of rescue would be greater than the market value of the ship or cargo. They are treated as totally lost.

推定全损指货物受损后进行施救、整理和恢复原状所需要的费用，或者再加上续运至目的地的费用总和，估计要超过货物在目的地的完好状态的价值。

2.2 Partial Loss 部分损失

It means a partial damage to or the total loss of part of the insured cargo.

部分损失指被保险货物的损失没有达到全部损失的程度。

2.2.1 General Average 共同海损

It is defined as a partial and deliberate sacrifice of the ship, freight, cargo, or the additional expense incurred to rescue a ship and its cargo from impending danger or for the common safety of the adventure under a peril of the sea or some other hazards.

There are four conditions forming GA:

1) The danger that threats the common safety of cargo and/or vessel shall be materially existent and is not foreseen.

2) The measures taken by the master shall be conscious and reasonable, which means, GA is man-made but not an accidental loss.

3) The sacrifice shall be specialized and not caused by perils directly and the expense

incurred shall be additional expense which is not within the operation budget.

4) The loss of sacrifice and expenses should ultimately be effective.

The loss of sacrifice as well as the expenses incurred in a general average shall be shared among all parties, including the carrier and all cargo owners, in proportion to their respective interested value benefited from the general average, and such proportion is called a general average contribution. As to each party involved, the amounts benefited from GA may be less than the intrinsic value of the vessel, cargo and transportation costs. So GA belongs to partial loss.

载货船舶在海运途中遇到危难，船长为了维护船舶和所有货物的共同安全或使航程得以继续完成，有意并且合理地做出的某些牺牲或支出的特殊费用。

构成共同海损的条件包括：

（1）船方在采取紧急措施时，必须确有危及船、货共同安全的危险存在。

（2）船方所采取的措施必须是有意识的、合理的。所谓有意识的是指共同海损的发生必须是人为的、有意识行为的结果，而不是一种意外的损失。

（3）所做出的牺牲或支出的费用必须是非常性质的。所谓非常性质是指这种牺牲或费用不是通常业务中所必然会遇到或支出的。

（4）构成共同海损的牺牲和费用支出，最终还必须是有效的。

共同海损的牺牲和费用应由船、货或运费三方按最后获救的价值共同按比例分摊，即共同海损的分摊。对个别有关当事人而言，分摊到的金额均小于船、货、运费的本身价值。因此，从这个意义上说，共同海损属于部分损失。

2.2.2 Particular Average 单独海损

It is a partial loss of the subject matter insured, caused by an event that had been insured against. It falls entirely upon the particular owner of the property which has suffered the damage. For instance, collision or breakage is irrelevant to cargo owners and ship owners and it causes only partial loss, which is called particular average.

The differences between GA and PA are:

1) GA is caused directly by risks; PA is man-made loss in order to remove or alleviate risks.

2) The damaged party is responsible for losses incurred in a PA; the loss of sacrifice as well as the expenses incurred in a GA shall be shared among all parties.

单独海损是指货物受损后未达到全损程度，而是单独一方的利益受损，并只能由该利益所有者单独负担的一种部分损失。如瓷器碰撞、破碎，与其他货主、船东无关，而损失又未达到全损程度，称为单独海损。

单独海损与共同海损的区别如下：

（1）前者是风险直接导致的损失；后者是为了解除或减轻这些风险而人为造成的损失。

（2）前者的损失由受损方自己承担；后者由受益各方按受益大小的比例分摊。

Lesson 2 Ocean Marine Cargo Clauses of CIC
我国海运货物保险条款

China Insurance Clauses (CIC) are constituted according to both practices and conventions in the international insurance market and China's real needs for insurance. The latest revision is in 2009, Abr. Cargo Clauses 2009. Insurance coverage refers to the scope of responsibility the insurer takes and it is the basis of not only performing rights and obligations, but also the basis of collecting insurance premium.

The following mainly introduces the China Ocean Marine Cargo Clauses stipulated by the People's Insurance Company of China (PICC 2009).

China insurance coverage consists of basic ocean marine cargo insurance and additional risks.

中国人民保险公司根据我国保险业务的实际需要并参照国际保险市场的习惯做法制定了各种不同运输方式的货物运输保险条款以及附加险条款，总称“中国保险条款”。最近一次的修订是在2009年，简称2009保险条款。保险险别是保险人对风险和损失的承保责任范围，它是保险人与被保险人履行权利与义务的基础，也是保险人承保责任的大小和被保险人缴付保险费多少的依据。

本节主要介绍中国人民保险公司2009年制定的《海洋运输货物保险条款》。

我国保险条款将保险险别分成基本险和附加险两大类。

1. Basic Ocean Marine Cargo Insurance 基本险

1.1 Free from Particular Average (FPA) 平安险

FPA means the compensation does not cover Particular Average. The coverage of FPA includes: Total loss due to natural disasters and total or partial loss caused by fortuitous accidents. FPA is not responsible for the partial loss due to natural disasters. In fact, FPA covers sacrifice in and contribution to General Average and salvage charges, that is, FPA is not applicable to Particular Average due to natural disasters.

It indicates non-liability of indemnification. This insurance covers:

1) Actual total loss or constructive total loss of the consignment caused by natural calamities such as heavy weather, tsunami, earthquake, flood, etc..

2) Total loss or partial loss caused by fortuitous accidents such as stranding, striking upon the rocks, icebergs or other objects, collision, fire and explosion.

3) Partial loss of the insured cargo attributable to heavy weather, lightning, and/or tsunami, where the conveyance has been grounded, stranded, sunk or burnt irrespective of whether the event or events took place before or after such accidents.

4) Partial or total loss resulting from the failing of entire package or packages into sea during loading, transshipment or discharge.

5) Reasonable cost incurred by the insurant on salvaging the cargo or averting or minimizing a loss recoverable under the policy, provided that such cost shall not exceed the sum insured of the consignment.

6) Losses attributable to discharge of the insured cargo at a port of distress following a sea peril as well as special charges arising from loading, warehousing and forwarding of the cargo at an intermediate port of call or refuge.

7) Sacrifice in and contribution to general average and salvage charges.

8) Such proportion of losses sustained by the ship owners as is to be reimbursed by the cargo owner under the contract of affreightment both to blame collision clause.

It needs to point out that the insurance covers the loss that the conveyance has been grounded, stranded, sunk or burnt in transit irrespective of whether the event or events took place before or after such accidents.

平安险旧译为“单独海损不赔”。其责任范围包括自然灾害导致的全部损失和意外事故造成的全部损失或部分损失。平安险对自然灾害造成的部分损失不赔，实际上部分损失中的共同海损以及共同海损的牺牲和分摊及救助费用和对受损保险货物进行施救的费用等是保险公司的赔偿责任范围。也就是说，平安险只是对自然灾害造成的“单独海损不赔”。

投保了平安险，保险公司对下列损失负赔偿责任：

（1）被保险的货物在运输途中由于恶劣气候、雷电、海啸、地震、洪水等自然灾害造成整批货物的全部损失或推定全损。若被保险的货物用驳船运往或运离海轮，则每一驳船所装的货物可视作一个整批。

（2）由于运输工具遭遇搁浅、触礁、沉没、互撞，与流冰或其他物体碰撞以及失火、爆炸等意外事故所造成的货物全部或部分损失。

（3）在运输工具已经发生搁浅、触礁、沉没、焚毁等意外事故的情况下，货物在此前后又在海上遭受恶劣气候、雷电、海啸等自然灾害所造成的部分损失。

（4）在装卸或转船时由于一件或数件甚至整批货物落海所造成的全部或部分损失。

（5）被保险人对遭受承保责任内的货物采取抢救、防止或减少货损的措施所支付的合理费用，但以不超过该批被毁货物的保险金额为限。

（6）运输工具遭遇海难后，在避难港由于卸货引起的损失，以及在中途港或避难港由于卸货、存仓和运送货物所产生的特殊费用。

（7）共同海损的牺牲、分摊和救助费用。

（8）运输契约中如订有“船舶互撞责任”条款，则根据该条款规定应由货方偿还船方的损失。

需要注意的是，如在运输过程中运输工具发生搁浅、触礁、沉没、焚毁等意外事故，则不论在事故发生之前或之后由于自然灾害所造成的单独海损，保险公司也要负赔偿责任。

1.2 With Particular Average: WPA or WA 水渍险

Aside from the risks covered under FPA conditions as above, this insurance also covers partial losses of the insured goods caused by natural calamities such as heavy weather, lightning, tsunami, earthquake or flood (excluding FPA).

水渍险直译为“单独海损也赔”，水渍险的责任范围包括平安险的责任范围，外加由于自然灾害如恶劣天气、闪电、海啸、地震及洪水造成的部分损失，都给予赔偿（平安险不赔）。

1.3 All Risks (AR) 一切险

Aside from the risks covered under the FPA and WA conditions as above, this insurance covers 11 additional risks. In other words, all risks are the most comprehensive coverage among the three.

一切险的责任范围：水渍险的各项责任再加 11 种一般附加险。也就是说，一切险是平安险、水渍险、一般附加险的总和。

1.4 Exclusions 三种基本险的除外责任

1）Loss or damage caused by the intentional act of fault of the insured;

2）Loss or damage falling under the liability of the consignor;

3）Loss or damage arising from the inferior quality or shortage of the insured goods prior to the attachment of this insurance;

4）Loss or damage arising from normal loss, inherent vice or nature of the insured goods, loss of market and/or delay in transit and any expenses arising therefore;

5）Risks and liabilities excluded by the ocean marine cargo war risks clauses and strike, riot and civil commotion clauses of CIC.

（1）被保险人的故意行为或过失所造成的损失；

（2）属于发货人的责任所造成的损失；

（3）在保险责任开始前，被保险货物已存在的品质不良或数量短量所造成的损失；

（4）被保险货物的自然损耗、本质缺陷或本身特性以及市场跌落、运输延迟所引起的损失或费用；

（5）属于海洋运输货物战争险和罢工险条款规定的责任范围和除外责任。

1.5 Insurance Duration 保险期限（保险责任的起讫）

We take the practice stipulated by the International Insurance Market called Warehouse to Warehouse Clause to decide the insurance duration.

W/W indicates that the insurance company undertakes an insurance liability over the insured cargo from the warehouse or the place of storage of the shipper named in the policy until the cargo has arrived at the warehouse or the place of storage of the receiver named in the policy. The insurance liability terminates once the cargo arrives at the warehouse of the receiver.

我国采用国际保险市场上有关保险责任起讫规定的惯例——仓至仓条款。

仓至仓条款是保险责任起讫的条款。它是指自被保险货物运离保险单所载明的起运地发货人的仓库时生效，包括正常的运输过程，直至该货物运交保险单所载明的目的地收货人的仓库时为止。一旦货物进入收货人的仓库，保险责任即告终止。

2. Additional Risks 附加险

Additional Risks include General Additional Risks and Special Additional Risks.

Additional Risks cover losses caused by Extraneous Risks and Extraneous Risks including General Extraneous Risks and Special Extraneous Risks, so Additional Risks are divided into General Additional Risks and Special Additional Risks.

General Additional Risks shall go with FPA and WPA according to the characteristics of the cargo. If General Additional Risks are insured, All Risks are insured. Therefore, General Additional Risks are in the coverage of All Risks. There is no need to apply for General Additional Risks if All Risks are obtained.

附加险包括一般附加险和特殊附加险。

由于附加险承保的是外来风险造成的损失，而外来风险又有一般外来风险和特殊外来风险之分，所以附加险也可分为一般附加险和特殊附加险。

一般附加险不能作为一个单独的项目投保，而只能在投保平安险或水渍险的基础上，根据货物的特性和需要加保一种或若干种一般附加险。如加保所有的一般附加险，这就叫投保一切险，可见一般附加险被包括在一切险的承保范围内。故在投保一切险时，不存在再加保一般附加险的问题。

2.1 General Additional Risks 一般附加险（11 种）

1) Risk of Theft, Pilferage and Non-delivery 偷窃、提货不着险；

2) Risk of Fresh Water Rain Damage; F.W.R. 淡水雨淋险；

3) Risk of Shortage 短量险；

4) Risk of Intermixture & Contamination 混杂、沾污险；

5) Risk of Leakage 渗漏险；

6) Risk of Clash & Breakage 碰撞、破碎险；

7) Risk of Odor 串味险；

8) Risk of Damage Caused by Heating & Sweating 受热、受潮险；

9) Risk of Hook Damage 钩损险；

10) Risk of Loss or Damage Caused by Breakage of Packing 包装破裂险；

11) Risk of Rust 锈损险。

Rust should be in transit. Compensation is not suitable for rust in packing.

All these additional risks should go with three basic types of risks as one type or several types of risks added.

All Risks cover all these eleven general additional risks; therefore, it is not necessary to insure General Additional Risks if All Risks are obtained (excluding Special Additional Risks).

锈损必须发生在运输过程中，对于原装时就已发生的锈损则不予赔偿。

这些附加险都不能单独投保，只能在投保一种基本险别的基础上加保一种或若干种附加险。

一切险已包含所有 11 种一般附加险。所以，不需要再加保一般附加险（不包含特殊附加险）。

2.2 Special Additional Risks 特殊附加险

Special Additional Risks are not in the coverage of All Risks. There are 8 types of Special Additional Risks, among which War Risk and Strikes Risk are the main ones.

特殊附加险不包括在一切险范围内。特殊附加险目前共有八种，战争险和罢工险是其中最主要的。

2.2.1 War Risk 战争险

War Risk shall go with one of the three types of basic insurance coverage.

War Risk is one of the main types of Special Additional Risks. Though it cannot be solely insured, it is more independent than other additional risks. It includes insurance coverage, exclusions, and commencement and termination.

In conclusion, Commencement and Termination of War Risk is from the port of shipment to the port of destination, which does not conform to Warehouse to Warehouse Clauses.

战争险不能单独投保，必须在投保一种基本险别的基础上加保。

战争险是特殊附加险的主要险别之一，它虽然不能独立投保，但对其他附加险而言又有很强的独立性，其内容包括责任范围、除外责任、责任起讫等。

战争险的保险责任起讫，不适用于仓至仓条款，而是从货物在装运港装上船，保险责任开始生效，到目的港卸离海轮终止。

2.2.2 Strikes Risk; S.R.C.C. Strike Riots and Civil Commotions 罢工险

It covers loss of or damage to the cargo insured directly caused by acts of strikers and locked-out workmen. But it does not cover loss of or damage to the cargo caused by lack of labor force or failure to apply the workforce. For instance, cargo suffers losses without fuel added or due to the malfunction of the air-conditioner.

According to the international insurance practice, the insured shall not be charged with any other expense as long as the insurant has already covered War Risk and generally War Risk is covered together with Strikes Risk.

罢工险是指对罢工人员行为所造成的损失进行保险，但对由于罢工劳力不足或不能运用劳力而造成的货物受损不赔。例如，货物因无人加油、空调不工作而受损，是不能获得赔偿的。

根据国际保险业的惯例，承保这一险别时，只要投保人已投保战争险就不再另收保费，而且一般都是与战争险同时承保。

Lesson 3 Other Types of Cargo Insurance
其他运输方式下的货运保险

1. Overland Transportation Insurance 陆上运输货物保险

According to CIC, it covers rail and road transportation and it is applicable to Warehouse-to-Warehouse Clauses.

中国人民保险公司《陆上运输货物保险条款》规定，责任范围仅限于火车和汽车运输，也采用仓至仓条款。

1.1 Coverage of Overland Transportation Insurance (Similar to WPA) 陆运险（与水渍险相似）的承保责任范围

The risks covered under Overland Transportation Risks are somewhat similar to those under WPA for marine cargo insurance. It covers total or partial loss of the insured cargo caused by natural calamities, such as storm, thunder, flood and earthquake, or resulting from the clashing, overturning, and derailing of the transportation in transit. It also covers total or partial loss of the insured cargo due to the lightering transportation being grounded, stranded, sunk or clashed in the course of lightering. It covers total or partial loss of the insured cargo caused by accidents, such as tunnel wrack, cliff crack, fire or explosion, too. In addition, the insurance covers the reasonable cost incurred by the insurant on salvaging the cargo or averting or minimizing a loss recoverable under the policy, provided that such cost shall not exceed the sum for which the consignment is insured. The insurant shall cover one or more types of General Additional Risks if needed.

The risks covered under Overland Transportation All Risks are somewhat similar to those under All Risks for marine cargo insurance. Aside from the risks covered under Overland Transportation Risks, this insurance also covers all risks of loss of or damage to the insured goods, whether partial or total, arising from external causes in transit.

The exclusions of overland transportation risks are just the same as those of marine cargo insurance.

陆运险的承保责任范围与海洋运输货物保险条款中的水渍险相似。保险公司负责赔偿被保险货物在运输途中遭受暴风、雷电、洪水、地震等自然灾害，或由于运输工具遭受碰撞、倾覆、出轨，或在驳运过程中因驳运工具遭受搁浅、触礁、沉没、碰撞，或由于遭受隧道坍塌、崖崩或失火、爆炸等意外事故所造成的全部或部分损失。此外，被保险人对遭受承保责任内危险的货物采取抢救、防止或减少货损的措施而支付的合理费用，保险公司也负责赔偿，但以不超过该批被救货物的保险金额为限。在投保陆运险的情况下，被保险人可根据需要加保一种或数种一般附加险。

陆运一切险的承保责任范围与海上运输货物保险条款中的一切险相似。保险公司除承担上述陆运险的赔偿责任外，还负责保险货物在运输途中由于一般外来原因所造成的全部或部分损失。

陆上运输险的除外责任与海洋运输货物险的除外责任相同。

1.2 Duration 保险责任的起讫期限

It also follows the W/W clause. The insurance company undertakes an insurance liability over the insured cargo from the warehouse or the place of storage of the shipper named in the policy until the cargo has arrived at the warehouse or place of storage of the receiver named in the policy. The insurance shall be limited to sixty days after completion of discharge of the insured goods at the final port of discharge before they reach the above mentioned warehouse of storage.

陆上运输货物险的责任起讫也采用仓至仓责任条款。保险人责任在被保险货物离开保险单所载明的起运地仓库或储存处所开始运输时生效，包括正常运输过程中的陆上和与其有关的水上舶运在内，直至该项货物运达保险单所载目的地收货人的最后仓库或储存处所或被保险人用作分配、分派的其他储存处所为止。如未运抵上述仓库或储存处所，则以被保险货物运抵最后卸载的车站满 60 天为止。

1.3 Overland Additional Risks 陆运附加险

It includes Overland General Additional Risks and Overland Special Additional Risks. Attention should be paid to the following.

1) One or more types of General Additional Risks and Special Additional Risks could be covered together with Overland Transportation Risks;

2) If the added risk is War Risk, the coverage shall be limited to the railway, and the duration does not follow W/W clause but is limited by the time when the cargo is loaded on the transportation;

3) If there is no transshipment, the duration is 48 hours after the cargo arrives at the destination; if there is transshipment, the duration is 10 days and the coverage continues to be valid once the cargo is loaded on the transportation.

陆运附加险包括陆运一般附加险和陆运特殊附加险。需要注意以下问题。

（1）在投保陆运险的基础上可加保一种或若干种一般附加险和特殊附加险；

（2）投保陆运一切险时，如加保战争险则仅以铁路运输为限，其责任起讫不是仓至仓条款，而是以货物置于运输工具时为限；

（3）从货物装上车开始至卸车时为止如果不卸车，则从货物到站当日午夜起满 48 小时为止；如中途转车，不论卸车与否以 10 天为限，装上车续运则继续有效。

2. Air Transportation Cargo Insurance 航空运输货物保险

2.1 Basic Air Transportation Cargo Insurance of PICC 中国人民保险公司规定的基本险别

1) Coverage of Air Transportation Risk (WPA in Marine Cargo Insurance) 航空运输险（海运水渍险）的承保责任范围

The coverage of Air Transportation Risk is almost as extensive as that of WPA in marine cargo insurance. It covers total or partial loss of or damage to the insured cargo caused in transit by lightning, fire, explosion, jettison due to the aircraft encountering bad weather or other perils, collision, overturning, crashing or missing and other accidents.

航空运输险的承保责任范围与海洋货物运输保险条款中的“水渍险”相似，包括被保险货物在运输途中遭受雷电、火灾、爆炸或由于飞机遭受恶劣气候或其他危难事故而被抛弃，或由于飞机遭受碰撞、倾覆、坠落或失踪等自然灾害和意外事故所造成的全部或部分损失。

2) Coverage of Air Transportation All Risks (external causes) 航空运输一切险（一般附加险外来原因造成）的承保责任范围

In addition to what are covered under Air Transportation Risks, the coverage of Air Transportation All Risks also covers total loss or partial loss of or damage to the insured cargo arising from external causes in transit.

航空运输一切险的承保责任范围与海洋运输保险条款中的“一切险”相似，除包括航空运输险的各项责任外，还包括被保险货物由于一般外来原因所造成的全部或部分损失。

2.2 Duration 航空运输货物保险责任起讫

It follows W/W clauses, but the insurance shall be limited to 30 days after completion of discharge of the insured cargo from the aircraft at the final airport of discharge. And if the cargo shall be transferred to the destination not indicated in the insurance policy, the insurance liability ends when transferring begins.

虽然也是仓至仓条款，但不同的是如果货物运达保险单所载明的目的地而货物未进仓，以货物在最后卸载地卸离飞机后满 30 天为止。如在上述 30 天内，该保险货物需转运到非保险单所载明的目的地时，保险责任于该项货物开始转运时终止。

2.3 Coverage of Air Transportation Cargo War Risk 航空运输货物战争险的承保责任范围

It is one type of Additional Risks to Air Transportation Risk based on Air Transportation Risk and Air Transportation All Risks.

The insurance company undertakes loss of or damage to cargo caused by war, military events, armed conflicts, regular weapons and bombs, excluding losses caused by atomic or heated nuclear weapons.

航空运输货物战争险是航空运输货物险的一种特殊附加险，只有在投保了航空运输险或航空运输一切险的基础上方可加保。

加保航空运输货物战争险后，保险公司赔偿在航空运输途中由于战争、敌对行为或武装冲突以及各种常规武器和炸弹所造成的货物的损失，但不包括因使用原子或热核制造的武器所造成的损失。

2.4 Duration of Air Transportation Cargo War Risk 空运战争险的起讫责任

It is from charging the cargo on the plane to discharging from the plane at the destination indicated in the policy. But the insurance shall be limited to 15 days after the cargo arrives at the final airport of discharge. If the cargo is transferred during the trip, the insurance shall be limited to 15 days after the cargo arrives at the transshipment point. The insurance continues to be valid once the cargo is reloaded on the plane.

这一保险从被保险货物装上飞机开始，直到卸离保险单所载明的目的地的飞机时为止。如不卸机，则以载货飞机到达目的地的当日午夜起计算满 15 天为止。如被保险货物在中途转机，保险责任以飞机到达转运地当日起满 15 天为止。重新装上飞机，保险责任恢复有效。

Lesson 4 Institute Cargo Clauses
伦敦保险协会海运货物保险条款

Insurance business originating from England enormously affects the whole world. The Institute Cargo Clauses (I.C.C.) were initially published by the Institute of London Underwriters in 1912 and were revised in 2009 and the newest clauses came into effect on January 1, 2009.

保险业源于英国，对世界各国影响很大。英国伦敦保险协会货物条款最早制定于 1912 年，最近的一次修订完成于 2009 年，并于 2009 年 1 月 1 日起实行。

1. Different Kinds of ICC Clauses 伦敦保险协会修订的海运货物保险条款种类

It is mainly composed of the following 6 clauses:

主要有以下六种：

1) Institute Cargo Clauses A, ICC A 协会货物条款（A）

2) Institute Cargo Clauses B, ICC B 协会货物条款（B）

3) Institute Cargo Clauses C, ICC C 协会货物条款（C）

4) Institute War Clauses (Cargo) 协会战争险条款

5) Institute Strikes Clauses (Cargo) 协会罢工险条款

6) Malicious Damage Clauses 恶意损害险条款

The first 5 kinds can be independently covered without being attached to any other particular coverage. Meanwhile, ICC A clauses include malicious damage clauses, but malicious damage clauses should be attached to ICC B or ICC C.

前五种险别可以单独投保。另外，协会货物条款（A）险中包括恶意损害险，但在投保协会货物条款（B）险或协会货物条款（C）险时，应另行投保恶意损害险。

2. Coverage of Marine Cargo Insurance of ICC 伦敦保险协会货物保险条款规定保险责任的方法

2.1 ICC A 协会货物条款（A）

It is similar to that of All Risks under China Marine Cargo Insurance Clauses.

It adopts the method of "all risks except for exclusions", that is to say, except for exclusions; the insurer is responsible for the rest risks. In comparison, ICC B and ICC C cover named perils.

协会货物条款（A）相当于我国海洋货物运输保险条款的一切险。

协会货物条款（A）采取“一切风险减除外责任的方法”，即除了“除外责任”项下所列的风险保险人不予负责外，其他风险均予负责。而协会货物条款（B）、（C）险为“列明风险”。

Exclusions:

1) General Exclusions: Willful misconduct of the assured; ordinary leakage, ordinary loss in weight or volume, ordinary wear and tear; unsuitable packing; inherent vice; delay; insolvency or financial default of the owners, managers, characters or operators of the vessel; any weapon or device employing atomic or nuclear fission and/or fusion.

2) Exclusions of Unseaworthiness and Unfitness: Unseaworthiness and unfitness of vessel for the safe carriage of the subject-matter insured, where the assured are privy to such unseaworthiness or unfitness, at the time the subject-matter insured is loaded; unfitness of container or conveyance for the safe carriage of the subject-matter insured.

3) Exclusions of War: War, civil war, revolution, rebellion, insurrection, civil strike, or any hostile act by or against a belligerent power; capture, seizure, arrest, restraint or detainment, and the consequence thereof or any attempt threat; derelict mines, torpedoes, bombs or other derelict weapons of war.

4) Exclusions of Strikes: Strikers, locked-out workmen, or persons taking part in labor disturbances, riots or civil commotions; strikes, lock-outs, labor disturbances, riots or civil

commotions; any act of terrorism being an act of any person acting on behalf of, or in connection with, any organization; any person acting from a political, ideological or religious motive.

协会货物条款（A）的除外责任：

（1）一般除外责任包括：归因于被保险人故意的不法行为造成的损失或费用；自然渗漏、重量或容量的自然损耗或自然磨损；包装或准备不足或不当所造成的损失或费用；保险标的内在缺陷或特性所造成的损失或费用；直接由于迟延所引起的损失或费用；由于船舶所有人、经理人、租船人或经营破产或不履行债务造成的损失或费用；由于使用任何原子或热核武器所造成的损失或费用。

（2）不适航和不适货除外责任是指：在装船时，被保险人或其受雇人已经知道船舶不适航，以及船舶、装运工具、集装箱等不适货，如违反适航、适货的默示保证为被保险人或其受雇人所知道。

（3）战争除外责任是指：由于战争、内战、敌对行为等造成的损失或费用；由于捕获、拘留、扣留等（海盗除外）所造成的损失或费用；由于漂流水雷、鱼雷等造成的损失或费用。

罢工除外责任是指：由于罢工者、被迫停工工人等造成的损失或费用；任何恐怖主义者或出于政治动机或宗教信仰而行动的人所造成的损失或费用。

2.2 ICC B 协会货物条款（B）

It is similar to WPA Clauses.

协会货物条款（B）相当于我国保险条款的水渍险。

2.2.1 Insurance Coverage 协会货物条款（B）规定保险责任的方法

In short, it covers named perils, namely, it specifies insurable risks one by one for the insurant's choice and is convenient for settlement of compensation. The indemnity is determined by degree of loss, but not types of risks. There is no indication for franchise ratio.

简短来说，规定保险责任的方法可以概括为四个字——“列明风险”，即将承保范围内风险一一列举出来，便于投保人选择险别，又便于保险公司处理损害赔偿。一律按损失程度给予赔偿，不因险别不同而对部分损失赔偿。无免赔率的规定。

2.2.2 Specific Coverage 协会货物条款（B）险具体承保的风险

1) Losses or damages caused by fire, explosion, vessels or crafts being stranded, grounded, sunk, capsized, overturning, derailment of land conveyance, collision, contact of vessel craft or conveyance with any external object other than water, discharge of cargo at a port of distress, earthquake, volcanic eruption or lightning.

2) General average sacrifice, jettison or washing overboard, entry of sea, lake or river water into vessel, craft hold, conveyance, container, lift van or place of storage; total loss of any package lost overboard or dropped whist loading on to, or unloading from, vessel or craft.

（1）灭失或损害合理归因于下列原因：火灾、爆炸；船舶或驳船触礁、搁浅、沉没或倾覆；陆上运输工具倾覆或出轨；船舶、驳船或运输工具同水以外的外界物体碰撞；在避难港卸货；地震、火山爆发、雷电。

（2）灭失或损害由下列原因造成：共同海损牺牲；抛货；浪击落海；海水、湖水或河水进入船舶、驳船、运输工具、集装箱、大型海运箱或贮存处所；货物在装卸时落海或摔落造成整件的全损。

2.2.3 Exclusions 协会货物条款（B）的除外责任

In addition to the exclusions of ICC A, it shall not cover deliberate damage to or deliberate destruction of the subject-matter insured or any part thereof by the wrongful act of any person or persons only excluding losses, damage or expenses attributable to willful misconduct of the assured.

协会货物条款（B）的除外责任包括了协会货物条款（A）的除外责任的内容，另外加上了海盗造成的损失和第三方的恶意损害。也就是说，针对这些情况协会货物条款（B）都不予赔偿。

2.3 ICC C 协会货物条款（C）

It is similar to FPA Clauses.

协会货物条款（C）相当于我国海洋货物运输保险的平安险。

2.3.1 Insurance Coverage 协会货物条款（C）规定保险责任的方法

It only covers losses caused by important events and is not liable for unimportant accidents and natural calamities. In detail, it does not cover jettison or washing overboard, entry of sea, lake or river water into vessel, craft hold and total loss of any package lost overboard or dropped whist loading on to, or unloading from vessel or craft.

协会货物条款（C）只赔偿重大意外事故造成的损失，对非重大意外事故和自然灾害造成的损失都不予赔偿。对浪击落海，海水、湖水进入船舱和集装箱以及货物装卸时单件或数件落海都不予赔偿。

2.3.2 Exclusions 协会货物条款（B）的除外责任

The exclusions of ICC C are the same as those of ICC B. The coverage of ICC A and ICC B is wider than that of WPA and FPA under China Marine Cargo Insurance Clauses. ICC A adds regulations on compensations for the third party's intentional and paretic damages to the cargo. Moreover, it covers entry of sea, lake or river water into vessel, craft hold, which is not indicated in China Marine Cargo Insurance Clauses.

协会货物条款（A）和协会货物条款（B）比我国海洋货物运输的一切险和水渍险的范围要大。协会货物条款（A）增加了对第三方恶意损害进行赔偿和对海盗造成的损失进行赔偿的内容。另外，对浪击落海，海水、湖水进入船舱给予赔偿。这两个条款是我国海洋货物运输保险条款所没有的。

Lesson 5 Insurance Terms in Sales Contract
国际货物买卖合同中的保险条款

The insurance terms are one of the most important parts of the international sales contract, which relates to both parties' benefits. Insurance terms include insurance amount, the risks covered, the insurance premium, the insurance policy and the insurance clauses applied.

保险条款是国际货物买卖合同的重要组成部分之一。它涉及买卖双方的利益。保险条款包括保险金额、投保险别、保险费、保险单证和保险适用条款等。

1. Insurance Terms in Sales Contract 销售合同中的保险条款

Insurance terms may differ under different trade terms.

销售中的保险条款，因采用不同的贸易术语而有所区别。

Under FOB, CFR, FCA or CPT terms, insurance terms may simply be stipulated as: "Insurance to be covered by the buyer." Under CIF or CIP terms, the sales contract shall indicate "specific insurance amount and risks covered." For example: "Insurance is to be covered by the seller for 110% of the invoice value against All Risks and War Risk as per Ocean Marine Cargo Clauses of the People's Insurance Company of China 2009".

如按 FOB、CFR、FCA、CPT 条件成交，合同中只需规定："保险由买方办理。"如按 CIF、CIP 术语成交，出口合同则需具体规定保险金额、保险险别。例如："由卖方按发票金额的 110%投保一切险加战争险，按 2009 年《中国人民保险公司海洋运输货物保险条款》修订本"。

2. Insurance Practice of China Export Companies 我国外贸企业办理货物运输保险的做法

2.1 Export Insurance 出口货物运输保险——逐笔投保

According to the export contract or the Letter of Credit, after preparing the goods and confirming shipping tools and shipping dates, the seller shall apply for insurance and fill in an insurance policy which indicates name of the insurant, name and quantity of the cargo insured, packing methods, shipping marks, port of shipment and destination, name of vessel and voyage number, insurance amount, risks covered, insurance date and place for settlement.

Several ways of calculating the insurance premium are listed as follows.

外贸企业在装船前根据出口合同或信用证的规定，在备妥货物、确定运输工具和装运日期后即可申请投保、填写投保单：列明被保险人名称，保险标的物名称、数量、包装方式、运输标志、起止地点、船名、航次、开航日期、保险金额、险别、投保日期、赔款地点等。

保险费的计算方法有以下几种。

2.1.1 Amount Insured 保险金额——投保金额

It is the maximal indemnity paid by the insurer, which is the basis of checking the insurance premium.

Customarily, Amount Insured=CIF×(1+10%)

投保金额是保险公司可以赔偿的最高金额，也是核算保险费的基础。

习惯上按发票金额加一成（即 10%）投保加成：预期利润、业务费用。

保险金额＝CIF（总值）×（1＋10%）

2.1.2 Premium 保险费

It is the consideration paid by the insurer to the insurant, laying the pre-conditions for the insurer to undertake the insurance liability.

保险费是投保人给保险人的对价，是保险人承担保险责任的前提条件。

2.1.3 Premium Rate 保费率

Insurance Premium is determined by the amount insured and the premium rate. The Premium Rate is determined by risks covered and loss rate.

Insurance Premium=Insurance Amount×Premium Rate= [CIF×(1+10%)] × Premium Rate

E.g. Some 10,000 pieces of cargo exported to the USA by USD 10/pc CIF New York to be covered against All Risks and War Risk and the premium rates are respectively 0.6% and 0.4%.

Then Amount Insured=CIF×(1+10%) and Insurance Premium=Insurance Amount×Premium Rate=CIF×(1+10%)×Premium Rate=10×10,000×(1+10%)×(0.6%+0.4%)=110,000×1%=1,100 USD

保费率是计收保险费的依据。保险人交纳保险费的多少主要取决于保险金额和保费率，保费率是根据保险险别、风险大小、损失率高低制定的。

保险费的计算公式：

保险费＝保险金额×保费率＝[CIF×（1＋10%（投保加成率）]×保费率

例如：某商品出口美国，共 10 000 件，每件 USD 10/PC，CIF New York。投保一切险加战争险保费率分别为 0.6%和 0.4%，试计算保险费。

答：保险金额=[CIF×(1+10%)]×保费率

保险费= [10×10 000×(1+10%)]×(0.6%+0.4%)=110 000×1%=1 100（美元）

2.2 Import Insurance 进口货物运输保险

It includes open cover and open policy. Under FOB, CFR, CPT and FCA import trade terms, insurance is covered by the importer. We usually adopt simplified measures, that is, our exporter signs various kinds of open insurance contracts with insurance companies. As to opening insurance contracts, exporter does not need to sign insurance policies one by one, but to hand over shipping notice from the seller to the insurer, thus finishing import insurance procedures.

进口货物运输保险分为进口预约保险合同和预约保单。凡按 FOB、CFR、CPT、FCA 签订的进口合同，由进口方投保。外贸企业为了简化手续，大多采用预约保险的做法，也就是由外贸企业与保险公司签订各种不同运输方式的进口预约保险合同。按照预约保险合同的规定，外贸企业无须逐笔填写投保单，只需将国外卖方出口商的装运通知送交保险公司，即办妥了进口保险手续。

3. Insurance Documents 保险单据

3.1 Definition 保险单据的定义

An insurance document is the evidence of the insurance contract entered into by the insurer and the applicant or the insurant. It serves as a document defining the obligations of the insurer and the insurant. It is also the document according to which the insurant lodges a claim and the insurer settles a claim when the loss or damage which is answerable under the terms of the coverage occurs. Under CIF and CIP contracts, the seller must provide the buyer with insurance documents. And insurance documents are negotiable by endorsement.

Under CIF and CIP terms, the insured is the seller or the exporter, which is also called beneficiary in letter of credit and the principal in collection.

According to UCP600 Section 28 Item e: “The date of the insurance document must be no later than the date of shipment, unless it appears from the insurance document that the cover is effective from a date not later than the date of shipment”.

保险单据是保险公司在接受投保后签发的承保凭证，是保险人和被保险人之间订立的保险合同，在被保险货物遭受保险合同责任范围内的损失时，它是被保险人索赔和保险人理赔的主要依据。在 CIF、CIP 合同中，保险单据是卖方必须向买方提供的主要单据之一。保险单是可以背书转让的。

在 CIF 或 CIP 价格条件下，被保险人即为卖方（出口商），信用证方式下指的是受益人（卖方），托收方式下为委托人（卖方）。

UCP600 第 28 条 e 款规定：“保险单据日期不得晚于发运日期，除非保险单据表明保险责任不迟于发运日生效。”

3.2 Types of Insurance Documents 保险单据的种类

3.2.1 Insurance Policy 保险单

Insurance Policy is a formal insurance policy. It is the most commonly used document that contains all the details concerning the name, quantity of the cargo, coverage, premium and the insured amount on the face and the detailed contract terms including the rights and obligations of the insured and insurer at the back.

保险单俗称大保单，是一种正规的保险合同。保险单除载明被保险人名称，被保险货物名称、数量、重量、运输标志、运输工具、航次、起讫地点、承保险别、保险币别和保险金额、保费是否已付、赔偿地点，出具保单日期外，在背面还印有保险人的责任范围以及保险人与被保险人各自的权利、义务等内容的详细条款。

3.2.2 Insurance Certificate 保险凭证

It is the simplified form of the insurance policy certifying that insurance has been affected and that a policy has been issued. It does not list all the details at the back but it is of the same legal validity as an insurance policy.

保险凭证俗称小保单，是一种简化的保险凭证，除正面内容与大保单相同外，背面未印有详细条款。在法律上与保险单具有同等的法律效力。

Case Study 本章案例

Case 1: Our exporter exported a load of cargo to a Middle-East country under CIF terms and covered WPA in addition to TPND, but the vessel was detained as a result of the Iran-Iraq war. The importer lodged a claim to the insurance company. Can the importer be compensated?

【案例 1】我国某外贸公司按 CIF 条件向中东某国出口一批货物，根据合同投保了水渍险附加偷窃提货不着险（TPND）。但在海运途中，因两伊战争船被扣押，进口商因提货不着向保险公司索赔。问：是否能得到赔偿？

Case Analysis: TPND refers to the cargo being stolen partially or totally and leads to non-delivery by the consignee at destination. From this instance, it does not belong to the above case, so the insurance company shall not compensate.

【案例分析】偷窃提货不着险是指被保货物整件被偷或从整件中窃取一部分，以致货到目的地后收货人提取不着整件的货物。从本例来看，显然不属于这种情况，所以保险公司将不予赔偿。

Case 2: In the previous case, which type of insurance should be covered so that the insurance shall make indemnity?

【案例 2】上例应保什么险保险公司方予赔偿？

Case Analysis: Failure to deliver risk shall be covered. Failure to deliver risk refers to the risk, once loaded on board the seagoing vessel; fail to be delivered at the destination within six months of scheduled date for arrival due to whatever cause it might be. However, the insured shall handle equity-transferring procedures so as to get compensation.

【案例分析】应保交货不到险。交货不到险是指从货物装上船开始，六个月内不能运到目的地，不论什么原因，保险公司要按全部损失赔偿。不过被保险人要向保险人办理权益转让手续，否则保险人不予赔偿。

Questions 思考题

1. What are the conditions of General Average?

构成共同海损应具备哪些条件？

2. How can the insurance amount be determined under CIF term when the cargo is exported? What about the insurance premium?

按 CIF 条件出口的货物，其保险金额如何确定？保险费如何计算？

3. How does PICC stipulate the coverage and duration of War Risk for Ocean Marine Cargo Transportation?

中国人民保险公司对海运货物战争险条款的承保责任范围和保险起讫是怎样规定的？

4. How does PICC stipulate the duration of Basic Risks for Ocean Marine Cargo Transportation?

中国人民保险公司对基本险的责任起讫是怎样规定的？

Chapter 11

Price of Commodity

商品的价格

Terms of price are the core terms in a contract. The content, which is related to buyers and sellers' mutual vital interests and the feasibility of a transaction, is playing a great role in constituting other terms in the contract. Legitimately grasping the methods of pricing and reasonably establishing the terms of price have significance on fulfilling missions of importing and exporting and improving economic benefits.

买卖合同中的价格条款是合同中的核心条款，其内容直接对合同中的其他条款产生重大影响，关系买卖双方切身利益、双方能否成交的实质问题。正确掌握成交价格、合理采用各种作价方法、订好合同中的价格条款，对贯彻外贸政策、完成进出口任务、提高经济效益意义重大。

Lesson 1　Pricing 定价

1. Correctly Implement Pricing Principles 正确贯彻作价原则

Before the prices of import and export commodities are determined, these three principles should be followed.

1）Determine the appropriate price on the basis of international price combined with our purchasing intention.

International price is determined in the international market competition on the basis of the international value of commodity, which can be accepted by both sides and will be the objective basis of importing and exporting commodity.

2）Pricing should take into account other countries' policies and regional rules in order to make the international trading conform to diplomacy.

3）Pricing should combine with purchasing intention. The determined price can be slightly higher or lower than the international price. The core principle is that pricing should be in line with the international price.

在确定进出口商品价格前，必须遵循下列三项原则。

（1）按照国际市场价格水平作价，结合我们的购销意图确定适当的价格。

国际市场价格是以商品的国际价值为基础并在国际市场竞争中形成的，它是交易双方都能接受的价格，是我们确定进出口商品价格的客观依据。

（2）外贸配合外交——结合国别、地区规定作价。

（3）作价应结合购销意图。价格可略高或略低于国际市场价格。作价的核心原则是：按国际市场价格水平确定价格。

2. Price Components of Export Commodities 出口商品价格构成

2.1 Four Components 出口商品单价的四个组成部分

The price of export commodity is composed of four indispensable parts: Pricing Currency, Units of Measurement, Unit Value (Price), Trade Terms. For instance, USD 100/MT CIF HAMBURG.

The international price fluctuates according to the supply and demand relation. Sometimes the price changes dramatically within a short time; therefore, it is necessary to be aware of the changes of the supply and demand relation and the trend of the international price fluctuation when setting the pricing strategies.

出口商品单价由四个部分组成，缺一不可：计价货币；计量单位；单位金额（单价）；贸易术语。例如：USD 100/MT CIF HAMBURG。

国际市场价格因受供求关系的影响而上下波动，有时甚至瞬息万变。因此，在确定成交价格时，必须注意市场供求关系的变化和国际市场价格涨落的趋势。

2.2 Components of FOB, CFR and CIF FOB、CFR、CIF 三种贸易术语的构成

Price of FOB=Purchase Cost + Domestic Cost + Net Profit

FOB 价=进货成本价+国内费用+净利润

Price of CFR = Purchase Cost + Domestic Cost + Overseas Freight + Net Profit

CFR 价=进货成本价+国内费用+国外运费+净利润

Price of CIF=Purchase Cost + Domestic Cost + Overseas Freight
+ Overseas Insurance + Net Profit

CIF 价=进货成本价＋国内费用+国外运费+国外保险费+净利润

3. Export Exchange Cost 出口换汇成本

3.1 Definition 定义

It refers to the amount of RMB required for a unit of foreign currency of certain export commodity.

出口换汇成本指某商品出口净收入一个单位的外汇所需要的人民币成本。一个单位的外汇通常按美元计。

3.2 Formula 计算公式

$$\text{Export Exchange Cost}=\frac{\text{Total Export Cost (RMB)}}{\text{Export Foreign Exchange Net Income (dollars)}}$$

$$\text{出口商品换汇成本}=\frac{\text{出口总成本(人民币)}}{\text{出口销售外汇净收入(美元)}}$$

3.2.1 Total Export Cost 出口总成本

Total Export Cost is composed of purchase cost, domestic cost and export tax, which means the total domestic cost paid by foreign trade enterprises for export commodities. The export cost price is calculated on the basis of total export cost, excluding any overseas cost; Transaction price of exports includes overseas freight, insurance premiums, and commissions etc.

Domestic Cost includes circulation cost, processing fees, packaging fees, custodial fees (warehouse rental and fire insurance), domestic transportation cost (from warehouse to harbor), documents fees (inspection fees, notary fees, consular fees, certificate of origin and licensing fees, customs declaration fees, customs fees), freight (discount interest, loaded container cost, lifting cost and shipping fees), banking charges (discount interest and other charges) and postal fees.

出口总成本包括进货成本（购货成本）、国内费用和出口税，它是外贸企业为出口商品支付的国内总成本。出口成本价格是以企业出口总成本为基础计算出来的单位价格，并不涉及国外任何费用；出口成交价格包括单位商品的国外运费、保费、佣金等。

国内费用包括流通费用、加工整理费用、包装费用、保管费（仓租、火险等）、国内运输费用（仓库至码头）、证件费用（包括商检费、公证费、领事签证费、原产地证书费、许可证费、报关单费、海关规费）、装船费（贴现利息、装集装箱费、起吊费和轮船费）、银行费用（贴现利息、手续费用）、邮电费。

3.2.2 Export Foreign Exchange Net Income 出口外汇净收入

Export Foreign Exchange Net Income comprises total export foreign exchange excluding labor cost and other non-trade foreign exchange (freight, insurance premiums, and banking charges).

FOB—Foreign Exchange Net Income.

CIF — Foreign Exchange Net Income excluding freight, insurance premiums and commissions.

出口外汇净收入指出口外汇总收入扣除劳务费用等非贸易外汇（运费、保费、银行费用）后的收入。

按 FOB 价格术语——外汇净收入。

按 CIF 价格术语——扣除运费、保费、佣金得出外汇净收入。

3.2.3 Overseas Cost 国外费用

Overseas cost mainly comprises overseas freight, overseas premiums and commissions.

国外费用主要包括国外运费（装运港—目的港运费）、国外保费和佣金。

3.2.4 Relationship among Variables 各变量之间的关系

Export Exchange Cost is directly proportional to Total Export Cost and inversely proportional to Export Foreign Exchange Net Income. Compared with Foreign Exchange Rate of BOC (Bank of China), the lower Export Exchange Cost is, the more profits will be gained. For instance, in an export transaction, the Export Exchange Cost is calculated as 7.26, while Foreign Exchange Rate is 7.61. This means every dollar gained will earn 0.35 RMB. The Export Exchange Cost is measured by RMB, so the lower the number is, the lower the cost is.

出口换汇成本与出口总成本成正比，与出口外汇净收入成反比。出口换汇成本越低越好，与中国银行外汇牌价相比，能直接反映出口商品是否盈利。例如，在一笔出口交易中，计算出的出口换汇成本为 7.26，外汇牌价为 7.61，那么就意味着每收入 1 美元，则盈利 0.35 元人民币。换汇成本得出的数值为人民币，数值越低说明成本越低。

Case Study: A trading company exports 10,000 units of arts and crafts which cost 300,000 Yuan (30 Yuan per unit), other domestic cost: 8,000 RMB, expected profit: 10%, freight: 10 units/CTN, 1,000 cartons, carton size: 25cm×56cm×32cm, GW: 32kg, NW: 30kg, the freight to Europe is calculated by W/M as 120 Dollars per ton. The price of 40 containers to Europe: 3,500 Dollars, insurance by 11% of the invoice value against all risks at the premium rate of 0.8%, foreign sales price: USD 4.85/PC CIF London. Please calculate the export exchange cost respectively by container and by cargo.

1) Cost by container

Total Export Cost=300,000+8,000=308,000 yuan

Premiums=CIF×(1+10%)×Premium rate=4.85×10,000×110%×0.8%=426.80 Dollars

Export Foreign Exchange Net Income: 4.85×10,000–3,500–426.8=44,573.20 Dollars

$$\text{Export Exchange Cost} = \frac{308{,}000}{44{,}573.20} = 6.91 \text{ yuan}$$

That means 6.91 yuan per US dollar.

Tips: The foreign exchange rate of BOC is USD 1=RMB7.61 (bid price), every dollar that is gained earns 0.70 yuan.

2) Cost by tons (not shipped by containers, calculated by cargo)

$$\text{Stowage factor=M/W=}\frac{0.56\times0.32\times0.25}{0.032}=\frac{0.045}{0.032}>1\text{, calculated by volume.}$$

Freight=0.56×0.32×0.25×1,000×120=5,376.00 USD

$$\text{Export Exchange Cost=}\frac{300{,}000+8{,}000}{48{,}500-53{,}76.00-426.8}-\frac{308{,}000}{42{,}697.2}=7.21\text{ yuan}$$

例：我某公司出口工艺品一批，收购价 30 万元人民币，每件 30 元人民币，共 10 000 件，国内其他费用 8 000 元人民币。预期利润 10%。运费：10 件/箱，1 000 箱，箱规为 25 厘米×56 厘米×32 厘米，毛重 32kg，净重 30kg，到欧洲每运费吨 120 美元，按 W/M 计费。40 英尺货柜到欧洲价格 3 500 美元。保费按发票金额 11%投保一切险，保费率在 0.8%，对外销售价 USD 4.85/PC CIF London。试按集装箱运输和按件杂货分别计算该笔交易的出口换汇成本。

解：（1）按集装箱运输计算成本

出口总成本：300 000+8 000=308 000（元人民币）

保费＝CIF×(1+10%)×保费率＝4.85×10 000×110%×0.8%=426.80（美元）

出口外汇净收入：4.85×10 000−3 500－426.8=44 573.20（美元）

$$\text{出口换汇成本=}\frac{308\ 000}{44\ 573.20}=6.91\text{（元人民币）}$$

即每 6.91 元人民币换 1 美元外汇。

提示：若中国银行美元外汇牌价 USD 1＝RMB7.61（买入价）， 这笔交易每净收入 1 美元盈利 0.70 元人民币。

（2）按运费吨计算（不走集装箱，按件杂货计算）

$$\text{积载系数=M/W=}\frac{0.56\times0.32\times0.25}{0.032}=\frac{0.045}{0.032}>1\text{，属于轻货，应按体积计费。}$$

运费=0.56×0.32×0.25×1 000×120=5 376.00（美元）

$$\text{出口换汇成本=}\frac{300\ 000+8\ 000}{48\ 500-5\ 376.00-426.8}-\frac{308\ 000}{42\ 697.2}=7.21\text{（元人民币）}$$

4. Profit and Loss Ratio of Export Commodities 出口商品盈亏率

4.1 Definition 定义

Profit and Loss Ratio of Export Commodities demonstrates the ratio between the volume of export profit and total export cost. The volume of export profit indicates the balance between net RMB income of export sales and total export cost. If the balance is a positive number, it means making a profit, and vice versa. The very ratio is perceived as an important index to measure the degree of export profit or loss.

出口商品盈亏率指出口盈亏额与出口总成本的比例，出口盈亏额是指出口销售的人民币净收入与出口总成本的差额。如果差额是正数，为盈余；如果是负数，就是亏损。它是衡量出口盈亏程度的一个重要指标。

4.2 Formula 计算公式

$$\text{Profit and Loss Ratio of Export Commodities}=\frac{\text{RMB Net Income of Export Sales} - \text{Total Export Cost}}{\text{Total Export Cost}}\times 100\%$$

RMB Net Income of Export Sales = Foreign Exchange Sales FOB× Foreign Exchange Rate (Bid Price)

$$\text{出口商品盈亏率}=\frac{\text{出口销售人民币净收入}-\text{出口总成本}}{\text{出口总成本}}\times 100\%$$

出口销售人民币净收入=外汇销售收入 FOB×外汇牌价（买入价）

Case Study: connected to the previous one

Please calculate the profit and loss ratio of export commodities

Net income of export sales = 44,573.20 dollars ×7.61=339,202.05 yuan

Total cost =308,000 yuan

Balance =339,202.05－308,000=31,202.05 yuan

Profit and loss ratio of export commodities＝31,202.05/308,000×100%＝10%

例： 接上例，计算出口商品盈亏率。

出口商品人民币净收入=44 573.20 美元×7.61=339 202.05（元人民币）

出口总成本=308 000（元人民币）

盈亏额=339 202.05–308 000=31 202.05（元人民币）

出口商品盈亏率＝31 202.05/308 000×100%＝10%

5. Foreign Exchange Earned through Export (Exchange Rate Appreciation) 出口创汇率（外汇增值率）

5.1 Definition 定义

Foreign exchange earned through export is concluded by the ratio between certain difference calculated by export foreign exchange net income minus foreign exchange cost of raw materials and foreign exchange cost of raw materials. The ratio is universally adopted in imported materials processing and supplied materials processing to calculate exchange rate appreciation.

出口创汇率指出口成品外汇净收入减去原料外汇成本后与原料外汇成本的比率，用于进料加工、来料加工计算外汇增值率。

5.2 Formula 计算公式

$$\text{Foreign Exchange Earned through Export (Exchange Rate Appreciation)} = \frac{\text{Export Foreign Exchange Net Income} - \text{Foreign Exchange Cost of Raw Materials}}{\text{Foreign Exchange Cost of Raw Materials}} \times 100\%$$

Through calculation of exchange rate appreciation, the profit of foreign exchange earned can be revealed, i.e. whether raw materials export profitable is profitable or finished products export is profitable.

$$\text{出口成品创汇率（外汇增值率）} = \frac{\text{出口成品外汇净收入} - \text{原料外汇成本}}{\text{原料外汇成本}} \times 100\%$$

通过外汇增值率的计算，可看出成品出口的创汇情况，即出口原料有利还是出口成品有利。

Case Study: A trading company imports fabric to proceed to clothing at an amount of 100,000 Dollars in CIF terms (USD 9/PC CIF HAMBURG per garment). The total freight: 8,000 Dollars, premiums: 2,000 Dollars. Please calculate the exchange rate appreciation.

$$\text{Exchange rate appreciation} = \frac{9 \times 20{,}000 - 8{,}000 - 2{,}000 - 100{,}000}{100{,}000} \times 100\% = 70\%$$

例：我国某外贸公司用 CIF 贸易术语进口布料 100 000 美元，加工成成衣 20 000 件，每件 USD 9/PC CIF HAMBURG。已知出口运费共计 8 000 美元，保费共计 2 000 美元，求该商品的出口创汇率。

出口成品创汇率＝出口成品外汇净收入－原料外汇成本/原料外汇成本×100%

$$\text{出口成品创汇率} = \frac{9 \times 20\,000 - 8\,000 - 2\,000 - 100\,000}{100\,000} \times 100\% = 70\%$$

Lesson 2 Commission and Discount
佣金和折扣

1. Commission 佣金

Commission is the remuneration for the agents who provide service for principals. During trading, commission is usually in the form of remuneration which either side of a trade provides to the middleman. For example, exporters pay commissions to sales agents, or importers pay commissions to purchase agents. Therefore, commission applies to the contract signed by the exporter/importer and the agents. Certain trading occurs through middlemen or agents who need to be paid commissions. If the ratio of commission is defined, we call them the defined commission; otherwise, we call them undefined commissions which agents may require from both sides.

Commission can be defined as follows:

1) Labeled by words. E.g., this price includes 5 percent commission.

2) Trading terms. E.g., CIFC2 San Francisco.

3) Defined by number. E.g., Commission: USD 25 per Metric Ton.

佣金指代理人或经纪人为委托人服务而收取的报酬。在货物买卖中，佣金常常表现为交易一方支付给中间商的报酬。例如，出口商支付佣金给销售代理人，或进口商支付佣金给采购代理人。因此，它适用于进出口商与代理人或佣金商签订的合同。有些交易是通过中间商、代理商进行的，这就要向其支付一定的酬金——佣金。凡货价中包含佣金的即为含佣金价。如明确规定佣金的百分比，则为明佣；如不标明百分比，甚至连佣金字样也不标示出来，则为暗佣，中间商两头签佣。

佣金的规定方法有如下几种：

（1）用文字说明，如：This price includes 5 percent commission。

（2）用贸易术语表示，如：CIFC2 San Francisco。

（3）用绝对数表示，如：Commission: USD 25 per Metric Ton。

2. Calculation and Payment Methods of Commissions 佣金的计算与支付方法

2.1 Calculation by Turnover Value 计算方法：按成交金额计算

It should be defined in a contract whether commission is calculated on the basis of FOB or CIF. It is more sensible to adopt FOB which nevertheless cannot be accepted by agents. It is conventional that CIF serves as the basis of commission's calculation in a CIF contract. If it is not clearly defined in the contract, it usually turns to the invoice.

Calculate the Commission on the basis of the invoice value.

Formula

$$\text{Commission}=\text{Price with Commission}\times\text{Commission Rate}$$

$$\text{Net Price}=\text{Price with Commission}-\text{Commission per Unit}=\text{Price with Commission}\times(1-\text{Commission Rate})$$

$$\text{Price with Commission}=\frac{\text{Net Price}}{1-\text{Commission Rate}}$$

E.g.: Net price: 100 USD, CIF London commission rate: 3%. Calculate the price with commission: USD 100/(1–3%) =USD 103.09

计算佣金的基数按 FOB 值还是 CIF 值应在合同中订明。按 FOB 值的基数计算佣金，这种计算方法比较合理，但是中间商往往不同意。按习惯做法，如 CIF 合同就按 CIF 总值作为佣金计算的基数。如合同中未订明，通常按发票金额计算。

按发票金额计算佣金的基数。

佣金公式：佣金额=含佣价×佣金率

净价=含佣价−单位货物佣金额=含佣价×（1−佣金率）

$$含佣价=\frac{净价}{1-佣金率}$$

例：净价为USD 100，CIF London 佣金为3%，则含佣价为：USD 100/(1−3%)=USD 103.09。

2.2 Payment Methods of Commission 支付方法

Remove from exporting/importing price.

Remittance from principals in a defined rate.

委托人收清货款后再按约定佣金比率另行汇付。

中间商直接从货价扣除。

3. Discount (Rebate) 折扣

3.1 Definition 定义

Discount is aimed to motivate the initiatives of the buyer, which is provided by the seller as a concession in the contract.

The differentiation between the commission and the discount: commissions are offered by the seller to the middlemen, while discounts are concessions provided by the seller.

所谓折扣是指为了调动买方的积极性，在合同中订明卖方按原价给买方一定百分比的减让。

佣金与折扣的区别在于：佣金为卖方给第三者的手续费，折扣为卖方直接给予买方的减让。

3.2 Types 种类

Quantity Discount: discount offered if the buyers reach certain quantity.

Special Discount: discount offered for frequent client.

Turnover Bonus.

Defined Discount: defined discount rate in a contract.

Undefined Discount: not mentioned in a contract, but mentioned in other agreements.

数量折扣：如买方购买达到一定的数量给予折扣。

特别折扣：对于常年购买的老顾客给予价格优惠。

年终回扣。

明扣：在合同中明确规定折扣率。

暗扣：合同中不标示出来，另有协议。

3.3 Defined Methods 折扣的规定方法

1) Literally Defined 用文字明确表示

It is usual that the discount rate should be defined literally in a pricing terms. For instance, USD 1,000 per metric ton CIF Hong Kong including 2% discount, or USD 1,000 per metric ton CIF Hong Kong less discount 2%.

在价格条款中，一般用文字明确表示给予折扣的比例。例如：CIF 香港每公吨 1 000 美元，折扣 2%或者写成：CIF 香港，每公吨 1 000 美元，减 2%折扣。

2) Defined by determined number 用绝对数表示

For instance, USD 1,000.00/mt less discount USD 5.00

例如：每公吨 1 000 美元，折扣 5 美元。

3.4 Calculation and Payment Methods of Discount 折扣的计算与支付方法

Discount can be calculated on the basis of turnover value or invoice value.

Discount per Unit=Original Price × Discount Rate

Net Seller's Revenue=Original Price × (1−Discount Rate)

E.g.: Original price: USD 100.00/PC CIF HK, discount rate: 2%, discount offered by the seller to buyer: USD 100.00×2%=USD 2.00, net revenue of the seller: USD 100.00×(1−2%) =USD 98.00

The payment method of discount can be offered directly during issuing; Sellers remove the discount from the invoice value.

以成交额或发票金额为基础：

单位货物折扣额=原价×折扣率

卖方净收入=原价×（1−折扣率）

例如：原价 USD 100.00/PC CIF HK，折扣为 2%，则卖方给买方的折扣为 USD 100.00×2%=USD 2.00，卖方的净收入为 USD 100.00×(1−2%)=USD 98.00。

折扣的支付方法可在开证中直接扣除金额或开证为原价，卖方在发票中扣除折扣额。

Case Study 本章案例

Case 1: A trading company exports a number of commodities abroad, the original price: 2,000 USD per metric ton CIF 3% London, and the buyer require CIF 5% London. Insurance coverage for the original premiums is against all risks including war risks, and the rates was 0.8 USD and 6%, in accordance with 110% CIF price. Please calculate CFRC 5% London.

【**案例 1**】某公司出口货物一批，原报价为每公吨 2 000 美元 CIF 3% London，客户要求改报 CFRC5% London 价。查原报价保险险别为一切险加战争险，其费率分别为 0.8 美元和 0.6%，按 CIF 价加一成投保。试计算 CFRC 5% London 价。

Case Analysis:

(1) CIF=2,000×(1−3%) =2,000×0.97=1,940 dollars

(2) CFR=CIF−I

In that, I=1,940× (1+10%) × (0.008+0.006) =1,940×1.1×0.014=29.88 dollars

Then, CFR=1,940−29.88=1,910.12 dollars

Or, CFR=1,940 × [1−(1+10%) × (0.008+0.006)]

=1,940 × (1−1.1×0.014) = 1,940 × (1−0.015,4)

=1,940 × 0.984,6

=1,910.12 dollars

(3) CFRC 5%=1,910.12÷(1−5%)=1,910.12÷0.95=2,010.65 dollars

Therefore, CFRC 5% London is 2,010.65 Dollars.

【**案例分析**】

(1) CIF=2 000×(1−3%)=2 000×0.97=1 940 美元

(2) CFR=CIF−I

因为 I=1 940×(1+10%)×(0.008+0.006)=1 940×1.1×0.014=29.88 美元

则 CFR=1 940−29.88=1 910.12 美元

或：CFR=1 940×[1−(1+10%)×(0.008+0.006)]

=1 940×(1−1.1×0.014)=1 940×(1−0.015 4)

=1 940×0.984 6

=1 910.12 美元

(3) CFRC 5%=1 910.12÷(1−5%)=1 910.12÷0.95=2 010.65 美元

因此，应报 CFRC 5% London 价 2 010.65 美元。

Case 2: A UK client ordered 1,000 traveling bags, requiring CIF 3% Liverpool, other conditions: domestic purchase cost of traveling bags is 50 yuan per piece, other dominate cost is 5,000 yuan; the expected profit rate is 10%. The bags are packaged in cartons, 20 per carton. Freight is 20 dollars per carton from start port to Liverpool. Overseas shipping premium is defined as 0.8% by CIF, which adds 10% insurance against all risks and war risk. (P.S.: Exchange rate of RMB against USD is 6.2:1)

【**案例 2**】我国某外贸公司收到英国某客户来电，询购 1 000 只旅行包，要求按下列条件报出每只旅行包 CIFC 3%利物浦的美元价格。条件：旅行包国内购货成本为每只 50 元人民币，国内其他费用总计为 5 000 元人民币，我国某外贸公司的预期利润为 10%。该旅行包为纸箱装，每箱 20 只。从装运港至利物浦的海运费为每箱 20 美元。海运出口保险按 CIF 价加一成投保一切险、战争险，费率为 0.8%（注：人民币对美元汇率为 6.2:1）。

Case Analysis:

FOB=Purchase cost + domestic cost + net profit = (50+5 000÷1 000)×110%= 60.5 RMB/bag=9.76 USD/bag

Freight (F) =20 USD÷20= 1 USD/bag

CFR = FOB+F=9.76+1= 10.76 USD/bag

CIF=CFR÷ (1–110%× premium rate) =10.76÷ (1–110%×0.8%) =10.86 USD/bag

CIFC 3%=CIF price÷ (1–3%) =10.86÷0.97=11.20 USD/bag

Therefore, CIFC 3% is 11.20 USD/bag.

【案例分析】

FOB 价=成本+费用+利润=（50+5 000÷1 000）×110%=60.5 元/只=9.76 美元/只

运费（F）=20 美元÷20 只/=1 美元/只

CFR 价=FOB+F=9.76+1=10.76 美元/只

CIF=CFR÷（1–110%×保险费率）=10.76÷（1–110%×0.8%）=10.86 美元/只

CIFC 3%=CIF 单价÷（1–3%）=10.86÷0.97=10.86 美元/只

因此，每只旅行包的 CIFC 3%价为 11.20 美元。

Questions 思考题

1. What does the price term of a contract consist of? Please exemplify.
   我国进出口商品合同的作价原则是什么？
2. What is Export Foreign Exchange Net Income?
   什么是出口外汇净收入？
3. What is Export Exchange Cost?
   什么是出口换汇成本？
4. Explain the calculation of Profit and Loss Ratio and Export Exchange Cost.
   解释盈亏率和换汇成本的计算问题。
5. Explain the calculation of Export Quotation.
   解释对外报价的计算问题。

Chapter 12

International Payment and Settlement

国际货款支付与结算

Lesson 1　Instruments of Payment

支 付 工 具

Bill is a frequently used instrument of payment in international trade. It is a kind of security which is often used as a substitute for cash in circulation. The three mainly adopted bills and notes are bill of exchange (draft), promissory note and cheque (check).

票据是一种可以代替现金流通的有价证券，在国际贸易中，主要使用的有汇票、本票和支票。

1. Bill of Exchange (Draft, Bill) 汇票

1.1 Definition 定义

1) The definition from Bills of Exchange Act 1882 of the UK《英国票据法》的定义

A Bill of Exchange is defined as “an unconditional order in writing, addressed by one person (drawer) to another (drawee), signed by the person giving it, requiring the person to whom it is addressed to pay on demand, or at a fixed or determinable future time, a sum certain in money, to or to the order of, a specified person (payee), or to bearer”.

《英国票据法》的定义：汇票是一个人向另一个人签发的，要求见票时或在将来的固定时间或可以确定的时间，对某人或其指定的人或持票人支付一定金额的无条件的支付命令。

2) The definition from Negotiable Instruments Law of the People’s Republic of China《中华人民共和国票据法》的定义

A draft is a bill signed by the drawer, requiring the entrusted payer to make unconditional payment in a fixed amount at the sight of the bill or on a fixed date to the payee or the holder.

《中华人民共和国票据法》的定义：汇票是出票人签发的，委托付款人在见票时或者在指定日期应无条件支付确定金额给收款人或持票人的票据。

1.2 Contents 内容

1) The words of “Bill of Exchange” or “Draft” are required to be on the draft, to distinguish it from other paying instruments (Promissory Note, Check), but it is not required in Bills of Exchange Act.

应载明“汇票”字样，以示与其他票据支付工具（本票、支票）的区别，但《英国汇票法》无此要求。

2) It is an unconditional pay order, with the unlimited payment, without proviso.

表现为无条件支付命令，支付不受限制，不附带条件。

3) A certain sum, which is indicated in Arabic numbers and words in a definite currency including the interest, not allowed to be described with ambiguous words and approximate sum.

一定金额。表明以一定的货币表示的确切数目，不能用大约或模棱两可的描述，要用文字（大写）、阿拉伯数字（小写）分别列明金额。

4) Drawer, the one who issues the draft (namely debtee). The property of the draft is different according to different drawers. The drawer of a commercial draft is an exporter while the drawer of the banker’s draft is a bank.

出票人即签发汇票的人（债权人）。出票人不同，汇票的性质也不同。商业汇票的出票人为出口人，银行汇票的出票人为银行。

5) Drawee, the one who is ordered to make payment by the drawer. The drawee of a commercial draft can be the buyer, importer or bank, while the drawee of the banker’s draft is definitely a bank.

受票人，即付款人，出票人命令付款的人。商业汇票的受票人可以是买方、进口人或银行，银行汇票的受票人为银行。

6) Payee, who is entitled to the sum of the draft, in the import and export business, can be an exporter, seller, an appointed bank or a normal holder of the draft.

受款人，又称汇票的抬头，即受领汇票所规定金额的人，在进出口业务中可以是出口人、卖方、指定的银行或正当持票人。

The payee can be classified into the following 3 kinds:

① Restrictive. Writing the words on the draft, like “pay ×× Co. only”, “pay ×× Co., not negotiable”. The type of draft is not transferable, and only the payee is qualified to accept the payment.

② Demonstrative Order. Writing the words on the draft like “To ×× Co. or to order”, and transferable to others with endorsement.

③ Payable to Bearer. It is transferable with the draft without endorsement.

受款人按抬头分，有三种做法：

① 限制性抬头。在汇票上注明："仅付××公司"（pay ××co. only），"付××公司，不准流通"（Pay ×× Co.not negotiable）。此种汇票不能流通转让，仅限××人或××公司收取货款。

② 指示式抬头。在汇票上注明"付××公司或其指定的人"（记名抬头）；除××公司可以收取货款外，也可以经过自己背书转让给第三者。

③ 持票人或来人抬头。无须背书，仅交付汇票即可转让。

7) Payment Due Date 付款期限

① Payment Time Regulation

a. At Sight. Payment at sight refers to the payment that is made by the payer at sight of the draft, and the due date is the day that the payee presents the draft to the payer.

b. Payable ×× Days after Sight. The draft holder makes presentation of the draft to the payer, demanding the payer to accept the draft and make payment on the due date. The due date is confirmed according to the presentation date.

c. Payable ×× Days after Date. Payable within ×× days after the draft issuance date.

d. Payable 30 Days after B/L Date. Payable within 30 days after the B/L issuance date.

e. Fixed Date. Payable on a fixed date.

② Payment time stipulated in the *Negotiable Instruments Law of the People's Republic of China*

a. Payable at sight

b. Payable on a fixed date

c. Payable on a fixed date after the draft is issued

d. Payable on a fixed date after the sight of the draft

① 规定付款期限的方法：

a. 见票即付。见票即付又称即期付款，即付款人见票即付，受款人向付款人提示汇票的当天作为到期日。

b. 见票后××天付。持票人向付款人提示付款，要求承兑，根据承兑日确定付款到期日，提示见票日为依据。

c. 出票后××天付。从出票之日的第二天起算，直至第××天付款。

d. 提单日后××天付。

e. 指定日期付款。

②《中华人民共和国票据法》规定的付款期限：

a. 见票即付；

b. 定日付款；

c. 出票后定期付款；

d. 见票后定期付款。

The time calculation: not including the sight date, the issuance date or B/L date. The draft is not recognized if the payment time is not definite or the conditions attached to it are not met. According to *Negotiable Instruments Law of the People's Republic of China*, the draft without the specific payment time requirement will be regarded as being payable at sight.

时间的计算方法：均不包括见票日、出票日或提单日，算尾不算头。付款日期不确定或根据某种条件不视为汇票。《中华人民共和国票据法》规定：汇票上未记载付款日期的，为见票即付。

8) The Date and Place of Draft Issuance 出票日期和地点

The issuance date must be written on the draft so as to confirm the qualification of the drawer and calculate the payment date.

The place of draft issuance: written next to the date. It is necessary to write the issuance place in order to confirm the applicable law and complete the draft. According to *Negotiable Instruments Law of the People's Republic of China*, if a draft does not bear the place of draft, which can be the business operation place, the habitation, or the regular dwelling place of the drawer.

汇票上必须记载出票日期，以便凭以确定出票人在签发汇票时有无行为能力以及以出票日作为计算付款日。

出票地点：与日期连在一起。载明出票地点的必要性：确定以哪个国家的法律为依据，必须具备齐全的项目。《中华人民共和国票据法》规定：汇票上未记载出票地的，出票人的营业场所、住所或经常居住地为出票地。

9) Payment Place 付款地点

It is written next to the name of the payer, namely the place of making payment against the draft. According to *Negotiable Instruments Law of the People's Republic of China*, the payment place can be the business operation place, the habitation, or the regular dwelling place of the drawer in case that the specific payment place is not written on the draft.

付款地点指付款人名字旁边的地点，即汇票金额支付地。《中华人民共和国票据法》规定：汇票上未记载付款地的，付款人的营业场所、住所或经常居住地为付款地。

10) Signature of the Drawer 出票人签字

After signing the draft, the drawer is regarded as the main debtor and to be committed to the draft fulfillment. If the signature is fake or not authorized, the draft is invalid.

出票人签字后即承担汇票的责任，成为主债务人。如果伪造签字，或未经授权人签字，均视为无效。

11) Other Items Maybe Written on the Draft 任意记载事项

① The draft is issued in duplicate, the drawee makes payment against one draft, and then the other one is cancelled accordingly.

② Consideration clause, for value received.

①"付一不付二"。汇票一般做成两张，受票人对其中一张付款，另一张则自动作废。

② 对价条款，对价收讫。

12) In *Negotiable Instruments Law of the People's Republic of China*, the draft is regarded as being invalid in case that the following items are stated on the draft: ① the word "draft"; ② unconditional appointment; ③ definite sum; ④ name of payer; ⑤ name of payee; ⑥ draft issuance date; ⑦ the signature of the drawer.

根据《中华人民共和国票据法》，下述规定事项未记载则汇票无效：① 表明“汇票”字样；② 无条件支付委托；③ 确定的金额；④ 付款人的名称；⑤ 收款人的名称；⑥ 出票日期；⑦ 出票人签章。

1.3 The Classification of the Draft 汇票的种类

1.3.1 According to Different Drawers 按出票人不同划分

1) Banker's Draft 银行汇票

The draft is drawn by a bank, and the drawer is a bank. A banker's draft is sent to payee by remitter, with which the payee can exchange the money from the payer (the bank).

The characteristics of banker's draft: both the drawer and the drawee are banks.

银行汇票是一种汇款凭证，由银行签发，出票人为银行，通常交由汇款人寄给受款人或亲自交给受款人，凭票向付款人（银行）兑取票款。

银行汇票的特点：出票人和受票人都是银行。

2) Commercial Draft 商业汇票

The draft is made out by the seller of one country (exporter) and presented to the importer or the payment bank. Usually, the draft is presented to the importer or the payment bank (L/C opening bank) through the bank in the exporter's place or the correspondent bank of it in the importer's place.

The characteristics of commercial draft: the drawer is a firm or an individual, and the payer (the drawee) is a firm, an individual, or a bank.

商业汇票是由一国的卖方（出口人）向另一国的进口人或委托银行开出，通常是通过出口地银行或其在进口地的代理行向进口人或其委托银行（信用证开证行）收取票款。

商业汇票的特点：出票人是商号或个人；付款人（即受票人）可以是商号、个人，也可以是银行。

1.3.2 According to the Documents Accompanied 按流通转让时有无随附单据划分

1) Clean Bill 光票

Without shipment documents to accompany, the banker's draft is usually a clean bill.

不附带货运单据的汇票，银行汇票多为光票。

2) Documentary Bill 跟单汇票

The draft is accompanied with shipment documents, which is guaranteed by exporter's credit as well as the goods. The commercial draft is usually a documentary bill.

随附货运单据的汇票，这种汇票既有人的信用担保，又有物的担保。商业汇票多为跟单汇票。

1.3.3 According to Payment Time 按付款时间不同划分

1) Sight Draft 即期汇票

To make payment at sight of the draft.

见票提示即付。

2) Time Bill or Usance Bill 远期汇票

To make payment within ×× days or on a fixed date.

在一定期限或特定日期付款的汇票。

1.4 Procedure of Using a Bill of Exchange 汇票的使用步骤

1.4.1 Issuance 出票

It is made out in written form. The drawer fills in the contents including the payer's name, payment sum, payment time, place, payee's name etc., and signs his name.

做成书面汇票，出票人在汇票上填写付款人名称、付款金额、付款日期、地点、受款人名称等项目，最后由出票人签字。

The issuance is regarded to be fulfilled only after the bill is sent to the drawee.

将汇票交给受票人，只有经交付才算完成出票行为。

1.4.2 Presentation 提示

The holder of the draft presents the draft to the drawee, asking for the acceptance or payment.

Presentation for Payment. The draft holder presents the draft to the payer asking for the sight payment.

Presentation for Acceptance. The draft holder presents the draft to the payer asking for the acceptance at sight of the draft and making payment on the maturity time.

提示指持票人将汇票提交受票人，要求承兑或付款的行为。

付款提示。持票人向付款人提交汇票，要求付款（即期付款）。

承兑提示。持票人向付款人提交汇票，付款人见票后办理承兑手续，到期时付款。

1.4.3 Acceptance 承兑

It is a promise made by the payer that it will make payment against a time draft.

The payer writes the word "acceptance" on the bill remarking the acceptance date and affixes its signature, then returns the bill to the draft holder. The payer is regarded as the acceptor after making acceptance for the draft. The first debtor of the draft is the drawer before making acceptance, and it changes into the payer after making acceptance while the drawer becomes the second debtor. Before the payer's acceptance, all the bearers are allowed to recourse to the drawer as the draft is transferable.

承兑指远期汇票的付款人对远期汇票表示承担到期付款责任的行为。

付款人在汇票上写明"承兑"字样，注明承兑日期并签字，然后交还持票人。付款人对汇票做出承兑，即成为承兑人。汇票在付款人承兑前，主债务人是出票人，在付款人承兑后，主债务人是付款人。出票人成为第二债务人。因为出票人可转让其汇票，在付款人承兑前，所有后手都可以向出票人追索。

1.4.4 Payment 付款

For the sight payment, the payer shall make payment against the presentation of the draft; for the time bill, the payer makes payment on the maturity time after the acceptance and all the debts on the draft come to an end after the payment.

对于即期汇票，付款人应见票时付款；对于远期汇票，付款人经过承兑后，在汇票到期日付款。付款后，汇票的一切债务即告终止。

1.4.5 Endorsement 背书

The endorsement of the draft includes two points: to make endorsement on the overleaf of the draft; to transfer the bill to the endorsee. The two points are both necessary for the fulfillment of the endorsement.

In international market, the draft is a kind of transfer instrument, which is negotiable and transferable in the bill market. The endorsement is one legal procedure of transferring the bill, that is to say, the holder of draft signs its name on the back of the bill or adds the name of the bearer (endorsee), and then transfers the draft to the bearer. After the endorsement, the claim for the payment is transferred to the bearer, too.

汇票的背书包括两个方面：在汇票背面背书；交付给被背书人。只有通过交付，才算完成背书。

在国际市场上，汇票是一种流通工具，可以在票据市场上流通转让。背书是转让汇票权利的一种法定手续，就是由汇票持有人在汇票背面签上自己的名字，或再加上受让人（被背书人）的名字，并把汇票交给受让人的行为。经背书后，汇票的收款权利便转移给受让人。

1.4.6 Discounting 贴现

Discounting means that the usance bill after the acceptance but undue is sold to a bank or a discounting house for the immediate payment with the discounting interest deducted from the payment sum based on a certain discounting rate.

In the international market, in order to receive the payment immediately, a time bill holder may transfer the draft to the others by making endorsement before the bill is mature.

贴现是指远期汇票承兑后尚未到期，由银行或贴现公司从票面金额中扣除按一定贴现率计算的贴现利息后，将余款付给持票人的行为。

在国际市场上，一张远期汇票的持票人如想在付款人付款前取得票款，可以通过在到期前背书转让汇票，将汇票进行贴现。

1.4.7 Dishonor 拒付

It is called the dishonor by non-acceptance or by non-payment in case that the bill is not accepted or not paid when the bill is presented by the bill holder for the acceptance. Dishonor also happens when the payer returns the bill, keeps away from the bill, dies, or is bankrupted.

持票人要求承兑汇票时，遭到拒绝，或遭遇拒绝付款，均称为拒付。退票，付款人避不见票、死亡、破产，也称拒付。

1.4.8 Right of Recourse 追索权

Upon the dishonor, the bill holder has the right to claim for the settlement of the payment and the relevant charges against the prior endorser (or the drawer).

To exercise the right of recourse, the bill holder shall present the protest (or certificate of dishonor). The protest is an official document made by the local notary public, bank, chamber of commerce or court testifying that the draft has been dishonored. It is the legal proof with which the bill holder can take the right of the recourse against the prior endorser. If the dishonored bill has been accepted, the bill holder can go to court claiming for the payment against the acceptor.

汇票遭到拒付，持票人对其前手（即背书人、出票人）有请求其偿还汇票金额及费用的权利。

在行使追索权时，持票人必须提供拒付证书。拒付证书是可以由付款地法定公证人如银行、商会、法院提供的证明拒付事实的文件，这是持票人凭以向其前手进行追索的法律依据。如被拒付的汇票已经承兑，出票人可凭以向法院起诉，要求承兑人付款。

2. Promissory Note 本票

2.1 Definition 定义

2.1.1 The Definition from Bills of Exchange Act of the United Kingdom《英国票据法》的定义

The promissory note is an unconditional promise in writing made by one person (the maker) to another (the payee) and signed by the maker engaging to pay on demand or at a fixed or determinable future time a sum certain in money to or to the order of a specified person or bearer.

In accordance with "Convention on the Unification of the Law Relating to Bills of Exchange and Promissory Notes", the promissory note shall include the following contents:

① the words of "promissory note";

② unconditional payment promise;

③ the payee or the specified person by the payee;

④ the drawer;

⑤ the date and place of the issuance;

⑥ a period for payment;

⑦ a sum certain in money;

⑧ the payment place.

本票是一个人向另一个人签发的，保证即期或定期或在可能确定的将来时间，对某人或其他持票人支付一定金额的无条件承诺，即：本票是出票人对受款人承诺无条件支付一定金额的票据。

根据《日内瓦统一汇票和本票法》，本票必须包括以下各项内容：

① 写明“本票”字样；

② 无条件支付承诺；

③ 收款人或其指定的人；

④ 出票人；

⑤ 出票日期、地点；

⑥ 付款期限；

⑦ 一定金额；

⑧ 付款地点。

2.1.2 The Definition from *The Negotiable Instruments Law of the People's Republic of China*《中华人民共和国票据法》的定义

The promissory note is the note issued by the drawer, promising to make unconditionally a definite sum of money to the payee or the note holder at sight of the note. It is stipulated in *Negotiable Instruments Law of the People's Republic of China* that "The term 'promissory note' used in this Law refers to the bank note." There are only bank promissory notes in China but no commercial promissory note.

The key elements in the promissory note are as follows:

① the words of "promissory note";

② unconditional payment promise;

③ a sum certain in money;

④ the name of payee;

⑤ the issuance date;

⑥ the signature of the drawer.

本票是出票人签发的、承诺自己在见票时无条件支付确定的金额给收款人或者持票人的票据。《中华人民共和国票据法》规定：“本法所称本票，指银行本票。”我国只有银行本票，没有商业本票。

《中华人民共和国票据法》规定的本票要项包括：

① 表明“本票”的字样；

② 无条件支付的承诺；

③ 确定的金额；

④ 收款人名称；

⑤ 出票日期；

⑥ 出票人签章。

2.2 Classification of the Promissory Notes 本票的种类

Commercial promissory notes are also called general promissory notes, drawn by the commercial firms. The general promissory notes are divided into sight promissory note and time promissory note.

Bank promissory notes are issued and signed by banks. The bank promissory notes are sight, which are mostly adopted in international trade.

商业本票也称一般本票，由工商企业签发。一般本票可分为即期一般本票与远期一般本票。

银行本票是由银行签发的本票。银行本票都是即期的。国际贸易中使用的本票大都是银行本票。

2.3 The Involved Parties to the Promissory Notes 本票的当事人

There are two parties usually: the drawer and the payee. The payer of the promissory note is the drawer himself. The time promissory notes needn't the acceptance.

Some banks issue the promissory note which is at sight, without stating the payee or the words of "to the order". The kind of promissory note is equal to the currency circulated in the market.

本票涉及的当事人主要有两个：出票人和受款人。本票的付款人即出票人本人。远期本票不需承兑。

有的银行发行见票即付、不记载收款人或来人抬头的本票，这种本票相当于在市场上流通的纸币。

2.4 The Differences between the Promissory Note and the Bill of Exchange 本票与汇票的区别

The promissory note is a promise made by the drawer to make payment to the note holder; the B/E is an order made by one party to the other party requiring it to make payment.

There are only 2 parties in a promissory note, but 3 parties in a B/E.

The drawer of a promissory note is the payer, and a time promissory note doesn't need acceptance; the drawee of a B/E is the payer.

In whatever situation, for a promissory note, the drawer is the first debtor; for a B/E, the drawer is the first debtor before the bill is accepted, the acceptor becomes the first debtor after the acceptance and the drawer turns into the second debtor.

The promissory note is made out in only one original; the B/E is made out in duplicate.

本票是出票人承诺自己向持票人付款，汇票是一个人向另一个人发出的支付命令。

本票只有两个当事人，汇票有三个当事人。

本票的出票人即是付款人，远期本票不需承兑；汇票的受票人是付款人。

本票在任何情况下，出票人都是主债务人；汇票在付款人承兑前，出票人是它的主债务人，在承兑后，承兑人是主债务人，出票人成为次债务人。

本票只能开出一张，汇票可开出两张。

3. Check (Cheque) 支票

3.1 Definition 定义

It is stipulated in *The Bills of Exchange Act of UK* that a check is a sight B/E with the bank as the payer, that is to say, it is an unconditional order drawn on a banker by the drawer, requiring the banker to pay on demand a sum certain in money to or to the order of a specified person or to the bearer.

In *Negotiable Instruments Law of the People's Republic of China*, a check means a bill issued and signed by the drawer, appointing the bank or other financial institutes to make payment of a certain sum of money unconditionally to the payee or the check holder.

The key elements in a check according to *Negotiable Instruments Law of the People's Republic of China* are as follows:

1) the words of "Check" or "Cheque";

2) unconditional payment commission;

3) amount fixed;

4) the name of the payer;

5) the issuance date;

6) the signature of the drawer.

The drawer writes a sum certain in money on the check and draw on a banker requiring the banker to pay the sum to the specified person or to the bearer. The drawer shall be committed to the obligation for the check and on the law. The obligation of the check means that the drawer shall take the responsibility of making payment to the payee; the legal obligation means the drawer shall keep an account in the paying bank with the deposit not lower than the sum on the check. If the deposit is less, the check will be dishonored when the bearer presents the check to the paying bank for the payment. In this case, the drawer shall be held for the legal responsibility. The check is only at sight.

《英国票据法》规定：支票是以银行为付款人的即期汇票，即存款人对银行无条件支付一定金额的委托或命令。

《中华人民共和国票据法》规定：支票是出票人签发的，委托办理支票存款业务的银行或者其他机构在见票时无条件支付确定金额给收款人或持票人的票据。

《中华人民共和国票据法》规定的支票要项包括：

（1）表明“支票”的字样；
（2）无条件支付的委托；
（3）确定的金额；
（4）付款人名称；
（5）出票日期；
（6）出票人签章。

出票人在支票上签发一定的金额，要求受票的银行见票即付一定金额给特定人或持票人。出票人在签发支票后，应负票据上的责任和法律上的责任。前者是指出票人对收款人担保支票的付款；后者是指出票人签发支票时，应在付款的银行存有不低于票面金额的存款。如存款不足，支票持有人在向付款银行提示支票要求付款时，就会遭到拒付。这种支票叫空头支票。开出空头支票的出票人要负法律上的责任。支票只有即期，没有远期。

3.2 Classification 支票的种类

According to the relevant law of China, checks are classified into cash check and transfer check.

In other countries, checks are divided into crossed check and uncrossed check. The crossed check is crossed with two parallel lines on the up-left of the check, and the payee cannot cash the check but receive the payment through the bank transfer. The uncrossed check can both cash the money and make transfer.

《中华人民共和国票据法》规定：支票可分为现金支票和转账支票。

在其他国家，支票可分为划线支票和未划线支票。划线支票在支票左上角被划上两道平行线，受款人只能通过银行代为收款转账，不能提取现金。未划线支票既可转账也可提取现金。

Lesson 2 Remittance 汇付

1. The Definition of Remittance 汇付的定义

Remittance means that the payer makes payment to the payee through a bank or other institutions.

For the remittance in the international trade, the buyer makes payment to the seller by bank according to the conditions and the payment time stipulated in the contract.

汇付是指付款人主动通过银行或其他机构将款项汇交收款人。

国际贸易货款采用汇付，一般是由买方按合同约定条件（如收到单据或货物）和时间，将货款通过银行汇交给卖方。

2. The Involved Parties in the Remittance 汇付当事人

Remitter is the party who makes payment by remittance. Usually the importer or the buyer is the remitter.

Payee or Beneficiary is the party who receives payment. Usually the seller is the payee or beneficiary.

Remitting Bank is the bank which issues a remittance instruction at the request of the buyer. Usually, the remitting bank is the bank in the importer's country.

Paying Bank is the bank that transfers the money to the account of the seller following the instruction of the remitting bank. The paying bank is usually the bank in the exporter's country.

The application form of remittance is a contract concluded between the buyer and the remitting bank, and the paying bank is the agency bank of the remitting bank, committed to the obligation of making payment.

汇款人，即汇出款项的人，一般为进口人、买方。

收款人，即为收取款项的人，在进出口业务中一般为卖方。

汇出行，即接受买方的委托汇出款项的银行，通常是进口地银行。

汇入行，即解付汇款的银行，一般是出口地银行。

汇款申请书是买方与汇出行之间的一项合同，汇出行与汇入行是代理合同，承担解付汇款的义务。

3. The Classification of Remittance 汇付的种类

3.1 Mail Transfer (M/T) 信汇

Mail Transfer means that the remitting bank sends a remittance instruction letter by mail to the paying bank at the request of the payer, authorizing the paying bank to make payment of a sum of money to the payee.

Advantage: low cost; disadvantage: long time for receiving the payment.

信汇指汇出行应汇款人申请，将信汇委托书寄给汇入行，授权解付一定金额给收款人。

优点是费用低；缺点是收取汇款时间长。

3.2 Telegraphic Transfer (T/T) 电汇

Telegraphic transfer means that the remitting bank sends the remittance instruction to the paying bank by telex, tele-transmission or SWIFT at the request of the payer.

Advantages: speedy, beneficial to the seller's capital running as it can receive the payment in a short time; disadvantage: high cost.

电汇指汇出行应汇款人的申请，拍发加押电报或电传或通过 SWIFT（环球同业银行金融电信协会）指示另一个国家的分行或代理行（汇入行）解付一定金额给收款人的付款方式。

优点是速度快，卖方能尽快收到货款，有利于卖方资金周转；缺点是费用高。

3.3 Remittance by Banker's Demand Draft (D/D) 票汇

The remitting bank draws a banker's sight draft on its branch bank or agency bank on behalf of the payer after the payer pays some charges for the draft, and sends the draft to the payee; the payee gets the payment from the paying bank with draft.

票汇是汇出行应汇款人的申请，在汇款人向汇出行交款并支付一定费用的条件下，代替汇款人开立的以其分行或代理行为解付行、支付一定金额给收款人的银行即期汇票，寄交收款人，由收款人凭以向汇入行取款。

3.4 The Usage of the Remittance 汇付的应用

The remittance can be divided into the following two kinds:

汇付还可分为货到付款和预付货款两种。

3.4.1 Cash on Delivery, COD 货到付款

The buyer will make payment on receipt of the documents or goods from the seller. Actually, it is a kind of credit offered by the seller to the buyer as well as a kind of Open Account Transaction. For the seller, the risk of it is the greatest. It totally depends on the credit of the buyer whether the seller will be paid after the delivery of the goods.

货到付款：买方在收到卖方的单据或货物后再付款。实际上，它是卖方向买方提供的一种信用，也是一种赊销。对卖方来说，风险最大，卖方交货以后能否得到偿付全凭买方的商业信用。

3.4.2 Payment in Advance 预付货款

The buyer will make payment prior to the seller's delivery of the goods. In this way, the buyer offers credit to the seller while the buyer takes some risks. It is sometimes called Cash with Order. The buyer will make payment to the seller by T/T or M/T in a few days after the conclusion of the contract.

预付货款：预付货款在卖方还未生产交货时，买方预付货款。这种方式下买方向卖方提供了信用，买方存在一定的风险，这种做法有时叫作随订单付现。或者，在合同签订后若干天，买方即将货款电汇或信汇给卖方。

Lesson 3　Collection 托收

1. Conception of Collection 托收的概念

1.1 Definition 定义

Collection is an arrangement whereby the seller draws a draft on the buyer and authorizes its bank to collect.

The definition of the International Chamber of Commerce (ICC): The collection is the handling by banks, on instructions received, of documents (financial documents and/or commercial documents), in order to: obtain acceptance and/or, as the case may be, payment; or deliver commercial documents against acceptance and/or, as the case may be, against payment; or deliver documents on other terms and conditions.

托收指债权人（卖方）出具汇票，委托银行向债务人（买方）收取货款的一种支付方式。

国际商会《托收统一规则》522 号给托收下的定义：托收是指由接到托收指示的银行根据所收到的指示处理金融单据以便取得付款或承兑，或凭付款或承兑交付商业单据，或凭其他条款或条件交出单据。

1.2 Nature of Collection 托收的性质

Collection is a kind of commercial credit, offered to each other by firms and merchants. The collection bank acts only as collector of funds on behalf of the seller and is not committed to the obligation whether the buyer makes payment or not. It is dependent on the commercial credit of the buyer if the seller will be paid after the delivery of goods. Therefore, a collection transaction puts the seller under a great risk.

托收是一种商业信用，也就是商人之间互相提供的信用。通过银行办理托收，银行属于代办性质，对买方是否付款不承担责任。卖方交货后能否收回货款，完全要看买方个人的信誉。托收虽然通过银行办理，但银行只是代收代付，并不承担付款责任，所以托收对卖方仍然存在较大的风险。

2. The Involved Parties in Collection 托收的当事人

2.1 Principal 委托人

Usually, the principal is the seller. 委托人也称本人，通常是卖方。

2.2 Remitting Bank 托收银行

The bank in the exporter’s country is authorized by the principal to effect the collection on behalf of the principal.

出口地银行（委托行）接受委托人委托办理托收业务的银行。

2.3 Collecting Bank 代收行

The bank in the importer’s country who receives the authorization from the remitting bank to collect the funds from the payer.

进口地银行，即买方所在国银行。它接受托收行的委托，向付款人收取货款。

2.4 Payer 付款人

Namely the buyer, the drawee.

付款人即买方、受票人。

2.5 Presenting Bank 提示行

The bank who presents the shipment documents with draft to the payer.

向付款人做出提示汇票和单据的银行。

3. Types of Collection 托收的种类

The collection is classified into two kinds which are clean collection and documentary collection. The documentary collection is divided into Documents against Payment (D/P) and Documents against Acceptance (D/A).

托收可分为光票托收和跟单托收，跟单托收又可分为付款交单和承兑交单。

3.1 Documents against Payment（D/P）付款交单

3.1.1 Definition 定义

The document against payment refers to that the seller delivers the documents upon receipt of the payment from the buyer (importer). The buyer cannot get the documents until it makes the payment to the seller.

The documents are vital for a documentary collection, for the delivery of documents means the transfer of the ownership of cargo. The collecting bank in the importer's country will make presentation to the importer with the bill and the documents received from the remitting bank, but will not release the documents to the importer until the importer makes payment to the collecting bank.

付款交单指卖方的交单是以买方（进口人）的付款为条件。先付款后交单，以付款为交单的前提。

跟单托收中的单据很重要。在象征性交货的国际贸易中，货物的买卖实际上是一种单据的买卖，代表货物所有权的单据不能轻易脱手。国外代收行将托收行寄来的汇票和单据向进口人提示后，进口人必须先向代收行付款。付款后，代收行才可将单据交付进口人。

3.1.2 Classification 分类

1）D/P at Sight 即期付款交单

After the shipment, the seller draws a sight draft and makes presentation of it with the full set of shipment documents to the buyer through the banks, and the buyer makes the payment at sight of the bill; the bank releases the documents to the buyer on receipt of the full payment from the buyer.

卖方装运后开具即期汇票，随附全套单据，通过银行向买方提示，买方见票后立即付款。买方付清货款后取得全套单据。以买方先付款为条件，银行向其交单。

2）D/P after Sight 远期付款交单

After the shipment, the seller draws a sight draft and makes presentation of it with the full set of shipment documents to the buyer through the banks, and the buyer accepts the bill after confirming it and makes the payment on the mature date; then the bank releases the documents to the buyer.

The above shows that only after the payment has been made can the buyer obtain the shipping documents, and take delivery of or resell the goods, whether it is D/P at sight or D/P after sight. Therefore, using D/P sight or D/P after sight represents less risk for the seller compared with using remittance.

卖方装运后开出远期汇票，随附商业单据，通过银行向买方提示，买方审核无误后，即在汇票上承兑，于汇票到期日付清货款后，银行向其交单。

以上说明，不论是即期付款交单还是远期付款交单，都是买方付清货款后才能取得代表货物所有权的单据，才能提货或转售货物。所以，与汇付相比，托收的风险对卖方来说略小。

3.2 Documents against Acceptance（D/A）承兑交单

After the shipment, the seller draws a usance bill and makes presentation to the buyer through banks with the full set of documents, and the collecting bank releases the documents to the buyer upon receipt of the acceptance of the buyer. The buyer will fulfill the payment when the bill falls due. Documents against Acceptance means that the buyer obtains the ownership of cargo before making payment and thus the seller is put into a great risk. The seller will get into the loss of goods and money in case of the buyer's failure in payment. Therefore, the international trade companies in our country are very cautious about the payment by D/A.

承兑交单即卖方在装运后开出远期汇票，随附全套单据，通过银行向买方提示，买方承兑汇票后，代收行即将全套单据交给买方。在汇票到期后买方再履行付款义务。承兑交单实际上是买方先取得货物所有权，之后再付款，所以对卖方来说风险非常大。一旦买方到期不付款，卖方就会遭到货款两空的损失，所以现在我国的外贸公司对使用承兑交单非常谨慎。

4. The Property, Advantages and Disadvantages 托收的性质及利弊

Collection is a kind of commercial credit in favor of the buyer. The payment by collection needn't go through as complicated procedures as the L/C, without the requirement of bank deposit, with lower bank service charges, and not occupying capital. The remitting banks and collecting banks are not committed to the obligation of payment, and thus it is completely dependent on the buyer's credit whether the seller can receive payment or not. The buyer is in the risk of failure or delay of being paid in case that the buyer goes bankruptcy, loses the ability of discharging debt or refuses to pay in purpose. Although D/P is to deliver the documents on receipt of payment, the buyer may refuse to make payment and give up the documents when the market is shrinking. In this case, the seller will bear the loss of money and goods as well. The banks are not committed to the obligation of keeping and delivery of the shipment, but the seller has to pay for the settlement charges of delivery, customs clearance, warehouse storage, insurance, resale, auction or shipping back, etc. For the payment by D/A, the risk for the seller is larger.

托收是一种商业信用，对买方有利，它不需要像信用证那样办理烦琐的手续，不需银行押金，减少了费用支出，不占用资金。银行并不承担付款的责任，卖方能否收到货款完全依赖买方的个人信用。如买方破产或丧失清偿债务的能力或有意赖账，出口人则有可能收不回或延迟收回货款。虽然付款交单是以买方首先付款为条件，但在市场行情下跌时，信誉不好的买方可能溜之大吉，既不赎单，也不付款，那么卖方同样要遭受货款两空的损失。在这种情况下，银行没有义务代为保管或提取货物，出口人还要承担在进口地办理提货、缴纳进口关税、存仓、保险、转售以至于被低价拍卖或运回国内的损失。在承兑交单的情况下，卖方的损失会更大，风险也更大。

Questions 思考题

1. What are the differences between the commercial bill and the banker's bill?
商业汇票与银行汇票的区别是什么？

2. Who are the involved parties in a bill of exchange? Why is the drawer the main debtor (before the acceptance of the draft)?
汇票的当事人有哪些？为什么说出票人是主债务人（在汇票承兑前）？

3. Which one is the payer in the involved parties in B/E, promissory note and check?
汇票、本票、支票的当事人中哪一个是付款人？

4. What is the title of the B/E? How many ways are there for the title of the B/E?
什么是汇票的抬头？汇票抬头有哪几种做法？

5. What is the endorsement of the B/E? How many types are there for the endorsement?
什么是汇票的背书？背书有几种？

6. What is the property of the collection? How to use it in the international trade?
汇付方式的性质是什么？在国际贸易中如何使用？

7. What are the differences between D/P after 30 days sight and D/A after 30 days sight?
30 天即期付款交单与 30 天即期承兑交单有何区别？

Chapter 13

Letter of Credit and Letter of Guarantee

信用证和银行保函

Lesson 1 Letter of Credit 信用证

Letter of credit (L/C) is a payment term mainly used in international trade. Under the circumstance that the seller and the buyer don't know much of each other, lacking mutual trust, the payment term of L/C is a good solution to this difficult problem, which replaces commercial credit with bank credit, getting a bank involved in the payment obligation. The availability of the payment promise to the seller from a bank before the delivery of goods helps the transactions go well, further boosting the development of international trade.

L/C payment is in favor of buyers, too. In a sales transaction by L/C, the buyer can restrict the seller with the clauses of L/C to the fulfillment of the contract, ensuring the quality, quantity and delivery time of the goods. The seller cannot be paid if it breaches the contract.

信用证是目前我国外贸进出口结算的一种主要方式。它以银行信用取代商业信用，以银行的付款责任取代买方的付款责任。在买卖双方缺乏信任、互不熟悉的情况下，信用证的付款方式很好地解决了支付中的难题，使卖方在交货以前就能得到银行付款的承诺，使交易得以顺利进行，有利于国际贸易的快速发展。

信用证交易也给买方带来好处。在信用证交易中，买方可以利用信用证条款约束卖方履行合同，保证所购买货物的品质、数量、交货期符合合同的规定，卖方如果违约将得不到偿付。

1. Definition of L/C 信用证的定义

Letter of Credit is a kind of conditional document in written form, opened by a bank, with a promise to make payment. In detail, it is a kind of warrant issued by a bank at the request of the seller, addressed to the exporter, in a certain amount, under a certain condition, promising to make payment. The said “a certain amount, a certain condition” means that the payment made by the opening bank is under the condition that the seller presents the documents complying with the L/C clauses.

As defined in the UCP 600, a letter of credit means “any arrangement, however named or described, whereby a bank acting at the request and on the instructions of a customer or on its own behalf, is to make a payment to or to the order of a third party, or is to accept and pay bill of exchange drawn by the third party”.

信用证是一种银行开立的、有条件的、承诺付款的书面文件。具体地说，信用证就是银行（开证行）应进口人的请求和指示，向出口人开立的、一定金额的、在一定条件下保证付款的凭证。所谓“一定金额，一定条件”，是指开证行的付款是以卖方提交符合信用证的单据为条件。

UCP 600 给信用证下的定义是“一项不可撤销的安排，无论其名称或描述如何，该项安排构成开证行对相符交单予以承付的确定承诺”。

2. Parties Involved 信用证的当事人

Opener, Applicant: the party which applies to the bank for the opening of a letter of credit, namely, the importer or the buyer under a contract.

Issuing/Opening Bank: the bank which issues a credit to the seller, and usually, the bank located in the country of the importer.

Beneficiary: the party entitled to be reimbursed under a credit and specified in the credit, usually the exporter.

Advising/Notifying Bank: the bank nominated by the issuing bank to transfer a credit to the bank of the exporter’s country, usually the branch bank or the correspondent bank of the issuing bank.

Negotiating Bank: the bank which is ready to purchase or discount the documentary bill presented by the beneficiary under a letter of credit. It may be a bank designated by the issuing bank or another bank which is able to negotiate under the credit. Negotiation means that, after confirming the documents in compliance with the L/C, the negotiating bank discounts the documentary bill and pays for the shipping documents under the L/C according to the L/C clauses, and the reimbursement sum is the balance after the interests accrued from the negotiation date to the estimated payment date are deducted. Negotiation is actually a kind of financing way for the beneficiary; after negotiation the bank becomes the holder of the draft with recourse.

Paying/Drawee Bank: the bank which is specified in an L/C, usually an issuing bank, or a branch bank/correspondent bank of the issuing bank. Due to the transfer of money, the issuing bank will nominate another bank as the paying bank. The paying bank and issuing bank are on the same legal status, without recourse.

Reimbursing Bank: the bank which is specified in an L/C to make reimbursement on behalf of the issuing bank or paying bank. The bank is not committed to checking the documents but makes payment upon the authorization of the issuing bank, and the payment is final. The reimbursing bank is requested to fulfill the payment resulting from the capital of the issuing bank deposited in the third party country.

Confirming Bank: the bank which adds the confirmation to a letter of credit at the request of the issuing bank. The confirming bank is responsible to the L/C separately with the commitment of making payment or negotiation. The confirming bank holds the same obligation and status as the opening bank. The confirming bank can be the advising bank at the same time. The Confirming Bank can be acted by Advising/Notifying Bank or other kinds of banks.

开证申请人指向银行申请开立信用证的人，即进口人、买卖合同中的买方。

开证行指受开证人委托，向卖方开立信用证的银行，一般为进口人所在地银行。

受益人指信用证上所指定的有权使用该证得到偿付的人，一般为出口人。

通知行指受开证行的委托，将信用证转交出口人的银行，出口地银行通常是开证行的代理行。

议付银行指愿意对受益人交来的跟单汇票买入或贴现的银行，可以是开证行指定的银行，也可以是公开议付的银行。议付又称押汇、买单，是指议付行在审单无误的情况下，按信用证的条款贴现受益人的汇票，买入信用证项下的货运单据，从票面金额中扣除从议付日到估计收到票款之日的利息，将余款先行支付给受益人。议付实际上是银行向受益人先行垫付资金，银行在议付之后就成为汇票的正当持票人，具有追索权。

付款行指信用证上指定的付款银行，一般是开证行，也可以是开证行以外的分行或代理行。由于资金调拨的原因，开证行指定另一家银行为付款银行。付款行与开证行具有同等的法律地位，都是终局性的，没有追索权。

偿付行指信用证指定的代开证行或付款行清偿货款的银行，其不负责审单，只根据开证行的授权付款，付款也是终局性的。偿付行的出现，往往由于开证行的资金调度或集中在该第三国银行的缘故而要求该银行代为偿付信用证规定的款项。

保兑行指根据开证行的请求，在信用证上加具保兑的银行。保兑行在信用证上加具保兑后，即对信用证独立负责，承担必须付款或议付的责任。保兑行具有与开证行相同的责任和地位。保兑行可以由通知行兼任，也可由其他银行加具保兑。

3. Nature and Characteristics of Letter of Credit 信用证的性质

With the payment obligation of importer transferred to a bank through L/C payment, a bank is undertaking an absolute responsibility for payment.

There are three important legal principles as follows:

1）Undertaking an absolute responsibility, a bank is in the first place to make payment.

2）Being an independent instrument, L/C is a kind of promise or contract independent from the sales contract.

3）With the principle of strict compliance, a bank makes payment upon the strict compliance of documents with L/C.

信用证把原来由进口人履行的凭单付款责任转由银行来履行，在商业信用之上加上银行信用，银行负绝对责任。

信用证的性质基于三个非常重要的法律原则：

（1）银行承担的是绝对责任，超越原来的担保责任，银行承担第一位的责任。

（2）自足文件，信用证是独立于买卖合同的一种契约。

（3）严格相符原则，单据和信用证严格相符，这也是银行付款的依据。

4. Characteristics of Payment by L/C 信用证支付的特点

4.1 Opening Bank undertaking the Responsibility of the First Payer 开证行承担第一付款人的责任

It is a kind of absolute and primary responsibility. That is to say, after opening an L/C, the L/C opening bank has to fulfill the payment according to L/C terms whatever the buyer is bankrupt, with a solvency or not, dead. Without the consent of the beneficiary, an L/C cannot be revoked or revised.

这种责任是一种绝对的责任、第一位的责任。也就是说，开证行在开出信用证后，只要卖方提交了符合信用证规定的单据，无论买方是否破产、是否有清偿能力、是否死亡都与卖方无关，开证行必须按照信用证的承诺对卖方付款，未经受益人同意，银行不得撤销或者更改信用证。

4.2 An Independent Instrument 信用证是一种自足文件

A letter of credit is another contract, which is issued based on the sales contract, but independent from the sales contract and application form. A letter of credit is a contract between the issuing bank and the beneficiary. The rights and obligations of the parties involved in an L/C are subject to the L/C, not bound by the sales contract. Therefore, a payment or acceptance promise made by a bank is not bound by the restriction of the claims or defenses between the L/C applicant and the issuing bank or the beneficiary based on the existing relationships.

信用证是基于买卖合同开立的，但是信用证一旦开立就独立于买卖合同，独立于开证申请书，成为与买卖合同无关的另一个契约。信用证实际上是开证行与受益人之间的一个合同。信用证的各方当事人的权利、义务都以信用证为准，不受买卖合同的约束。因此，一家银行做出付款、承兑的承诺，不受申请人与开证行或与受益人之间在已有关系上产生索偿或抗辩的制约。

4.3 L/C Is a Kind of Transaction of Documents 信用证业务是一种单据的买卖

Under a letter of credit, a bank makes payment against documents. A bank makes payment depending on the documentary compliant with the shipping documents and credit, which is neither concerned with the goods, nor sales contract even the truth or false of documents.

Under a letter of credit, with the principle of strict compliance, the documents must comply with credit as well as each other. The paying bank must make payment as long as a presentation of documents is complying even though the actual shipment has something wrong. The paying bank can refuse payment too if a presentation is not complying even though the shipment is right. In case that the goods have something wrong or the seller is deceiving, the solution to make refusal of payment is to find out the documentary discrepancies.

在信用证项下，银行遵循的是凭单付款的原则，银行付款的依据仅仅是单据和信用证的规定表面相符，银行与货物无关，与买卖合同无关，与单据的真假无关。

在信用证条件下实行严格相符的原则，不仅要做到单证一致，还要做到单单一致。在信用证项下，只要交单正确，即使货物有假，银行也必须付款。如果单据有错误，即使货物准确，银行也可以拒付。如果发现货物有假或者卖方存在欺诈行为，买方如果想让银行拒付，唯一的办法就是寻找单据的不符点。

5. Form of Opening Letter of Credit 开立信用证的形式

Currently, SWIFT is the main way to transmit L/C in international trade.

"SWIFT" (namely BIC) is the abbreviation of Society for Worldwide Interbank Financial Telecommunication. The organization is a non-profitable international cooperation organization of international banks, established in May of 1973 in Belgium, with membership management, and including more than 200 countries, over 3,000 banks, over 8,000 working sites. Each member bank of the association has its own code, namely SWIFT code, equaling to the identification card of the bank. In order to ensure a speedy and accurate payment transfer to the payee's account, the applicant of remittance by cable fills the SWIFT code of the payee bank. The swift code can be searched out through Internet. Most of China's banks are the members of the association. For a credit with SWIFT, the credit must be issued according to the regulations in the SWIFT manual, adopting the tag stipulated in the SWIFT manual, and the undertaking clauses of banks can be omitted in the credit but the undertaking of bank cannot be exempted according to UCP 600.

Before the SWIFT, the credits are issued through cable or telex with different bank criteria, in different clauses and forms, and in complex words. Since SWIFT is adopted, L/C is issued in standard, fixed, and unified form, with speedy transmission and low cost; therefore, SWIFT has been widely used in European countries, American countries and Asian countries.

For the time being, the SWIFT format code is MT700 and MT701, and the revision of L/C is transmitted through SWIFT standard format MT707.

目前，在国际贸易中以 SWIFT 传递信用证是一种主要形式。

“SWIFT”（又称 BIC）是环球银行金融电信协会的简称。该组织是一个国际银行同业间非营利性的国际合作组织，于 1973 年 5 月在比利时成立，采用会员制，目前已有 200 多个会员、3 000 多个会员银行、8 000 多个站点。凡该协会的成员银行都有自己的代码，即 SWIFT CODE，相当于银行的身份证。电汇申请人在电汇时填写收入行 SWIFT CODE 能保证汇款快速准确地到达收款人账户。如不清楚对方银行的 SWIFT CODE，可上网查询。我国的主要银行大都是该协会会员。采用 SWIFT 信用证，必须遵守 SWIFT 使用手册的规定，使用 SWIFT 手册规定的代号，信用证必须按国际商会制定的 UCP 600 的规定，在信用证中可以省去银行的承诺条款，但不能免去银行所应承担的义务。

在 SWIFT 之前实行全电开证时，都采用电报或电传开证，各国银行标准不一，条款格式也各不相同，而且文字烦琐；采用 SWIFT 开证后，信用证具有了标准化、固定化、统一格式的特性，而且传递速度快、成本低，现在已被西北欧、美洲、亚洲等国家的银行广泛使用。

目前开立的 SWIFT 格式信用证代号为 MT700 和 MT701，如对开出的 SWIFT 信用证进行修改，则采用 MT707 标准格式传递信息。

6. Contents of Letter of Credit 信用证的内容

6.1 General Information of L/C 对信用证本身的说明

The general information of a credit is mainly as follows: 1) Whether the credit is confirmable or not, and transferrable or not; the conception of revocable credit has been deleted from UCP 600, and all credits are irrevocable; 2) credit number; 3) sum, currency, and spelling in words and figures; 4) expiry date and place; 5) whether there is an expiry date outside territory.

信用证的内容主要包括：（1）信用证是否可保兑、是否可转让，UCP 600 取消了可撤销信用证的概念，所有信用证都是不可撤销的；（2）编号；（3）金额、货币、大小写；（4）有效期及到期地点；（5）是否有境外有效期。

6.2 Information Required on the Draft 对汇票的要求

Under a letter of credit with draft, the information about drawer, drawee, payee, sum, and other main terms, must be specified in the draft. In Clause 6 (c) of UCP 600, it is written as follows: a credit must not be issued available by a draft drawn on the applicant.

Usually, it is stipulated in a credit for a draft as follows: “we hereby open our irrevocable letter of credit in your favor which is available by your drafts at sight drawn on us for full invoice value accompanied by the following documents."

在信用证项下，如使用汇票，要明确汇票的出票人、受票人、受款人、汇票金额、主要条款等内容。UCP 600 第 6 条 c 款规定："信用证不得开成凭以申请人为付款人的汇票兑用。"

通常，在信用证中规定："兹开出以你方为受益人的不可撤销信用证，本证凭你方按发票金额全额开出的以我行为受票人的即期汇票付款，并随附下列单据。"

6.3 Description of the Goods 对货物的要求

The details including name, types, specification, quantity, packing, price, must be stated in a credit, as well as the contract which the credit is subject to.

在信用证中要注明货物的名称、品种、规格、数量、包装、价格，并注明根据某某买卖合同。

6.4 Shipment Clauses 对装运的要求

In a credit, the details of loading port (place), destination port (place), time of shipment and partial shipment/transshipment or not, etc. must be specified.

在信用证中应列明装运港（地）、目的港（地）、装运期限以及可否分批、转运等项内容。

6.5 Documents about the Goods 货物单据

In a credit, the documents required shall be specified as follows:

They include invoice, packing list, certificate of origin, inspection certificate, etc.

It is written in UCP 600 that "a commercial invoice must be issued by the beneficiary, with the name of the applicant as letterhead, and in the same currency as the credit, and the goods, service or the performance of the contract must be described in the same way as the credit".

在信用证中应列明所需的各种货运单据，主要有以下几种：

货物单据包括发票、装箱单（包装清单）、原产地证、商检证明等。

UCP 600 规定："商业发票必须看似由受益人出具"，"须出具成以申请人为抬头"，"必须与信用证的货币相同"，"商业发票上的货物、服务或履约行为的描述应该与信用证中的描述一致。"

6.6 Shipping Documents 运输单据

The most important one is the ocean bill of lading, which is the warranty of cargo ownership.

Usually, a bill of lading is described in a credit as: "Full set clean on board ocean bills of lading, made out to order, blank endorsed marked freight prepaid notify applicant."

运输单据中最重要的是海运提单，它是货物所有权的凭证。

通常将提单描述为："全套清洁的已装船提单，凭指定的空白背书，注明运费已付，通知申请人。"

6.7 Special Clause 特殊条款

It means some special instruction or special requirement for the negotiation, or payment route, or confirmation or not.

银行对议付或付款路线或是否保兑，做出特别指示，或有特别要求。

Bank's Promise of Payment. For example:

We hereby agree with the drawers, endorsers and bona fide holders of drafts drawn under and in compliance with the terms of this credit that such drafts will be duly honored on due presentation to the drawee if negotiated on or before expiry date and paid on maturity.

The advising bank is requested to notify the beneficiary without adding their confirmation.

银行保证付款的承诺。例如：

我们兹向根据本证开出并符合本证条款的汇票的出票人、背书人和正当持票人承诺，只要你们在汇票的效期内向付款行提示或议付（远期汇票在汇票的到期日向付款行提示），将立即得到付款。

请通知行通知受益人本证未加以保兑。

6.8 A Declaration of Being Subject to UCP 600 声明本证遵循惯例 UCP 600

For example: this credit is subject to *the Uniform Customs and Practice for Documentary Credit 2007 Revision* by ICC (International Chamber of Commerce) and Publication No. 600.

例如：本证遵循国际商会《跟单信用证统一惯例》2007 年修订本第 600 号出版物的规定。

7. Types of Letters of Credit 信用证的种类

7.1 Irrevocable L/C 不可撤销信用证

Before the publication of UCP 600, credits are classified into being revocable and irrevocable. Since UCP 600 was put into effect on 1st July, 2007, the conception of revocable credit is deleted, that is to say, "a credit is irrevocable even if there is no indication to that effect".

An irrevocable letter of credit means that the issuing bank is irrevocably bound to honor as of the time it issues the credit. That is to say, an issuing bank cannot amend or revoke a credit without the approval of the party involved; an issuing bank must effect payment so long as the beneficiary makes a presentation of flawless documents.

在 UCP 600 之前，信用证还分为可撤销信用证和不可撤销信用证。在 UCP 600 于 2007 年 7 月 1 日生效之后，已经没有了可撤销信用证的概念，“凡是信用证都是不可撤销的，即使未如此表明”。

所谓不可撤销信用证，是指开证行自开立信用证之时起即不可撤销地承担承付责任。也就是说，未经信用证的有关当事人同意，开证行不得片面修改和撤销信用证，只要受益人提交了符合信用证的单据，开证行必须履行付款义务。

7.2 Sight L/C 即期信用证

7.2.1 Definition 定义

Sight letter of credit means under sight L/C, the issuing bank or paying bank effects payment immediately upon the presentation of the documentary draft and shipping documents complying with the letter of credit by the beneficiary. The payment in this way is speedy and safe, in favor of capital turnover.

In sight letter of credit, T/T Reimbursement Clause is also added sometimes, which means the issuing bank allows the negotiating bank to notify the issuing bank or the nominated paying bank by cable or fax that the documents presented are complying with the L/C clauses, and the issuing bank is responsible for effecting payment to the negotiating bank by T/T upon receipt of the above-mentioned notification.

即期信用证是指开证行或付款行收到符合信用证条款的跟单汇票或装运单据后，立即履行付款义务的信用证。这种方式收汇迅速、安全，有利于资金周转。

在即期信用证中，有时还加列电汇索偿条款，指开证行允许议付行用电报或电传通知开证行或指定付款行，说明各种单据与信用证要求相符，开证行接到电报或电传通知后，有义务立即用电汇将货款拨交议付行。

7.2.2 Sight Payment L/C 即期付款信用证

It is a letter of credit with payment to be made immediately upon a presentation of flawless documents, remarked with the words such as “Available by Payment” in the credit, and generally not demanding the beneficiary to issue a draft. The paying bank of sight payment L/C may be the issuing bank itself, the advising bank or the nominated bank in a third country.

A sight payment L/C taking the bank of exporter’s country as the paying bank, and with the maturity place of presentation in the export place, is most favorable to the beneficiary as the payment can be made promptly. If the paying bank is the issuing bank or the bank in a third country, usually the presentation is required to be made in the place where the paying bank is located.

即期付款信用证是指采用即期兑现方式的信用证，证中通常注明“付款兑现”字样，一般不要求受益人开立汇票。即期付款信用证的付款行可以是开证行本身，也可以是出口地的通知行或指定的第三国银行。

以出口地银行为付款人的即期付款信用证的交单到期地点在出口地，可以及时得到偿付，对受益人最为有利。付款行为开证行本身或第三国银行，交单也是通常规定在付款行所在地进行。

7.3 Usance L/C 远期信用证

A usance L/C is a letter of credit under which the payment is made by the issuing bank or paying bank within the stipulated time upon receipt of documents. A time draft is issued by the beneficiary. There are 3 types of usance L/C.

远期信用证指开证行或付款行收到信用证的单据时，在规定期限内履行付款义务的信用证。受益人开出的是远期汇票，远期信用证主要有三种。

7.3.1 Acceptance L/C 承兑信用证

It is a letter of credit accepted by a bank, that is to say, the nominated bank will make acceptance upon receipt of the shipping documents with a time draft drawn on which by the beneficiary, and make payment on the maturity date.

For the draft under the credit, the bank, based on the rights and obligations subject to the credit before the acceptance, undertakes payment to the bill drawer, holder, or endorser after the acceptance. This kind of credit is also referred to as bank acceptance L/C.

承兑信用证指由某一银行承兑的信用证，即当受益人向指定银行开具远期汇票并提示时，指定行即行承兑，并于汇票到期日履行付款。

这种信用证项下的汇票，在承兑前，银行对出口商的权利义务以信用证为准；承兑后，银行作为汇票承兑人对出票人、持票人、背书人承担付款责任。这种信用证也称为银行承兑信用证。

7.3.2 Deferred Payment L/C 延期付款信用证

It is stipulated in a letter of credit by the issuing bank that the payment is to be made within ×× days after shipment or on receipt of documents. Under this kind of L/C, the exporter is not required to issue a draft, so the exporter cannot discount draft to get money in advance, but pay for the goods itself or borrow money from bank. In export businesses, the price of goods under this kind of L/C will be a little higher than the bank acceptance L/C in order to balance the difference between the interest rate and discount rate. For a transaction in large amount, it is better to combine this kind of L/C payment with the export loan of government.

延期付款信用证指开证行在信用证中规定，货物装船后若干天内付款，或开证行收到单据后若干天内付款的信用证。这种信用证不要求出口商开立汇票，所以出口商不能利用其贴现市场资金，只能自己垫付或向银行借款。在出口业务中，使用这种信用证的货价应比银行承兑信用证高些，以便拉平利息率与贴现率之间的差额。成交金额较大时，要与政府的出口信贷结合起来使用。

7.3.3 Usance L/C Payable at Sight 假远期信用证

It is also named as “buyer’s usance L/C”. In this kind of L/C, a usance draft is drawn by the beneficiary, and discounted by the paying bank, with all interests paid by the importer.

The kind of credit appears to be a usance L/C, but actually the exporter can receive the payment in full amount at sight. So, it is called usance L/C payable at sight.

假远期信用证也称“买方远期信用证”。信用证规定受益人开立远期汇票，由付款行负责贴现，并规定一切利息由进口人承担。这种信用证表面上看是远期信用证，但从上述条款规定来看，出口人可以即期收到十足的货款。因此，被称为“假远期信用证”。

7.4 Transferable L/C 可转让信用证

It can be divided into transferable L/C and non-transferable L/C according to the beneficiary's right of transferring L/C.

Transferable Letter of Credit is a credit under which the beneficiary (first beneficiary) may request the bank authorized to pay, incur a deferred payment undertaking, accept or negotiate (the transferring bank), or in the case of freely negotiable credit, the bank specifically authorized in the credit as a transferring bank, to make the credit available in whole or in part to one or more other beneficiary(ies) (second beneficiary(-ies)). In UCP 600, it's stipulated that "transferrable credit means a credit that specifically states it is transferable". A transferable credit may be made available in whole or in part to another beneficiary ("second beneficiary") at the request of the beneficiary ("first beneficiary").

According to UCP 600, a credit is not transferable unless the words "transferable" is specifically stated in the credit by the issuing bank. Transferable credit can only be transferred once, i.e. it can only be transferred by the first beneficiary to the second beneficiary who shall not have the right to transfer the credit to any third beneficiary.

根据受益人对信用证的权利可否转让,信用证分为可转让信用证和不可转让信用证。

可转让信用证是指信用证的受益人（第一受益人）可以要求授权付款、承担延期付款责任、承兑议付的银行（统称“转让银行”），或当信用证是自由议付时，可以要求信用证中特别授权的转让银行，将信用证全部或部分转让给一个或数个受益人（第二受益人）使用的信用证。UCP 600 规定：“可转让信用证系指特别注明‘可转让’字样的信用证。可转让信用证可应受益人（第一受益人）的要求转为全部或部分由另一受益人（第二受益人）兑用。”

根据 UCP 600 的规定，唯有开证行在信用证中明确注明“可转让”，信用证方可转让。可转让信用证只能转让一次，即只能由第一受益人转让给第二受益人，第二受益人不得要求将信用证转让给其后的第三受益人。

7.5 Revolving L/C 循环信用证

A credit is established for a certain sum and quantity of goods with a provision that when a shipment has been made and documents presented re-available in its original from, another shipment can be made so on until to the stipulated time or total amount.

Revolving L/C can be divided into L/C by time and L/C by amount. A revolving L/C by time means that the beneficiary can draw money by L/C repeatedly in a certain period. A revolving L/C by amount means that the full amount will be automatically re-available for negotiation and payment again after the L/C negotiation until the preset total amount is used up.

循环信用证是指信用证被全部或部分使用后，其金额又恢复到原金额，可再次使用，直到达到规定的次数或规定的总金额为止。

循环信用证又分为按时间循环的信用证和按金额循环的信用证。按时间循环的信用证是指受益人在一定的时间内可多次支取信用证规定的金额；按金额循环的信用证是指信用证金额议付后，仍恢复到原金额可再次使用，直到用完规定的总额为止。

7.6 Reciprocal L/C 对开信用证

A reciprocal L/C is that two parties open letters of credit in favor of each other. The features of reciprocal L/C: the drawer and beneficiary of one L/C are usually the drawee and payer of another one; the opening bank of one L/C is the advising bank of another one. The amount of the two credits is the same or almost the same. The two credits can be opened to each other at the same time or one by one. Reciprocal L/C is often used in barter trade, processing trade etc., The both parties are afraid that the counterpart will not fulfill the obligation of import or export after one party has exported or imported by the first credit, Then they can restrict each other in the way of being mutually involved and conditioned.

对开信用证是指两张信用证的开证申请人互以对方为受益人而开立的信用证。对开信用证的特点是第一张信用证的受益人（出口人）和开证申请人（进口人）就是第二张信用证的申请人和受益人，第一张信用证的通知行通常就是第二张信用证的开证行。两张信用证的金额相等或大体相等，两证可同时互开，也可先后开立。对开信用证多用于易货贸易或进料加工贸易方式，交易的双方都担心对方凭第一张信用证出口或进口后，另外一方不履行进口或出口的义务，于是采用这种互相联系、互为条件的开证办法，彼此得以约束。

7.7 Back to Back L/C 背对背信用证

Back to back letter of credit means that beneficiary requires the advising bank of the original credit or other bank to issue a new credit with similar contents on the basis of the original L/C. The beneficiary of back to back L/C can be a foreign or domestic player. A back to back letter of credit must be irrevocable.

背对背信用证又称转开信用证，是指受益人要求原证的通知行或其他银行以原证为基础，另开一张内容相似的新信用证。背对背信用证的受益人可以是国外的，也可以是国内的。背对背信用证的开证银行只能根据不可撤销信用证开立。

7.8 Standby L/C 备用信用证

It is also called Commercial Paper L/C or Guarantee L/C, which is a guaranty issued by the opening bank on behalf of the applicant declaring that the bank will undertake certain obligations. That is to say, the opening bank guarantees that when the applicant fails to fulfill its obligation that has to be done, the beneficiary can make a bill of exchange on the applicant according to the stipulations of the standby letter of credit or present to the opening bank the statements or evidence papers which can testify the applicant's failure to fulfill his obligations to effect the payment.

备用信用证又称商业票据信用证、担保信用证或保证信用证，指开证行根据开证申请人的请求对受益人开立的承诺承担某项义务，受益人只要凭备用信用证的规定向开证行开具汇票（或不开汇票），并提交开证申请人未履行义务的声明或证明文件，即可取得开证行的偿付。备用信用证属于银行信用，开证银行保证在开证申请人未履行其义务时，即由开证银行付款。因此，备用信用证对受益人来说是备用于开证申请人发生违约时取得赔款的一种方式。备用信用证下，银行承担的也是第一位的责任。

7.9 Confirmed L/C 保兑信用证

There are two kinds of credits, which are confirmed L/C and unconfirmed L/C.

A confirmed L/C is a credit issued by the issuing bank, and guaranteed by another bank to fulfill the payment for the consistent presentation of documents. The bank who adds its confirmation to the credit is called as Confirming Bank.

信用证按是否有另一家银行加保兑，可以分为保兑信用证和不保兑信用证。

保兑信用证是指开证行开出的信用证，由另一家银行保证对符合信用证条款规定的单据履行付款义务。对信用证加保兑的银行，叫作保兑行。

Lesson 2 Letter of Guarantee
银行保函

In international trade, due to the lack of mutual understanding and trust between both parties in a transaction, it is hindered to conclude deals and fulfill contracts smoothly. In order to solve these problems, the banks and other financial institutions with excellent credit offer the service of letter of guarantee, through which, the warrantor promises the L/G applicant will fulfill the liability or obligation under the concerning business contract or other economic contracts, further in favor of the transaction's fulfillment.

在国际贸易中，交易双方往往缺乏了解和信任，因而给达成交易和履行合同造成一定障碍。为了解决这些问题，就出现了由信誉卓著的银行以及其他金融机构办理的保函业务，担保人保证申请人履行双方签订的有关商务合同或其他经济合同项下的某种责任或义务，从而有利于交易的顺利进行。

1. Definition and Nature of L/G 银行保函的定义及性质

Letter of Guarantee is a guaranty in written form issued by bank, insurance company, guarantee company or individual upon request of the applicant, promising to fulfill the payment or compensation to some extent in a certain amount of money in case that the applicant fails to fulfill the obligation. Bank's L/G is a kind of guaranty issued by bank, undertaking the obligation of payment. Under a bank's L/G, the bank undertakes absolute payment obligation according to the regulation of L/G. So, most of bank's L/G are Demand L/G.

According to the payment conditions under the L/G, the L/G can be divided into the following two kinds:

保函（简称 L/G）又称保证书，是指银行、保险公司、担保公司或个人（保证人）应申请人的请求，向第三方（受益人）开立的一种书面信用担保凭证，保证在申请人未能按双方协议履行其责任或义务时，由担保人代其履行一定金额、一定期限范围内的某种支付责任或经济赔偿责任。银行保函是由银行开立的、承担付款责任的一种担保凭证。银行根据保函的规定承担绝对付款责任。所以，银行保函大多属于见索即付保函。

在保函项下，受益人在什么条件下才能取得保证人的偿付，按索偿条件分，通常可分为以下两种。

1.1 Demand L/G 见索即付保函

Demand L/G is also named as unconditional L/G, with bank's undertaking of the payment in the first place, which is a kind of independent warranty separated from the basic contract, with the rights and liabilities of beneficiary subject to the contents of L/G, not limited by the basic contract. The guarantor must fulfill payment so long as the beneficiary presents the documents complying with the requests of L/G. All letters of guarantee are irrevocable. Letter of guarantee is in form of writing, including telecommunication messages with encrypted EDI information.

见索即付保函又称无条件保函，银行承担的是第一性的责任，是一种与基础合同相脱离的独立性担保文件，受益人的权利与担保人的义务完全以保函所载内容为准，不受基础合同的约束。受益人只要提交了符合保函要求的单据，担保人就必须付款。所有保函均为不可撤销的文件。保函必须是书面的，“书面”包括有效的电信信息加密押的 EDI 信息。

1.2 Conditional L/G 有条件保函

A conditional L/G means guarantor makes payment to beneficiary conditionally, and guarantor will fulfill payment only under the condition of complying with the regulation of L/G. So, the guarantor of a conditional L/G is undertaking a subordinate payment obligation.

有条件保函指保证人向受益人付款是有条件的，只有在符合保函规定的条件下，保证人才予付款。可见，有条件保函的担保人承担的是第二性的、附属的付款责任。

2. Types of L/G 银行保函的种类

Letter of guarantee is widely used in the practical operation of businesses, applicable to the transactions of goods as well as other economic fields, such as the international construction contracts, bid and loan businesses. According to the usage, letter of guarantee can be divided into tender L/G, performance L/G, and repayment L/G.

银行保函在实际业务中的使用范围很广，它不仅适用于货物的买卖，而且广泛适用于其他国际经济领域。例如，在国际工程承包、招标与投标以及借贷业务中都有使用。银行保证书按其用途可分为投标保证书、履约保证书和还款保证书。

2.1 Tender Guarantee 投标保证书

A tender guarantee means bank, insurance company or other involving party (guarantor) makes promise to beneficiary (tenderee), sometimes according to the instruction of the authorized bank by the guarantee applicant, that guarantor shall fulfill payment with the stipulated sum in case that applicant (tender) fails to fulfill the obligation resulted from his tender.

A tender guarantee mainly guarantees that tender will not revoke or revise the tender without the agreement with tenderee, and will sign the contract paying the fulfillment deposit after winning the bid. Otherwise, the bank will be committed to the compensation for the loss of the tenderee.

投标保证书指银行、保险公司或其他当事人（保证人）向受益人（招标人）承诺，或按照担保申请人所授权的银行的指示向受益人（招标人）承诺，当申请人（投标人）不履行其投标所产生的义务时，保证人应在规定的金额限度内向受益人付款。

投标保证书主要担保投标人在开标前不撤销投标和片面修改投标条件，中标后要保证签约和交付履约金。否则，银行负责赔偿招标人的损失。

2.2 Performance Guarantee 履约保证书

A performance guarantee is a promise made by a guarantor, that a guarantor will make payment to beneficiary with the agreed sum in case that guarantee applicant (contractor) fails to fulfill the contract concluded by beneficiary (owner) and contractor.

Performance guarantee is widely used in the normal import and export businesses. Performance guarantees are divided into import performance guarantee and export performance guarantee.

履约保证书指保证人承诺，如果担保申请人（承包人）不履行他与受益人（业主）之间订立的合同，应由保证人在约定的金额限度内向受益人付款。

履约保证书的适用范围很广泛，在一般货物进出口交易中也有使用。履约保证书可分为进口履约保证书和出口履约保证书。

2.2.1 Import Performance Guarantee 进口履约保证书

It is a guarantee issued by guarantor (bank) upon request of importer to exporter (beneficiary). It is stipulated in the guarantee, that the bank is committed to making compensation for payment if the importer fails to make payment in a timely manner after exporter fulfills the delivery of goods as requested in the contract. The kind of guarantee is a convenient, prompt and assured guarantee for the exporter.

进口履约保证书指保证人（银行）应进口人的申请开给出口人（受益人）的保证书。保证书规定，如出口人按合同交货后，进口人未能按期付款，由银行负责偿还。这种履约保证书对出口人来说是一种简便、及时和确定的保障。

2.2.2 Export Performance Guarantee 出口履约保证书

It is a guarantee issued by guarantor (bank) upon request of exporter to importer (beneficiary). It is stipulated in the guarantee, that the bank is committed to making compensation for the loss of the importer if the exporter fails to make delivery of goods on time as requested in the contract. The importer is ensured by the kind of guarantee.

出口履约保证书指保证人（银行）应出口人的申请开给进口人（受益人）的保证书。保证书规定，如出口人按合同未能按期交货，银行负责赔偿进口人的损失。这种履约保证书对进口人是有保障的。

2.3 Repayment Guarantee 还款保证书

Repayment guarantee is a guarantee issued by bank, insurance company or other involving party upon the application of one party of a contract to the other party of a contract. It is stipulated in the repayment guarantee, that the bank is committed to making reimbursement in case that the applicant fails to fulfill the obligation agreed in the contract, not returning or repaying the deposit or paid amount to the beneficiary.

A repayment guarantee used in an international project contract is offered by a contractor to the project owner through a bank. As stipulated in the guarantee, the bank is committed to making reimbursement in case that the applicant fails to fulfill the obligation agreed in the contract, not returning or repaying the deposit or paid amount to the beneficiary.

Repayment guarantee is also applicable in the import and export business of goods, service trade, technology trade etc. For example, in a contract of whole set equipment and large vehicles with the payment by installment or deferred payment usually adopted, a performance guarantee is issued by the importer to the exporter after signing the contract, in which the importer is ensured by a bank to make payment as requested in the contract, and at the same time, a repayment guarantee is issued by the exporter to his counterpart, in which the bank promises to make reimbursement of the principal paid by the importer and the related interests if the exporter fails to make delivery on time.

In addition to the above mentioned guarantees, there are also other kinds of guarantees according to different functions and usages, such as technology imported guarantee, processing with imported materials guarantee, tender guarantee, offset trade guarantee, financial leasing guarantee, loaning guarantee, deferred payment guarantee under trade, etc.

还款保证书指银行、保险公司或其他当事人应合同一方当事人的申请向合同另一方当事人开立的保证书。保证书规定，如申请人不履行他与受益人订立的合同的义务，不将受益人预付、支付的款项退还或还款给受益人，银行则向受益人退还或支付款项。

还款保证书在国际承包业务中使用时，由承包人通过银行向业主提供。保证书规定，如申请人不履行他与受益人订立的合同的义务，不将受益人预付、支付的款项退还或还款给受益人，则由银行向受益人退还该款项。

还款保证书除在国际工程承包项目中使用外，也适用于货物进出口、劳务使用和技术贸易等业务。例如，在成套设备及大型交通工具的合同中，通常采用带有预付性质的分期或延期支付部分价款的方式。在这种交易中，进口人在签订合同后向出口人开立履约保证书，由银行保证进口人按合同规定按期支付价款，同时，出口人也向对方开立还款保证书。如出口人不能按期交货，银行保证及时偿还进口人已付款项的本金及所产生的利息。

除上述几种保函外，还可以根据其他功能和应用的不同，分为其他种类，如技术引进保函、来料加工保函、投标保函、补偿贸易保函、融资租赁保函、借款保函、贸易项下的延期付款保函等。

Lesson 3 Combination of Payment Modes
支付方式的选用

In order to meet the demand in our country's international trade development, we shall adopt all kinds of payment terms flexibly based on the research of the payment terms used widely in international market. In the practical operation of international trade, in order to conclude the deal, both parties may adopt two or more payment terms combined together if they fail to reach an agreement on a certain payment term. The frequently used combination of payment terms are listed as follows.

为了适应我国外贸发展的需要，国际市场各种惯用的支付方式必须要在认真研究的基础上灵活地加以运用。实践中，有时为了促成交易，在双方未能就某一种支付方式达成协议时，也可以采用两种或多种方式结合使用的方式，常见的有以下几种。

1. Combination of Letter of Credit and Collection 信用证与托收相结合

It means that the payment is made partially by L/C and the balance by collection. It is usually operated in the way as follows: two bills of exchange are issued under the credit, the payment by L/C is made with the clean draft and the payment by collection is made by sight or time D/P with the presentation of the full set of documents. For the sake of safety, the clause such as "the documents delivered upon the full payment" must be stated in the letter of credit.

这种方式是指部分货款用信用证支付，余款用托收方式结算。一般做法是，信用证规定出口人开立两张汇票，属于信用证部分的货款凭光票付款，而全套单据附在托收部分汇票项下，按即期或远期付款交单方式托收。但信用证上必须订明“在发票金额全部付清后才可交单”的条款，以确保安全。

2. Combination of Collection and Standby L/C or L/G 托收与备用信用证或银行保函相结合

Collection is a kind of commercial credit, putting great risk on the seller. However, collection is in favor of the buyer as it is low costly with simple procedures. To promote its products, the seller may adopt the collection combining with L/G, which is in favor of the buyer as well as avoiding risks. The specific operation is that the exporter may collect the payment from the bank with clean bill and L/G after receiving the standby L/C and L/G complying with the contract.

Before the seller makes delivery, the buyer issues a standby L/C or L/G in advance. For example, under collection, the bank is committed to fulfilling payment if the buyer fails to make payment. Through the settlement method, the expiry date of standby L/C or L/G shall be after the expiry date of collection so that the seller has sufficient time to claim for reimbursement against the bank after the collection is refused.

托收是一种商业信用，对卖方来说风险较大。但是，托收对买方而言费用较低且手续简便。卖方为了推销商品可以采用托收和银行保函相结合的方法，既给了买方优惠，又避免了风险。具体做法是，出口人在收到符合合同规定的备用信用证或银行保函后就可凭光票与声明书向银行收回货款。

卖方在交货前，买方先开立一份备用信用证或保函。如托收项下买方不能够履行付款义务，则由银行承担付款义务。使用这种结算方式，备用信用证或保函的有效期应当迟于托收付款期限的一定时间，以便托收被拒付后，卖方有足够的时间向银行追偿货款。

3. Combination of Remittance, Collection and L/C 汇付、托收、信用证三者相结合

For the transaction of whole set equipment, large mechanical products and vehicles, due to the large contract sum and long production cycle of the product, the payment is usually made by installment according to the project schedule and delivery schedule.

在成套设备、大型机械产品和交通工具的交易中，因为成交金额较大，产品生产周期较长，一般采取按工程进度和交货进度分若干期付清货款，即分期付款和延期付款的

方法，采用汇付、托收和信用证相结合的方式。

3.1 Pay by Installments 分期付款

With the payment by installments, the payment is settled upon the goods are delivered to the buyer. Without interests involved in the transaction, to some extent, the seller makes use of the capital of the buyer. The details are as follows.

It is agreed by both the seller and the buyer in the contract that the buyer may pay part of payment as deposit to seller through remittance before the production, and the seller shall offer the photocopy of export license and letter of guarantee issued by bank to the buyer before the deposit is paid. Except for the deposit, the balance payment may be paid by installments, with letter of credit at sight issued by the buyer, and the balance of payment is usually paid off on the delivery time of goods or the expiry time of seller's quality warranty. The ownership of the goods will be transferred when the balance of payment is paid off. With the payment by installments, the payment will be paid off or almost paid off on the delivery time. Therefore, the contract with payment by installments is a contract with payment at sight.

采用分期付款，卖方在交货时，买方的货款基本付清。这种交易不牵涉利息，在某种意义上，卖方甚至利用了买方的资金。其具体做法如下。

买卖双方在合同中规定，在产品投产前，买方可采用汇付方式，先交部分货款作为定金，卖方在买方付出定金前，应向买方提供出口许可证影印本和银行开具的保函。除订金外，其余货款可按不同阶段分期支付，买方开立不可撤销的信用证，即期付款，但最后一笔货款一般是在交货或卖方承担质量保证期满时付清。货物所有权则在付清最后一笔货款时转移。在分期付款的条件下，货款在交货时付清或基本付清。因此，按分期付款条件签订的合同是一种即期合同。

3.2 Deferred Payment 延期付款

With this payment term, most of payment will be paid in the future years or by installments within a long future period after the goods are delivered to the buyer. So, the transaction is a credit sale with the buyer utilizing the capital of the seller, so the interests shall be added to price of goods. The details are as follows.

For the transaction of the whole set equipment and in large sum, the deferred payment is adopted as the buyer hardly pays off once for all. After signing the contract, the buyer will make a small part of payment as deposit. It is also stipulated in some contracts that, part of payment will be paid according to project schedule or delivery schedule, but most of the payment will be paid by installments in the following years after the delivery of goods, namely by the usance L/C. The payment term means a commercial credit offered to the buyer by the seller, so the buyer shall undertake the interests of the deferred payment. The ownership will be transferred upon the delivery.

采用这种支付方式，在卖方交货时，买方大部分货款要在将来若干年或相当长的一段时间分期摊付，属于一种赊销性质的交易。买方实际上是占用了卖方的资金，在货价中要加上利息的成本。具体做法如下。

在成套设备和大宗交易的情况下，由于成交金额较大，买方一时难以付清全部货款，可采用延期付款的办法。买卖双方签订合同后，买方一般要预付一小部分货款作为定金。有的合同还规定，按工程进度和交货进度分期支付部分货款，但大部分货款是在交货后若干年内分期摊付，即采用远期信用证支付。这种支付方式等于是卖方给买方提供的商业信贷。因此，买方应承担延期付款的利息。在延期付款的条件下，货物所有权一般在交货时转移。

Appendix: A Letter of Credit in Chinese and English
附录：信用证中英对照翻译

E.g.

实例：

MSGACK DWS765I Auth OK, key B004121903FOE71E, BKCHCNBJ SHBK**** record

Basic Header	F 01 BKCHCNBJA720 1325 634817	
<银行密押>		
Application Header	O 700 1755 051116	SHBKKRSEA××× 7103 891281 051116 1655 N
开证行	<银行代码>	* SHINHAN BANK * SHINHAN 银行 *SEOUL *首尔
User Header	Service Code	103:
<银行代码>	Bank. Priority	113:
	Msg User Ref.	108: 0001598759
	Info. From CI	115:

Sequence of Total	27:	1/1
报文页次	27:	1/1
Form of Doc. Credit	40A:	IRREVOCABLE
信用证的形式	40A:	不可撤销
Doc. Credit Number	20:	M42V5511RS150
信用证号	20:	M42V5511RS150
Date of Issue	31C:	081115

开证日期	31C:	2008 年 11 月 15 日
Expiry	31D:	Date 090214 Place IN THE BENEFICIARY COUNTRY
有效期	31D:	2009 年 2 月 14 日 在受益人国家到期
Applicant	50:	GANIL MANPOWER CO., LTD 950-1 DOGOK-DONG KANGNAM-GU SEOUL KOREA
开证申请人	50:	GANIL MANPOWER CO., LTD 950-2 DOGOK-DONG KANGNAM-GU SEOUL KOREA
Beneficiary	*59:	FUJIAN ZHONGYI IMPORT AND EXPORT CO., LTD F.18 FuXiang Building NO.119 WuSi Fuzhou Fujian P.R. China
受益人	*59:	FUJIAN ZHONGYI IMPORT AND EXPORT CO., LTD F.18 FuXiang Building NO. 119 WuSi Fuzhou Fujian P.R.China
Amount	32B:	CURRENCY USD AMOUNT 11,772.00
总金额	32B:	11 772.00 美元
Available with/by	41D:	ANY BANK BY NEGOTIATION
指定的有关银行及信用证兑付的方式	41D:	任何银行议付
Drafts at...	42C:	AT SIGHT
汇票付款日期	42C:	见票即付
Drawee	42D:	SHINHAN BANK, SEOUL
汇票付款人	42D:	SHINHAN 银行，首尔
Partial Shipments	43P:	ALLOWED
分批装运	43P:	允许
Transshipments	43T:	ALLOWED
转船	43T:	允许
Loading in Charges	44A:	CHINESE PORT
装运港	44A:	中国港口
For Transport to ...	44B:	JAPANESE PORT
转运港	44B:	日本港口
Latest Date of Ship	44C:	090204
最迟装运日期	44C:	2009 年 2 月 4 日
Descript of Goods	45A:	
货物描述	45A:	

	GENERAL MERCHANDISE
	一般商品
03-3205	CUTE FLOWER POT (BOAT SHAPE)
03-3207	精美花瓶（船形）
	5 400 PCS USD 0.70/PC USD 3 780.00
	5 400 个 USD 0.70/个 USD 3 780.00
03-3206	CUTE FLOWER POT (SQUARE SHAPE)
03-3208	精美花瓶（方形）
	5 400 PCS USD 0.68/PC USD 3 672.00
	5 400 个 USD 0.68/个 USD 3 672.00
03-3204	CUTE FLOWER POT (BASKET SHAPE)
03-3204	精美花瓶（花篮形）
	5 400 PCS USD 0.80/PC USD 4 320.00
	5 400 个 USD 0.80/个 USD 4 320.00
	—— USD 11 772.00
	ORIGIN CHINA 中国原产地
	FOB CHINESE PORT 价格条件：FOB 中国港口
Documents Required	46A:
要求的单据	46A:

+SIGNED COMMERCIAL INVOICES IN 2 FOLD

+已签署的商业发票一式两份

+FULL SET AND 1 COPY OF CLEAN ON BOARD OCEAN BILLS OF LADING MADE OUT TO THE ORDER OF SHIPPER AND BLANK ENDORSED MARKED FREIGHT COLLECT AND NOTIFY APPLICANT

+全套正本（另加一份副本）清洁已装船的海运提单，做成托运人抬头，空白背书，并注明“运费到付”，通知开证申请人

+PACKING LIST IN 2 FOLD

+装箱单一式两份

+G.S.P CHINA CERTIFICATE OF ORIGIN FORM-A 1 COPY ISSUED TO CONSIGNEE: DAISO INDUSTRIES CO., LTD. 1-4-14 SAIJYO YOSHIYUKIHIGASHI HIGASHIHIROSHIMA- CITY 739-8501 JAPAN

+普惠制原产地证书格式 A 一份做成由“DAISO INDUSTRIES CO., LTD. 1-4-14 SAIJYO YOSHIYUKIHIGASHI HIGASHIHIROSHIMA-CITY 739-8501 JAPAN”为抬头

+ONE COPY OF RECEIPT FOR SENDING ORIGINAL G.S.P AND SHIPPING DOCUMENTS COPY TO THE GANIL MANPOWER SHANGHAI OFFICE DIRECTLY

+一份直寄给 GANIL MANPOWER SHANGHAI 的正本普惠制原产地证书和副本装运单据的收据副本

+A COPY OF THE FINAL SHIPPING NOTICE (FSN) ISSUED BY GANIL MANPOWER

+一份由 GANIL MANPOWER 签发的最后装运通知的副本
Additional Cond. 47A:
特别条款 47A:
PLEASE SEND ORIGINAL G.S.P FORM-A AND COPY OF SHIPPING DOCUMENTS TO THE GANIL MANPOWER SHANGHAI OFFICE (ROOM B, GF, BLDG, 8, FOURTUNE GARDEN NO. 1369 SUNFANG ROAD, PUDONG, SHANGHAI, CHINA) BY COURIER SERVICE WITHIN 3 DAYS AFTER SAILING DIRECTLY
在开船后三天内，请将一份正本普惠制原产地证书格式 A 和一份副本的装运单据以快件方式直接寄给 GANIL MANPOWER SHANGHA 驻上海办事处(中国上海浦东尚芳路1369号温泉花园 8 号楼 B 室)。
THE NUMBER OF CARTONS PER ITEM PER CONTAINER NUMBER SHALL BE SHOWN ON THE BILL OF LADING.
每个货号的箱数和集装箱号必须在提单上显示。
Details of Charges 71B: ALL BANKING CHARGES OTHER THAN ISSUEING CHARGES ARE FOR ACCOUNT OF BENEFICIARY
费用情况 71B: 所有开证行以外的费用由受益人承担
PRESENTATION PERIOD 48: DOCUMENTS TO BE PERSENTED WITHIN 21 DAYS AFTER SHIPMENT DATE BUT PRIOR TO CREDIT EXPIRY
交单期限 48: 所有的单据必须在装运后的 21 天内提交银行，同时必须在信用证的效期内
Confirmation *49: WITHOUT
保兑 *49: 不需要
Instructions 78:
指示 78:
T/T REIMBURSEMENT NOT ALLOWED
不允许 T/T 电汇索偿
THE DISCREPANCY FEE OF USD 70.00 (OR EQUIVALENT) SHOULD BE DEDUCTED FROM YOUR REIBMURSEMENT CLAIM TO THE REIBMURSING BANK OR WILL BE DEDUCTED FROM PROCEEDS BY US IF DOCUMENTS ARE PRESENTED WITH DISCREPANCY (IES).
如交单时含不符点，每一笔不符点的费用 70 美元或等值 70 美元将在你们从偿付行索偿时扣除，或者是向我们提交单据（含不符点）时，在索偿时从金额中扣除（不符点费用）。
UPON RECEIPT OF ALL DOCS AND DRAFTS IN CONFORMITY WITH TERMS AND CONDITIONS OF THIS CREDIT WE SHALL REMIT THE PROCEEDS TO THE BANK DESIGNATED BY NEGOTIATING BANK.
一俟收到与本信用证规定相符的单据和汇票，我们将立即把信用证的款项汇入议付行指定的银行（账户）。
ALL DOCUMENTS MUST BE DESPATCHED BY COURIER IN ONE LOT TO SHINHAN

BANK, TRADE SERVICE OFFICE, 2ND FL., 120, 2-KATAEPYUNG-RO, SHUNG-KU, SEOUL 100-724, KOREA.
所有的单据必须一次性以快件形式寄交 SHINHAN BANK，地址是 TRADE SERVICE OFFICE, 2ND FL., 120, 2-KATAEPYUNG-RO, SHUNG-KU, SEOUL 100-724, KOREA。
REIBMURSEMENT IS SUBJECT TO ICC URR525.
我们将根据国际商会 URR525 惯例进行付款。

Case Study 本章案例

Case 1: A Chinese exporter reached a contract with a UK buyer about some commodities in a large quantity in terms of CIF and irrevocable sight L/C payment, stipulating the shipment shall be effected in November in the contract, but no specific L/C issuing date mentioned therein. Later, the UK buyer delayed the issuance of L/C because of the decrease of market price of the commodity. To avoid the delay of the shipment, the exporter had urged the buyer to issue L/C for many times since the middle of OCT., and the buyer finally issued the L/C up to 8th Nov. However, it is too late for the exporter to arrange for the shipment as scheduled, who therefore required the buyer to extend the shipment time and the L/C negotiation expiry date for one more month. The UK buyer refused the requirement, and cancelled the contract unilaterally excusing that the exporter failed to effect shipment on time. The exporter did nothing but accepted it. Please make an analysis and comment about it: Had the exporter settled the matter in a proper way? And what shall we learn from it?

【案例 1】我国某外贸公司与英商就某商品按 CIF、即期信用证付款条件签署一项数量较大的出口合同。合同规定 11 月装运，但未规定具体开证日期，后因该商品市场价格趋降，外商便拖延开证。我方为防止延误装运期，从 10 月中旬起多次电催开证，终于使该商在 11 月 8 日开来了信用证。但由于该商品开证太晚，我方安排装运发生困难，遂要求对方对信用证的装运期和议付有效期进行修改，分别推迟一个月。但英商拒不同意，并以我方未能按期装运为由单方面解除合同，我方也就此作罢。试分析我方如此处理是否适当，应从中吸取哪些教训？

Case Analysis: The exporter did not settle it properly, the lessons we shall learn are as follows:

1) The issuance time of L/C shall be stipulated in the contract.

2) In accordance with the international usual practice, the buyer shall issue the L/C before the shipment month even though the issuance date is not mentioned in the contract; the exporter shall keep the claim right against the buyer for the buyer's failure of issuing the L/C on time.

3) As to the buyer cancelling the contract unilaterally without the permit of exporter, the exporter shall not let it be.

【案例分析】我方处理不恰当。应吸取的教训有：（1）在合同中未规定信用证开到日期不妥;（2）按惯例，即使合同未规定开证期限，买方也应于装运月前开到信用证，买方未及时开到信用证，我方应保留索赔权;（3）对于外商以我方未能按时装运为由，单方面宣布解除合同，我方不能就此作罢。

Case 2: An exporter makes an offer to a Japanese client in terms of payment by D/P at sight, and the client's reply is that the offer is acceptable in terms of the payment by D/P in sight of 90 days and collection by Bank A nominated by the client. Please make an analysis of the reason why the Japanese client brings about the requirement.

【案例 2】我国某公司向日本某商以付款交单见票即付方式推销某商品，对方答复：如我方接受付款交单见票后 90 天付款，并通过其指定的 A 银行代收则可接受。请分析日方提出此项要求的出发点。

Case Analysis: Obviously, the Japanese client tends to put off the payment time through changing the D/P at sight into D/P in sight of 90 days, which is in favor of his capital running. The nomination of collecting bank is for buyer's borrowing shipment documents from the bank which is also beneficial to the buyer. In a usance D/P business, the collecting bank usually will not allow the payer to borrow the documents. So, the Japanese client is supposed to have financial relationship with bank A, and then he is permitted to borrow the documents from the bank in order to make full use of the exporter's capital.

【案例分析】日商提出将付款交单即期改为 90 天远期，很显然旨在推迟付款，以利其资金周转。而日商指定 A 银行作为该批托收业务的代收行，则是为了便于向该银行借单，以便早日获取经济利益。在一般的远期付款交单托收业务中，代收行在未经授权的情况下通常是不会轻易同意付款人的借单的。该日商之所以提出通过 A 银行代收货款的，很可能是该商与 A 银行有既定融资关系，从中可取得提前借单的便利，以达到进一步利用我方资金的目的。

Questions 思考题

1. What are the main contents included in a letter of credit?
信用证中的主要内容有哪些？

2. What is L/C at sight? And what is usance L/C?
什么是即期信用证？什么是远期信用证？

3. What is back to back letter of credit? What are the differences between a back to back L/C and a transferrable L/C?
什么是背对背信用证？它与可转让信用证有什么区别？

4. What is a standby letter of credit? What are the differences between a standby credit and a documentary credit?
什么是备用信用证？备用信用证与跟单信用证的区别是什么？

5. What is the payment by L/C combined with D/P? How to face a payment term of 50% L/C and 50% by D/P? And in the payment term how to make the documents and draft?

什么是信用证与付款交单方式相结合？50%信用证、50%付款交单应当怎么办理？单据、汇票应怎么开？

6. What is a payment combination of D/P, standby L/C and bank guaranty letter?

什么是付款交单与备用信用证、银行保函相结合？

7. What is Usance Letter of Credit Payable at sight? What is the difference of it from a usance L/C?

什么是假远期信用证？假远期信用证与远期信用证的区别是什么？

8. How many kinds of bank guaranty letters are there? And what are their definitions and usages?

银行保函有哪几种？它们的含义和作用是什么？

Chapter 14

Commodity Inspection

商 品 检 验

1. General Introduction 概述

1.1 Definition 定义

In the international trade, most of sellers and buyers are far away from each other. They cannot make delivery face to face, which is quite different from the domestic trade, so the damage due to the long distance transportation is hard to avoid. In order to verify the reasons for the damages, and clarify the respective responsibilities of the parties involved, a usual practice has come into being, that is to say, the qualified third party who has no conflict of interest with the concerning parties is authorized to inspect the quality, quantity, weight, packing of goods etc., and issues the relevant certificate as the evidence for the delivery of goods, and the settlement of payment and claims. Commodity inspection has become an indispensable part in international trade, which is the extension of the quality clause of contract and the warranty of it as well.

国际贸易的买卖双方大都远隔重洋，与国内贸易不同的是，他们不能当面交接货物，商品在长途运输途中，发生残损在所难免。为了便于查明事故的起因、分清各方当事人的责任，在长期的贸易实践中形成了一种习惯做法，即由一个有资格的、与有关当事人无任何利害关系的第三者对商品的质量、数量、重量、包装等进行检验并出具证书，作为交接货物、结算货款、处理索赔、理赔的依据。商品检验已成为国际贸易中不可缺少的环节，它是合同中品质条款的延续，是品质条款的保证。

1.2 Buyer's Inspection Right 买方对货物的检验权

According to "Sale of Goods Act, 1893" (revised in 1979), the buyer who has not made inspection on the goods cannot be assumed to accept the goods, so he is not deprived of the right of refusing the goods until he is granted reasonable opportunity to inspect.

According to "United Nations Convention on Contracts for the International Sale of Goods", the buyers shall implement the inspection or have others to do it in the shortest practical time. The inspection can be put off to the time when the goods arrive at the destination in case of the involvement of the transportation.

There is a common principle in the above-mentioned law and convention: the buyer shall be granted the inspection right before accepting the goods unless there is another agreement between the buyers and the sellers.

根据英国《1893 年货物买卖法》（1979 年修订本）的规定，凡是事先未经检验的货物，都不能认为是买方已经接受了货物，其没有丧失拒收货物的权利，直至有合理的机会检验货物为止。

根据《联合国国际货物销售合同公约》的规定，买方必须在按实际情况可行的最短时间内检验货物或由他人检验货物。如果合同涉及运输，检验可推迟到货物到达目的地后进行。

上述有关法律和公约都体现了一个共同的原则：除非买卖双方另有约定，否则买方在接受货物之前应享有对货物进行检验的权利。

2. Import and Export Inspection in China 我国对进出口商品实施检验的规定

2.1 Law of the People's Republic of China on Import and Export Commodity Inspection《中华人民共和国进出口商品检验法》

The law stipulates the work of the inspection authorities of China and the range of the legal inspection. The commodity inspection is the inspection and supervision on the production, sales of the exported commodities and the imported commodities, which is performed by the government according to the related regulations and rules.

该法规定了我国商检机构的任务和法定检验的实施范围。商品检验体现为国家对进出口商品的生产、销售和进口商品按规定实施检验和监管。

2.2 Inspection Range of the Inspection Organization in China 我国商检机构实施法定检验的范围

The governmental inspection authorities are committed to implementing the compulsory inspection on the important imported and exported commodities related to the national economy and the people's livelihood in accordance with the concerning laws and regulations. The commodities, which are not inspected or failed to pass the inspection, are not released by the customs.

国家检验机构根据有关的法律、法规，对关系国计民生的重要进出口商品实施强制性检验。未经检验或检验不合格的商品，海关不予放行。

3. Inspection Clauses 检验条款的主要内容

The inspection clauses cover these as follows: inspection time and place; inspection authority; inspection certificate; inspection methods, contents and standards; re-inspection.

检验条款主要包括：检验时间、地点；检验机构；检验证书；检验方法、内容、依据；商品复验。

3.1 Inspection Time and Place 检验的时间和地点

The inspection time and the inspection place refer to when and where the inspection is implemented to the goods. The so-called inspection right means that the buyer or the seller has the right to exercise inspection on the traded goods, with the inspection result as the evidence for the delivery and the acceptance of the goods. The confirmation of the inspection time and place means confirming which party exerts the inspection right, that is to say, confirming which party's inspection certificate is taken as the final inspection result.

There are the following four ways to regulate the inspection time and place.

检验的时间和地点是指在何时、何地行使对货物的检验权。所谓检验权，是指买方或卖方有权对所交易的货物进行检验，其检验结果即作为交付与接受货物的依据。确定检验的时间和地点，实际上就是确定买卖双方中的哪一方行使对货物的检验权，也就是确定检验结果以哪一方提供的检验证书为准。

关于检验的时间和地点，有以下四种规定。

3.1.1 Inspection in Export Country 在出口国检验

There are two ways including the inspection at manufacturing place (factory) and the inspection at the loading port.

For the inspection at the loading port, it is also called as "Shipping Quality, Shipping Weight", which means the inspection authority specified in the sales contracts makes the inspection and appraisal on the cargo's quality, weight (quantity) and the like, and the inspection certificate issued by the authority is taken as the final evidence. The seller is not responsible for the changes of the cargo after the delivery. Therefore, the clause is a great disadvantage to the buyer as it denies the re-inspection right of the buyer.

这种方法又分为在产地（工厂）检验和在装运港检验两种。

在装运港检验，也称“离岸品质，离岸重量”，是指货物在装运港或装运地交货前，由买卖合同中规定的检验机构对货物的品质、重量（数量）等项内容进行检验鉴定，并以该机构出具的检验证书作为最后依据。卖方对交货后货物所发生的变化不承担责任。因此，这种规定和办法从根本上否定了买方的复验权，对买方极为不利。

3.1.2 Inspection in Import Country 在进口国检验

It is also divided into the inspection at the destination port and the inspection in the buyer's business location or the final user's location.

The inspection at the destination port or discharging port is also called “Landed quality, Landed weight”, which means that the cargo is inspected by the inspection authority specified in the contract within the specified time on the spot after the cargo arrives in the destination port or place, and the inspection certificate issued by the organization is taken as the final evidence of the cargo delivered by the seller. In the way, the buyer has right to claim for the compensation with the inspection result made at the destination port or place in case that the quality, weight (quantity) are not in conformity with the involving requirement.

The clause is disadvantageous to the seller. Under the trade term of CIF (CIP, CFR, CRT), the seller is responsible for carrying the goods to the destination, but according to “International Rules for the Interpretation of Trade Terms of 2020”, the obligation of the seller has been completed after the goods are loaded on the ship (delivered to the carrier) in the export country, the risk has been transferred to the buyer when the goods are on the board. The regulation of the inspection time and place means that the conditions of the goods are subject to the final inspection result in the destination, actually transferring the risks of the cargo losses occurred during the transportation to the seller. During the transportation, the goods have been out of supervision of the seller, but under the control of the carrier, so it is quite unfair to the seller with the inspection clause against the regulation of the seller’s obligation in the above-mentioned trade terms.

这种方法又分为在目的港/地检验和在买方营业处所或最终用户所在地检验。

在目的港/地卸货后检验，也称“到岸品质，到岸重量”，是指货物运达目的港或目的地时，由合同规定的检验机构在规定的时间内，就地对商品进行检验，并以该机构出具的检验证书作为卖方所交货物品质、重量（数量）的最后依据。采用这种方法时，买方有权根据货物运抵目的港或目的地时的检验结果，就属于卖方责任的品质、重量（数量）不符合向卖方索赔。

这种规定方法对卖方不利。因为在使用 CIF（CIP、CFR、CPT）术语的情况下，虽然卖方要负责把货运到目的地，但按照《国际贸易术语解释通则 2020》的解释，卖方的交货义务实际上是在出口国装运港装上船（或交承运人）时即完成，风险在装运港装上船时转移至买方。这种检验时间、地点的规定方法以最后到目的港的检验为准，实际上要把运输途中产生的货损、货差的风险转由卖方承担。在运输途中，货物已经脱离了卖方的监管，并在承运人的监控之下，这对卖方极不公平，违反了上述贸易术语有关卖方义务的规定。

3.1.3 Inspection in Export Country and Re-inspection in Import Country 出口国检验，进口国复验

The inspection certificate issued by the export county’s inspection authority is taken as one of the bank negotiating documents for payment, but not the final inspection proof. After the arrival of the cargo, the inspection certificate issued by the import country’s inspection authority is taken as the final inspection result to confirm if the quantity and the quality of the goods are right and the proof for the buyer's claims.

It is fair and reasonable for the buyer and the seller to regulate the inspection time and inspection place in this way, so it is the way used mostly in international trade, complying with the international usual practice.

以出口国检验机构出具的检验证书作为卖方向银行议付货款的单据之一，不作为最后的依据。货到目的港后，以进口国检验机构出具的检验证书作为卖方交货品质数量合格与否的最后依据，也是买方索赔的依据。

这种检验时间、地点的规定方法对买卖双方都公平合理，因而它是国际贸易中目前最常用的一种规定方法，符合国际惯例。

3.1.4 Weight Inspection in Export Country and Quality Inspection in Import Country 出口国检验重量，进口国检验品质

It is also called as "Shipping Weight, Landed Quality", which means that for the inspection of goods in large amount, in order to conciliate the conflict of the buyer and the seller on the inspection, the inspection on the weight and the quality are respectively carried out. That is to say, the inspection certificate issued by the inspection authority at the loading port or place is taken as the final proof for the weight of the delivered goods, and the quality inspection certificate issued by the inspection authority at the destination port is taken as the final proof of the commodity quality.

出口国检验重量，进口国检验品质也称“离岸重量，到岸品质”，是指在大宗商品交易的检验中，为了调和买卖双方在商品检验问题上存在的矛盾，常分别进行商品的重量和品质检验，即以装运港或装运地验货后检验机构出具的重量检验证书作为卖方所交货物重量的最后依据，以目的港或目的地检验机构出具的品质检验证书作为商品品质的最后依据。

3.2 Inspection Authority 检验机构

The inspection organizations are divided into the following three types, which are governmental inspection authority, government related inspection authority, and non-governmental inspection authority.

According to the regulation of "Law of the People's Republic of China on Import and Export Commodity Inspection" ("Law of Inspection" for short), General Administration of Customs is in charge of the inspection of the imported and exported commodities throughout the whole country, and the local customs are in charge of the local inspection of the imported and exported commodities.

检验机构的类型大体可归纳为官方检验机构、半官方检验机构和非官方检验机构。

根据《中华人民共和国进出口商品检验法》（简称《商检法》）的规定，海关总署主管全国进出口商品检验工作，各地海关下属的出入境检验检疫机构管理其所辖地区内的进出口商品检验工作。

3.3 Inspection Certificate 检验证书

An inspection certificate is a kind of testifying document in written form issued and signed by the inspection authority after the inspection and appraisal of the imported and exported commodities.

Functions:

1) to certify if the quality, quantity, packing and the clean situation of the goods delivered by the seller are complying with the requirements stipulated in the contract;

2) for customs to release the goods;

3) for the sellers to settle the payment;

4) as the evidence of making claims and the settlement.

检验证书是检验机构对进出口商品进行检验、鉴定后签发的书面证明文件。

作用：

（1）是证明卖方所交货物的品质、数量、包装以及卫生条件等方面是否符合合同规定的依据；

（2）是海关验关放行的依据；

（3）是卖方办理货款结算的依据；

（4）是办理索赔和理赔的依据。

Case Study 本章案例

Case 1: An import & export company in our country is in export of 1,000 cartons of foodstuff with term of "CIF Rotterdam", and arranges for insurance with PICC covering all risks. After the arrival of the goods, the importer finds the following problems after the re-inspection: (1) there are attaint in one batch (100 cartons) after sampling 20 cartons from 10 batches (1,000 cartons); (2) the shortage of 2 cartons with receiving 998 cartons actually; (3) the shortage of 60 KGS totally for 15 cartons with good appearance outside. According to the above situation, who shall be claimed against by the importer?

【案例 1】我国某进出口公司以“CIF 鹿特丹”条件出口食品 1 000 箱，并向中国人民保险公司投保一切险。货到目的港后，经进口商复验发现下列情况：（1）该批货物共 10 个批号，抽查 20 箱，发现其中 1 个批号，即 100 箱内出现沾污现象；（2）收货人实收 998 箱，短少 2 箱；（3）有 15 箱货物外表良好，但箱内货物共短少 60 千克。根据以上情况，进口商应当分别向谁索赔？

Case Analysis: (1) It belongs to General Additional Insurance Coverage, included in All Risks, which can be claimed against the insurance company; (2) it belongs to Risk of Shortage, one type of General Additional Insurance Coverage, which can be claimed against the insurance company; (3) it is supposed that the exporter didn't load the cargo in full before the delivery with good appearance outside, so the importer shall make claim against the exporter.

【案例分析】（1）属于一般附加险，包含在一切险范围内，应向保险公司索赔；（2）属于短量险，应向保险公司索赔；（3）由于外表良好，应为出口商所装食品量不足，是交货以前发生的，应向出口商索赔。

Case 2: In April 2003, one foreign trade company of China signed a tea export contract with a Canadian importer, requiring a proper packing, with trade term of "CIF Ottawa", covering all risks by PICC. The manufacturer lowered down the humidity of tea to the scale specified in the contract at the last procedure, and packed the tea in the containers made of hard paper then in cartons with double layers. The goods were shipped in container and arrived in Ottawa on May 2003. But, the result of the inspection at destination port indicates: all tea has gone off and moldy, and the total loss reached one hundred thousand dollars. But, the temperature and humidity in the manufacturing place and the import country are modest, the transportation is normal and smooth. Who shall take the responsibility and make compensation for the loss? Why?

【案例 2】2003 年 4 月，我国某外贸公司与加拿大进口商签订一份茶叶出口合同，并要求采用合适的包装运输，成交术语为"CIF 渥太华"，向中国人民保险公司投保一切险。生产厂家在最后一道工序将茶叶的湿度降低到了合同规定值，并用硬纸筒盒作为容器装入双层纸箱，在装入集装箱后，货物于 2003 年 5 月到渥太华。检验结果表明：全部茶叶变质、湿霉，总共损失价值达 10 万美元。但是，当时货物出口地温度与湿度适中，进口地温度与湿度也适中，运输途中并无异常发生，完全为正常运输。试问以上货物的损失该由谁来赔偿，为什么？

Case Analysis: Although the goods shall be covered in All Risks, the main reason is not from the carrier as the transportation is normal. On the other hand, the package for the tea cannot meet the requirement of the anti-humidity for the common transportation, so the problem is due to the package which occurred before the transportation, and the manufacturer shall take the responsibility and make compensation for the loss.

【案例分析】尽管属于一切险赔偿范围，但是应当找到主要责任原因。一方面，由于运输过程正常，因此船方无责任；另一方面，由于茶叶包装并不能满足其一般运输防潮要求，因此货物问题应当是由于包装不能满足基本运输要求所引起的，这是在运输交货前发生的，所以责任应当是在生产厂家，货物损失应当由出口厂家赔偿。

Questions 思考题

1. What is legal inspection? Which commodities belong to the range of the legal inspection?

   什么是法定检验？哪些商品为法定检验？

2. How is it stipulated about the time and the place in the international trade?
在国际贸易中关于时间和地点是怎样规定的？
3. What are included in the import and export commodity inspection items?
进出口商品检验条款包括哪些内容？
4. What kinds of import and export commodities need to be inspected?
我国进出口商品实施检验的范围是什么？

Chapter 15

Force Majeure and Arbitration in International Trade
不可抗力和国际贸易仲裁

Lesson 1 Force Majeure 不可抗力

1. Definition of Force Majeure 不可抗力的含义

Force Majeure, also called Act of God, refers to an event that can neither be anticipated nor be preventable, avoidable and controllable after the conclusion of the contract, not resulted from the fault or neglect of the parties involved, leading to the failure or the delay of the fulfillment of contract; the party who fails to fulfill or delays fulfilling the contract due to such an event can be free from the liabilities, or is to be given an option of terminating the contract or postponing the performance of the contract.

Force Majeure clause is an escape clause in a contract, a legal principle as well. In international trade, different laws and rules have their own regulations and rules about it. In United Nations Convention on Contracts for the International Sales of Goods of 1980, the exemption is regulated as follows: "A party is not liable for a failure to perform any of its obligation if it proves that the failure was due to an impediment beyond its control and that it could not reasonably be expected to have taken the impediment into account at the time of the conclusion of the contract or have avoided or have overcome it or the consequence of it." The Convention has pointed out that the party who fails to perform the contract due to the occurrence of an impediment beyond his control, which cannot be expected, avoided or overcome, can be free from the liability.

The definitions of a Force Majeure event in different laws and rules are not explanatorily unified, nor its descriptions, however the basic principles are the same generally, which include the following points:

1) The occurrence of a Force Majeure event is after the conclusion of the contract.

2) The event is not resulting from the fault or neglect of the parties involved.

3) The event is beyond of the control of the parties involved, such as the market risk, fluctuation of commodity prices, change of foreign exchange rates, etc.

不可抗力又称人力不可抗拒，指在买卖合同签订后，不是由于合同当事人的过失或疏忽，而是由于发生了合同当事人无法预见、无法预防、无法避免和无法控制的事件，以致不能履行合同或不能如期履行合同，发生意外事件的一方可以免除履行合同的责任或推迟履行合同。

不可抗力是合同中的一项免责条款，也是一项法律原则。对此，在国际贸易中不同的法律、法规等各有自己的规定。1980 年《联合国国际货物销售合同公约》（简称《公约》）在其免责一节中做了如下规定："如果他（指当事人）能证明此种不履行义务是由于某种非他所能控制的障碍，而且对于这种障碍没有理由预期他在订立合同时能考虑到或能避免或能克服它或它的后果。"该《公约》指明了一方当事人不能履行义务，是由于发生了他不能控制的障碍，而且这种障碍在订约时是无法预见、避免或克服的，可予以免责。

国际贸易中不同法律、法规对不可抗力的确切含义在解释上并不统一，叫法也不一致，但其精神、原则大体相同，主要包括以下几点：

（1）意外事故必须发生在合同签订以后；

（2）不是因为合同当事人双方自身的过失或疏忽而导致的；

（3）意外事故是当事人双方所不能控制的、无能为力的。市场风险、商品价格波动、汇率变化等均不能视为不可抗力事件。

2. Significance of Force Majeure Clause 约定不可抗力的意义

With a view to avoiding the unnecessary disputes due to a Force Majeure event, and preventing the arbitrary explanation of the Force Majeure event, unreasonable requirement proposed, or unreasonable refusal of the reasonable requirement proposed by the other party, it is very necessary to make a Force Majeure clause in a sales contract, specifying the nature, scope, principle, and settlement of the Force Majeure clearly so as to execute the contract.

为避免因发生不可抗力事件而引起的不必要纠纷，防止合同当事人对发生不可抗力事件的性质、范围做任意的解释，或提出不合理的要求，或无理拒绝对方的合理要求，有必要在买卖合同中订立不可抗力条款，明确规定不可抗力事件的性质、范围、处理原则和处理办法，以利于合同的履行。

3. Stipulation of Force Majeure Clause 不可抗力条款的规定

3.1 Scope of Force Majeure Events 不可抗力事件的范围

- Natural disasters such as flood, fire, ice damage, storm, heavy snow, earthquake, etc.
- Social disasters such as war, strike, the governmental ban, etc.

- 由自然力量引起的，如水灾、火灾、冰灾、暴风雨、大雪、地震等。
- 由社会力量引起的，如战争、罢工、政府禁令等。

3.2 Synthesized Stipulation 综合式规定

Force Majeure: If the shipment of the contracted goods is prevented or delayed in whole or in part by reason of war, earthquake, flood, fire, storm, heavy snow or other causes of Force Majeure, the Seller shall not be liable for non-shipment or late shipment of the goods or non-performance of this contract. However, the Seller shall notify the Buyer by cable or telex and furnish the latter within 15 days by registered airmail with a certificate issued by the China Council for the Promotion of International Trade attesting such event or events.

In the above mentioned clause, besides the various force majeure events recognized in common by both parties, the words "other causes of Force Majeure" are added too. It is helpful to identify the unlisted force majeure events by the both parties. This way of stipulation is specific and flexible, widely adopted in Chinese international trade practice.

人力不可抗拒：如由于战争、地震、水灾、火灾、暴风雨、雪灾或其他不可抗力，卖方不能全部或部分装运或延迟装运合同货物，卖方对于这种不能装运或延迟装运或不能履行合同的情形均不负责任。但卖方须用电传或电报通知买方并必须在 15 天内以航空挂号信件向买方提交由中国国际贸易促进会出具的证明此类事故的证明书。

上述规定方法既列明了双方当事人已经取得共识的各种不可抗力事故，又加列上"其他不可抗力"这一句，这就使得将来如果发生合同未列明的意外事故，双方当事人可据以共同确定是否作为不可抗力事故。因此，这种规定方法既明确具体，又有一定的灵活性，比较科学实用。我国的业务实践中多采用这一种。

3.3 Settlement of Force Majeure Events 不可抗力事件的处理

There are two kinds of legal consequences arising from a force majeure event: termination of the contract; postponement of the contract fulfillment.

The adoption of the settlement ways is dependent on the effect of the force majeure event.

不可抗力引起的法律后果有两种：解除合同；延期履行合同。

至于什么情况下可以解除合同，什么情况下只能延期履行合同，要看不可抗力事故对履行合同的影响程度。

3.4 Notification and Proof of Force Majeure Events 不可抗力事件的通知和证明

Example: one party shall notify the other party by cable or telex and furnish the details and the effect of the event or events within 15 days by registered airmail with the documents attesting such an event or events.

例如：一方遭受不可抗力事故后，应以电报通知对方，并应在 15 天内以航空挂号信提供事故的详情及影响合同履行程度的证明文件。

4. Notes to Quoting Force Majeure Clause 援引不可抗力条款应注意的事项

The party who suffers from force majeure event shall notify the other party immediately.

The party who receives the notification and supporting document about the force majeure event from the other party shall reply to the other party promptly as required.

After the confirmation of a force majeure event, the settlement of the event shall be made according to the requirements of the contract.

任何一方发生不可抗力事故后，应按规定立即通知对方。

一方接到另一方关于不可抗力事故的通知和证明文件后，应按规定及时答复对方。

不可抗力事故成立后，应按合同规定处理问题。

Lesson 2 Arbitration 国际贸易仲裁

1. Definition and Characteristics 仲裁的含义和特点

Arbitration is an important way to settle the disputes incurred in international trade. The Arbitration means that the two parties, before or after the disputes arise, reach a written agreement that they will submit the disputes which cannot be settled through amicable negotiations to a third party for arbitration. Both parties shall settle the disputes complying with the result of arbitration as the arbitration result has legally binding force.

In international trade practice, for the disputes between exporters and importers, both parties usually settle them through amicable negotiation. If both parties fail to reach an agreement through negotiation, they may resort to other ways like Conciliation, Litigation, etc., depending on the different situations.

仲裁是解决对外贸易争议的一种重要方式。仲裁又称公断，是指买卖双方在争议发生之前或发生之后签订书面协议，自愿将争议提交双方所同意的第三者予以裁决以解决争议的一种方式。由于仲裁是依照法律所允许的仲裁程序裁定争端，因而仲裁裁决具有法律约束力，当事人双方必须遵照执行。

在国际贸易中，当双方发生争议时，一般通过友好协商解决。如协商得不到解决，则根据不同情况采取调解或诉讼等方式进行处理。

2. Function of Arbitration Agreement 仲裁协议的作用

An arbitration agreement is a kind of agreement in written form, concluded at the will of both parties concerned before or after the disputes arise, agreeing to settle the disputes through arbitration. It is a necessary document for the application for arbitration. As an agreement signed by both parties concerned, it is on the basis of willingness, amicable negotiation, equality and mutual benefit. An arbitration agreement is the evidence, in accordance with which the arbitral body and the arbitrators settle the case. It is not acceptable for arbitral bodies to settle the disputes without an arbitration agreement.

1) The both parties involved are bound to the arbitration agreement. Where a dispute arises, it shall be settled through arbitration, instead of resorting to litigation. If one party files a suit at the court, the other party has the right to require the court to stop the proceedings of the case.

2) If one party breaches the arbitration agreement and has resort to the court at its own will, the other party may require the court to refuse the case according to the arbitration agreement, and bring the case to the arbitral tribunal for judgment. An arbitration agreement can exclude the jurisdiction of court effectively.

3) The arbitration tribunal or arbitrator is granted the jurisdiction of the case concerning the dispute.

The core of the above-mentioned functions is the second item, namely the exclusion of the court's jurisdiction of the case. Therefore, the both parties involved shall stipulate arbitration clauses in the contract before the disputes arise if they are not likely to resort to the court for the settlement of disputes, in order to avoid the possibility of having resorts to litigation in case of disputes arising in the future and failing to reach an arbitration agreement. In a word, it is very important to conclude arbitration clause in a sales contract.

仲裁协议是买卖双方在争议发生之前或争议发生之后自愿将争议通过仲裁解决的一种书面协议，是申请仲裁的必备材料。作为双方当事人的协议，它必须建立在自愿、协商、平等互利的基础之上，不允许一方强加于另一方。仲裁协议是仲裁机构和仲裁员受理争议案件的依据，仲裁机关不受理没有仲裁协议的争议纠纷。

（1）双方当事人均须受仲裁协议的约束，如果发生争议，应以仲裁的方式解决而不向法院起诉。如一方去法院起诉，另一方有权要求法院停止审理，并将有关争议案件发还给仲裁庭审理。

（2）排除法院对有关案件的管辖权，如果一方违背仲裁协议，自行向法院起诉，另一方可根据仲裁协议要求法院不予受理，并将争议案件退交仲裁庭裁断。有了仲裁协议，可以有效地排除法院对有关争议案件的管辖权。

（3）使仲裁庭或仲裁员取得对有关争议案件的管辖权。

上述三项作用的中心是第二项，即排除法院对争议案件的管辖权。因此，双方当事人不愿将争议提交法院审理时，就应在争议发生前在合同中规定仲裁条款，以免将来发生争议后由于达不成仲裁协议而不得不诉诸法庭。这反映出在买卖合同中订立仲裁条款的重要性。

3. Arbitration Clause in Contract 合同中的仲裁条款

The arbitration place is the main content and the key element in an arbitration clause since the arbitration place generally determines the arbitration rules and the relevant laws. The selection and arrangement of arbitration place in international practice are generally in the following ways: the country of buyer, the country of seller, the third country, the country of defendant, the country of complaint, the location of the goods, etc. There are three ways to stipulate the arbitration place according to our country's law.

仲裁地点是仲裁条款的主要内容，也是一个关键问题，因为在什么地点仲裁就适用哪个国家的仲裁规则或有关法律。国际上对仲裁地点的选择与安排，一般有以下几种情形：在买方所在国、在卖方所在国、在第三国、在被告所在国、在原告所在国、在货物所在地等进行仲裁。我国法律规定了三种关于仲裁地点的方法。

3.1 Arbitration in Our Country 规定在我国仲裁

For example, any dispute, controversy or claim arising out of or relating to this contract, or the breach, termination or invalidity thereof, shall be settled amicably through negotiation. In case no settlement can be reached through negotiation, the case shall then be submitted to the China International Economic and Trade Arbitration Commission of the China Council for the Promotion of International Trade, Beijing, for arbitration in accordance with its Rules of Arbitration. The arbitral award is final and binding upon both parties.

例如：由于本合同或者由于违背合同、终止合同或者合同无效而发生的或与此有关的任何争端、争议或要求，双方应通过友好协商解决；如果协商不能解决，应提交北京中国国际贸易促进委员会对外经济贸易仲裁委员会，根据该会仲裁程序暂行规则进行仲裁。仲裁裁决是终局的，对双方都有约束力。

3.2 Arbitration Tribunal Formation and Arbitrators Appointment 组织仲裁庭与仲裁员的指定

The stipulation about the numbers of arbitrators and the appointment ways varies in different countries. In most countries, arbitration tribunal is composed of three arbitrators, but there is sole-arbitrator tribunal in the U.K. and the U.S.A., and there is also arbitration tribunal composed of two persons or even numbers in a few countries. In a temporary arbitration, the sole arbitrator is appointed by both parties in the arbitration agreement. For an arbitration tribunal with three arbitrators, two of them are appointed by both parties respectively, and the third arbitrator so called chief arbitrator is appointed by the two arbitrators together. The arbitrator can also be appointed by the chairman of the arbitration body and the chief arbitrator is chosen by the chairman from the panel of arbitrators. In order to have the case settled fairly and reasonably, the arbitrators appointed by both parties respectively shall neither have any interest in the case, nor represent any party's interest. If the appointed arbitrator has any interest in the case, it shall ask for abstaining from the arbitration. It is decided by the arbitration body if the arbitrator shall abstain from the case. When the arbitrator abstains from the case or fails to fulfill the duty, a new arbitrator shall be appointed according to the procedures.

关于仲裁员人数和选定办法，各国法律规定不同，多数国家规定为三人制，但英、美等国一般为一人独任制，少数国家也允许二人制或采用双数制。在临时仲裁中，独任仲裁员都是由双方当事人在仲裁协议中指定。三人制中的三名仲裁员则是由双方当事人各指定一名，再由这两名仲裁员指定第三名首席仲裁员。如当事人不指定，也可委托仲裁委员会主席指定。首席仲裁员由仲裁委员会主席在仲裁员名册中另行指定。由当事人双方分别指定一名仲裁员，目的在于使争议案件能得到公平合理的裁决，而被指定的仲裁员并非是指定一方的代理人。被指定的仲裁员如果与案件有利害关系，应当自行向仲裁委员会请求回避。回避的决定由仲裁委员会做出，仲裁员因回避或其他原因不能履行其职责时则应按照原指定仲裁员的程序重新指定。当事人所指定的仲裁员并不代表当事人的利益。

3.3 Proceedings of Case 审理案件

There are two forms of proceedings of arbitration case: one is a closed proceeding. It is usually required or agreed by the parties involved that the arbitration tribunal may examine the case and issue an award on the basis of documents only; the other one is an open proceeding. The arbitration usually is not in public according to the arbitration rules. Upon the request of both parties involved, an open proceeding can be exercised dependent on the decision of the arbitration tribunal.

仲裁庭审理案件的形式有两种：一是不开庭审理，即一般是经当事人申请，或由仲裁庭征得当事人同意，只以书面文件进行审理并裁决。二是开庭审理。按照仲裁规则的规定，一般采取不公开审理的形式，但如果双方当事人要求公开进行审理则由仲裁庭做出决定。

3.4 Award Issuance 做出裁决

To issue an award is the last section of the whole arbitration process. After an award is issued, the procedure of arbitration has come to an end, so the judgment is final. According to the Arbitration Rules of our country, the arbitration tribunal may issue an intermediate award or a partial award with respect to any problem of the case. An intermediate award means an award temporarily issued for the dispute which has been examined and handled clearly, in favor of further handling of the case; a partial award is a final one issued separately for some problems which have been handled clearly in the case, and the partial award is regarded as the part of the final award for the whole case.

An award of arbitration must be issued in written form within 45 days after the closing of the case. Except for the verdict issued through mediation, an arbitration award shall specify the reasons for issuing the award, and state that the award is final with the date and place of award issuing as well as the signature of the arbitrators.

The parties involved shall enforce the award within the time limit stipulated in the award. For the award without a time limit, the award shall be enforced immediately. In case that one party fails to fulfill the award, the other party may have resorts to the court of China for applying for the enforcement in accordance with the law of China, or settle it according to the relevant international convention and practice.

In the arbitration clause of a sales contract, the arbitration rules of which country or region and arbitration body adopted shall be specified. For the applicable arbitration rules in China, it refers to *China International Economic and Trade Arbitration Commission Rules*. There are different arbitration rules in different countries and regions. It shall be noted that, the adopted arbitration rules must not be in compliance with the arbitration place though the arbitration rules of the arbitration place are usually adopted according to the international practice. It is also allowed in law to adopt the arbitration rules of other countries or regions rather than the arbitration place based on the agreement of both parties.

In addition, about the cost of arbitration, which party shall bear the arbitration cost is usually specified clearly in the arbitration clause. Usually, it is stipulated that the arbitration cost is borne by the losing party, or depending on the arbitration tribunal's decision.

裁决是仲裁程序的最后一个环节，裁决做出后审理案件的程序即告终结，因而这种裁决被称为最终裁决。根据我国仲裁规则的规定，除最终裁决外，仲裁庭认为有必要接受当事人之提议，在仲裁过程中，可就案件的任何问题做出中间裁决或者部分裁决。中间裁决是指对审理清楚的争议所做的暂时性裁决，以利于对案件的进一步审理；部分裁决是指仲裁庭对整个争议中的某些问题已经审理清楚，而先行做出的部分终局性裁决，它构成最终裁决的一部分。

仲裁裁决必须于案件审理终结之日起 45 天内以书面形式做出，仲裁裁决除由于调解达成和解而做出的裁决书外，应说明裁决所依据的理由，并写明裁决是终局的和做出裁决书的日期与地点以及仲裁员的署名等。

当事人应依照仲裁裁决书中所规定的期限自动履行。裁决书未规定期限的，应立即履行。一方当事人不履行的，另一方当事人可以根据中国法律的规定向中国法院申请执行，或根据有关国际公约或中国缔结或参加的其他国际条约的规定办理。

在买卖合同的仲裁条款中还应确定采用哪个国家（地区）和哪个仲裁机构的仲裁规则进行仲裁。适用我国的仲裁程序规则，是指适用《中国国际经济贸易仲裁委员会仲裁规则》。其他国家的仲裁机构也都有自己的仲裁程序规则，应注意的是，所采用的仲裁程序规则与仲裁地点并非绝对一致，按照国际仲裁的一般做法，原则上采用仲裁所在地的仲裁规则，但在法律上也允许根据双方当事人的约定，采用仲裁地点以外的其他国家（地区）仲裁机构的仲裁规则进行仲裁。

此外，在仲裁费用的负担问题上，通常在仲裁条款中明确规定仲裁费用由谁承担。一般规定由败诉方承担，也有的规定由仲裁庭酌情决定。

4. Enforcing an Award 仲裁裁决的承认与执行

The recognition and enforcement of an arbitral award are involved with the enforcement of the award in another country different from the country where the award is issued. It is stipulated in the laws of various countries that the award shall be enforced by the losing party voluntarily and the arbitration body is not with coercive force and obligation to enforce it. In case that the losing party is not willing to enforce the award, the wining party may resort to the courts of local country or the losing party's country for the help to force the losing party to enforce the award.

In order to have the award executed smoothly, some international conventions have been concluded and signed. On 10th June, 1958, the UN had a meeting on international business arbitration, and signed *Convention on the Recognition and Enforcement of Foreign Arbitral Award, New York Convention* for short, which is the most important international convention about the execution of foreign arbitration award. The following two points are stressed in the Convention: firstly, to recognize the effectiveness of the arbitration agreement signed by both parties concerned; secondly, the convention states to recognize the force of the award under the arbitration agreement and enforce it. Our country and other many countries have become parties of the Convention. In the stipulation of the Convention, the awards made in the territory of the convention states may be executed according to the Convention; the awards made in non-convention states may be executed according to the Convention unless the award enforcement place belongs to the non-convention country completely. Nevertheless, it is stipulated in the Convention that the convention state may propose some reservation when the state is approved to join the Convention.

仲裁裁决的承认与执行涉及一个国家的仲裁机构所做出的裁决要由另一个国家的当事人去执行的问题。各国法律规定，仲裁裁决应由败诉方自动执行，仲裁机构无强制执行裁决的权力和义务。如果败诉方不愿执行裁决，胜诉方只能求助于本国或败诉方所在国的法院，请其协助强制败诉方执行。

为了解决仲裁裁决的顺利执行问题，国际上曾签订了一些国际仲裁公约。1958 年 6 月 10 日，联合国在纽约召开了国际商事仲裁会议，签订了《承认和执行外国仲裁裁决公约》（简称《纽约公约》），成为当前国际上关于执行国外仲裁裁决的最主要公约。该公约强调了两点：一是承认双方当事人所签订的仲裁协议有效；二是根据仲裁协议所做出的仲裁裁决，缔约方应承认其效力并有义务执行。我国和许多国家（地区）参加了这个公约。公约规定，凡在缔约方领土内做出的仲裁裁决，都可以运用本公约予以执行；在非缔约方领土内做出的裁决，只要执行地不认为这完全属于其内部仲裁，也可以运用本公约加以执行。但该公约又规定，允许缔约方在批准参加时可提出某些保留。

Case Study 本章案例

Case 1: A Chinese importer had concluded a contract with a foreign company to import chemical products, however the foreign seller found he would be at a loss as the price of the products in the international market was rising. So he required to cancel the contract due to Force Majeure. Then as the Chinese importer, how to deal with the situation?

【案例 1】我国某外贸公司与外商订立一份化工产品进口合同，订约后由于该产品的国际市场行情上扬，外商亏本。于是外商以不可抗力为由要求撤约。问：进口商应如何对待此问题？

Case Analysis: The seller's requirement is not valid. The price rise is a kind of commercial risk instead of a Force Majeure. The buyer shall refuse the seller's requirement and urge the seller to make delivery promptly.

【案例分析】外商的撤约要求不能成立。因为合同货物市价上扬属商业风险，不构成不可抗力事故。故此，我方应拒绝外商的撤约要求，催促对方按时发货。

Case 2: An institute in China signed an import contract with a Japanese seller to buy a set of precision appliance. It was stipulated to make delivery in September in contract, but the Japanese government declared the kind of appliance was a high-tech product which was prohibited for export on 7th September and the regulation came into effect 7 days after the declaration. Then the Japanese seller required removing the contract due to force majeure. Question: Is the requirement of Japanese seller reasonable? How to settle the matter as the Chinese buyer?

【案例 2】国内某研究所与某日商签订了一项进口合同，欲引进一台精密仪表。合同规定 9 月交货，但到 9 月 7 日，日本政府宣布该仪表属高科技产品，禁止出口，自宣布之日起 7 天后生效。后日方来电以不可抗力为由要求解除合同。问：日方的要求是否合理？我方应如何处置较为妥当？

Case Analysis: The Japanese seller's requirement is unreasonable. The time of the interdictory act coming into effect is after the delivery time, so it cannot be taken as a Force Majeure. The Japanese seller is capable of fulfilling the delivery in September. The Chinese buyer may not accept the requirement but urge the seller to execute the contract as soon as possible.

【案例分析】日方的要求是不合理的。日本政府颁布的禁令的生效日是在合同规定的最后交货日之后，因此，不构成履约的"不可抗力"。日方完全可以在 9 月份装船发货，履行合同。因此，日本政府的禁令对本合同不构成不可抗力条款的规定，日方要求不合理，我方可向日方回电拒绝其无理要求，敦促其尽快履约。

Questions 思考题

1. What is Force Majeure? What are the three characteristics of it and its application scope?

   什么是不可抗力？其三个特征是什么？范围是怎样的？

2. What are the legal result of Force Majeure and the principles of settling it?

不可抗力的法律后果及其处理原则是什么？

3. How to make a regulation of Force Majeure in a sales contract?

   在买卖合同中，如何规定不可抗力条款？

4. What are the roles of arbitration agreement?

   仲裁协议的作用有哪些？

5. What are the varieties of arbitrament and the contents included?

   仲裁裁决的种类是怎样的？

Chapter 16

The Conclusion of Sales Contracts

国际货物买卖合同的订立

Lesson 1 The Procedure for the Conclusion of Sales Contracts

国际货物买卖合同订立的程序

The international business made between the Buyer and the Seller is mainly the conclusion of the contract and the fulfillment of the contract. The establishment of a contract includes the following four legal steps: inquiry, offer, counter offer and acceptance, in which the offer and the acceptance are indispensable and necessary.

买卖双方进行国际贸易的商务活动归根结底就是双方签订和履行国际贸易买卖合同的过程。合同的成立有四个法律步骤：询盘、发盘、还盘和接受。其中，发盘和接受是达成交易、合同成立不可缺少的两个基本环节和必经的法律步骤。

1. Definition of Contract 合同的定义

A contract is an agreement reached by two or more than two parties concerned, in order to establish, modify or terminate the civil rights and obligation of the parties. According to the definition given in Common Law, a contract is an accord of both parties, which can be explained in short as follows:

"The contract is formed on the promise of the offer."

"The contract is formed upon the acceptance of the offer."

"The establishment time of a contract is also the time when the acceptance comes into effect."

合同是两个或两个以上的当事人以发生变更或者消灭民事法律关系为目的所达成协议。按照英美法给合同下的定义，合同是双方的一种合意。

可概括为：

“要约一经承诺，合同即告成立。”

“发盘一经接受，合同即告成立。”

“接受生效的时间即是合同成立的时间。”

2. Offer 发盘

2.1 Definition 定义

An offer is a proposal of terms and conditions presented in a potential contract by one party, called the offerer, to anther party, called the offeree. Once the other side accepts, the contract is concluded. It is also called offer or quotation in commercial laws.

The party which makes offer is named as offerer, the party which accept the offer is named as offeree.

An offer may be proposed by the seller or the buyer. The offer proposed by the buyer is referred to as bid.

发盘是指一方当事人以缔结合同为目的，将交易的全部条件十分明确、肯定地向另一方所做出的一种意思表示。只要对方表示接受，合同即告成立。在商法中也称为要约或发价。

发出要约的人称为发盘人，接受发盘的人称为受盘人。

发盘既可以由卖方提出，也可以由买方提出。由买方提出的发盘，称为递盘。

2.2 Necessary Conditions for a Valid Offer in Law 构成一项法律上有效的发盘必须具备的条件

2.2.1 An Offer Must Be Addressed to One or More Specific Persons 发盘必须向一个或一个以上特定的人提出

An offer shall be addressed to a specific person, who may be a natural person or a corporation. The common commercial advertisement，the catalogues and a price list sent to clients are not an offer usually, but an invitation of offer. It should not be the common commercial advertisement, the catalogues or a price list distributed to the public. Proposals of this kind are also regarded as invitation for offer.

发盘应向特定的人提出，即向有名有姓的个人或公司提出。普通商业广告及向国外客商寄发的商品目录、价目单等行为一般不能构成发盘，通常只能视为邀请发盘。

2.2.2 The Contents of an Offer Must Be Sufficiently Definite 发盘的内容必须十分确定

For an effective offer, the contents shall be definite, that is to say the terms of the offer shall be complete, definite, and final. It is stipulated in CISG Art.14. A proposal is sufficiently definite if it indicates the goods and expressly or implicitly fixes or makes provision for determining the quantity and the price.

It shows that three basic elements are necessary for the proposal of an offer:

1) indicating name of commodity;

2) indicating explicitly or implicitly the quantity or the way of confirming the quantity;

3) indicating explicitly or implicitly the price or the way of confirming the price.

A proposal of establishing a contract with the above three elements may be regarded as an effective offer. A sales contract is established upon the acceptance of the offeree.

一项有效的发盘其内容必须是确定的，即发盘中的交易条件必须是完整的、确定的和终局性的。《联合国国际货物销售合同公约》（以下简称《公约》）第 14 条规定，一项订立合同的建议“如果写明货物，并且明示或默示地规定数量和价格或如何确定数量和价格，即为十分确定”。

可见，在提出的订约建议中，至少应包括下列三个基本要素：

（1）标明货物的名称；

（2）明示或默示地规定货物的数量或规定数量的方法；

（3）明示或默示地规定货物的价格或规定确定价格的方法。

凡包含上述三项基本因素的订约建议，即可构成一项有效的发盘。如该发盘被受盘人接受，买卖合同即告成立。

2.2.3 With the Indication that the Offer Is Binding upon the Offerer 表明发盘对发盘人有约束力

The offerer shall indicate that, he is committed to establishing a contract with the offeree upon an effective acceptance made by the offeree. If an offerer makes a proposal tending to negotiate with the offeree on some trade terms, not meaning to be bound by the proposal, the proposal is not regarded as an offer. For example, a proposal remarked with words such as “for reference only”, “subject to the final confirmation of the offerer” or other reservation conditions, is not an offer but an invitation for offer.

发盘人在发盘中应表明，自己有责任在受盘人对发盘做出有效接受时与其订立合同。如发盘人只是就某些交易条件建议同对方进行磋商，而根本没有受其建议约束的意思，则此项建议不能被认为是一项发盘。例如，发盘人在其提出的订约建议中加注诸如“仅供参考”“须以发盘人的最后确认为准”或其他保留条件，这样的订约建议就不是发盘，而只是邀请对方发盘。

2.2.4 An Offer Comes into Effect Only When It Reaches the Offeree 发盘必须送达受盘人才能生效

An offer is effective when it reaches a specific offeree. The offeree cannot make acceptance initiatively before receiving the offer even though he has been informed of the contents of the offer in other ways.

Such as: Offer firm metal silicon 98% 500 MT. Price: USD 1,150/ metric ton CIF London export standard packing shipment: During July/August 2006 payment: irrevocable L/C sight. Subject to your reply reach here before 20th June, Beijing time.

一项发盘于送达特定的受盘人时才有效。即使受盘人在此之前已通过其他途径知道了发盘的内容，也不能在收到发盘前主动对该发盘表示接受。

例如："发盘（实盘）：金属硅；含量98%；数量500公吨。价格：USD 1 150/公吨；CIF 伦敦；出口包装。装运：7、8月间，2006年。付款方式：即期信用证；（效期）以你方最后复到北京时间6月20日前为准。"

2.3 Validity Time of an Offer 发盘的有效期

An offer is usually with a validity, the acceptance made by an offeree is effective merely within the period and the offerer is bound to the obligation to conclude the contract with the offeree upon the offer terms within the period. When the validity time is not specified in the offer, the offeree's acceptance shall be made within a reasonable time. So-called "reasonable time" is depending on the specific situation.

通常，发盘都有一个有效期，只有在有效期内，受盘人对发盘的接受才有效，发盘人也才承担按发盘条件与受盘人成交的责任。当发盘未具体列明有效期时，受盘人应在合理时间内接受才能有效。何谓"合理时间"需根据具体情况而定。

2.4 Withdrawal and the Revocation of an Offer 发盘的撤回与撤销

In legal sense, the withdrawal and the revocation of an offer are different. The withdrawal of an offer means that the offeror takes some measures to prevent the offer from taking effect before the offer becomes effective. The revocation of an offer means that the offer's effect is removed by the offerer after the offer comes into effect.

在法律上，发盘的撤回与撤销属于两个不同的概念，发盘的撤回是指发盘尚未生效时发盘人采取某种方式阻止它生效的行为。发盘的撤销是指在发盘已生效后发盘人以一定方式解除发盘的效力。

2.4.1 Withdrawal of an Offer 发盘的撤回

An offer (including an irrevocable offer) may be amended or withdrawn before it comes into effect, and the withdrawal notification must reach the offeree before or at the same time as the offer reaches the offeree.

一项发盘（包括注明不可撤销的发盘）只要在其尚未生效以前，都是可以修改或撤回的，撤回发盘的通知应赶在受盘人收到该发盘之前或同时送达受盘人。

2.4.2 Revocation of an Offer 发盘的撤销

The revocation of an offer which has becomes effective in law, means the offer is not binding upon the offeror if it is revocable. There is a great difference between Common Law system and Continental Law system about the offer's revocation. According to the principle in the Common Law, an offer is not binding upon the offeror in principle, and the offerer may revoke or amend the offer anytime before the offeree accepts the offer although the offer is within a validity time, which is in favor of the offeror obviously. The principle is also blamed in the countries adopting the Common Law system. For example, the principle has been abandoned to some extent during making and modifying Uniform Commercial Code in America. In the Uniform Commercial Code, it is stipulated that the offer cannot be revoked if it is made by a merchant. In the countries adopting the Continental Law system, the opinion that whether an offer is revocable or not is on the contrary, and they think the offerer is bound to an offer which is irrevocable. For instance, it is stipulated in the law of Germany, an offer in its validity time, or without a validity time, cannot be revoked before it is replied by the offeree usually. In France law, an offer may be revoked by the offeree, but the offerer shall take the responsibility of compensation in case of an improper revocation.

Splitting the difference, it is stipulated in Article 16 of the CISG, an offer may be revoked if the revocation reaches the offeree before he has dispatched an acceptance, endorsing the opinion of the Common Law system. However, it is also stipulated in the 2nd part of Article 16, that the offer cannot be revoked in the following cases: ① if it indicates, whether by stating a fixed time for acceptance or otherwise, it is irrevocable; or ② if it was reasonable for the offeree to rely on the offer as being irrevocable and the offeree has acted in reliance on the offer.

It actually agrees with the principle of the Continental Law system, that an offer is irrevocable in the regulated validity time. Even though the offer is not with validity time, an offer is irrevocable so long as it was reasonable for the offeree to believe the offer is irrevocable and act relying on it.

所谓发盘的撤销，实质上是针对一项法律上已经生效的发盘而言，也就是发盘对发盘人有无约束力的问题，即发盘人在做出要约后能否反悔，能否把发盘的内容加以变更或取消。关于这一问题，英美法与大陆法存在着严重的分歧。英美法认为，发盘原则上对发盘人没有约束力，发盘人在受盘人对发盘表示接受之前的任何时候都可撤销发盘或变更其内容。在受盘人表示接受之前，即使发盘中规定了有效期，发盘人也可以随时予以撤销，这显然对发盘人有利而对受盘人极为不利。这种原则在英美法国家中也不断受到责难。例如，美国在制订或修改《美国统一商法典》时，实际上已在不同程度上放弃了这一原则。如果一项发盘是由商人做出的，那么它就是不可撤销的。大陆法系国家对“一项发盘是否可以撤销”的看法相反，认为发盘人原则上应受发盘的约束，不得随意将其发盘撤销。例如，德国法律规定，发盘在有效期内，或没有规定有效期，则依通常情况在可望得到答复之前不得将其撤销。法国的法律虽规定发盘在受盘人接受之前可以撤销，但若撤销不当，发盘人应承担损害赔偿责任。

《公约》采取了折中的办法，第 16 条规定，在发盘已送达受盘人，即发盘已经生效，但受盘人尚未表示接受这一段时间内，只要发盘人及时将撤销通知送达受盘人，仍可将其发盘撤销。受盘人一旦发出接受通知，则发盘人无权撤销该发盘。这实际上是肯定了英美法的观点。在《公约》16 条第 2 款又规定，在下列情况下发盘不得撤销：① 发盘写明接受发盘的期限或以其他方式表示发盘是不可撤销的；② 被发盘人有理由信赖该项发盘是不可撤销的，而且被发盘人已本着对该项发价的信赖行事。

这实际上是肯定了大陆法的原则，一项发盘在规定的有效期内是不能撤销的。即使没有规定有效期，只要受盘人有理由相信该项发盘是不可撤销的并且已经本着对该项发盘的信赖行事，那么该项发盘仍然是不可撤销的。

3. Inquiry 询盘

The non-firm offer is legally called as invitation for offer, meaning with an intention to purchase or sell some certain commodities, one party inquires the trade terms of the other party, or brings about a proposal for business transaction with some terms. There are some ways to make an invitation to offer, and the inquiry is widely used. It is not with legal force, nor constituting an offer.

In an inquiry, the details such as the quality, specification, quantity, packing, price or shipment of the commodities may also be involved in, and the demand of samples included as well.

询盘在法律上称为邀请发盘，在商法上称为要约引诱，在我国外贸实践中称为虚盘。询盘是指交易的一方打算购买或出售某种商品，向另一方询问该项商品的有关交易条件，或者就该项交易提出带有保留条件的建议。邀请发盘可有不同的形式，其中最常见的是询盘，询盘不具有法律上的约束力，且其本身并不构成发盘。

在询盘中也会涉及商品的品质、规格、数量、包装、价格和装运等成交条件，也可以索取样品。

4. Counter-offer 还盘

Counter-offer means a reply to the offer made by the offeree, not accepting completely the terms of the offer and with the proposal to modify or change it.

A counter-offer is also a reply to the offer containing the additions, limitations or other modifications, which constitutes a rejection to the offer. Then, the original offer is not valid any more, which the offerer is not bound to. In accordance with the CISG, the offeree's modification on the price, payment, quality, quantity, delivery time and place, the compensation scope or the settlement ways on disputes, is regarded as the substantial change on the offer's terms.

In addition, a conditional acceptance to the offer is also a kind of counter offer, for example, the offeree's reply to the offer with the extra conditions such as "subject to the final confirmation", "valid until it is sold out" etc. The kind of reply is taken as a counter-offer or an invitation of an offer. A counter-offer without the offer's terms is regarded as an invitation of an offer. Whereas, a counter-offer containing an offer's terms is taken as a new offer with the counter-offerer as the new offerer and the original offerer as the new offeree. The new offeree is granted with the right to accept, refuse or make a counter-offer again.

还盘，又称还价，在法律上称为反要约。还盘是指受盘人不同意或不完全同意发盘提出的各项条件，并提出了修改或变更的表示。

还盘是对发盘条件进行添加、限制或其他更改的答复。还盘实际上构成了对原发盘的拒绝，使原发盘失效，原发盘人就不再受其约束。根据《公约》的规定，受盘人对货物的价格、付款、品质、数量、交货时间与地点、一方当事人对另一方当事人的赔偿责任范围或解决争端的办法等条件提出添加或更改要求，均作为实质性变更发盘条件。

此外，对发盘表示有条件的接受也是还盘的一种形式。例如，受盘人在答复发盘人时，附加有“以最后确认为准”“未售有效”等规定或类似的附加条件，这种答复只能视作还盘或邀请发盘。还盘的内容，凡不具备发盘条件，即为“邀请发盘”。如还盘的内容具备发盘条件，就构成一个新的发盘，还盘人成为新发盘人，原发盘人成为新受盘人，拥有对新发盘作出接受、拒绝或再还盘的权利。

5. Acceptance 接受

5.1 Implication of an Acceptance 接受的含义

Acceptance means that the offeree agrees with the trade terms of the offer unconditionally within the validity period of the offer, and is willing to conclude the contract with the offerer based on these terms. The contract is established once the offer is accepted. The both parties concerned shall perform the obligation stipulated in the contract and own the relevant rights.

接受，在法律上称为“承诺”，是指受盘人在发盘的有效期内，无条件地同意发盘中提出的各项交易条件，愿意按这些条件和对方达成交易、订立合同的一种意思表示。发盘一经接受，合同即告成立。双方均应履行合同所规定的义务并拥有相应的权利。

5.2 Key Elements Constituting an Acceptance 构成接受的要件

Based on the interpretation of the CISG, an effective acceptance must contain the following elements:

1) An acceptance must be made by the specific offeree. The assent indicated by others cannot be taken as an acceptance, but a new offer.

2) The contents of the acceptance must be in compliance with the offer, that is to say, the modification on the offer is usually regarded as a counter offer as stated above. If the contents of the acceptance are not in compliance with the offer, that is to say, there is some modifications to the condition of the offer, in common, as we stated above, it should be regarded as a counter-offer.

The CISG distinguishes the substantial acceptance and the unsubstantial acceptance according to the alteration of 6 elements as follows: “Additional or different terms relating, among other things, to the price, payment, quality and quantity of the goods, place and time of delivery, extent of one party’s liability to the other or the settlement of disputes are considered to alter the terms of the offer materially.”

In case that the offeree makes an acceptance and proposes to alter the offer unsubstantially, such as adding the copies of the contract, asking to sign the sales confirmation, proposal of making notarization etc., the acceptance is regarded as a valid acceptance unless the offerer objects to it or indicates explicitly in the offer that any amendment cannot be made to the offer.

3) The acceptance made and delivered to the offeror within the effective period of the offer.

In case that the offer is made orally, the offeree shall make a reply to accept or not immediately unless the offerer and the offeree have agreed otherwise on the period for the acceptance.

In case that the offer is made in writing (such as telegram, fax, letter etc.), the acceptance shall reach the offeror within the fixed effective period or a reasonable time if not fixed.

4) The transmission way of the acceptance notice conforming to the requirement of the offer.

When an offer is made by the offeror, the transmission way is stipulated sometimes or not. In case that the transmission way is not stipulated, the offeree may adopt the same way as the offer's or the faster way to dispatch the acceptance notice to the offerer.

5) An acceptance must be indicated.

根据《公约》的解释，构成有效的接受必须具备以下几个条件：

（1）接受必须由特定的受盘人做出。其他人对发盘表示同意，不能构成接受，只能视为一项新的发盘。

（2）接受的内容必须与发盘相符（即接受必须是同意发盘提出的交易条件）。接受的内容如果与发盘不一致，也就是对发盘的条件做出了修改，在一般的情况下，正如前面所述，应被视为一项还盘。

《公约》区分实质性接受和非实质性接受是根据以下六个条款是否改变："有关货物的价格、付款、货物质量和数量、交货地点和时间、一方当事人对另一方当事人的赔偿责任范围或解决争端等的添加或不同条件均视为在实质上变更发盘的条件。"

如果受盘人对发盘的内容提出非实质性变更的修改意见，这里所说的非实质性变更，如增加合同的副本数、要求签订确认书、建议对合同进行公证等（如前所述），在这种情况下，除非发盘人及时表示反对或者发盘中明确表示不得对发盘的内容做出任何变更，否则该接受构成一项有效的接受。

（3）接受必须在发盘的有效期内表示并送达发盘人。

如果是以口头方式做出发盘的，那么除非发盘人与受盘人另有约定接受的具体期限，否则，受盘人应立即做出接受与否的意思表示。

如果是以书面（电报、传真、信函等）的非口头方式做出的发盘，接受应当在规定的有效期内或合理的期限内到达发盘人。

（4）接受通知的传递方式应符合发盘的要求。

发盘人发盘时，有的具体规定接受通知的传递方式，也有未做规定的。如发盘没有规定传递方式，则受盘人可按发盘所采用的，或采用比其更快的传递方式将接受通知送达发盘人。

（5）接受必须表示出来。

5.3 Period for an Acceptance Coming into Effect 接受生效的时间

A contract is established upon the acceptance of an offer, so the time of an acceptance to become effective is involved in the establishment of a contract.

About the time for an acceptance to become effective, there is a great difference in the provisions between the Common Law and the Continental Law. In the Common Law, an acceptance becomes effective as soon as the notice of it is dispatched or posted; whereas in the Continental Law, an acceptance comes into effect when the notice of an acceptance reaches the offeree. In the CISG, it is stipulated definitely that an acceptance becomes effective when it reaches the offeree, standing on the side of the Continental Law. In our country, the stipulation of it is also in compliance with the CISG.

发盘一经接受合同即告成立。接受生效的时间关系合同的成立与否。

在接受生效的时间问题上，英美法和大陆法存在严重分歧。英美法采用投邮生效的原则，即接受通知书一经投邮或发出，立即生效；而大陆法采用到达生效的原则，也称为到达主义，即接受通知书必须到达发盘人时才生效。《公约》则明确规定，接受送达发盘人时生效，支持了大陆法的立场。我国也采取了到达生效的原则。

5.4 Late Acceptance 逾期接受

A late acceptance means the notice of an acceptance reaches the offerer after the effective time or a reasonable time if the effective time is not fixed. In accordance with the laws of various countries, a late acceptance is not effective, but a new offer. The CISG also takes the opinion that a late acceptance is not valid, however, in favor of the establishment of the contract, the acceptance is still effective and the contract can be concluded.

(1) A late acceptance is invalid in principle. However, a late acceptance is still effective if the offerer notifies the offeree without delay orally or in writing that a late acceptance is effective. So, it is decided by the offerer whether a late acceptance is effective or not.

2) If a letter or other writing containing a late acceptance shows that it has been sent in such circumstances that if its transmission had been normal it would have reached the offeror in due time, the late acceptance is effective as an acceptance unless, without delay, the offerer orally informs the offeree that he considers his offer as having lapsed or dispatches a notice to that effect.

逾期接受又称为迟到的接受，是指接受通知到达发盘人的时间已经超过了发盘所规定的有效期，或者在发盘未规定有效期时，已超过了合理的时间。按照各国的法律，逾期接受不能认为是有效的接受，而只是一项新的发盘。《公约》亦认为逾期的接受原则上是无效的，但为了有利于双方合同的成立，《公约》对逾期的接受亦采用了一些灵活的处理方法，使它在符合某些条件的情况下，仍然具有接受的效力，合同仍得以成立。

（1）逾期接受原则上无效。但如发盘人毫不迟延地用口头或书面通知受盘人，他认为逾期接受仍然有效，则逾期接受仍具有接受的效力。该种情况下，逾期接受是否有效的决定权在发盘人手中。

（2）如果载有逾期接受的信件或其他书面文件表明它是在传递正常、能及时送达发盘人的情况下寄发的，则该项逾期接受具有接受的效力，除非发盘人毫不迟延地口头或书面通知受盘人他的发盘已经失效。

5.5 Withdrawal of an Acceptance 接受的撤回

The withdrawal of an acceptance means that the offeree takes some measures to prevent the acceptance from coming into effect when he has made acceptance to the offerer.

The CISG has adopted the principle of the Continental Law, namely the acceptance becomes effective upon reaching it. However, the countries under the Common Law system still comply with the principle that the acceptance becomes effective upon being dispatched, taking the opinion that an acceptance has become effective as soon as it is dispatched, so it cannot be withdrawn. In our practice, we shall take the difference into account.

接受的撤回也就是受盘人在对原发盘人发出接受通知时，采取某种方式阻止该接受生效的行为。

《公约》采取了大陆法送达生效的原则。但英美法系国家遵循的是投邮原则，认为接受在发出时间即生效，因此接受不能撤回。在实际业务中，一定要注意法律规定的这种差别。

Lesson 2 Establishment of International Business Contracts
国际贸易合同的签订

A contract for the sales and purchase of international commodity established according to the law is the verification of a business relationship as well as a legal relationship between the buyer and the seller. A contract complying with the law can be performed smoothly under the law frame and with binding force. Meantime, the party's benefit involved can be protected from being damaged.

A contract becomes effective since it is established. However, the establishment of a contract is different from its coming into effect. The establishment of a contract is dependent upon the effectiveness of an acceptance, whereas a contract becoming effective means a contract with legal binding force. Usually, the moment of the establishment of a contract is also the time that the contract comes into effect, because they are on the same time. However, sometimes a contract is established without coming into effect immediately, it will become effective when other conditions are available.

依法成立的国际货物买卖合同不仅体现了买卖双方的经济关系，还体现了它们之间的法律关系。只有符合法律规范的合同才能在法律的约束下顺利履行。依法成立的合同才具有法律约束力，当一方当事人的利益受到损害时，其才能依据合同得到法律的保护。

合同自成立时生效。但是，合同成立与合同生效是两个不同的概念。合同成立的判断依据是接受是否生效；而合同生效是指合同是否具有法律上的效力。在通常情况下，合同成立之时就是合同生效之日，二者在时间上是同步的。但有时，合同虽然成立却不立即产生法律效力，而是需要其他条件成立时合同才开始生效。

1. Establishment of Contract 合同的成立

1.1 Time of Establishment of a Contract 合同成立的时间

In accordance with the CISG, a contract is concluded when the offeree accepts the offer and sends the acceptance to the offeror with in the validity time of the offer. In the practice, the time of the establishment of a contract is subject to the date indicated on the contract signed, or the date of confirming the contract from the other party.

根据《公约》的规定，受盘人接受发盘并在发盘有效期内将接受送达发盘人，合同即告成立。在实际业务中，合同成立的时间以订约时合同上所写明的日期为准，或以收到对方确认合同的日期为准。

1.2 Key Elements for an Effective Contract 合同生效的要件

In accordance with the contract laws of countries, after the buyer and the seller have reached an agreement through offer and acceptance, an effective contract must be based on the following elements.

根据各国合同法规定，一项合同，除买卖双方通过发盘和接受就交易条件达成协议后，还需具备以下要件才是一项有效的合同，才是一项有法律约束力的合同。

1) The parties concerned must be with the conduct capacity to sign a contract 合同当事人必须具有签订合同的行为能力

The parties concerned of a contract shall be natural persons or juridical persons. For a natural person, he shall be a mentally normal adult, a minor or a mentally ill person or the like shall be limited to conclude a contract. In case that the parties concerned are juridical persons, the laws of most countries take the opinion in common, that the contract must be signed by the authorized representative within the business scope of his. The contract out of the scope is not effective.

签订买卖合同的当事人应是自然人或法人。自然人必须是精神正常的成年人，未成年人、精神病人等订立合同必须受到限制；如果当事人是法人，各国法律一般认为，必须通过其代理人在法人的经营范围内签订合同，即越权的合同不发生法律效力。

2) A contract must be with consideration or cause 合同必须有对价或约因

Consideration is a concept in the Common Law system, an important element for the establishment of a contract. It is called as Consideration in the Common Law system and Cause in France law. The so-called consideration refers to the price the party concerned has to pay for the benefit of the contract. "Some rights, benefit, profit or favor obtained by one party, or the restraint to perform a right, the suffer from a loss or the undertaking of an obligation."

Cause refers to a direct objective pursued by the party concerned in the contract signed. In accordance with the rules of the Common Law system and the Continental Law system, a contract which is effective in law must be with Consideration or Cause.

对价是英美法的概念，是合同成立的一个重要因素，英美法称之为对价，大陆法称之为约因。所谓对价是指当事人为了取得合同利益所付出的代价。“合同一方得到的某种权利、利益、利润或好处，或是他方当事人克制自己不行使某项权利或遭受某项损失或承担某项义务。”

约因是指当事人签订合同所追求的直接目的。按照英美法和大陆法的规定，合同只在具有对价或约因时，才是法律上有效的合同。

3) The objective of a contract must be legal 合同的标的物必须合法

The goods involved in a contract shall be legal, which shall be allowed to be imported and exported by government. For the goods under the supervision and limitation of a government, the concerning licence or quota shall be obtained at first; a contract shall not be against law, public order or public policy as well as custom and morality.

合同涉及的货物必须合法。货物应是政府允许自由进出口的商品，如果属于政府管制，应先取得有关许可证或配额；合同内容必须合法，包括不得违反法律、不得违反公共秩序或公共政策，以及不得违反善良的风俗习惯或道德三个方面。

4) A contract shall be in compliance with the stipulated form by law 合同必须符合法律规定的形式

The form of a contract is not limited in principle in the CISG. Nevertheless, the member states in the CISG are permitted to make declaration for the reservation about it.

《公约》原则上对国际货物买卖合同的形式不加以限制，但允许缔约方对此声明予以保留。

5) The party concerned of a contract shall be in true willingness 合同当事人的意思表达必须真实

In international business, the buyer and the seller shall reach an agreement voluntarily and true willingness. The contract involving fraud, intimidation, or violence is invalid.

在国际贸易中，买卖双方必须在自愿和真实的基础上达成协议。任何一方采取欺诈、威胁或暴力行为与对方订立的合同无效。

2. Significance of Signing a Contract 签订书面合同的意义

In business negotiation, a deal is concluded after an offer is accepted, and then a contract relationship is established by the buyer and the seller. The correspondence between two parties in negotiation is taken as the written proof of the contract. Nevertheless, the buyer and the seller will sign a written contract to further make sure the rights and obligations of both sides.

It's not necessary for an effective contract to sign a contract in written form. It is stated in the CISG, "A sales contract is not bound to be concluded or certified in written form, unlimited in the form. A sales contract may be certified in any ways including witnesses." However, in the international business practice, the parties concerned will usually sign a contract in written form after reaching an agreement through negotiation.

在交易磋商过程中，一方发盘经另一方接受以后，交易即告成立，买卖双方就构成了合同关系。双方在磋商过程中的往返函电即是合同的书面证明。但根据国际贸易习惯，买卖双方还要签订书面合同，以进一步明确双方的权利和义务。

签订书面合同不是合同有效成立的必要条件。《公约》规定："销售合同无须以书面订立或书面证明，在形式方面也不受任何其他条件的限制。销售合同可以用包括人证在内的任何方法证明。"但是，在国际贸易实践中，在当事人双方经过磋商一致，达成交易以后，一般均须另行签订一份具有一定格式的书面合同。

Case Study 本章案例

Case 1: As an exporter, we cable an American businessman to export agricultural products. Beside the necessary items stated in the offer, the clause "Packing in Sound bags" is also added in. During the validity of the offer, the American businessman replies "Refer to your telex first accepted, Packing in new bags." When we receive the above reply, we are ready for shipment. The international market price for the agricultural products tumbled a few days ago. The American businessman replies that the contract is established because we did not confirm when they changed the packing condition. We insists that the contract has been established. So argument occurs between both parties. How to handle this case?

【案例 1】我国某出口公司于 2 月 1 日向美商电报出口某农产品，在发盘中除列明必要条件外，还表示"Packing in Sound bags"。在发盘有效期内，美商复电称："Refer to your telex first accepted, Packing in new bags."我方收到上述复电后，即着手备货。数日后该农产品国际市场价格猛跌，美商来电称："我方对包装条件做了变更，你方未确认，合同并未成立。"而我国出口公司则坚持合同已经成立，于是双方对此发生争执。此案应如何处理？

Case Analysis: The contract has been established. In this case the American businessman's packing change belongs to a substantial change. It constitutes the effective acceptance. So the contract is established. And the conditions on the contract are subject to the conditions on the offer and the changes on the acceptance.

【案例分析】合同成立。该案例中美商对包装的变更属于非实质性变更，仍构成了有效接受，而使合同得以成立，并且合同的条件以该项发盘的条件以及在接受中所载更改为准，即该合同除包装条款改为"in new bags"外其他仍按该出口公司在发盘中列明的条款，双方应按此合同承担义务与责任。

Case 2: A Chinese international engineering contracting company asks an Italian supplier to make an offer for us to sell a batch of steel on May 3 by telex. In our telex statement: We require that this offer is to calculate the bid price of a building and determine whether or not to participate in bidding; we must tender on May 15 and the bid opening date is on May 31. The Italian supplier cables us the offer on May 5 for the above mentioned steel. We calculate the price on his offer and submit the tender to the tenderer on May 15. The Italian supplier sends a telex to revoke his May 5 offer on May 20, because of the rising price of the steel market. We immediately reply them that we don't agree to revoke the offer. So, both sides make a dispute over the revocation of the offer. Then on May 31, we bid successfully. We immediately telex the Italian supplier to accept the May 5 offer. But the Italian supplier insists that they have cancelled the offer on May 20. The contract is not established. However we believe that the contract is established. Neither could convince the other. Hence both sides agree to submit it to arbitration. Question: if you are an arbitrator, what will you arbitrate? Explain your reasons.

【案例 2】我国某对外工程承包公司于 5 月 3 日以电传请意大利某供应商发盘出售一批钢材。我方在电传中声明：要求这一发盘是为了计算承建一幢大楼的标价和确定是否参加投标之用；我方必须于 5 月 15 日向招标人送交投标书，而开标日期为 5 月 31 日。意供应商于 5 月 5 日用电传就上述钢材向我方发盘。我方据以计算标价，并于 5 月 15 日向招标人递交投标书。5 月 20 日意供应商因钢材市价上涨，发来电传通知撤销他 5 月 5 日的发盘。我方当即复电表示不同意撤盘。于是，双方为能否撤销发盘发生争执。5 月 31 日招标人开标，我方中标，随即电传通知意供应商我方接受该商 5 月 5 日的发盘。但意供应商坚持该发盘已于 5 月 20 日撤销，合同不能成立，而我方则认为合同已经成立。对此，双方争执不下，遂协议提交仲裁。试问，如你为仲裁员，将如何裁决？说明理由。

Case Analysis: The contract is established. The reasons are as follows:

1) Both Italy and China are the member states in the CISG. The telexes exchanged by the two parties have not ruled out the CISG, so this case should be restricted by the CISG.

2) The Italian supplier's offer is irrevocable:

① We have definitely notified the Italian supplier the intentions of inviting this offer in our inquiry;

② The Italian supplier is aware of our intention and makes an offer for us. We have the reason to believe that the offer is irrevocable, and participate in the bid with the trust;

③ The offer does not stipulate the validity and it should be regarded the time is reasonable and effective. In this case the reasonable time should be regarded as several days after the opening date;

3) The Italian supplier cabled us revoking the offer on May 20, we made a immediate rejection, so the revocation cannot be established. According to the regulations of the CISG, the offeree has the reasons to trust that the offer is irrevocable and acts in the trust, and the

offer cannot be revoked.

4) When we bid successfully, we advise the Italian supplier immediately that the acceptance is effective. The contract comes into effect.

【案例分析】本案裁决：合同已成立，理由是：

（1）意大利与中国均为《联合国国际货物销售公约》之缔约方，双方当事人交换的电传也未排除《公约》，因此本案应受《公约》制约。

（2）意大利供应商发盘是不可撤销的：

① 我方询盘中已明确告知对方我方邀请发盘的意图；

② 意方知悉我方意图后向我方发盘，我方有理由相信该项发盘是不可撤销的，并已本着该项信赖，参与了投标；

③ 该项发盘未规定有效期，应视为合理时间有效，本例合理时间应为开标后若干天。

（3）意大利供应商5月20日来电撤销发盘，我方立即拒绝，撤销不能成立。《公约》规定，对于一项发盘，受盘人有理由信赖该项发盘是不可撤销并已本着该项信赖行事，该项发盘不能撤销。

（4）我方中标后立即通知意方接受，接受生效，双方合同成立。

Case 3: A Britain businessman (businessman A) makes an offer to a federal German businessman (businessman B) on May 3 to sell a certain of goods. Businessman B is in the receipt of this offer the next day (May 6). Businessman B makes a complete answer to accept the offer on the morning of May 6. After Businessman A sends the offer, he finds the commodity prices upward, hence he cabled Businessman B to withdraw the offer in the afternoon of May 7. It is in the morning of May 8 that Businessman A receives the acceptance from Businessman B. Question: (1) According to the Britain law, is it legal for Businessman A to withdraw the offer? (2) If the case is applied to the CISG, does the contract relationship exist?

【案例3】英国A客商于5月3日向联邦德国B客商发出一项要约，供售某商品一批，B商于收到该要约的次日（5月6日）上午答复A商，表示完全同意要约内容。但A商在发出要约后发现该商品行情趋涨，遂于5月7日下午致电B商，要求撤销其要约。A商收到B商承诺（接受）通知的时间是5月8日上午。试简要回答：（1）若按英国法律，A商提出撤销要约的要求是否合法？（2）若此案适用《公约》，A商、B商双方是否存在合同关系？

Case Analysis: (1) According to the Britain law, it is illegal for Businessman A to withdraw the offer. According to the British law: once an acceptance is sent out, it is effective immediately, and in this case Businessman B makes a promise in the morning of May 6, the contract between them has come into effect.

(2) According to the CISG, the contract relationship exists between the two parties. According to the CISG, an offer can be withdrawn before the offeree advises the commitment. However in this case Businessman B has made a commitment before Businessman A makes the withdrawal advice. So Businessman A cannot withdraw the offer. The commitment made

by Businessman B has come into effect when it reaches Businessman A in the afternoon of May 8. The contract is formed.

【案例分析】（1）按英国法律，A 商提出撤销要约的要求不合法，英国法律规定：承诺一经发出，立即生效，本例 B 商 5 月 6 日上午做出承诺，A 商、B 商之间的合同已经成立。

（2）根据《公约》，A 商、B 商双方存在合同关系。按《公约》规定：一项发价在被发价人发出承诺通知前通知被发价人，发价可以撤销，但本案 A 商做出撤销要约通知前，B 商已做出承诺，A 商撤销不能成立，B 商承诺于 5 月 8 日下午到达 A 商时生效，合同成立。

Case 4: One day morning a French businessman pays a visit to one of our exporters to purchase a certain of goods. We make an oral offer, they do not answer. He visited again that day afternoon and accepted the morning's offer unconditionally. At that time we have also learned that there is an upward tendency in the international market. So how to handle this situation , why?

【案例 4】某法国商人于某日上午走访我国外贸企业洽购某商品。我方口头发盘后，对方未置可否，当日下午法商再次来访表示无条件接受我方上午的发盘，那时，我方已获知该项商品的国际市场价格有趋涨的迹象。对此，你认为我方应如何处理为好，为什么？

Case Analysis: France and China are the member states in the CISG. Both parties shall be bound by the CISG. According to the CISG, as for oral offer, the contract can be established on the condition that it should be immediately accepted. When we offer that morning, the French businessman did not reply or put forward any requirement, the contract will not be established. Accordingly, we can refuse or raise the price to make a new quotation according to the upward price.

【案例分析】中国与法国均系《公约》缔约方，因此，双方当事人均应受该《公约》约束。按《公约》规定：对口头要约，须立即接受方能成立合同。上午我方发盘后，法商未置可否，也未提出任何要求，则合同没有成立。据此，我方鉴于市场有趋涨迹象，可以予以拒绝或提高售价另行报价。

Case 5: One of our exporters makes an offer to an Italian businessman, and the offer is subject to the reply reaching here on 10th of this month. Then the Italian businessman cables us accepting this offer on 9th. Because of the delay of the Telegraph Office, we receive his acceptance notice in the morning of the 11st of this month. However, we get the message that the market price is upward. So what shall we do ?

【案例 5】我国某出口企业对意大利某商人发盘限 10 日复到有效，9 日意商用电报通知我方接受该发盘。由于电报局传递延误，我方于 11 日上午才收到对方的接受通知，而我方在收到接受通知前获悉市场价格已上涨。对此，我方应如何处理？

Case Analysis: Italy and China are the member states in the CISG. During the negotiation the two parties did not exclude or make any reservations, and therefore, both parties shall be bound by the CISG. According to the CISG the late acceptance can be accepted if there are some late acceptance letters or written documents stating that the acceptance was sent in time and in the normal transport to the offeror. The late acceptance was invalid unless the offeror informs the offeree in oral or written way without delay. According to the CISG, the acceptance cable which we receive from the Italy businessman on the 11st of this month is caused by the transport delay. Therefore if we don't agree on this deal, we shall inform them by cable as soon as possible that the offer is invalid. If we are willing to conclude this deal and make a contract on the basis of the offer for some reasons, we can reply the Italy businessman to confirm. If we don't reply, we will be in default.

【案例分析】中国与意大利均系《公约》缔约方，该案在双方洽谈过程中，均未排除或做出任何保留。因此，双方当事人均应受《公约》约束。按《公约》规定，如果载有逾期接受的信件或其他书面文件表明它是在传递正常能及时传达到发盘人的情况下寄发的，则该项逾期接受具有接受效力，除非发盘人毫不迟延地用口头或书面通知受盘人，他认为发盘已经失效。据此，我方于 11 日收到意商的接受电报属因传递延误而造成的逾期接受。因此，如我方不同意此项交易，应即复电通知对方：我方原发盘已经失效。如我方鉴于其他原因愿按原发盘达成交易、订立合同，可回电确认；也可不予答复，予以默认。

Case 6: One of our foreign trade company received an offer from the D company which is in Paris, France on July 16 , 2009. " 500 MERTICTON TINPLATE US DOLLARS 540 CFR CHINA PORT AUGUST SHIPMENT SIGHT L/C SUBJECT TO YOUR REPLY REACHING US BY JULY 20." We replied on July 17 stating that we can accept the offer if the unit price is USD 500.00 CFR CHINA PORT. If there are some disputes, arbitration in China. The D company replied by cable that the market is firm, the price can not be reduced, the arbitration can be accepted, lease reply as soon as possible. There is an upward tendency in the tinplate's price at the same time. So we replied by cable that we accept your firm of 16th.The L/C has been established through the Bank of China, please confirm. However the French businessman did not confirm and returned the L/C. Question: Whether is the contract establish? Does we make any mistakes? Explain the reasons.

【案例 6】我国某外贸公司 C 于 2009 年 7 月 16 日收到法国巴黎 D 公司发盘："马口铁 500 公吨，每吨 540 美元 CFR 中国口岸，8 月装运，即期信用证支付，限 20 日复到有效。"我方于 17 日复电："若单价为 500 美元 CFR 中国口岸可接受 500 公吨马口铁，履约中如有争议，在中国仲裁"。法国 D 公司 18 日复电"市场坚挺，价格不能减，仲裁条件可接受，速复。"此时马口铁价格确实趋涨。我方于 19 日复电："接受你 16 日发盘，信用证已由中国银行开出，请确认。"但法商未确认并退回信用证。试问：合同是否成立？我方有无失误？说明理由。

Case Analysis: The contract is not established. The reason is that the D company made an offer on July 16th, the C company made a counter-offer on July 17th, then the offer of July 16th was invalid. We have two mistakes (1) we should not accept the D company's offer of

July 16th, we had better accept the offer of July 18th. (2) When we make acceptance, we shall not use the wording or the sentence such as please confirm.

【案例分析】合同不能成立。理由是 D 公司 16 日发盘，经 C 公司 17 日还盘已失效。

我方有失误，具体失误有两点；（1）我国某出口企业不应接受 D 公司 16 日发盘，而应接受其 18 日发盘；（2）在作“接受”时，不应用“请确认”字样或文句。

Questions 思考题

1. What is offer? What are the necessary conditions for a valid offer?

什么是发盘?构成一项有效发盘的条件是什么?

2. What are the different provisions in the offer coming into effect? What is the meaning for the time for the offer coming into effect?

在发盘生效问题上国际上有哪些不同的规定?明确发盘生效的时间有何意义?

3. Whether the offer can be withdrawn or revoked? What are the provisions for the offer's withdrawal and revocation?

发盘能否撤回和撤销?《公约》关于发盘的撤回与撤销问题是怎样规定的?

4. What is the acceptance? What are the conditions for a valid acceptance?

什么是接受?构成一项有效接受的条件是什么?

5. What is the late acceptance? What is the consequence for a late acceptance in law?

什么是逾期接受？逾期接受的法律后果如何?

6. Whether can the acceptance be withdrawn?

接受能否撤回?

7. Which are the conditions for a legally binding contract?

一项有法律约束力的合同应具备哪些条件?